Bibliography of English Translations from Medieval Sources, 1943–1967

NUMBER LXXXVIII OF THE

RECORDS OF CIVILIZATION

SOURCES AND STUDIES

W. T. H. Jackson, Editor

Bibliography of English Translations from Medieval Sources, 1943-1967

BY

Mary Anne Heyward Ferguson

COLUMBIA UNIVERSITY PRESS
NEW YORK

Library of Congress Cataloging in Publication Data
Ferguson, Mary Anne.
Bibliography of English translations from medieval sources, 1943–1967.
(Records of civilization; sources and studies, no. 88)
Supplement to Bibliography of English translations from medieval sources, by C. P. Farrar and A. P. Evans, published in 1946.
1. Literature, Medieval—Translations into English—Bibliography. 2. English literature—Translations from foreign literature—Bibliography. I. Farrar, Clarissa Palmer. Bibliography of English translations from medieval sources. II. Title. III. Series.
Z6517.F47 016.08 73-7751
ISBN 0-231-03435-0

Printed in the United States of America
10 9 8 7 6 5 4 3 2

Preface

Though not a revision, this Supplement to Farrar and Evans' *Bibliography of English Translations from Medieval Sources* (1946) attempts in general to follow the same principles of inclusion as that work and is intended to be used in conjunction with it. Above all, Farrar and Evans' principle of usefulness to potential users as the decisive criterion has been followed. But, paradoxically, that principle has caused departure from some of the original guidelines. The main changes are as follows:

1. *Change in time limits for inclusion.* Though the period of Constantine the Great was the beginning date for Farrar and Evans, they were not entirely consistent; they included some earlier Christian works, such as those of the Apostolic Fathers of the 1st century. In view of our present knowledge of the importance of Jewish exegesis of the Bible for medieval practice, it seemed logical to include Philo Judaeus, Talmudic material, and such recent discoveries as the Dead Sea Scrolls. Works such as the fables of Aesop and the Arabian Nights, which took form during the medieval period, have also been included, as well as material of doubtful provenience such as riddles and proverbs. At the other end of the time limit, 1500, this volume includes the late 15th century travel records which did not appear in the original volume.

2. *Inclusion of documentary material.* It may be that Farrar and Evans excluded Columbus on the basis of their policy to omit most documentary material—a policy based on their expectation of issuing a separate list or volume for such material, which lends itself to different classification from that adopted. That expectation and their hope for the early appearance of a new edition of Charles Gross's *Sources and Literature of English History* were not fulfilled; nor has a supplement to the 2d edition of Paetow's *Guide to the Study of Medieval History* yet appeared. It seemed wise, therefore, to include major documents such as translations of the Roman and Byzantine law codes and other collections of laws and documents.

3. *Expansion of subject categories.* Partly to meet the problem of classifying documents, this Supplement contains more subject categories than did Farrar and Evans, although their general principle of including works under their authors' names or, if anonymous, under the title has been adhered to. Their heading *Historical sources. Collections,* has been subdivided: separate headings now appear not only as formerly for specific countries (e.g., England, France), but also for regions (Caucasus) and religious communities (Jews, Islam). Collections

of religious works are divided into *Christian literature, Judaism,* and *Islamic literature*; and the category *Liturgy and Ritual* lists Jewish as well as Christian rites. Islamic rituals and traditions as well as *belles lettres* appear under *Islamic literature. Collections.* The category *Literature. Collections* and its subheadings such as *English literature, Hebrew literature, Russian literature,* include anthologies of belletristic works only. Other new categories include *Philosophy. Collections; Art, works about; Scientific works,* all of which were established in order to group the anthologies in those fields. Extensive cross references in the index will, it is hoped, enable the reader to locate works in all fields; the index includes further categories such as medicine, laws, mysticism, logic, political writings, and the major medieval genres: romances, epics, sagas, letters, sermons, saints' lives.

4. *Exclusion of reprints.* Farrar and Evans noted reprints; this volume does not. No consistent effort has been made, furthermore, to indicate publication simultaneously in two countries, though such information is noted when it was available in the copy examined. To list reprints would amount to a partial revision of Farrar and Evans, since many of the works listed there have been often reprinted; works listed in the present volume may have been reprinted since listing. As often as possible works designated as new *editions* have been examined; they are noted when the change is substantive. But many so-called new editions are really reprints with the bibliography updated or a new section added without any real change in the medieval material translated. Such new "editions" are not noted here, simply to avoid prolonging the compilation of this volume, which has been five years in process. An examination of *Books in Print* will indicate the status of any of the works listed in both volumes; many of them, of course will be out of print and available only in libraries. The main libraries in which copies of the works listed were found are Harvard, Ohio State, and the New York Public; but many books had to be sent for on interlibrary loan or be examined by a researcher in England. The location of a book has been indicated when it has been particularly difficult to find.

5. *Changes in nomenclature.* In following Library of Congress procedures, as Farrar and Evans did, this volume introduces changes made by the Library during the past quarter century. A major change in the system of Arab nomenclature has occurred. Some names formerly entered under the given names now appear under a later part of the name, the patronymic or the nisbah: *e.g.,* Muḥammad ibn Aḥmad, Abū al-Raihan, al-Bīrūnī, is now entered under al-Bīrūnī; 'Abd al-Malik ibn Hishām under Ibn Hishām. But this system has not been followed consistently by the Library when confusion might result; 'Abd al-Laṭīf and Ibn Ṭāhir, for example, are not listed under their common nisbah, al-Baghdādī. I have tried through cross references in the index to note names

which may be confused. When an Arabic name was not recorded by the Library of Congress, the version used by the *Encyclopedia of Islam* or in some cases by the editor of the work in question, has been adopted; this has resulted in rather eclectic use of diacritical marks.

In the index I have also cross-referenced the English version of titles which according to the Library's system are listed in the original language: *e.g.*, *Igor, prince, raid of*, for *Slovo o Polku Igoreve; Book of rights* for *Leabhar na g-cert*.

The long process of compiling this volume began with checking the *Index Translationum*, an annual publication of the United Nations since 1948. The *Index* proved to include only about half of the works eventually listed here; it omits many monographs and other works of which translation is a part, and it excludes periodicals. Medieval bibliographies such as the *Bulletin of the Progress of Medieval Studies* (1923–60) and the *International Guide to Medieval Studies* (1961–) were consulted. Useful also were general bibliographies such as *The Literatures of the World in English Translation*, edited by George Parks and others; Professor Parks kindly let me see material for unpublished volumes. The *Reader's Adviser: an Annotated Guide to the Best in Print*, was useful especially for paperbacks. Also consulted were bibliographies for specific fields, such as *Isis* for science, *Publications of the Modern Language Association* for literature, *Byzantinische Zeitschrift*, as well as more specialized works such as Wilfred Bonser's *An Anglo-Celtic Bibliography (450–1087)*, C. A. Storey's *Persian Literature: a Bio-bibliographical Survey*, and Nicholas Rescher's *al-Fārābī: an Annotated Bibliography*. The appearance in 1969 of *Serial Bibliographies for Medieval Studies* by Richard H. Rouse facilitated the search for such specialized bibliographies. I was also aided by Professor Ruth Erlandson, Research Consultant at the Ohio State library. Unfortunately, few bibliographies note translations *per se*; it has been necessary to read reviews in such works as *Speculum* and the *Bulletin of the School of Oriental and African Studies* to find clues to translations which appear in monographs or collections of texts.

The process has been long, and though I have attempted to be complete, I do not assume that I have in fact been so for any field. I should appreciate notice of omissions and corrections from users of the *Bibliography*; I have made use of notices sent to Farrar and Evans. I hope soon to publish a further supplement for 1968 and 1969 in the journal *Manuscripta* (St. Louis University) and eventually to bring the bibliography of translations up through 1972; additions and corrections to the present volume could be included in these projected supplements.

The journal *Speculum* in January of 1973 began publishing a list of editions and translations from medieval works; I hope that its listing and continued progress of the *Repertorium Fontium Historiae Medii Aevii*, which indicates translations into all languages, will make further supplements on translations only unnecessary. For specific authors a great new source of bibliography through 1956 is gradually becoming available; the National Union Catalogue of the Library of Congress is publishing a retrospective catalogue which is not merely a conflation of former volumes but a completely new bibliography. I was able to verify my listings up through the letter G in this new catalogue and feel surer about completeness for this part of the bibliography.

Although I have worked primarily alone, many people have been of help to me. Without two research grants from the University of Massachusetts/Boston and the Elizabeth Howald Postdoctoral Fellowship from the Ohio State University, the work would have been much longer in process. Both institutions also supplied me with research assistants; of those I wish to thank especially Edward F. Flaherty from Massachusetts and Deborah Fleming of Ohio who were particularly painstaking in their assistance.

Professor W. T. H. Jackson of Columbia University, editor-in-chief of the series Records of Civilization of which this volume is a part, and Mr. Henry Wiggins, Assistant Director of the Columbia University Press, have been helpful in making decisions about policy. Professor D. M. Dunlop of Columbia and Ms. Margaret Anderson, Arabic cataloguer at Ohio State, have been most helpful in an area in which I am especially ignorant. Miss Elisabeth L. Shoemaker of the Columbia University Press has faithfully seen a most difficult text through the press. Neither she nor I had any advice from anyone connected with the original bibliography, all of whom had died before this work was undertaken. Nonetheless, my greatest debt is to Farrar and Evans, whose guidance I have felt throughout and whose standards I despair of approaching. Omissions and errors are due, to quote Dr. Johnson, to ignorance, sheer ignorance. But I hope that, like its predecessor, this volume will be useful wherever English is understood better than the some twenty medieval languages from which the translations have been made.

Mary Anne Heyward Ferguson

University of Massachusetts/Boston

July, 1973

Bibliography of English Translations from Medieval Sources, 1943–1967

Bibliography of English Translations from Medieval Sources, 1943–1967

A

Aaron ben Elijah, Karaite, *c. 1300–69.* The tree of life, by Aaron ben Elijah of Nicomedia, tr. with intro. and notes by Morris Charner. [New York, printed by Saprograph Co.], 1949. xxi, 188 p. 1

The first part (chs. 1–78 of one hundred fourteen chapters) is translated; the work is a treatise attempting to give a philosophical basis for revelation; the first half is a vindication of God's unity.

Abailard, Pierre, *1079–1142.* Abelard's Christian theology, tr. by J. Ramsay McCallum. Oxford, Blackwell, 1948. vii, 117 p. 2

Translation of extracts from Abailard's Theologiae Christianae, with an abstract of the entire work. Appendix E has a translation of Abailard's Morning hymn.

—— The Story of Abelard's adversities, a translation with notes of the Historia calamitatum by J. T. Muckle, intro. by Etienne Gilsòn. Toronto, The Pontifical Institute of Medieval Studies, 1954. 70 p. 3

Abān ibn ʿAbd al-Hamīd al-Lāḥiqī, *d. c. 815–16.* "The poetry of Abān al-Lāḥiqī," by K. A. Fariq, *Journal of the Royal Asiatic Society,* 1952, 46–59. 4

Contains translations of some of al-Lāḥiqī's poems and of comments on his life and works by later writers. According to the Encyclopedia of Islam (2d ed.), al-Lāḥiqī is also known as al-Raḳāshī.

ʿAbd al-Laṭīf, al-Baghdādī, *1162–1231.* The Eastern key (Kitāb al-ifādah waʿl-iʿtibar), tr. by K. Hafuth Zand and John A. and Ivy E. Videan. London, Allen & Unwin [1965]. 293 p. 5

Text and facing translation of a history of Egypt, with much geographical description and description of plants and animals.

Aberconway Abbey, Chronicle of. The History of the abbey of Aberconway, 1186–1537, by Rhŷs W. Hays. Cardiff, University of Wales Press, 1963. xiii, 210 p. 6

The Chronicle, the last entry of which is for 1283, is translated on pp. 146–50; it was previously translated, according to the editor, by W. Bezant Lowe in The heart of Northern Wales (2 vols., Llanfairfechan, privately printed, 1912–18), I, 448–58. The abbey moved to a new site in 1284 and was then known as Maenan Abbey.

Abinnaeus, Flavius, *fl. c. 340.* The Abinnaeus archive; papers of a Roman officer in the reign of Constantius II, [ed. and tr.] by H. I. Bell, *et al.* Oxford, Clarendon Press, 1962. xiv, 191 p. 7

Latin and Greek texts with following translation of the Abinnaeus papyri in the British Museum and Geneva University Library, plus two still in private hands; these documents, discovered in 1892, are here edited and translated for the first time. Many of the documents are official petitions but some are letters of a private nature.

ABOTH

Aboth. Pirke Aboth. The tractate "Fathers" from the Mishnah, commonly called "Sayings of the Fathers," ed. with intro., translation, and commentary by R. Travers Herford. New York, Jewish Institute of Religion, 1945. 176 p. (3d rev. ed.; 1st ed., 1925). **8**

—— Sayings of the fathers; or Pirke Aboth, tr. by Joseph H. Hertz. New York, Behrman House [1945]. 128 p. **9**

Hebrew text and translation, with commentary.

—— Ethics of the fathers, tr. and annotated, with an intro. by Philip Birnbaum. New York, Hebrew Publishing Co. [c. 1949]. 58 p. **10**

—— The living Talmud, the wisdom of the fathers and its classical commentaries, selections, tr. by Judah Goldin. Chicago, University of Chicago Press [1957], 244 p.; New York, Heritage Press [c. 1960]. xxxi, 165 p. **11**

Translation of Pirke Aboth and of nine medieval commentaries. The 1960 edition has the Hebrew text for Pirke Aboth.

—— Ethics from Sinai, an eclectic, wide-ranging commentary on Pirke Avoth, by Irving M. Bunim. New York, Feldheim [c. 1964]. xxiii, 360 p. **12**

Text and parallel translation of Pirke Aboth with extensive commentary.

—— Pirke Abot, Sayings of the Fathers, ed. with translation and commentaries by Isaac Unterman. New York, Twayne Publishers, 1964. 408 p. **13**

Includes the Midrash and commentators.

—— Chapters of the Fathers, commentary by Samson Raphael Hirsch, [tr. by Gertrude Hirschler]. New York, Feldheim, 1967. 117 p. **14**

Text and translation of Pirke Aboth parallel; commentary at bottom of page.

Aboth de-Rabbi Nathan. The Fathers according to Rabbi Nathan, tr. by Judah Goldin. New Haven, Yale University Press, 1955. xxvi, 277 p. *Yale Judaica series,* 10. **15**

According to the translator, Rabbi Nathan lived probably in the 2d century, but the commentary as we have it is probably a redaction of the 7th to the 9th century. The Pirke Aboth, translated by Herbert Danby, is given in an appendix. An earlier version of part of this translation appeared in the Mordecai M. Kaplan Jubilee Volume, ed. Mosheh Davis, New York, 1953, pp. 263–80.

Abraham bar Hiyya, ha-Nasi, *1065–1143.* Judaism as a philosophy; the philosophy of Abraham bar Hiyya (1065–1143), by Leon D. Stitskin. [New York], Bloch Publishing Co. for Yeshiva University, 1960. xiii, 251 p. **16**

Contains paraphrase and translation of excerpts from works many of which are commentaries on Aristotle, and an attempt to correlate Aristotle's ideas with Jewish thought.

Abraham ben David, ha-Levi, *c. 1100–c. 1180.* "The biology of Abraham ben David Halevi of Toledo," by F. S. Bodenheimer, *Archive des Sciences,* 4 (1951), 39–62. **17**

Contains abridged translation of chapters 1 and 6 of the Emunah Ramah ("The exalted faith"), from a Hebrew version of the original Arabic work.

—— "The story of the four captives," by Gerson D. Cohen, *Proceedings of the American Academy for Jewish Research,* 29 (1960–61), 55–131. **18**

Contains translation of a "romance with a moral," a homily meant to serve as a consolation to Jews, about four great scholars captured by Muslim Spaniards; from the Sefer ha-qaballah.

—— A critical edition with a translation and notes of the book of tradition (Sefer ha-qaballah) by Abraham Ibn Daud, by Gerson D. Cohen. Philadelphia, Jewish Publication Society of America, 1967. lxii, 348, 74, 22 p. **19**

A polemic against the Karaites, supporting Talmudic authorities, written *c.* 1161. Hebrew text at back.

Abraham ben David of Posquières, *d. 1198.* Rabad of Posquières, a twelfth-century Talmudist, by Isadore Twersky. Cambridge, Harvard University Press, 1962. xii, 336 p. **20**

This monograph contains *passim* translation of excerpts from Rabad's commentary on Maimonides' Mishneh Torah and from Rabad's other works, not elsewhere translated.

Abraham ben Mēʼīr ibn Ezra, *c. 1092–1167.* "The muwashshahs of Abraham ibn Ezra," by S. M. Stern, pp. 368–86 in Hispanic studies in honour of I. Gonzales Llubera, ed. by Frank Pierce. Oxford, Dolphin Book Co., 1959. 440 p. **21**

Contains translation of Ibn Ezra's poems.

Abraham ben Simeon, *of Worms, 15th cent.* The book of the sacred magic of Abra-Melin the mage, delivered by Abraham the Jew unto his son Lamech, A.D. 1458, tr. from the original Hebrew into the French, and now rendered from the latter language into English . . . by S. L. MacGregor-Mathers. . . . London, J. M. Watkins, 1956. xlviii, 268 p. [1st ed. 1898]. **22**

The translation, made for students of the occult, is from a 17th-century French manuscript in the Bibliothèque de l'Arsenal. Abraham, who lived chiefly in Würzburg, according to the translator, transmitted kabalistic mysteries learned from his father to his son; he performed "marvels" for the Emperor Sigismund of Germany and Henry VI of England.

Abraham Sholom, *d. 1492.* The philosophy of Abraham Shalom, a 15th-century exposition and defense of Maimonides, by Herbert A. Davidson. Berkeley, University of California Press, 1964. viii, 111 p. *University of California Near Eastern studies,* 5. **23**

Translation *passim* of excerpts with Hebrew text in footnotes; contains summary of and commentary on Neweh Shalom, the Abode of Peace.

Abū ʻAlī b. al-Bannāʻ, *1005–1080.* "Autograph diary of an eleventh-century historian of Baghdad," by George Makdisi, *Bulletin of the School of Oriental and African Studies,* 18 (1956), 1–31, 239–60; 19 (1957), 13–48, 281–303, 426–43. **24**

Arabic text and following translation of contemporary's history of Baghdad for the year 1068–69.

Abū al-Faraj al-Iṣfahānī, *897–967.* "The song captions in the Kitāb al-Alghānī al-Kabīr," by Henry G. Farmer, *Transactions of the Glasgow University Oriental Society,* 15 (1953–54), 1–10. **25**

Contains translation of the captions of the songs, designating the rhythmical mode of the music, and of excerpts from other writings which help to define the modes.

Abū al-Fidā, *of Hebron, d. 1429.* Palestine—Mohammedan Holy Land, by Charles D. Matthews. New Haven, Yale University Press, 1949. xxx, 176 p. *Yale Oriental series, researches,* 25. **26**

Contains translation of Abū al-Fidā's Book of inciting desire to visit Abraham or Kitāb Muthīr al-Gharām li-Zyārat al-Khalīl . . ., which describes Hebron and its shrines; see pp. 43–137.

Abū al-Ḥasan, Aḥmad ibn Ibrāhīm al-Uqlīdisī, *10th cent.* "The earliest extant arabic arithmetic: Kitāb al Fusūl fī al Hisāb al-Hindī of Ab al-Ḥasan, Aḥmad ibn Ibrāhīm al-Uqlīdisī", by A. S. Saidan, *Isis*, 57 (1966), 475–90. **27**

Summary and commentary with extensive illustrative excerpts in translation of a work written 952/3.

Abū al-Ḥasan ibn Abī Dharr, *10th cent.* "Some Plato in an Arabic epitome," by A. J. Arberry, *Islamic Quarterly*, 2 (1955), 86–99. **28**

Text and translation of an Arabic extract from Plato's Republic, the longest continuous extract from the Republic in Arabic, according to Professor Arberry, who assigns a 10th rather than a 13th century date for its origin. The section translated is on justice. I have accepted Professor Arberry's designation of authorship which I could not verify elsewhere.

Abū Ḥayyān, *1256–1344.* "A noteworthy passage from an Arab grammatical text," by S. Glazer, *Journal of the American Oriental Society*, 62 (1942), 106–8. **29**

Abū Kāmil Shujā' ibn Aslam, *c. 850–930.* The algebra of Abū Kāmil: Kitāb fī al-jābr wa'l-muqābala, in a commentary by Mordecai Finzi. Hebrew text, translation and commentary, with special reference to the Arabic text, [ed. and tr. by] Martin Levey. Madison, University of Wisconsin Press, 1966. xii, 226 p. *University of Wisconsin publications in medieval science.* **30**

Text and facing translation of an early Arabic algebra, in a 15th-century version.

Abū Ma'shar, *805 or-6–886.* "Albumasar in Sadan," by Lynn Thorndike, *Isis*, 45 (1954), 22–32. **31**

Description, paraphrase, and translation of illustrative excerpts from work on astrology in dialogue form.

Abū al-Minā al-Kūhīn, al 'Aṭṭar, *13th cent.* "The Arabic pharmacopoeia of Abū al-Minā al-Kūhīn, al-Aṭṭar," by Leon Nemoy, *Hebrew Medical Journal*, 1941, 68–76, 156–66; 1942, 88–93, 144–48; 1943, 77–85, 144–50. **32**

Excerpts from the introduction and from each chapter are translated; an appendix lists the English, Latin, and Arabic technical terms. This manual of pharmacology represents a major Jewish contribution to Arabic medicine, according to the translator; the author's Hebrew name may have been Abraham ha-Kohen. The manual was probably written *c.* A.D. 1260, in Cairo.

Abū al-Qāsim Khalaf ibn 'Abbas al-Zahrāwī, *d. 1013?* A pharmaceutical view of Abulcasis Al Zahrawi in Moorish Spain, with special reference to the "Adhan," by Sami Khalaf Hamarneh and Glenn Sonnedecker. Leiden, Brill, 1963. xii, 176 p. **33**

Text and translation of excerpts from the 25th treatise of al-Tasrif, Manual for physicians, the "Adhān" on oils and ointments.

—— Tacuinum sanitatis in medicina, Codex Vindobonensis, series nova 2644 der Osterreichischen Nationalbibliothek . . . Englische Ubersetzung der Bildtexte, Heide Saxer und Charles H. Talbot. Graz, Austria, Akademische Druck- und Verlagsanstalt, 1967. 148 p. **34**

The captions of the illustrations in the 14th-century medical house book of the Cerruti family are translated in a companion volume to the facsimile edition.

Abū Yazīd, al-Bistāmī, *d. c. 874.* Hindu and Muslim mysticism, by Robert C. Zaehner. London, University of London, Athlone Press, 1960. viii, 234 p. **35**

Contains on pp. 198–218 (Appendix II) a translation of the "ascension" or mi ʿrāj of Abū Yazīd.

Adam of Eynsham, *fl. 1196–1232.* The Life of St. Hugh of Lincoln, ed. and tr. by Decima L. Douie and Hugh Farmer. London and New York, Nelson, [1961–62]. 2 v. *Medieval texts.* **36**

Text and facing translation of Magna vita Sancti Hugonis.

Adamnan, *Saint, 625?–704.* Adamnan's Life of Columba, ed. with translation and notes by Alan O. Anderson and Marjorie O. Anderson. London and New York, Nelson [1966]. xxiv, 590 p. **37**

Text from an early 8th-century manuscript and facing translation.

—— De locis sanctis, ed. and tr. by Denis Meehan. Dublin, Institute for Advanced Studies, 1958. 154 p. *Scriptores Latini Hiberniae,* 3. **38**

Description of a journey to Jerusalem supposedly taken by Arculf, late 7th century, who was described by Bede as "Galliarum episcopus", according to the editor, but about whom nothing else is known. Text and facing translation.

Adamus Bremensis, *d. 1081.* Adam of Bremen, History of the Archbishops of Hamburg–Bremen, tr. . . . by Francis J. Tschan. New York, Columbia University Press, 1959. xxxiv, 253 p. *Records of civilization,* 53. **39**

Translation of Gesta Hammaburgensis ecclesiae pontificum.

Aegidius of Assisi, *d. 1262.* Golden words; the sayings of Brother Giles of Assisi, with a biography by Nello Vian, tr. from the Italian by Ivo O'Sullivan. Chicago, Franciscan Herald Press [1966]. 159 p. **40**

Aesopus.

Although Farrar and Evans did not list translations of the Aesopian fables, translations are listed here which include medieval accretions to the genre, many of which cannot be regarded as mere redactions. For a discussion of the relationship of the medieval versions to their sources and among each other, see the introduction by Ben Edwin Perry to the Loeb Classics edition of Babrius and Phaedrus, Cambridge, Harvard University Press, 1965.

—— Caxton's Aesop (1484), ed. by R. T. Lenaghen. Cambridge, Harvard University Press, 1967. 264 p. **41**

Includes Life of Aesop and one hundred sixty-seven fables which Caxton translated from a French version by Julien Macho of the German collection of Heinrich Steinhöwel, 15th century. The collection includes fables from the Romulus collection, a medieval prose redaction of the Phaedrus 1st-century version; and from additions by Rinuccio da Castiglione of Arezzo, 15th century; Petrus Alphonsus, 12th century; and Poggio Bracciolini, 15th century.

—— Fables, a new translation by S. A. Handford. Baltimore, Penguin Books [1956]. xx, 228 p. **42**

A selection.

—— Fables of Aesop as first printed by William Caxton in 1484 with those of

AESOPUS

Avian, Alfonso, and Poggio, selected, told anew, and their history traced by Joseph Jacobs. New York, Macmillan, 1929; c. 1894. **43**

A partial translation.

—— "Two fables recovered," by B. E. Perry, *Byzantinische Zeitschrift,* 54 (1961), 4–14. **44**

Contains Greek text and translation of two fables from a 15th-century manuscript. According to the author, these fables do not derive from ancient sources but are original works from a "lost medieval story book" showing Arabic influence.

Aethelwold, *Saint, bp. of Winchester, 908?–84.* The monastic agreement of the monks and nuns of the English nation, ed. and tr. by Thomas Symons. London, Nelson [1953]. lix, 1–69, 1–69, [70]–77 p. *Medieval classics.* **45**

Text and facing translation of the Regularis concordia, marking "the final settlement . . . of the Benedictine revival" under Edgar at the Council of Winchester, *c.* 970.

Aetius of Amida, *6th cent.* Aetios of Amida; the gynecology and obstetrics of the 6th c. A.D., tr. from the Latin edition of Cornarius, 1542, . . . by James V. Ricci. Philadelphia, Blakiston, 1950. xiii, 215 p. **46**

The original Greek Tetrabiblon was translated by Janus Cornarius, 1500–58, into Latin. This is the 16th book of the encylopedic work.

Aḥmad ibn al-Ṭayyib, al-Sarakhsī, *d. 899.* Aḥmad b. at-Ṭayyib as-Saraẖsī, a scholar and littérateur of the ninth century, by Franz Rosenthal. New Haven, American Oriental Society, 1943. 135 p. *American Oriental series,* 26. **47**

Contains translation of excerpts of biographical material about al-Sarakhsī and of the fragments of his encyclopedic works quoted by later authors. A pupil of al-Kindī, al-Sarakhsī wrote about science, music, history, and philosophy.

Akathistos hymn. Ode to our blessed Lady . . . A.D. 626, translated by V. McNabb. Oxford, Blackfriars, 1948. 40 p. **48**

Translation of a poem celebrating the deliverance of Constantinople from the barbarians.

Albarus, Paulus, *d. c. 861.* Paul Albar of Cordoba, studies on his life and writings, by Carleton M. Sage. Washington, Catholic University of America Press, 1943. xii, 239 p. *Catholic University studies in medieval history,* n.s. 5. **49**

Includes a translation of Albar's Vita Eulogii, pp. 190–214.

Alberti, Leone Battista, *1404–72.* On painting, tr. by John R. Spencer. New Haven, Yale University Press, 1956. 141 p. Revised, 1966. **50**

Translation from Latin and Italian manuscripts of the "first modern treatise on the theory of painting," written *c.* 1435.

Albertus Magnus, *Saint, bp. of Ratisbon, 1193?–1280.* "Albertus Magnus on ore deposits," by Dorothy Wyckoff, *Isis,* 49 (1958), 109–22. **51**

Includes translations of many excerpts, later included in the complete translation of De mineralibus.

—— Arabic science in the West, by D. M. Dunlop. Karachi, Pakistan Historical Society [preface 1958]. v, 119 p. **52**

Includes some excerpts from De mineralibus in translation.

—— Book of Minerals, tr. by Dorothy Wyckoff. Oxford, Clarendon Press, 1967. xiii, 309 p. 53

A translation of De mineralibus, which contains much first-hand observation by Albertus on mining.

—— Latin treatises on comets, between 1238–1368, ed. and tr. by Lynn Thorndike. Chicago, University of Chicago Press [1950]. ix, 274 p. 54

Texts of several treatises; translations of those of Thomas Aquinas, pp. 77–86; Albertus Magnus, pp. 62–76 (Liber I Meteorum, tractatus III).

SUPPOSITIOUS WORKS

—— Of Cleaving to God; De adhaerando Deo, tr. from the 15th c. Latin Ms. attributed to St. Albert the Great by Elisabeth Stopp. Oxford, Blackfriars [1947]. 59 p.; London, Mowbray, 1954. 52 p. *Fleur de lys series*, 3. 55

A compilation attributed to Albertus Magnus but also to Johannes von Kastl.

—— "An alchemical tract attributed to Albertus Magnus," by Pearl Kibre, *Isis*, 35 (1944), 303–16. 56

Text and "analysis of contents" which is a loose paraphrase of a work probably not by Albertus but which is a pre-1500 "pseudo-scientific" tract.

—— Libellus de alchimia, ascribed to Albertus Magnus, tr. . . . by Virginia Heines. Berkeley, University of California Press, 1958. xxii, 79 p. 57

The "Little Book of Alchemy" was also known as Semita recta, "Right Path." Translated from the Borgnet edition.

Alcuin, *d. 804.* Son well-beloved, six poems by Alcuin, tr. by Benedictines of Stanbrook. Callow End, Worcester, Stanbrook Abbey Press, 1967. viii, 10 p. 58

This translation, published in a limited edition, has not been seen.

Alexandre de Villedieu, *1170–1250.* Ecclesiale by Alexander of Villa Dei, ed. with English translation by L. R. Lind. Lawrence, University of Kansas Press, 1958. x, 155 p. 59

Text and following prose translation of a verse computus, a treatise on the liturgical year, made from an unique manuscript.

ʻAlī ibn Riḍwān, *d. c. 1068.* "The Kitāb al-nāfiʻ of ʻAlī ibn Riḍwān," by M. C. Lyons, *Islamic Quarterly*, 6 (1961), 65–71. 60

Translation of selected passages from a work on medicine in 11th-century Egypt.

Alma rišaia rba. A pair of Naṣoraean commentaries; two priestly documents, the Great first world and the Lesser first world, tr. by E. S. Drower. Leiden, Brill, 1963. xi, 90 p. and two scrolls. 61

The scrolls are facsimiles of two manuscripts in the Bodleian Library, of the Alma rišaia rba and the Alma rišaia zuta, modern transcriptions of ancient rites in archaic language of the Mandaean sect of Gnostics.

Ambrosius, *Saint, bp. of Milan, c. 340–97.* The Brahman episode, St. Ambrose's version of the colloquy between Alexander the Great and the Brahmans of India, ed. . . . and tr. by S. V. Yankowski. Ansbach [privately printed by Elisabeth Kottmeier and E. G. Kostetzky], 1962. 47 p. [64 p. in some copies which include illustrations]. **62**

St. Ambrose's version of the Greek of Palladius (successively Bp. of Helenopolis and of Aspona, d. *c.* 430). The story tells of the meeting between Alexander and the leader of the Brahmans, the Sage of India.

—— The Explanatio symboli ad initiando, a work of St. Ambrose; a provisionally constructed text ed. with intro., notes, and a translation by R. H. Connolly. Cambridge [Eng.], Cambridge University Press, 1952. 39 p. *Texts and studies, contributions to Biblical and Patristic literature,* 10. **63**

Contains the text of an orally delivered work reconstructed from two manuscript versions; and a translation. The work is a commentary on the Apostle's Creed.

—— Funeral orations by Gregory Nazianen and Ambrose, tr. by Leo P. McCauley *et al.* New York, Fathers of the Church, 1953. xxi, 344. *Fathers of the Church,* 22. **64**

Includes the following orations of Ambrose: On his brother Satyrus (two), On Emperor Valentinian, On Emperor Theodosius.

—— Given to love, sermons preached at Milan and written out in three books for his sister Marcellina. . . . with a fourth book of other sermon notes, tr. by James Shiel. Chicago, Scepter Press, [1963]. 126 p. **65**

The first three books constitute De virginibus. According to the translator, the fourth book is a collection of notes from other sermons, "practically a phrase by phrase commentary on the Song of Solomon." This volume also appeared under the title The nun's ideals, same place and publisher, 1964.

—— Hexameron, Paradise, and Cain and Abel, tr. by John J. Savage. New York, Fathers of the Church, 1961. xi, 449 p. *Fathers of the Church,* 42. **66**

—— Letters, tr. by Mary Melchior Beyenka. New York, Fathers of the Church, 1954. xviii, 515 p. *Fathers of the Church,* 26. **67**

Ninety-one letters arranged according to addressees.

—— Theological and dogmatic works, tr. by Roy J. Deferrari. Washington, Catholic University of America Press, 1963. xxiii, 343 p. *Fathers of the Church,* 44. **68**

Contains translations of The mysteries, The Holy Spirit, The sacrament of the Incarnation of our Lord, The sacraments.

—— There came wise men: Magi venerunt, commentary by Saint Ambrose of Milan, tr. by Benedictines of Stanbrook Abbey. Callow End, Worcester, Stanbrook Abbey Press, 1959. 11 p. **69**

Text and translation from the Mass and Office of the sixth day within the octave of the Epiphany. A copy of this limited edition is in the Andover Library, Harvard University.

America, Norse discovery of. *Sagas.* The Vinland sagas; the Norse discovery of America, tr. with an intro. by Magnus Magnusson and Hermann Pálsson. [New York], New York University Press, 1966; Baltimore, Penguin Books [1965]. 124 p. **70**

Contains translation of Grœnlander þattr and Eiriks þattr Rauða.

—— Vinland the good, the saga of Leif Eiriksson and the Viking discovery of America, with a preface by Helge Ingstad, tr. by Joan Tindale Blindheim. Oslo, Tanum [1966]. 79 p. **71**

The translation is based on Anne Holtsmark's version *Vinland det gode*. Grœnlander þattr is translated from the Flateyjarbók codex; Eirik's from Skálboltsbók. For other translations, see *Icelandic literature. Collections.*

Amirani (*Georgian mythological epic*). Amiran Darejaniani; a cycle of medieval Georgian tales traditionally ascribed to Mose Khoneli, tr. by R. H. Stevenson. Oxford, Clarendon Press, 1958. xxxiii, 240 p. **72**

A 12th-century cycle. Passages from Khoneli's other works, as well as suggested emendations to this translation, appear in "Amiran-Darejaniani, a Georgian romance and its English rendering," by D. M. Lang and G. M. Meredith, *Bulletin of the School of Oriental and African Studies,* 22 (1959), 454–90.

Ancren riwle. The Ancrene riwle (the Corpus MS.: Ancrene wisse), tr. . . . by M. B. Salu, with an intro. by Gerard Sitwell and a preface by J. R. R. Tolkien. London, Burns & Oates, [1955]; Notre Dame, Ind., University of Notre Dame Press [1956]. xxvii, 196 p. **73**

This translation is from the Middle English version.

Andreas, *Saint, abp. of Crete, 660–740.* The great canon: a poem of Saint Andrew of Crete, recited during some of the Lenten offices of the Easten Orthodox Church, tr. by Derwas J. Chitty. London, Fellowship of St. Alban and St. Sergius, 1957. 47 p. **74**

Andrew, *Saint, apostle, legend.* Andrew, brother of Simon Peter, his history and his legends, by P. M. Peterson. Leiden, Brill, 1958. vii, 69 p. **75**

Contains translation *passim* and on pp. 49–66 of excerpts from the apocryphal Acts of Andrew, the Gospel of Peter, and other material in Greek and Syriac up to the 12th century.

Anglo-Saxon chronicle. The Anglo-Saxon chronicle, a revised translation ed. by Dorothy Whitelock, with David C. Douglas and Susie I. Tucker. London, Eyre and Spottiswoode [1961]; New Brunswick, N.J., Rutgers University Press [1962]. xxxii, 240 p. **76**

Translation revised from that which appeared in Vols. I and II of *English Historical Documents;* arranged so as "to make it easier for the reader to distinguish the information common to all or several mss. from those additions peculiar to single versions." *Cf.* below, *England. Historical sources.*

—— Anglo-Saxon chronicle, tr. by George N. Garmonsway. London, Dent, 1953. xlviii, 295 p. *Everyman's library.* **77**

Translation of the Parker Chronicle (A) and Laud Chronicle (E) in parallel columns.

—— The Peterborough chronicle, tr. by Harry A. Rositzke. New York, Columbia University Press, 1951. 193 p. *Records of civilization,* 44. **78**

This translation, based on the E text printed by Plummer, is of a single chronicle, rather than the usual conflation of several.

Anglure, Ogier VIII, *seigneur d', d. 1412?* "Le saint voyage de Jherusalem du seigneur d'Anglure," by Henry L. Savage, pp. 199–220 in The Arab heritage, ed. by Nabih Amin Faris. Princeton, Princeton University Press, 1944. xii, 279 p. **79**

ANNALES GANDENSES

The essay contains translations of illustrative quotations and a paraphrase of a travel record of 1395.

Annales Gandenses. Annals of Ghent, tr. . . . by Hilda Johnstone. New York, Oxford University Press; London, Nelson, 1951. xxix, 100, 100, 101–5 p. *Medieval classics.* **80**

Text and translation of annals covering 1297 to 1310.

Annals of Innisfallen. Annals of Innisfallen, ed. with translation by Sean MacAirt. Dublin, Institute for Advanced Studies, 1951. lii, 596 p. **81**

Text in Latin, Irish of some pre-Patrician, mostly post-Patrician annals (433–1450). The pre-Patrician annal, essentially an abridgment of the Latin "Irish World Chronicle," is translated completely; the later annals, in Latin and Irish, have only the Irish parts translated. These records, which record events of Munster and Southern Ireland, are to be distinguished from the "Dublin Annals of Innisfallen," compiled in 1765 from various sources.

Anonymous IV. [Concerning the measurement of polyphonic song], tr. and ed. by Luther Dittmer. Brooklyn, Institute of Medieval Music [1959]. 72 p. *Musical theorists in translation,* 1. **82**

A translation of De mensuris et discantu . . ., written *c.* 1275 by an author designated as Anonymous IV in Edmund de Coussemaker's (Cousse) Scriptorum de musica medii aevi . . ., 1854.

Anonymous VII. "Two XIII century treatises on modal rhythm and the discant," by Janet Knapp, *Journal of Music Theory,* 6 (1962), 200–216. **83**

Contains a translation of the anonymous De musica libellus.

Anselm, *Saint, abp. of Canterbury, 1033–1109.* The De grammatico of St. Anselm, the theory of paronymy, tr. by Desmond P. Henry. Notre Dame, Ind., University of Notre Dame Press, 1964. xiii, 169 p. *University of Notre Dame publications in medieval studies,* 18. **84**

Text and following translation of a logical work better described, the translator suggests, as a "Dialogue on paronymns." Excerpts from De grammatico as well as from expositions and parallel passages to it in other works of Anselm and other philosophers appear in The logic of Saint Anselm by Desmond P. Henry, Oxford, Clarendon Press, 1967. viii, 251 p.

—— The many-faced argument; recent studies on the ontological argument for the existence of God, ed. by John Hick and Arthur C. McGill. New York, Macmillan [1967]. vii, 373 p. **85**

Contains a new translation by Arthur C. McGill of chapters 2–4 of the Proslogion, Gaunilo's criticism, and Anselm's reply, pp. 3–32.

—— Prayers and meditations, sel. and tr. by a Religious of C.S.M.V. London, Mowbray; New York, Morehouse-Gorham [1952]. 54 p. **86**

—— St. Anselm's Proslogion, with A reply on behalf of the fool by Gaunilo, and the author's reply to Gaunilo, tr. with an intro. and philosophical commentary by M. J. Charlesworth. Oxford, Clarendon Press, 1965. vi, 196 p. **87**

Text and facing translation.

—— Theological treatises, ed. [and tr.] by Jasper Hopkins and Herbert Richardson [*et al.*] Cambridge, Harvard Divinity School Library [1965–67]. 3 v. **88**

Vol. I: Three philosophical dialogues: Concerning truth, On freedom of choice, the Fall of Satan was published in 1967 by Harper and Row as Truth, freedom and evil: three philosophical dialogues by Anselm of Canterbury, 196 p. Vol. II: contains On the procession of the Holy Spirit, Two letters concerning Roscelin, On the Incarnation of the Word, On the sacraments. Vol. III: On the Virgin conception and original sin, On the harmony of the foreknowledge, the pre-destination, and the grace of God with free choice.

Anthemius, *d. c. 534.* Anthemius of Tralles, a study in later Greek geometry, by George L. Huxley. Cambridge, Harvard University Press, 1959. *Greek, Roman and Byzantine monographs,* 1. **89**

Contains text and translation of Peri paradoxon mechanomaton and Fragmentum mathematicum Bobiense.

Anthologia graeca. The Greek anthology with an English translation by W. R. Paton. London, Heinemann; New York, Putnam, 1916–18. 5 v. *Loeb classics.* **90**

Text and facing translation. Contains also a bibliography of "the more important books containing verse translations from the Greek Anthology." Recent verse translations of selections include: Poems from the Greek anthology in English paraphrase, by Dudley Fitts. [New York], New Directions [1956], 141 p.; and Selections from the Greek anthology by Andrew Sinclair. New York, Macmillan [c. 1967], 150 p. [This heading omitted in Farrar and Evans.]

al-Anvār, Qāsim, *1356–1433–4.* "The Turkish verses of Qāsim al-Anvār," by G. M. Meredith-Owens, *Bulletin of the School of Oriental and African Studies,* 25 (1962), 155–61. **91**

Text (based on nine manuscripts) and translation of four poems written "playfully" in Turkish by Qāsim, who usually wrote in Arabic.

Apicius. The Roman cookery book, a critical translation of the art of cooking, tr. by Barbara Flower and Elisabeth Rosenbaum. London and New York, British Book Centre, 1958; London, Harrap [1958]. 240 p. **92**

A translation from two 9th-century manuscripts of a work now thought to have been compiled in the 4th century. For the date, see Mary Ella Milham, "Aspects of non-technical vocabulary in Apicius," *American Journal of Philology,* 80 (1959), 67–75.

Apocrypha of the New Testament.

Only major translations are listed here. For translations of excerpts, summaries, and bibliographies of all the apocrypha, see Johannes Quasten, Patrology (Westminster, Md., Newman Press, 1950–60), Vol. I, Ch. III, pp. 106–57. See also *Christian literature. Collections.*

COLLECTIONS

—— New Testament Apocrypha by Edgar Hennecke, ed. by William Schneemelcher; English translation [from German] ed. by R. McL. Wilson; tr. by R. McL. Wilson and others. Philadelphia, Westminster Press, 1963–65. 2 v. **93**

The English translation was made from the German by various translators but after comparison with original texts; the apocrypha and the commentary by Hennecke have been translated. Most apocrypha are translated in full but a few are abridged, *e.g.,* the Gospel of truth. Vol. I contains The Gospels and related writings; Vol. II, Writings related to the Apostles; Apocalypses and related subjects.

—— [Coptic Gospel of Philip.] The Gospel of Philip, tr. by Robert M. Wilson. New York, Harper [c. 1962]. vii, 198 p. **94**

A translation of a commentary on New Testament writings from the point of view of a Valentinian heretic.

—— "The Gospel according to Philip." by C. J. Catanzaro, *Journal of Theological Studies,* 13 (1962), 35–71. **95**

—— [Coptic Gospel of Thomas.] The Coptic Gospel of Thomas: a gnostic source of unknown sayings of Jesus from Chenoboskion, distributed as ms. by Princeton Theological Seminary. Princeton, N.J., 1959. 9 p. **96**

An English translation prepared by the New Testament Seminar of Princeton Theological Seminary, from a Coptic manuscript published in 1956 by Dr. Pahor Labib, Coptic Gnostic Papyri in the Coptic Museum in Old Cairo, I. The manuscript was discovered in 1945 in Nag-Hamadi, upper Egypt.

—— The Gospel according to Thomas, Coptic text established and tr. by A. Guillaumont, H-Ch. Puech, and G. Quispel. Leiden, Brill; London, Collins; New York, Harper, 1959; vii, 62 p. **97**

Text and facing translation. The text is a Sahidic Coptic version of an original Greek text, the editors think; they intend to publish a complete text and translation of the entire codex. This part is almost entirely "Sayings of Jesus."

—— The secret books of the Egyptian Gnostics, an intro. to the Gnostic Coptic manuscripts discovered at Chenoboskion, by Jean Doresse [tr. by Philip Mairet], with an English translation and critical evaluation of the Gospel according to Thomas. New York, Viking Press [1960]. xvii, 445 p. **98**

The Gospel has been translated by Leonard Johnston, from Doresse's French version.

—— The secret sayings of Jesus, by Robert M. Grant in collaboration with David Noel Freedman, with an English translation of the Gospel of Thomas by William R. Schoedel. Garden City, N. Y., Doubleday, 1960; London, Collins, 1960. 206 p. **99**

According to the author, the manuscript for the Gospel dates from the 4th century; Thomas probably lived in the 2d century.

—— [Gospel of John.] The Gospel of peace of Jesus Christ by the Disciple John. The Aramaic and Old Slavonic texts compared and ed. by Edmond Szekely, tr. by E. Szekely and Purcell Weaver. Rockford, England, C. W. Daniel Co., 1947. 62 p. **100**

This volume contains a translation of about one eighth of the Gospel; a complete edition promised by the editors has never appeared. The introduction to the 1947 version refers to the "1st ed., 1937" which has not been seen.

—— [Miracles at Christ's Birth.] "The Middle Irish Apocryphal account of 'The seventeen miracles at Christ's birth,'" by Vernam Hull, *Modern Philology,* 43 (1945–46), 25–39. **101**

Text and translation in prose and verse.

—— [Vision of Daniel.] "A commentary on the XIVth Vision of Daniel, according to the Coptic version," by Otto F. A. Meinardus, *Orientalia Christiana Periodica,* 32 (1966), 394–449. **102**

Contains translation of a Coptic version of an apocalyptic work; the translation seems to have been done by O. H. E. Khs.-Burmester.

Apollonius of Tyre. Historia Apollonii regis Tyri, tr. by Paul Turner. [London] Golden Cockerel Press, 1956. 68 p. **103**

The first translation from the Latin version since 1576, according to the translator; *cf.* Farrar and Evans, item 324. The translation is based on Codex Lauretianus, 9th or 10th century, and Codex Parisinus, 14th century.

Apostolias, Michaēl, *fl. 1462.* "A Byzantine looks at the Renaissance," by Dino Geanokoplos, *Greek, Roman and Byzantine Studies,* 1 (1958), 160–61. **104**

A brief but significant translation.

Apostolic Fathers. The Apostolic Fathers, tr. by Francis X. Glimm, Gerald G. Walsh, and Joseph Marique. New York, Cima Publishing Co. [1947]. xii, 401 p. *Fathers of the Church,* 1. **105**

Contents: Letter of St. Clement of Rome to the Corinthians; the so-called Second letter of Clement; Letters of St. Ignatius of Antioch; Martyrdom of St. Polycarp; the Didache; Letter of Barnabas; the Shepherd of Hermas (omitted after 1st printing); Letter to Diognetus; Fragments of Papias (in 1st printing only). No reason is given for omitting the Shepherd of Hermas, but this work seems now to be regarded as part of the Apocrypha rather than as a Patristic product.

—— The Didache, The epistle of Barnabas, The epistles and The martyrdom of St. Polycarp, The fragments of Papias, The epistle to Diognetus, newly tr. and annotated by James A. Kleist. Westminster, Md., Newman Press, 1948. vi, 235 p. *Ancient Christian writers,* 6. **106**

—— The Apostolic Fathers, an American translation by Edgar J. Goodspeed New York, Harper [1950]. xi, 321 p. **107**

Contents: the Didache; Letter of Barnabus; First and so-called Second letter of Clement; the Shepherd of Hermas; Letters of Ignatius; Letter of Polycarp; Martyrdom of Polycarp; Apology of Quadratus; Fragments of Papias. The translation is based on the Funk-Bihlmeyer edition, Tübingen, 1924.

—— The Apostolic Fathers; a new translation and commentary ed. by Robert M. Grant. New York, Nelson [1964–68]. 6 v. **108**

Contents: vol. I, Introduction by R. M. Grant; vol. 2, First and Second Clement, by R. M. Grant and H. H. Graham; vol. 3, Barnabas and the Didache, by R. A. Kraft; vol. 4, Ignatius of Antioch, by R. M. Grant; vol. 5, Polycarp, Martyrdom of Polycarp, Fragments of Papias, by W. R. Schoedel; vol. 6, the Shepherd of Hermas, by G. F. Snyder.

Arabian nights.

This category was not included by Farrar and Evans, but it has seemed advisable to include it here because of the new evidence for medieval provenience of many of the tales. Only major translations before 1942 and new ones since that date are listed. For a complete bibliography of translations into all languages up to 1963, see Mia I. Gerhardt, The art of story-telling, a literary study of the Thousand and One Nights, Leiden, Brill, 1963; see Ch. 1 of this work for a discussion of the medieval provenience. For a restatement of the problems of the Arabian Nights, see the article *s.v.* Alf laila wa laila in the Encyclopedia of Islam, 2d ed. Translations are listed here in chronological order.

—— The thousand and one nights, The Arabian nights' entertainment, tr. by Edward W. Lane. London, C. Knight, 1839–41. 3 v. **109**

According to de Bary and Embree, Guide to Oriental Classics, Columbia University Press, 1964, this is "the earliest important translation," "incomplete and literal . . . but valuable for its accuracy and extensive commentary."

ARABIAN NIGHTS

—— The book of the thousand and one nights, tr. by John Payne. London, 1882–88, 13 v. **110**

According to de Bary and Embree, this is the first complete translation into English, "noted for its literal rendering of the original."

—— The Arabian Nights' entertainments; or, The book of a thousand nights and a night, tr. by Richard F. Burton. Benares, 1885–88, 16 vols.; London, ed. Smithers, 1894–97, 12 vols; reprinted by Heritage Press, 1956, 6 v. in 3. **111**

A very full but incomplete "literal" translation.

—— Scheherezade, tales from the thousand and one nights, tr. by A. J. Arberry. London, Allen & Unwin, 1953. 221 p. **112**

Contains translations of Aladdin and the enchanted lamp, Judar and his brother, Aboukir and Abousir, The amorous goldsmith.

—— The Thousand and one nights, the Hunchback, Sinbad, and other tales, tr. by N. J. Dawood. Harmondsworth [Eng.], Penguin Books, 1954. 240 p. **113**

Tales included are those of the hunchback, the donkey, the fisherman and the jinee, the young woman and her five lovers, Sindbad the sailor, Kafur the black eunuch, Khalifah the fisherman, and Ma'aruf the cobbler.

—— Aladdin and other tales from the 1001 nights, tr. by N. J. Dawood. Harmondsworth [Eng.], Penguin Books, 1957. 210 p. **114**

This work has not been seen.

Arabic literature. *Collections.* Arabic-Andalusian casidas, tr. with intro. by Harold Morland. London, Phoenix, 1969. 57 p. **115**

Poems of the 9th to the 13th century translated into verse.

—— "The Arabic chess manuscripts in the John Rylands Library," by Joseph de Somogyi, *Bulletin of the John Rylands Library,* Manchester, 41 (March, 1959), 430–45. **116**

Description and summary-paraphrase of two 14th-century manuscripts.

—— Arabic poetry; a primer for stutents, ed. by A. J. Arberry. Cambridge [Eng.], Cambridge University Press, 1965. vi, 174 p. **117**

Arabic text and facing English translation of poems from twenty-five medieval poets and six later ones.

—— "Aspects of Arabic urban literature mostly in the ninth and tenth centuries," by G. E. von Grunebaum, *al-Andalus*, 20 (1955), 259–81. **118**

Contains *passim* translation of excerpts from poems about cities.

—— Eastern love; 101 ribald tales, a collection of amorous tales of the Orient as tr. by Edward Powys Mathers; unexpurgated abridgment ed. by Joseph Hilton Smyth. Greenwich, Conn., Fawcett Publications [1958]. 239 p. **119**

This is a partial reprint of a work published in London by John Rodker, 1927–29, 12 v. in 4; Mathers translated from the French version of René Basset. The work contains anecdotes and tales attributed to medieval Arabic authors.

—— Eastern love poems, tr. by [Edward] Powys Mathers. [London], Folio Society, 1953. 148 p. **120**

Most of the translations are from Far Eastern sources, but twelve poems from medieval Arabic and Persian sources are included.

—— "Four famous muwaṣṣahs from Ibn Buṣrā's Anthology," by S. M. Stern, *al-Andalus,* 23 (1958), 339–69. **121**

Arabic text and following prose translation of four poems from a work discovered in 1950; the poems are from the 11th or 12th century; written in Spain, they belong to Mozarabic literature.

—— Hispano-Arabic poetry and its relations with the old Provençal troubadours, by A. R. Nykl. Baltimore, J. H. Furst Co., 1946. xxvii, 416 p. **122**

Translation of selected poems written 711–1492 by some three hundred poets.

—— Humor in early Islam, a translation of the Ash'ab story, by Franz Rosenthal. Leiden, Brill; Philadelphia, University of Pennsylvania Press, 1956. x, 154 p. **123**

Anecdotes by Ash'ab telling political, religious, and urban jokes, from the 8th century.

—— Images from the Arab world; fragments of Arab literature tr. and paraphrased with variations and comments by Herbert Howarth and Ibrahim Shukrallah. London, Pilot Press, [1944]. xvi, 17–143 p. **124**

Both poetry and prose are translated, largely from medieval authors.

—— A Maltese anthology, ed. by Arthur J. Arberry. Oxford, Clarendon Press, 1960. xxxvii, 280 p. **125**

Contains on pp. 2–37 text and facing translation of folk materials which are "approximate specimens of medieval Maltese," a dialect of Arabic, according to the editor; no actual medieval Maltese documents survive.

—— Persian and Arabic riddles, a language-centered approach to genre definition, by Charles T. Scott. Bloomington, University of Indiana Press, 1965. vii, 135 p. *Publications of the Indiana University Research Center in Anthropology . . .,* 89. **126**

Contains text and "free translation" of many riddles *passim* and in appendices.

—— "Studies on Ibn Quzmān," by S. M. Stern, *al-Andalus,* 16 (1951), 379–425. **127**

Contains text and translation of four unpublished poems of the genre *zayāl* (strophic poems), two by Ibn Quzmān, one by Ibn Rāsid, a predecessor of Ibn Quzmān, and one anonymous.

—— A treasury of Asian literature, ed. by John D. Yohannan. New York, Day [1956]. 487 p. **128**

Short selections from many medieval sources, including Arabic and Persian.

Arabs. *Historical sources.* Arab seafaring in the Indian Ocean in ancient and early medieval times, by George F. Hourani. Princeton, Princeton University Press, 1951. 131 p. *Princeton Oriental studies,* 13 **129**

The Appendix, pp. 114–22, contains translation of four sea stories, three from Buzurg ibn Shahriyār, 10th century, and one from Muḥammad ibn Aḥmad, called Ibn Jubair, 1145–1217. Many excerpts from these and other sources are translated *passim* also.

—— "Events in Arabia in the 6th century A.D.," by Sidney Smith, *Bulletin of the School of Oriental and African Studies,* 16 (1954), 425–68. **130**

ARAMAIC TEXTS

Contains *passim* translations of many Greek as well as Arabic sources including contemporary inscriptions.

Aramaic texts. "An Aramaic exorcism," by Cyrus H. Gordon, *Archiv Orientalni (Journal of the Czechoslovakia Oriental Institute)*, 6 (1934), 466–74. **131**

Text and translation of 7th-century vase inscription of Jewish origin.

—— Aramaic incantation texts from Nippur, by James A. Montgomery. Philadelphia, University Museum, 1913. 326 p. *University of Pennsylvania, The Museum, Publications of the Babylonian section,* 3. **132**

Text and translation of inscriptions written in 600 and later in Aramaic, Syriac, Mandaic. This volume was omitted from Farrar and Evans.

—— "Aramaic magical bowls in the Istanbul and Baghdad Museums," by Cyrus H. Gordon, *Archiv Orientalni (Journal of the Czechoslovak Oriental Institute)*, 6 (1934), 319–34. **133**

Text and translation of inscriptions from the 7th century which reflect life in Babylonia at the time of the Islamic conquest.

—— Jewish and Mandaean incantation bowls in the Royal Ontario Museum, by William S. McCullough. Toronto, University of Toronto Press, 1967. 70 p. **134**

Decipherment and translation of inscriptions in Hebrew and Mandaic, *terminus ad quem,* 600.

Archelaos, *alchemist, 8th cent.?* "Rhetorical and religious aspects of Greek alchemy, including a commentary and translation of the poems of the philosopher Archelaos upon the sacred art," by C. A. Browne, *Ambix,* 2 (1946), 129–37. **135**

Metrical translation of a work very influential upon later writers, according to the author. Discussion of the poem is found in *Ambix*, 3 (1948), 15–25.

Arethas, *bp. of Caesarea, c. 860–c. 940.* "Eight letters of Arethas on the fourth marriage of Leo the Wise," by R. J. Jenkins and B. Laourdas, *Hellenika,* 14 (1956), 293–372. **136**

Contains Greek text, a summary in English, and commentary on the letters.

—— "Texts for the historical study of the Vita Euthymii," by P. Karlin-Hayter, *Byzantion,* 28 (1958), 363–89; 31 (1961), 273–307. **137**

Text and translation of documents concerning the fourth marriage of Leo the Wise.

Aristotle. Maqāla tas͟htamil ʻala fuṣūlmin kitāb al-hayawān liariṣtū (Tract comprising excerpts from Aristotle's Book of animals), ed. and tr. by J. N. Mattock. Cambridge [Eng.], Published for the Cambridge Middle East Centre by W. Heffer [c. 1966]. xvi, 110. *Arabic technical and scientific texts,* 2. **138**

Text and facing translation of a work sometimes attributed to Maimonides; it is "less of an epitome of Aristotle's biological works than a series of short paragraphs containing isolated fragments from three works of Aristotle on animals." The theoretical parts are omitted.

—— "The Nicomachean ethics in Arabic," by Arthur J. Arberry, *Bulletin of the School of Oriental and African Studies,* 17 (1955), 1–9. **139**

Includes text and translation of a fragment.

Aristotle, *life of.* Aristotle in the ancient biographical tradition, by Ingemar

Düring. Göteburg, 1957. 490 p. *Acta Universitatis Gothoburgensis, Göteborgs Universitets Årsskrift,* 63, no. 2. **140**

Part II, The Syriac and Arabic tradition on Aristotle's life and writings, pp. 184–248, has translation of the Vita Syriaca I and II, and of three Arabic lives, all based on Ptolemy-el-Garib, a non-extant work, with fictitious additions from Syriac and Arabic traditions. The Arabic authors are Ibn Abī Ya'qub an-Nadīm, who wrote before 987; Mubashshir ibn Fatik, Abū al-Wafā, 11th century; and Ibn Abī Uṣaibi 'a, 1203–70.

Armenian literature. Armenian legends and poems, compiled by Zabelle C. Boyajian . . . and a contribution [history of Armenian literature] by Aram Raffi. New York, Columbia University Press; London, Dent, 1916; reprint 1958. **141**

Contains translations from Moses of Khorene, 5th century; St. Gregory of Narck, 951–1009; St. Nerses Shnorhali, 1102–73; Hovhannes Erzingatzi, b. 1260; "Frik," d. 1330; Hovhannes Tulkourantzi, 1450–1525; Grigoris of Aghtamar, 15th century; Nahabed Kouchak, 15th century. This work was omitted by Farrar and Evans, perhaps because of the doubtfulness of some of the ascriptions to medieval sources.

—— Daredevils of Sassoun; the Armenian national epic, tr. by Leon Surmelian. Denver, A. Swallow [1964]. 279 p. **142**

A translation of Sasowntsi Davit', which though not written down until the 19th century, has traditional stories of supermen, "the possessed of Christian Armenia, . . . medieval beatniks!"

Arnaldus de Villanova, *1235?–1311.* "Bedside manners in the Middle Ages, the treatise De cautelis medicorum attributed to Arnald of Villanova," tr. by Henry E. Sigerist, *Northwestern University Medical School Quarterly Bulletin,* 20 (1946), 136–43. **143**

Contains advice on relationship with patients and on the practice of uroscopy. The translator thinks that Arnaldus was the compiler of material from at least one hundred years earlier, rather than the author of the treatise.

Arnobius Afer, *fl. c. 300.* The case against the pagans, newly tr. and annotated by George E. McCracken. Westminster, Md., Newman Press, 1949. 2 v. *Ancient Christian writers,* 7–8. **144**

A translation of Adversus nationes.

Arnórr Thórdarson Jarláskald, *b. c. 1012.* "Arnórr Thórdarson Jarláskald and his poem Hrynhent," by Lee M. Hollander, *Scandinavian Studies,* 17 (1942–43), 99–109. **145**

The poem and scattered biographical references to the author are translated; the poem is an enconium to King Magnus, d. 1047, son of St. Olaf.

Art. *Works about.* "Ars sine scientia nihil est, Gothic theory of architecture at the Cathedral of Milan," by James Ackermann, *Art Bulletin,* 31 (June, 1949), 84–111. **146**

Contains translation of excerpts from late 14th-century annals of the building of the cathedral; text in appendix.

—— Artists on art, from the XIV to the XX century, . . . ed. by Robert Goldwater and Marco Treves. [New York], Pantheon Books [1945]. xv, 497 p. **147**

Largely new translations by the editors of excerpts from Cennino Cennini, *c.* 1372; Lorenzo Ghiberti, 1378–1455; Leone Battista Alberti, 1404–72; Antonio Averlino, called Filarete, 1400–65; Piero della Francesco, 1416?–1492; and Leonardo da Vinci, 1452–1519.

ART

—— The literary sources of art history by Elizabeth Gilmore Holt. Princeton, Princeton University Press, 1947. 555 p. **148**

Republished in expanded form in 1957 as A documentary history of art, vol. I, The Middle Ages and the Renaissance, Garden City, N. Y., Doubleday, xix 380 p. Many of the works are here translated for the first time; pp. 1–288, 297–304 have translations from medieval sources, from the 10th through the 15th century. Short excerpts from many sources; longer ones from Suger, Abbot of St. Denis; Cenninno Cennini; Lorenzo Ghiberti; Leone Battista Alberti; Piero della Francesca; and Leonardo da Vinci.

Arthur, *King.* Arthur, king of Britain; history, romance, chronicle, and criticism, with texts in modern English from Gildas to Malory, ed. by Richard L. Brengle. New York, Appleton-Century-Crofts [1964]. xv, 439 p. **149**

Excerpts from medieval sources and modern criticism; various translations, including some new by the editor.

al-Asadābādī, ʻAbd al-Jabbār ibn Aḥmad, *fl. c. 1025–26.* The Jewish Christians of the early centuries of Christianity according to a new source, by Salomon Pines, *Israel Academy of Sciences and Humanities, Proceedings,* 2, no. 13 (1966). 74 p. **150**

Contains extensive translation of excerpts from an Arabic manuscript ostensibly a chapter of Moslem anti-Christian polemics but actually taken by ʻAbd al-Jabbār from a Jewish-Christian commentary to which he added a commentary.

Asʻad, Fakhr ul-Dīn, *called* **Fakhrī, Jurjānī,** *fl. 1040.* "Vis u Ramin, a Parthian romance," by V. Minorsky, *Bulletin of the School of Oriental and African Studies,* 11 (1946), 741–63; reprinted in *Iranica, twenty articles,* by V. Minorsky, Teheran University, 1964, pp. 151–99. **151**

Contains detailed summary of the plot of a romance similar in many respects to the Tristan and Isolde story.

al-Ashʻarī, ʻAlī ibn Ismāʻīl, *873?–935?* The theology of al-Ashʻari, the Arabic texts of al-Ashʻarī's Kitāb al Lumaʻ and Risālat Istiḥsān al Khawd fī ʻIlm al-Kalām, tr. by Richard J. McCarthy. Beirut, Impressions catholique, 1953. xxviii, 275 p. **152**

Text and facing translation of a work of polemic theology, by the founder of the largest school of Muslim theology, according to the editor. For a discussion of the translation of some difficult terms in al-Ash ʻarī's works, especially with reference to free will in man, see "The structure of created causality in Al-Aš ʻari," by Richard M. Frank, *Studia Islamica,* 25 (1966), 5–75.

Athanasius, *Saint, patriarch of Alexandria, d. 373.* Athanasiana Syrica. Part I. 1. De incarnatione; 2. Epistula ad Epictetum, ed. and tr. by Robert W. Thomson. Louvain, Secrétariat du Corpus SCO, 1965. 2 v. *Corpus scriptorum Christianorum orientalium,* 257 and 258; *Scriptores Syri,* 114, 115. **153**

The first volume contains the texts, the second the translation. The editors expect to publish the rest of Athanasius's works in Syriac in three more parts.

—— De incarnatione, tr. by a Religious of C.S.M.V., intro. by C. S. Lewis. London and New York, Mowbray, 1944. 120 p. **154**

The translation has occasional paraphrase and abridgment. A second edition (1953) has some revisions and adds a translation of the Epistola ad Marcellinum.

—— The letters of St. Athanasius concerning the Holy Spirit, tr. by C. R. B. Shapland. London and New York, Epworth Press, 1951. 204 p. **155**

Contains four epistles written 356–61 to Serapion, bishop of Thmuïs.

—— The life of Saint Antony, newly tr. and annotated by Robert T. Meyer. Westminster, Md., Newman Press, 1950. 154 p. *Ancient Christian writers*, 10. **156**

—— St. Athanasius on the Psalms, a letter rendered for the first time into English by a Religious of C.S.M.V. London, Mowbray, 1949. 43 p. **157**

This translation of the Epistola ad Marcellinum was reprinted with the 1953 edition of De incarnatione; see above.

SPURIOUS AND DOUBTFUL WORKS

—— The Armenian version of the pseudo-Athanasian letter to the Antiochenes [Sermo maior de fide] and of the Expositio fidei, by Robert P. Casey. London, Christophers; Philadelphia, University of Pennsylvania Press, 1947. 78 p. *Studies and documents*, 15. **158**

Text of a 7th-century Armenian version and of a few Greek fragments (Greek original lost) and translation of the Armenian. An anticipated second volume of commentary has apparently never appeared.

—— "A treatise attributed to Athanasius," by G. A. Egan, *Le Muséon*, 80 (1967), 139–51. **159**

Contains text and translation of an Armenian version of a work against heretical views of good and evil.

Athenagoras, *2d cent.* Embassy for the Christians, The resurrection of the dead, tr. and annotated by Joseph H. Crehan. Westminster, Md., Newman Press, 1956. 193 p. *Ancient Christian writers*, 23. **160**

Another translation of the Embassy appears in Early Christian fathers, by Cyril C. Richardson, London, 1953, pp. 290–340; *cf. Christian literature. Collections.*

Augustinus, Aurelius, *Saint, bp. of Hippo, 354–430.*

COLLECTIONS

—— The writings of St. Augustine. New York, Cima Publishing Co., 1947–48. *Fathers of the Church*, 2, 4, 5. **161**

The short treatises appeared in three volumes as follows: vol. 2: Christian instruction, tr. John J. Gavigan; Admonition and grace, tr. John C. Murray; The Christian combat, tr. Robert P. Russell; Faith, hope and charity [Enchiridion], tr. Bernard M. Peebles; vol. 4: The immortality of the soul, tr. Ludwig Schopp; The magnitude of the soul, tr. John J. McMahon; On music. tr. Robert C. Taliaferro; vol. 5: The happy life, tr. Ludwig Schopp; Answer to skeptics, tr. Denis J. Kavanagh; Divine providence and the problem of evil, tr. Robert P. Russell; Soliloquies, tr. Thomas F. Gilligan. The complete works of Augustine are translated in this series; other works are listed under their titles elsewhere. The heading "Writings of St. Augustine" used here is really a subtitle and there is some confusion about numbering the early volumes. Apparently Roy. J. Deferrari is the editor of these volumes, though no indication appears within any of these three.

—— Basic writings of St. Augustine, ed. by Whitney J. Oates. New York, Random House, 1948. 2 v. **162**

Vol. 1 contains the Confessions and twelve treatises; vol. 2, The city of God, On the trinity. Various translations have been used (many of them issued before in the edition of Marcus Dods, Edinburgh, 1872–76), some modified by the editor.

AUGUSTINUS, AURELIUS

—— The greatness of the soul [and] The teacher, tr. and annotated by Joseph M. Colleran. Westminster, Md., Newman Press, 1950. 255 p. *Ancient Christian writers*, 9. **163**

—— Treatises on various subjects, ed. by Roy J. Deferrari, tr. by Mary S. Muldowney *et al.* New York, Fathers of the Church, 1952. viii, 479 p. *Fathers of the Church*, 16. **164**

A collection of minor works classified as "Works of moral and practical theology," nine works by various translators, all newly done for this volume. The works are: De vita Christiana, De mendacio, Contra mendacium, De continentia, De patientia, De bono viduatitis, De opera monachorum, De utilitate jejuni, Quaestiones Dulcitii.

—— Earlier writings, selected and tr. with intro. by John H. S. Burleigh. Philadelphia, Westminster Press [1953]. 413 p. *Library of Christian classics*, 6. **165**

Includes Soliloquia, De magistro, De libero arbitrio, De vera religione, De utilitate credendi, De natura boni, De fide et symbolo (Faith and the Creed), De diversis quaestionibus (To Simplician).

—— Confessions and Enchiridion, newly tr. and ed. by Albert C. Outler. Philadelphia, Westminster Press [1955]. 423 p. *Library of Christian classics*, 7. **166**

—— Later works, selected and tr. with introductions by John Burnaby. Philadelphia, Westminster Press [1955]. 359 p. *Library of Christian classics*, 8. **167**

Includes De trinitate (Books 8, 9, 10, 14, 15), De spiritu et littera, Tractatus in Epistolam Iohannis (Ten homilies on the 1st Epistle General of St. John).

—— Treatises on marriage and other subjects, tr. by Charles T. Wilcox [and others], ed. by Roy J. Deferrari. New York, Fathers of the Church, 1955. vi, 456 p. *Fathers of the Church*, 27. **168**

Contains The good of marriage; Adulterous marriages; Holy virginity; Faith and works; The creed; In answer to the Jews; Faith and the Creed; The care to be taken for the dead; The divination of demons.

SINGLE WORKS

—— [Confessiones] The confessions of St. Augustine, tr. by Francis Joseph Sheed. New York, Sheed & Ward, 1943; London, Sheed and Ward, 1944. xxii, 354 p. **169**

This translation has been often reprinted with slightly varying number of pages. Selections from it have appeared also in the series *Catholic masterpiece tutorial series*, no. 7, New York, 1942 and 1943.

—— Confessions, in thirteen books, a new English translation from the original Latin, ed. by J. M. Lelen. New York, Catholic Book Publishing Co. [1952]. 384 p. **170**

The translation was apparently made by the editor.

—— Confessions, tr. by Vernon J. Bourke. New York, Fathers of the Church, 1953. *Fathers of the Church*, 21. **171**

—— The confessions of St. Augustine, Book VIII, ed. and tr. by C. S. C. Williams. Oxford, Blackwell, 1953. xxx, 55 p. **172**

Text and translation.

—— The confessions of St. Augustine, tr. by John K. Ryan. Garden City, N.Y., Image Books [1960]. 429 p. 173

—— Confessions, tr. by R. S. Pine-Coffin. Baltimore, Penguin Books [1961]. 346 p. 174

—— Confessions, a new translation by Rex Warner. [New York], New American Library [1963]. xv, 351 p. 175

—— [Contra academicos]. Answer to skeptics; a translation of St. Augustine's Contra academicos, by Denis J. Kavanagh . . . with an intro. by Rudolph Arbesmann . . . New York, Cosmopolitan science and art service company [*c.* 1943]. xxv, 269 p. 176

Text and facing translation; the translation alone appeared in the *Fathers of the Church* series; see above, item 161. With De beata vita and De ordine, this dialogue is part of Augustine's earliest work, the Dialogues of Cassiaciacum.

—— Against the academics, tr. . . . by John J. O'Meara. Westminster, Md., Newman Press, 1950 [*i.e.* 1951]. vi, 213 p. *Ancient Christian writers,* 12. 177

—— Against the academicians. Contra academicos, tr. . . . by Mary Patricia Garvey. Milwaukee, Marquette University Press, 1957. 85 p. *Medieval philosophical texts in translation,* 2. 178

—— [Contra Julianum] Against Julian, tr. by Matthew A. Schumacher. New York, Fathers of the Church, 1957. xx, 407 p. *Fathers of the Church,* 35. 179

A polemic against Julianus, Bp. of Eclanum, d. *c.* 454, in which St. Augustine discusses grace and predestination.

—— [De beata vita] De beata vita, tr. by Ruth Allison Brown. Washington, Catholic University of America Press, 1944. xvii, 193 p. *Patristic studies,* 72. 180

Text and facing translation.

—— [De catechizandis rudibus] The first catechetical instruction, tr. by Joseph P. Christopher. Westminster, Md., The Newman Bookshop, 1946. 171 p. *Ancient Christian writers,* 2. 181

A revision of the translator's 1926 edition published by the Catholic University of America Press.

—— [De civitate Dei] The City of God . . . by Saint Augustine [ed. by R. V. G. Tasker]. London, Dent; New York, Dutton, 1945. 2 v. *Everyman's library.* 182

This is a "thoroughly revised edition of John Healey's translation of 1610," made by comparison to the Latin text, modernization of the 17th-century vocabulary, and new translation of parts.

—— Introduction to St. Augustine. The City of God, being selections from De civitate Dei, including most of the xixth book, with text, translation, and running commentary by Reginald H. Barrow. London, Faber & Faber [1950]. 288 p. 183

Extracts from Books 1, 5, 12, 14, 15, 18; most of 19; text and translation are facing.

—— The city of God. Washington, Catholic University of America Press, 1950–54. 3 v. *Fathers of the Church*, 8, 14, and 24. 184

Books I-VII, tr. Gerald G. Walsh; books VIII-XVI, tr. Gerald G. Walsh and Grace Monahan; books XVII-XXII, tr. Demetrius B. Zema and Gerald G. Walsh. A selection from this translation edited by Vernon J. Bourke was published by Image Books, the Doubleday Company, Garden City, N. Y., 1958, as St. Augustine, The City of God, an abridged version.

—— The city of God against the Pagans, in seven volumes. Cambridge, Harvard University Press; London, Heinemann, 1957–60. *Loeb classics.* 185

Text and facing translation. Vol. 1, translated by George E. McCracken; vol. 2, William M. Green; vol. 3, David S. Wiesen; vol. 4, Philip Levine; vol. 5, Eva M. Sanford and William M. Green; vol. 6, William Chase Greene.

—— City of God, abr. and tr. by J. W. C. Wand. London, Oxford University Press, 1963. xxiii, 428 p. 186

The chapter headings of omitted parts are included.

—— [De doctrina christiana] On Christian doctrine, tr. with an intro. by D. W. Robertson, Jr. New York, Liberal Arts Press [1958]. xxii, 169 p. 187

—— [De dono perseverantiae] The De dono perseverantiae of St. Augustine, tr. by Mary A. Lesousky. Washington, Catholic University of America Press, 1956. xxii, 310 p. *Patristic studies,* 91. 188

Text and facing translation with a commentary.

—— [De excidio urbis Romae sermo] Sancti Aurelii Augustini, De excidio urbis Romae sermo, a critical text and translation . . . by Marie Vianney O'Reilly. Washington, Catholic University of America Press, 1955. xvii, 95 p. *Patristic studies,* 89. 189

—— [De haeresibus] The De haeresibus of St. Augustine, tr. with an intro. and commentary by Liguori G. Müller. Washington, Catholic University of America Press, 1956. xix, 229 p. *Patristic studies,* 90. 190

Text and facing translation.

—— [De libero arbitrio] De libero arbitrio voluntatis; St. Augustine on free will, tr. by Carroll M. Sparrow. Charlottesville, University of Virginia Press, 1947. xii, 149 p. *University of Virginia studies,* 4. 191

—— The problem of free choice, tr. and annotated by Mark Pontifex. Westminster, Md., Newman Press, 1955. vi, 291 p. *Ancient Christian writers,* 22. 192

The work is a dialogue on the problem of evil and the connection of free will and determinism to good and evil. Also translated in an appendix is ch. 9 of Book 1 of the Retractions.

—— On free choice of the will [by] Saint Augustine, tr. by Anna S. Benjamin and L. H. Hackstaff, with an intro. by L. H. Hackstaff. Indianapolis, Bobbs-Merrill [1964]. xxxi, 162 p. 193

Includes section of the Retractions dealing with De libero arbitrio.

—— [De moribus] The Catholic and Manichaean ways of life, De moribus ecclesiae Catholicae et de moribus Manichaeorum, tr. by Donald A. Gallagher and Idella J. Gallagher. Washington, Catholic University of America Press [1966]. xx, 135 p. *Fathers of the Church,* 56. **194**

—— [De musica] De musica, a synopsis, by William F. Jackson Knight. London, Orthological Institute [1949?]. 125 p. **195**

This is in effect a paraphrase. The main subject of the treatise is metric theory and theory of aesthetic psychology. For another translation, see item 161 above.

—— [De natura boni] De natura boni of St. Augustine, a translation with an intro. and commentary by A. Anthony Moon. Washington, Catholic University of America Press 1955., xvii, 281 p. *Partristic studies,* 88. **196**

Text and translation of a work on good and evil and the Manichaean heresy.

—— [De ordine] Divine providence and the problem of evil, a translation of St. Augustine's De ordine, with annotations by Robert P. Russell. New York, Cosmopolitan science and art service company [1942]. iv, 191 p. **197**

Text and facing translation. The translation appeared later in the *Fathers of the Church series*; see above, item 161

—— [De sermone Domini in monte] The Lord's sermon on the mount, tr. by John J. Jepson, with an intro. and notes by the editors. Westminster, Md., Newman Press, 1948. 227 p. *Ancient Christian writers,* 5. **198**

—— Commentary on the Lord's Sermon on the Mount, with seventeen related sermons, tr. by Denis J. Kavanagh. Washington, Catholic University of America Press, [c. 1951, 1963]. vi, 382 p. *Fathers of the Church,* 11. **199**

—— [De trinitate] The Trinity, tr. by Stephen McKenna. Washington, Catholic University of America Press [1963]. xvii, 529 p. *Fathers of the Church,* 45. **200**

A selection from this translation, edited and abridged by Charles Dollen, was published in Boston, St. Paul's Editions [1965].

—— [De utilitate Ieiunii] De utilitate Ieiunii, a text with a translation, intro., and commentary by S. Dominic Ruegg. Washington, Catholic University of America Press, 1951. xviii, 133 p. *Patristic studies,* 85. **201**

Text and facing translation of a work on the Usefulness of fasting.

—— [De vera religione] Of true religion, intro. by Louis O. Mink, tr. by J. H. S. Burleigh. Chicago, Regnery [c. 1959]. xix, 107 p. **202**

—— [Enchiridion] Faith, hope and charity, tr. and annotated by Louis A. Arand. Westminster, Md., Newman Bookshop, 1947. 165 p. *Ancient Christian writers,* 3. **203**

The full title of the work translated is Enchiridion de fide, spe, et caritate; it is often referred to, as here, by the title Concerning faith, hope, and charity.

—— Enchiridion, or, Manual to Laurentius concerning faith, hope, and charity, tr. from the Benedictine text, with an intro. and notes, by Ernest Evans. London, S.P.C.K., 1953. xxvii, 146 p. **204**

—— [Enerrationes in Psalmos] Like as the hart, by St. Augustine, being his *Enerratio super Psalmum XLI* tr. by an unknown sixteenth-century writer and ed. with an intro. by G. Desmond Schlegel. Oxford, Blackfriars Publications, [1947]. 55 p. 205

—— Nine sermons of Saint Augustine on the Psalms, tr. . . . by Edmund Hill. New York, Kenedy [1959]. xi, 176 p. 206

Translation of Enerrationes in Psalmos 18, 21, 25, 26, 29, 30, and 31; includes translation of Augustine's version of the Psalms.

—— St. Augustine on the Psalms, tr. and annotated by Scholastica Hebgin and Felicitas Corrigan. Westminster, Md., Newman Press, 1960. 2 v. *Ancient Christian writers,* 29. 207

Some of the works translated are labeled "sermons" in the Migne edition, according to the translators, but are here included as "discourses"; these include the Sermo ad plebem, Sermo ad populum. This is the same work as that translated in *Library of Fathers* (Oxford, 1848), vol. 39, as Expositions on the book of Psalms; *cf.* Farrar and Evans, item 426.

—— [Epistolae] St. Augustine, Letters, tr. by Wilfrid Parsons. New York, Fathers of the Church, 1951–56. 5 v. *Fathers of the Church,* 12, 18, 20, 30, 32. 208

Two hundred and seventy letters plus fifty written to St. Augustine.

—— [Regula] The Rule of our holy father St. Augustine, bishop of Hippo, a translation from the Latin by Francis E. Tourscher, rev. by Robert P. Russell. Villanova, Pa., Province of St. Thomas of Villanova, 1942. 27 p. 209

The translation is followed by the Latin text. The work has no introduction and no information about the translation process.

—— The Rule of St. Augustine, commentary by Blessed Alphonsus Orozco, tr. by Thomas A. Hand. Westminster, Md., Newman Press, 1956. 210

The Rule is on pp. 1–16, followed by the 16th-century commentary.

—— [Sermones] John shines through Augustine; selections from the sermons of Augustine on the Gospel according to Saint John, tr. by A. P. Carleton. London, United Society for Christian Literature [1960]; New York, Association Press [1961]. 79 p. 211

—— Selected Easter sermons, with intro., text of 30 sermons, notes and commentary, by Philip T. Weller. St. Louis, Herder [1959]. vii, 321 p. 212

Only the English translation is given here; the word *text* in the title is ambiguous.

—— Selected sermons, tr. and ed. by Quincy Howe, Jr. New York, Holt, Rinehart and Winston [1966]. xix, 234 p. 213

New translation of thirty from five hundred sermons, selected to give "as wide a representation as possible to St. Augustine's thought."

—— Sermons for Christmas and Epiphany, tr. and annotated by Thomas C. Lawler. Westminster, Md., Newman Press, 1952. 240 p. *Ancient Christian writers,* 15. 214

Twenty-three sermons, most of them translated for the first time into English, from Sermones ad populum.

—— Sermons on the liturgical seasons, tr. by Mary Sarah Muldowney. New

York, Fathers of the Church, 1959. xxii, 451 p. Writings of Saint Augustine, v. 17. *Fathers of the Church,* 38. **215**

Contains translations of seventy-nine sermons for feast days and other occasions of the liturgical year; these are from Sermones de tempore.

—— [Soliloquia] The Soliloquies of St. Augustine, translation and notes by Thomas Gilligan; intro. by Robert P. Russell. New York, Cosmopolitan science and art service company, 1943. xviii, 173 p. **216**

Text and facing translation of a work which, according to the introduction, is not to be confused with a spurious work of the same title; this is part of the Cassiciacum dialogues. The translation was published in the *Fathers of the Church* series; see above, item 161. In spite of the *caveat* in the introduction, the Library of Congress has catalogued this as a "Spurious and Doubtful Work" in the new National Union Catalog of pre-1956 imprints.

SELECTIONS

—— St. Augustine, a biographical sketch, compiled from the saint's own writings . . . by J. M. Flood, with an intro. by Martin C. D'Arcy. Dublin, Clonmore & Reynolds; London, Burns and Oates [1960]. 108 p. Published under title The mind and heart of St. Augustine: a biographical sketch, Fresno, Cal., Academy Guild Press, 1960. **217**

Excerpts from letters, sermons, the City of God, and the Confessions; no statement of source of translations.

—— Selected writings, ed. and with an intro. by Roger Hazelton. Cleveland, Meridian Books [1962]. 312 p. **218**

—— The political writings of St. Augustine, ed. . . . by Henry Paolucci, including an interpretive analysis by Dino Bigongiari. Chicago, Regnery [c. 1962]. xxiii, 358 p. **219**

Previously published translations "considerably revised," from seven works.

—— Unless the grain die. Saint Augustine of Hippo; Saint Ignatius of Antioch [tr. by Benedictines of Stanbrook]. Worcester [England], Stanbrook Abbey Press, 1963. 23 p. **220**

Contains translation of St. Augustine's Commentary on John VI and John XII, and St. Ignatius' Letter to the Romans written from Smyrna.

—— The essential Augustine, selected and with commentary by Vernon J. Bourke. [New York], New American Library [1964]. 272 p. **221**

—— Introduction to the philosophy of St. Augustine; selected readings and commentaries by John A. Mourant. University Park, Pa., State University Press, 1964. ix, 366 p. **222**

Mostly a compilation of previously published translations, but some new for this volume by Robert P. Russell; arranged by topics.

Aurelianus, Caelius, *5th cent.* On acute diseases and On chronic diseases, ed. and tr. by Israel E. Drabkin. [Chicago], University of Chicago Press [1950]. xxvi, 1019 p. **223**

This is a translation of a Latin translation, abridged and added to, of non-extant works of Soranos of Ephesos, Greek of the 1st century B.C. Text and English translation parallel.

Ausonius, Decimus Magnus, *c. 310–c.393.* "Two from Ausonius," tr. by Harold Isbell, *Arion,* 4 (1965), 221–32. **224**

Contains translation of two poems, Bissula and Mosella.

Auðunar þattr vestfirzka. Seven Icelandic short stories, ed. by Ásgeir Pétursson and Steingrímur J. Þorsteinsson. New York, American Scandinavian Foundation, 1960. 166 p. **225**

Contains a translation by G. Turville-Petre of "The story of Audunn and the bear," pp. 37–49; the translation is based on a 13th-century manuscript.

Avempace, *d. 1138 or 1139.* Ibn Bajjah's 'Ilm al-Nafs, translation and notes by M. S. Hasan Ma'sumi. Karachi, Pakistan Historical Society, 1961. iv, 208 p. **226**

Text and translation of a commentary on and paraphrase of Aristotle's De anima; the title means "Sayings concerning the soul."

—— "Ibn Bajjah's 'Tadbīru'l-mutawaḥḥid' (Rule of the solitary)," text in Arabic, ed., vowelled, and tr. . . . by D. M. Dunlop, *Journal of the Royal Asiatic Society,* 1945, 61–81. **227**

Arabic text and translation of a philosophical work, making the distinction between the human, animal, and inorganic actions of men.

—— "Ibn Bajjah on the human intellect," by M. Saghir Ḥasan Ma'sūmī, *Islamic Studies,* 4 (1965), 121–36. **228**

Text and translation.

Averroës, *1126–1198.* Averroes' commentary on Plato's Republic, ed. and tr. by E. I. J. Rosenthal. Cambridge [Eng.], Cambridge University Press, 1956; repr. 1966 with corrections. vi, 339 p. *University of Cambridge Oriental publications,* 1. **229**

The Arabic original is lost; this translation is from a Hebrew version by Samuel b. Yehūdā of Marseilles, *c.* 1320. Text and translation.

—— "Averroes on good and evil," by G. F. Hourani, *Studia Islamica,* 16 (1962), 13–40. **230**

Averroës wrote no specifically ethical work; here the author has culled ethical material from many writings and has translated excerpts, *passim.*

—— Epitome of Parva naturalia, tr. from the original Arabic and the Hebrew and Latin versions with notes and intro. by Harry Blumberg. Cambridge, Mediaeval Academy of America, 1961. xxii, 130 p. *Corpus commentariorum in Aristotelem. Versio Anglica,* v. 7. *Mediaeval Academy of America publications,* 71, *Corpus philosophorum Medii Aevi.* **231**

—— "Notes on Essence and Existence in Averroes and Avicenna," by Majid Fakhry, in Die Metaphysik im Mittelalter, ed. by Paul Wilpert. Berlin, Walter Gruyter, 1963, pp. 414–17. *Miscellanea medievalia* 2. **232**

Translation of important though brief passages from Averroës' Large commentary on the Metaphysics of Aristotle.

—— On Aristotle's De generatione et corruptione: middle commentary and epitome, tr. from the original Arabic and the Hebrew and Latin versions, with notes and intro., by Samuel Kurland. Cambridge, Mediaeval Academy of

America, 1958. xxv, 245 p. *Corpus commentariorum in Aristotelem, Versio Anglica,* iv, 1–2. *Mediaeval Academy of America publications* 67, *Corpus philosophorum Medii Aevi.* **233**

—— On the harmony of religions and philosophy, a translation, with intro. and notes, of Ibn Rushd's Kitāb faṣl al-maqāl, with its appendix (Ḍamīma) and an extract from Kitāb al-kashf'an manāhij al-adilla, by George F. Hourani. London, Luzac, 1961. viii, 128 p. *Gibb memorial series,* n.s. 21. UNESCO *collection of great works, Arabic series.* **234**

The translation is based on a text established in 1959 by Professor Hourani, based on a second manuscript "known but unused in previous editions."

—— Tahafut al-tahafut (The incoherence of the incoherence), tr. from the Arabic with intro. and notes by Simon van den Bergh. London, Luzac, 1954. 2 v. *Gibb memorial series,* n.s. 19. UNESCO *collection of great works, Arabic series.* **235**

Vol. 1 contains the translation; vol. 2, notes and index. This work is, according to the editor, "the most substantial production of Islamic philosophy"; it contains the theories of al-Farābī (d. *c.*950) and of Avicenna (d. 1037) on God and the world as summarized by al-Ghazzālī, and an almost complete redaction of al-Ghazzālī's Tahāfut al-falāsifa, completed in 1095, with Averroës' answer to al-Ghazzālī on behalf of Aristotle.

Avicenna, *980?–1037.* Arabic phonetics—Ibn Sīnā's Risālah on the points of articulation of the speech sounds, tr. by Khalil I. Semaan. Lahore, Ashraf, 1963. 62 p. *Arthur Jeffery memorial monographs,* 2. **236**

—— Avicenna and the visionary recital, by Henry Corbin; tr. from the French by Willard R. Trask. [New York], Pantheon Books [c. 1960]. xiii, 423 p. *Bollingen series,* 66. **237**

This includes a translation of Avicenna's Risālat Ḥayy ibn Yaqzān, Recital of the bird and the Recital of Salaman and Absal, allegories that seem to constitute a trilogy, according to the author; Part II is a translation of the Persian commentary on the Recital. A mystical work, the Recital deals with Avicenna's personal experience.

—— Avicenna on theology, tr. by Arthur J. Arberry. London, Murray, 1951. vi, 82 p. **238**

Contents: Avicenna's autobiography, a biography, On the nature of God, Predestination, On prophecy, On prayer, the After-life, Poem of the soul.

—— Avicenna's Poem on medicine, by Haven C. Krueger, with a foreword by Ralph H. Major. Springfield, Ill., Thomas [c. 1963]. xiii, 112 p. **239**

The translator, a doctor of medicine, has translated from a French version of 1956 by H. Jahier and A. Noureddine.

—— Avicenna's Psychology, an English translation of Kitāb al-najāt, Book II, Ch. VI, with historico-philosophical notes and textual improvements on the Cairo edition by F. Rahman. London, Oxford University Press, 1952. xii, 127 p. **240**

Book II is on physics, based on Aristotle but not a commentary; the Kitāb al-najāt, Book of salvation, is Avicenna's own abridgment of his larger work, Kitāb al-shifā'. No text is included here, but textual notes suggesting improvements to the Cairo edition of 1938 are included; the translation is based on the Cairo edition, that of Rome, 1593, and six manuscripts.

AVICENNA

—— Avicenna: scientist and philosopher, a millenary symposium, ed. by G. M. Wickens. London, Luzac, 1952. 128 p. **241**

Includes extensive excerpts in translation from Avicenna's autobiography, his Poem on the soul, and biographies.

—— The general principles of Avicenna's Canon of medicine [ed. and tr.] by Mazhar H. Shah. Karachi, Naveed Clinic, 1966. xlii, 459 p. **242**

Book I, General principles, is translated; Books II-V are summarized in an appendix; the names of drugs mentioned are translated in a separate appendix. The translation is based on the Arabic original and its Urdu translations; the previous translation (see Farrar and Evans, item 501) was made from a 12th-century Latin version, according to the present translator. Another partial translation of the Canon (Book 3, ch. 1, Anatomy of the eye) is listed by the bibliography in *Isis* (1958) as having appeared in "The story of a book" by W. Wells Thoms, *Medical Bulletin,* 22 (1956), pp. 227ff., but this work has not been seen.

—— "Ibn Sīnā's 'Essay on the secret of destiny,'" by George Hourani, *Bulletin of the School of Oriental and African Studies*, 29 (1966), 25–48. **243**

Contains text and translation of Risāla fī sirr al-qadar, with a commentary.

—— "A Treatise on love by Ibn Sina," by Emil L. Fackenheim, *Medieval Studies,* 7 (1945), 208–28. **244**

A translation of Risālah fī'l-'ishq based on the critical text of M. A. F. Mehren, 1894, with variants of other manuscripts noted.

—— A treatise on the soul ascribed to Ibn-i-Sina, by Saghir Ḥasan Ma'sūmī. [Panjab, University Press, 196?]. 14 p. **245**

The translation on pp. 4–8, is of a treatise which the author says "is neither a translation nor an abridgment of De anima nor any other work of Aristotle." The text is included.

SUPPOSITIOUS WORKS

—— "Two alchemical treatises attributed to Avicenna," by H. E. Stapleton, *Ambix,* 10 (1962), 41–83. **246**

Contains translations of two essays, Treatise for al-Sahli and Treatise for al-Baraqī, both of which are culled collections of excerpts from the Kitāb al-Asrār; the translation is from Arabic, and a Latin text is also included. The author believes the works not to be Avicenna's; they profess a belief in transmutation and other magical aspects of chemistry.

al-Awsī al-Anṣārī, 'Umar ibn Ibrāhīm, *fl. 1400*. A Muslim manual of war, being Tafrīj al-kurūb fī tadbīr al-ḥurūb, ed., tr. by George T. Scanlon. Cairo, The American University at Cairo Press, 1961. 130, 97 p. **247**

Translation followed by Arabic text.

B

Bagdad. Historical sources. "The topography of eleventh-century Bagdad: materials and notes," by George Makdisi, *Arabica,* 6 (1959), 178–97; 281–309. **248**

Contains translation of Ibn 'Aqīl's 11th-century description of Bagdad as well as of several other accounts from the 11th and 12th centuries.

Bahrāmī-yi Sarkhskī, Alī al-Dīn, *10th cent.* "Kanz al-Qāfiyah by Alī 'izz al-Dīn Bahrāmī-yi Sarkhsī," by Reuben Levy, pp. 135–38 in A locust's leg, studies in honor of S. H. Taqizadeh [ed. by W. B. Henning and E. Yarshater]. London, Lund, 1962. **249**

Contains a translation of an introduction to a Persian rhyming dictionary previously thought to be lost; the work is an addition to the "small stock of prose in Early Islamic Persian." The Persian itself is a translation of the Arabic original.

Bahya ben Joseph ibn Pakuda, *fl. 1040.* Duties of the heart, by Bachya ben Joseph ibn Paquda, tr. from the Arabic into Hebrew by Jehuda ibn Tibbon . . . with English translation by Moses Hyamson. Second treatise on the examination of created things and third treatise on the service of God. New York, Bloch, 1941. 78 [78] p. **250**

Translation with facing text. The first treatise appeared in 1925; *cf.* Farrar and Evans, item 513. Treatises 4–5 appeared in 1943, 6–8 in 1945, and 9–10 in 1947, completing the translation.

Baptista Mantuanus, *1447–1516.* "Baptista Mantuanus—amateur physician," by Gordon W. Jones, *Bulletin of the History of Medicine*, 36 (1962), 148–62. **251**

Contains translation of excerpts from a poem on the plague and from a prose work, De patientia, by the vicar general of the Carmelites in Mantua.

al-Bāqillānī, Muḥammad ibn al-Ṭayyib, *d. 1013.* A tenth-century document of Arabic literary theory and criticism: the sections on poetry of al-Bāqillānī's I'jāz al-Qur'an, tr. and annotated by Gustave E. von Grunebaum. Chicago, University of Chicago Press, 1950. xxii, 127 p. **252**

Excerpts from al-Bāqillānī's "On the uniqueness of the Koran" on stylistic devices of Arabic poetry, with detailed explication of examples from poetry.

Barbour, John, *d. 1395.* The Bruce, an epic poem written around the year A.D. 1375 . . . tr. and ed. by Archibald A. H. Douglas. Glasgow, McLellan, 1964. 476 p. **253**

A poetic translation made directly from manuscripts but no text is furnished.

Barlaam and Joasaph. The wisdom of Balahvar, a Christian legend of the Buddha, by David M. Lang. London, Allen & Unwin; New York, Macmillan [1957]. 135 p. *Ethical and religious classics of East and West,* 20. **254**

Contains translations of The wisdom of Balahvar from an old Georgian version and other fables of Balahvar from the Jerusalem Georgian text.

—— The Balavariani (Barlaam and Josaphat), a tale from the Christian East, tr. from the Old Georgian by David M. Lang; intro. by Ilia V. Abuladze. Berkeley, University of California Press, 1966. 187 p. UNESCO *collection of representative works, USSR series.* **255**

A 9th–10th-century version based on the Arabic non-Christian version, the editor thinks; based on a recently discovered 13th–14th century manuscript, this is a longer redaction than the one used for The wisdom of Balavar (see above). No text.

Bartolotti, Gian Giacomo, *15th cent.* Giovanni Tortelli, On medicine and physicians; Gian Giacomo Bartolotti, On the antiquity of medicine; two histories of medicine of the XVth century, ed. and tr. by Dorothy Schullian and Luigi Belloni. [Milan, Industrie Grafiche Italiane Stucchi, 1954]. xliv, 226 p. **256**

Text followed by translation into both English and Italian.

Baruc Teutonicus, *fl. 1320.* "The confession of a medieval Jewish convert," by Solomon Grayzel, *Historia Judaica,* 17 (1955), 89–120. **257**

Contains a translation of "The confession of Baruc at one time a Jew, who, having been baptized, reverted to Judaism," pp. 103–20. The confession is found in a Vatican manuscript of the records of the episcopal court of Pamiers.

Basilius, *Saint, the Great, abp. of Caesarea, c. 330–79.* Exegetic homilies, tr. by Agnes Clare Way. Washington, Catholic University of America Press [1963]. xvi, 378 p. *Fathers of the Church,* 46. **258**

Translation only of those homilies generally considered to be genuinely by St. Basil.

—— Letters, tr. by Agnes Clare Way, with notes by Roy J. Deferrari. New York, Fathers of the Church, 1951–55. 2 v. *Fathers of the Church,* 13, 28. **259**

The translation is based on an 1839 text revised by Professor Deferrari. In addition to the letters (1–185 in vol. 1, 186–368 in vol. 2) a translation of Basil's "Address to young men on reading Greek literature" is included, vol. 2, 378–435.

—— Writings of St. Basilius, Ascetical works, tr. by M. Monica Wagner. New York, Fathers of the Church, 1950. xii, 525 p. *Fathers of the Church,* 9. **260**

Contents: several ascetical discourses, the Long rules, Preface on the Judgment of God, Concerning faith, Concerning baptism, the Morals, On mercy and justice, five homilies.

al-Baydāwī, 'Abd Allah ibn 'Umār, *d. 1286?* Chrestomathia Baidawi, the light of inspiration and secret of interpretation, being a translation of the chapter of Joseph (Sūrat Yūsuf) with the commentary of Nasir-Id-Dīn al-Baidāwī, by Eric F. F. Bishop, with the help of Mohamed Kaddal. Glasgow, Jackson Press, 1957. 60 p. *Glasgow University publications, Oriental studies,* 1. **261**

The chapter from the Koran and Baydāwī's commentary are translated.

—— Baīdāwī's Commentary on Sūrah 12 of the Qur'ān, text accompanied by an interpretive rendering and notes by A. F. L. Beeston. Oxford, Clarendon Press, 1963. viii, 98 p. **262**

Translation of the commentary and the words and phrases from Sūrah Yūsuf upon which the commentary is based; these are excerpts from Baydāwī's Anwār al-tanzīl.

Bayeux tapestry. The Bayeux tapestry, by Eric Maclagan. London and New York, Penguin Books, 1943. 32 p. **263**

Contains a translation of the headings of the tapestry, with commentary. Another translation is found in *English Historical Documents,* vol. 2, 1042–1189, ed. by David Douglas and G. W. Greenaway, pp. 232–78. London and New York, Oxford University Press, 1953.

Beatrijs. The miracle of Beatrice, a Flemish legend of c. 1300, English-Flemish edition, translation by Adriaan J. Barnouw, intro. by Jan-Albert Goris. [New York], Pantheon [1944]. 107 p. **264**

A verse translation.

Beatus, *Saint, Presbyter of Liebana, 8th cent.* A new text of the Apocalypse from Spain, extracted and tr. from . . . the eighth-century commentary of the Spanish Presbyter Beatus, by E. S. Buchanan. New York, [n.p.], 1915. **265**

Only the translation of the Apocalypse, which differs from the Vulgate version, is given here, not Beatus' commentary.

Beda, *Venerabilis, 673–735.* "Bede's De schematibus et tropis, a translation," by Gussie Hecht Tanenhaus, *Quarterly Journal of Speech,* 48 (1962), 237–53. **266**

—— [Historia ecclesiastica] The ecclesiastical history of the English nation, books I–II, tr. . . . with notes and intro. by Michael Maclagan. Oxford, Blackwell, 1949. iii, 195. **267**

—— A history of the English church and people, tr. and with an intro. by Leo Sherley-Price. [Harmondsworth, Eng.], Penguin Books [1955]. 340 p. **268**

Benedetti, Alessandro, *c. 1450–1512.* Diary of the Caroline War, ed. and tr. with notes and intro. by Dorothy M. Schullian. New York, Ungar, for the Renaissance Society of America, 1967. ix, 276 p. **269**

Text and facing translation of an eyewitness account of the Battle of Fornovo and the Novara siege of 1495.

Benedictus, *Saint, abbot of Monte Cassino. 480–543.* The holy rule of our most holy father Benedict, tr. by a priest of the Abbey of our Lady of Gethsemane. Trappist, Ky., 1942. 263 p. **270**

Text and facing translation.

—— Rule for monasteries, tr. by Leonard J. Doyle. Collegeville, Minn., St. John's Abbey Press, 1948. vii, 92 p. **271**

—— The rule of St. Benedict, with intro., new translation of the rule and a commentary, all reviewed by Basilius Steidle. [Beuron], Beuroner Kunstverlag, c. 1952. 307 p. **272**

—— The rule of St. Benedict . . . tr. by Richard (John) Crotty. [Nedlands, Western Australia], University of Western Australia, 1963. 91 p. **273**

Text and facing translation.

—— The rule of Saint Benedict, ed. and tr. by Justin McCann. London, Burns and Oates [1952]. xxiv, 214 p. Westminster, Md., Newman Press, 1952. *Orchard books.* **274**

Abbott McCann published a translation in 1937 (Stanbrook Abbey); the present edition adds the text and revises the 1937 translation.

Benedictus Crispus of Milan, *d. 725 or 735.* "Benedictus Crispus, an eighth-century medical poet," by Jerry Stannard, *Journal of the History of Medicine,* 21 1966), 24–46. **275**

Contains a translation of "A book on medicine by Crispus, Dean of Milan," pp. 31–38.

Benzi, Ugo, *1376–1439.* Ugo Benzi, medieval philosopher and physician, 1376–1439, by Dean P. Lockwood. [Chicago], University of Chicago Press [1951]. xvi, 441 p. **276**

Translation of excerpts from and summaries of many of Ugo's Consilia, written directions for specific medical care; and a translation of Vita Ugonis by Socino Benzi, son of Ugo. Texts of documents in Appendices.

Beowulf. Beowulf in modern verse, with an essay . . ., tr. by Gavin Bone. Oxford, Blackwell, 1945. x, 84 p. **277**

An abridged verse translation with alternate rhymes.

BEOWULF

—— By his own might: the battles of Beowulf, by Dorothy Hosford. New York, Henry Holt and Company, 1947. [no pagination.] **278**

A very much abbreviated and "somewhat adapted" version.

—— Beowulf in modern English, tr. by Mary E. Waterhouse. Cambridge [Eng.], Bowes, 1949. xix, 129 p. **279**

A blank verse translation.

—— Beowulf; a verse translation into modern English, by Edwin Morgan. 1st ed., Aldington, Kent [Eng.], Hand and Flower Press, 1952. Berkeley, University of California Press, 1962 [c. 1952]; xxxiv, 94 p. **280**

—— Beowulf the warrior, tr. by Ian Serraillier. [London], Oxford University Press, 1954. 48 pp. **281**

A poetic translation of the three fights only.

—— Beowulf, a prose translation by David Wright. Harmondsworth [Eng.], Penguin Books, 1957. 122 p. **282**

Another prose translation of Beowulf is that of William Alfred, published in Medieval epics by Modern Library; see *Literature. Collections*.

—— Beowulf, a new translation with an intro. by Burton Raffel, afterword by Robert P. Creed. [New York], New American Library [1963]. 159 p. **283**

A fairly free verse translation.

—— Beowulf, tr. by Lucien D. Pearson, intro. by Rowland L. Collins. Bloomington, Indiana University Press, 1965. 127 p. **284**

A verse translation.

—— Beowulf, a new prose translation by E. Talbot Donaldson. New York, W. W. Norton [1966]. xv, 58 p. **285**

—— "Beowulf, a paraphrase," by W. K. Thomas, *Revue de l'Université d'Ottawa*, 37 (1967), 231–68. **286**

A blank verse translation omitting all references to historical happenings and to other poems familiar to the original audience but now unknown.

Berechiah ben Natronai, ha-Nakdan, *12th cent.* Fables of a Jewish Aesop, tr. by Moses Hadas. New York and London, Columbia University Press, 1967. xi, 233 p. **287**

The "Fox Fables" (Mishle shu'alim) of a French Jew also known as Benedictus le puncteur.

Bernard, *c. 1400*. The threefold gift of Christ, by Brother Bernard, tr. and ed. by a Religious of C.S.M.V. London, Mowbray; New York, Morehouse-Gorham [1954]. 45 p. *Fleur de lys series,* 4. **288**

Translation of Instructo sacerdoti, formerly ascribed to St. Bernard of Clairvaux, according to the editor.

Bernard de Clairvaux, *Saint, 1091?–1153.* The case of Peter Abelard, by Ailbe John Luddy. Dublin, M. H. Gill; Westminster, Md., Newman Bookshop, 1947. ix, 94 p. **289**

The appendix, pp. 58–94, contains a translation of a letter of St. Bernard addressed to Innocent II after the Council of Sens, known as the "Treatise against Abelard."

—— Lent with Saint Bernard, a devotional commentary on Psalm Ninety-One, ed. and tr. by a Religious of C.S.M.V. London, Mowbray; New York, Morehouse-Gorham [1953]. 79 p. *Fleur de lys series,* 1. **290**

From St. Bernard's Lenten course at Clairvaux between 1138 and 1153. Another translation of the seventh sermon appears as an appendix in Ancrene wisse, parts six and seven, ed. Geoffrey Shepherd, London, Nelson, 1959.

—— Letters, newly tr. by Bruno Scott James. Chicago, Regnery, 1953. xx, 530 p. **291**

Contains 479 letters, many newly discovered. Letters of doubtful authenticity have been omitted; letters to St. Bernard are summarized briefly.

—— St. Bernard of Clairvaux seen through his selected letters, newly tr. and with an intro. by Bruno Scott James, foreword by Thomas Merton. Chicago, Regnery, 1953. xii, 276 p. **292**

A selection from the larger edition of St. Bernard's letters by the same translator.

—— On the love of God, newly tr. by a Religious of C.S.M.V. London and New York, Mowbray, 1950. 76 p. **293**

This translation of De diligendo Deo was reprinted with omission of the last four chapters in the *Fleur de lys series,* 1961, 50 p.

—— St. Bernard on the Christian year, selections from his sermons, tr. and ed. by a Religious of C.S.M.V. London, Mowbray, 1954. 167 p. **294**

—— Saint Bernard On the Song of Songs; sermones in Cantica canticorum, tr. and ed. by a Religious of C.S.M.V. London, Mowbray; New York, Morehouse-Gorham [1952]. 272 p. **295**

An abridged translation.

—— The steps of humility, tr. by Geoffrey Webb and Adrian Walker. London, Mowbray; New York, Morehouse-Gorham [1957]. 87 p. *Fleurs de lys series,* 13. **296**

—— The story of his life as recorded in the Vita prima Bernardi by certain of his contemporaries, William of St. Thierry, Arnold of Bonnevaux, Geoffrey and Philip of Clairvaux, and Odo of Deuil, tr. by Geoffrey Webb and Adrian Walker. London, Mowbray, 1960. [2], 130 p. **297**

SPURIOUS AND DOUBTFUL WORKS

—— The School of self-knowledge, a symposium from medieval sources, tr. by Geoffrey Webb and Adrian Walker. London, Mowbray [1956]. *Fleur de lys series,* 8. **298**

Excerpts from three works written in the 12th–13th century by Cistercians of the school of St. Bernard: De cognitione sui, Meditatio piissima, De conscientia aedificando.

Bernardino da Siena, *Saint, 1380–1444.* "St. Bernardine's unedited Prediche Volgari," by Cuthbert Gumbinger, *Franciscan Studies,* 25 (n.s. 4, March, 1944), 7–33. **299**

Excerpts from sermons preached 1424, 1425, and 1443.

—— Sermon on St. Joseph, tr. by Eric May. Paterson, N. J., St. Anthony's Guild [1947]. 51 p. 300

Bernart de Ventadorn, *12th cent.* The Songs, tr. by Stephen G. Nichols, Jr., *et al.* Chapel Hill, University of North Carolina Press [c. 1962]. 235 p. *University of North Carolina studies in the Romance languages and literatures,* 39. 301

Text and facing prose translation of all the songs.

Bertrand de Mignanelli, *1370–1455.* "Ascensus Barcoch, a Latin biography of the Mamlūk Sultan Barqūq of Egypt (d. 1399), written by Bertrando de Mignanelli in 1416, rendered into English with an intro. and commentary by Walter J. Fischel," *Arabica,* 6 (1959), 64–74, 152–72. 302

—— "A new Latin source of Tamerlane's conquest of Damascus, (1400–1401)," by Walter J. Fischel, *Oriens* (1956), 201–32. 303

Contains a translation of Vita tamerlani.

Besa, *abbot of Athribis, 5th cent.* Letters and sermons, ed. [and tr.] by K. H. Kuhn. Louvain, L. Durbecq, 1956. 2 v. in 1. *Corpus scriptorum Christianorum orientalium,* 157, 158; *Scriptores Coptici,* 21, 22. 304

Vol. 1 contains the text, vol. 2 the translation. The letters are addressed to monks and nuns. Excerpts from this material were translated earlier by Professor Kuhn in "A Fifth-Century Egyptian abbot, I. Besa and his background" and II. "Monastic life in Besa's day," *Journal of Theological Studies,* n. s. 5 (1954), 36–48, 174–87.

Bestiary. The book of beasts, being a translation from a Latin bestiary of the twelfth century, made and ed. by T. H. White. London, Cape [1954]. 296 p. 305

A translation of Cambridge University Library manuscript Ii.4.26.

al-Bīrūnī, *973?–1048.* Al-Biruni on transits . . . tr. by Mohammed Saffouri and Adnan Ifran, with a commentary by E. S. Kennedy. Beirut, American University, 1959. 201 p. *Faculty of Arts and Sciences, Oriental studies,* 32. 306

A work of astronomical theory translated from a text published in 1948. The author's full name is Abū al-Rayhān, Muḥammad ibn Aḥmad, al-Bīrūnī. The Library of Congress at one time entered him as Albiruni; he should not be confused with Alberuni, 997–1030.

—— "Al-Bīrūnī's Arabic version of Patañjali's Yogasūtra: a translation of his first chapter and a comparison with related Sanskrit texts," by Shlomo Pines and Tuvia Gelblum, *Bulletin of the School of Oriental and African Studies,* 29 (1966), 302–25. 307

—— Al-Kanun-al-Masudi (Canon Masudicus) by Alberouni, tr. and ed. by Mohammed Farooq. Aligarh, Muslim University Press, 1929. 308

According to an entry in *Isis,* 35 (1944), 57, this volume contains a translation of Book 4, Ch. 1 of the Canon. The volume was not listed in Farrar and Evans and no copy has been located. A few pages from the Canon were translated by E. S. Kennedy *et al.* in "The Hindu calendar as described in al-Bīrūnī's Masudic canon," *Journal of the Near East Society,* 24 (1965), 273–84. The first Arabic edition of the Canon includes a summary, paraphrase, and some translation of excerpts; see al-Qānūnu'l-Mas'udi (An Encyclopedia of Astronomical Sciences), [intro. by H. J. J. Winter and Syed Hasan Barani], edited for Osmania Oriental Publications, Hyderabad, India, 1954–56, 3 v.

—— Commemoration volume, A.H. 362-A.H. 1362. Calcutta Iran Society [1951]. xxviii, 303 p. 309

A collection of essays by various authors who include excerpts from the scientific works of al-Bīrūnī and some of his predecessors, hitherto largely untranslated.

—— The determination of the coordinate of positions for the correction of distances between cities, Kitāb Tahdīd Nihāyāt al-Amākin Litashīh Masāfāt al-Masākin, tr. by Jamil Ali. Beirut, American University, 1967. xviii, 278 p. *Centennial publications.* **310**

The translation is based on an edition of 1962. Al-Bīrūnī has used Ghazna, his city, as the focus of his calculations.

Blaithmaic, *Saint, d. c. 827.* The poems of Blathmac, Son of Cú Brettan, together with the Irish Gospel of Thomas and a poem on the Virgin Mary, ed. [and tr.] by James Carney. Dublin, for the Irish Texts Society, 1964. xxxix, 170 p. *Irish Texts Society,* 47. **311**

Text and facing translation of poems of Blaithmaic to the Virgin, an anonymous poem to the Virgin, and a version of the Gospel of Thomas which the editor thinks may be a redaction of a 7th- or 8th-century Latin version.

Boccaccio, Giovanni, *1313–75.* Chamber of love: a selection of the complete works [tr. by Gertrude Flor], ed. by Wolfgang Kraus. New York, Philosophical Library [1958]. 158 p. **312**

The selections from the Decameron, Filocolo, Corbaccio, and other works seem to have been translated from German rather than from the original.

—— Concerning famous women, tr., with an intro. and notes, by Guido A. Guarino. New Brunswick, N. J., Rutgers University Press [1963]. xxxviii, 257 p. **313**

—— The fates of illustrious men, tr. and abr. by Louis B. Hall. New York, Ungar [1965]. xxii, 243 p. **314**

Contains about half of the original tales and links, according to the editor.

—— Forty-six lives, tr. from De claris mulieribus, by Henry Parker, lord Morley, ed. by Herbert G. Wright. London, Oxford University Press, 1943. cv, 200 p. *Early English Text Society,* original series, 214. **315**

Selections from the 104 lives of famous women translated in the 16th century (Lord Morley, 1476–1556) but apparently never before published. Text at bottom of each page.

—— The nymph of Fiesole (Il ninfale fiesolano), a translation by Daniel J. Donno. New York, Columbia University Press, 1960. xvii, 149 p. **316**

According to the editor, this is the first translation made from the Italian version rather than from an intervening French translation. The tale was written some two years before the Decameron.

Boethius, *d. 524.* The consolation of philosophy, tr. with an intro. and notes by Richard H. Green. Indianapolis and New York, Bobbs-Merrill [c. 1962]. 134 p. **317**

A prose translation throughout; based on the critical edition of 1934, checked against the new standard critical edition of 1957. There have been no other new translations of this work, but two editions of old translations should be mentioned. In The consolation of philosophy, in the translation of I.T., ed. by William Anderson, Carbondale, Southern Illinois University Press [1963], 118 p., the 1609 translation has been modernized and the Greek terms translated. The consolation of philosophy, ed. and abr. by James J. Buchanan, New York, Ungar [1957], 67 p., is based on W. V. Cooper's 1902 translation, with revisions. According to Edwin Quaim in *Thought*, December, 1946, the mysterious "I.T." was probably John Thorie, who saw the 1609 translation through the press; the actual translation was made by Michael Walpole, S.J.

Bonaventura, *Saint, cardinal, 1221–74.* The works of Bonaventure: cardinal, seraphic doctor, and saint, tr. from the Latin by José de Vinck. Paterson, N. J., St. Anthony Guild Press [c. 1960–]. **318**

Four volumes have appeared to date: Vol. 1, Mystical opuscula; vol. 2, The Breviloquium; vol. 3, Opuscula, 2d series; vol. 4, The defense of the mendicants. Vol. 5, the final one, now in preparation, will include the Collations on the six days.

—— Breviloquium . . . tr. by Erwin E. Nemmers. St. Louis and London, B. Herder, 1946. xxii, 248 p. **319**

One of the Tria opuscula, works of a philosophical-theological nature; according to the translator, this is not a mystical work but a compendium of Bonaventura's longer commentary on the Sentences of Peter Lombard.

—— The enkindling of love, also called The triple way, adapted, ed., and arr. by William I. Joffe. Paterson, N. J., St. Anthony Guild Press (c. 1956]. xiv, 71 p. **320**

An abridged translation of a mystical work about the soul's progress, De triplici via.

—— The mind's road to God, tr. with an intro., by George Boas. New York, Liberal Arts Press [1953]. 46 p. **321**

—— Saint Bonaventure's Itinerarium mentis in Deum, with an intro., translation and commentary by Philotheus Boehner. St. Bonaventure, N. Y., Franciscan Institute, 1956. 132 p. **322**

—— Introduction to the works of Bonaventure, by Jacques G. Bougerol, tr. from the French by José de Vinck. Paterson, N. J., St. Anthony Guild Press; distributor, Desclée, Paris, New York [1964]. xiv, 249 p. **323**

As an example of Bonaventura's thought and style, the Latin text and a translation of Bonaventura's commentary on the 3d book of the Sentences of Peter Lombard, distinction 24, article 2, question 39 are included; see pp. 60–72.

—— St. Bonaventure, Hymn to the Cross [tr. by José de Vinck]. Paterson, N. J., St. Anthony Guild Press [1960]. 14 p. **324**

—— The way of perfection, based on the Rule for novices of St. Bonaventura, tr. by Anselm Romb, ed. by Method C. Billy and Salvator Pantano. Chicago, Franciscan Herald Press [c. 1958]. 96 p. **325**

Includes translation of excerpts from other ascetical texts as well as a complete translation of the Regula.

SPURIOUS AND DOUBTFUL WORKS

—— Meditations on the life of Christ, an illustrated ms. of the 14th century, tr. by Isa Ragusa; completed from the Latin and ed. by Isa Ragusa and Rosalie B. Green. Princeton, Princeton University Press, 1961. xxxvi, 465 p. *Princeton monographs in art and archaeology*, 35. **326**

The editors have completed the Italian text by culling the last quarter of the work from published Latin texts. The work was attributed to Bonaventura until the 18th century, but the editors think that the only sure attribution is to "a Franciscan monk living in Tuscany in the second half of the thirteenth century." The editors claim that all previous translations of the work have been abridged.

—— The mystical vine: a treatise on the passion of our Lord by Saint Bonaventure, tr. by a Friar of S.S.F. London, Mowbray; New York, Morehouse-Gorham [1955]. 64 p. *Fleur de lys series, 5.* **327**

The translation is based on the shorter version of the Vitis mystica, which according to the translator is genuine, whereas the longer version is spurious. The Library of Congress, however, lists this version as spurious also.

Bonet, Honoré, *c. 1340–c. 1405.* The Tree of battles, tr. by G. W. Coopland. Cambridge, Harvard University Press, 1949. 316 p. **328**

Bonfils, Immanuel ben Jacob, *14th cent.* The book of the gests of Alexander of Macedon; Sefer toledot Alexandros ha-Makdoni; a medieval Hebrew version of the Alexander romance by Immanuel ben Jacob Bonfils, ed. and tr. by Israel J. Kazis. Cambridge, Medieval Academy of America, 1962. x, 227 p. plus Hebrew text. **329**

The Hebrew version is a translation from Latin by Bonfils, who flourished in France, 1340–56. The Latin version is by Leo, archipresbyter, 10th century.

Book of O'Hara. The Book of O'Hara. Leabhar I'Eadhra, ed. (and tr.) by Lambert McKenna. [Dublin], Dublin Institute for Advanced Studies, 1951 [*i.e.*, 1952]. xxxii, 458 p. **330**

Translation from a 16th-century manuscript containing a collection of Bardic poems of uncertain date dealing with the O'Hara clan.

Borgognoni, Teodorico, *bp., 1205–98.* The surgery of Theodoric, *c.* A.D. 1267, tr. . . . by Eldridge Campbell, M.D., and James Colton. New York, Appleton-Century-Crofts, 1955–60. 2 v. *History of medicine series,* 12. **331**

The editors refer to a translation from an early 16th-century manuscript by John Pickering as very much abbreviated, but such a translation has not been seen and is not mentioned in Farrar and Evans.

Boustronios, George, *fl. 15th cent.* The chronicle of George Boustronios, 1456–1489, tr. with an intro. by Richard M. Dawkins. [Victoria], University of Melbourne Press, 1964. xiii, 84 p. *University of Melbourne Cyprus Expedition publication* 2. **332**

The translation includes two paragraphs found in only one manuscript which carry the narrative to 1501.

Bozon, Nicole, *fl. 1300–1320.* Metaphors of Brother Bozon, a friar minor, tr. by J. R. London, Constable and Co., 1913. xii, 204 p. **333**

Translation by John Rose of selections from Les contes moralisés, a collection of anecdotes intended for use in sermons, with a tale after every 13th anecdote. This work was omitted by Farrar and Evans.

—— Seven more poems, ed. and tr. by M. Amelia Klenke. St. Bonaventure, N. Y., Franciscan Institute, 1951. ix, 162 p. *Franciscan Institute publications, history series,* 2. **334**

Anglo-Norman text and facing translation of "Le Evangel," from British Museum Ms. Cotton

Domitian XI, and of lives of six saints: St. Lucy, St. Elizabeth of Hungary, St. Cristine, St. Juliane, St. Agnes, and St. Agatha.

—— Three saints' lives, tr. by M. Amelia Klenke. St. Bonaventure, N. Y., Franciscan Institute, 1947. lxxviii, 123 p. *Franciscan Institute publications, history series,* 1. **335**

Anglo-Norman text with facing translation of the lives of Mary Magdalene, St. Margaret, and St. Martha.

Bradwardine, Thomas, *abp. of Canterbury, 1290?–1349.* Bradwardine and the Pelagians, a study of his "De causa Dei" and its opponents, by Gordon Leff. Cambridge [Eng.], Cambridge University Press, 1957. 282 p. *Cambridge studies in medieval life and thought,* n.s., 5. **336**

Ch. I, pp. 25–65, has detailed summary-paraphrase of Bradwardine's De causa Dei, with the Latin text cited in footnotes.

—— Thomas of Bradwardine, his Tractatus de proportionibus, its significance for the development of mathematical physics, tr. by H. Lamar Crosby, Jr. Madison, University of Wisconsin Press, 1955. xi, 203 p. *University of Wisconsin publications in medieval science,* 2. **337**

Text and facing translation of "one of the most widely influential works in medieval dynamics and kinematics," according to the translator.

Brant, Sebastian, *1457–1521.* Sebastian Brant, studies in religious aspects of his life and works with special reference to the Varia carmina, by Mary A. Rajewski. Washington, Catholic University of America Press, 1944. xvii, 270 p. *Catholic University studies in medieval German,* 20. **338**

Translation or paraphrase of many of Brant's poems both in German and Latin; many of the poems are in honor of the Virgin.

—— The ship of fools, tr. . . . with intro. and commentary by Edwin H. Zeydel . . . New York, Columbia University Press, 1944; Dover, 1962. viii, 399 p. *Records of civilization,* 36. **339**

A verse translation of Das Narrenschiff, written in 1494 as a series of rhyming sermons.

Brut y tywysogion. Brut y tywysogyon or the chronicle of the princes, from Peniarth Ms. 20 version, tr. by Thomas Jones. Cardiff, University of Wales Press, 1952. lxxvii, 272 p. *Board of Celtic studies, history and law series,* 11. **340**

The translation only.

—— Brut y tywysogyon, or The chronicle of the princes, Red Book of Hergest version, critical text and translation with intro. and notes by Thomas Jones. Cardiff, University of Wales Press, 1955. lxiv, 389 p. *Board of Celtic studies, history and law series,* 16. **341**

Text and facing translation of a work which, according to the editor, is attributed to Caradog of Llancarvan, to about 1150; the concluding portion, to 1282, was probably written by the monks of the monastery of Strata Florida.

al-Bukhārī, Muḥammad ibn Ismā'īl, *810–70.* Sahīh al-Bukhārī. Being traditions of the sayings and doings of the Prophet Muḥammad narrated by his companions . . . and compiled under the title Kitāb-al-Jāmiʻ aṣ-Ṣaḥīḥ, by Imām Abū ʻAbd Allāh Muḥammad ibn Ismāʻīl al-Bukhārī, tr. by Muhammad Asad [i.e., Leopold Weiss]. Model Town, Lahore, Arafat, 1938 [1941?]. 80 p. **342**

This work, labeled "Vol. 5, Installment 1–2," is all that appeared of a projected eight volumes; it contains Arabic text and facing translation of Chs. 50, 51, and 52, "The merits of the Prophet's companions," "The beginnings of Islam," and "The book of campaigns."

Burchard, Johann, *bp. of Orta and Cività Castellana, d. 1506.* At the court of Borgia, being an account of the reign of Pope Alexander VI, written by his master of ceremonies, Johann Burchard, ed. and tr. by Geoffrey Parker. London, Folio Society, 1963. 245 p. **343**

Selections from the Liber notarum, comprising about one fourth of Burchard's memoirs of 1492–1503. Pope Alexander was Rodrigo Borgia, father of Lucrezia and Cesare.

Burhān al-Dīn, *fl. 1203.* Instruction of the student: method of learning, tr. by G. E. von Grunebaum and Theodora M. Abel. New York, King's Crown Press, 1947. v, 78 p. **344**

At head of title: Talīm al-Muta ʻallim-ṭarīq al-taʻallūm. The author is also known as al-Zarnūji. The title should really be translated "Instructing the student in the method of learning," according to a review in *Speculum* by Philip Hitti (1948, p. 289).

Buridan, Jean, *c. 1328–1358.* Sophisms on meaning and truth, tr. by Theodore K. Scott. New York, Appleton-Century-Crofts, [1966]. xv, 223 p. **345**

A translation of the Sophismata based on a text established from two manuscripts and the 1500 edition, which the translator hopes to publish soon.

Byzantine empire. *Historical sources.* "Financial transactions of Aurelia Titoueis," by J. Day and S. B. Porges, *American Journal of Philology*, 81 (1960), 155–75. **346**

Contains text and translation of three papyri in the Columbia Collection, dated 372. The financial situation apparently caused resistance to military service.

—— The Oxyrhynchus papyri, ed. with translation and notes by Eric G. Turner *et al.* London, Egypt Exploration Society, 1962. xii, 224 p. **347**

This volume, part 27 of a series, includes text and translation of documents from the 4th–6th centuries. Earlier volumes included 1st–7th-century editions of classical texts as well as both public and private documents. The series was not included in Farrar and Evans apparently because of their intention to publish a separate volume on documentary material.

—— Papyri from Hermopolis and other documents of the Byzantine period, ed. with translation and notes by B. R. Rees. London, Egypt Exploration Society, 1964. 127 p. **348**

Contains text and translation of documents of 1st–6th-centuries, including some letters on the cult of Hermes Trismegistus.

—— The reign of Manuel II Palaelogus in Thessalonica, 1382–87, by George T. Dennis. Rome, Pontifical Institute for Oriental Studies, 1960. *Orientalia Christiana analecta,* 159. **349**

Has translation *passim* of excerpts from several sources, including letters of Manuel to Demetrius Cydones.

—— Social and political thought in Byzantium from Justinian I to the last

BYZANTINE EMPIRE

Paleologus: passages from Byzantine writers and documents, tr. with intro. and notes by E. Barker. Oxford, Clarendon Press, 1957. 256 p. 350

Translation of excerpts from works dealing with the character and nature of kingship, relations between church and state, and attempts at social and political reform.

—— "The will of a provincial magnate, Eustachios Boilas (1059)," by S. Vryonis, *Dumbarton Oaks Papers,* 11 (1957), 263–77. 351

Contains a translation and commentary.

C

Cabasilas, Nicolaus, *abp. of Thessalonica, 14th cent.* A commentary on the divine liturgy, tr. by J. M. Hussey and P. A. McNulty, with an intro. by R. M. French. London, S.P.C.K., 1960. xi, 120 p. 352

De divino altaris sacrificio is translated; the volume contains also a translation of the Liturgy of St. John Chrysostom.

—— "Nicolas Cabasilas' 'Anti-zealot' discourse, a reinterpretation," by Ihor Ševčenko, *Dumbarton Oaks Papers,* 11 (1957), 79–171. 353

Contains an edition of the text and a paraphrase-summary. Professor Ševčenko thinks that Nicolas was born probably *c.* 1320 rather than in 1300 as has been thought.

Caesarius, *Saint, bp. of Arles, 470?–543.* The rule for nuns of St. Caesarius of Arles, a translation with critical intro. by M. Caritas McCarthy. Washington, Catholic University of America Press, 1960. 230 p. *Catholic University studies in medieval history,* 16. 354

—— Sermons, tr. by Mary Magdeleine Mueller. New York, Fathers of the Church, 1956–63. 2 v. *Fathers of the Church,* 31, 47. 355

Cáin Domnaig. "Cáin Domnaig," ed. and tr. by Vernam Hull, *Ériu,* 20 (1966), 151–77. 356

Contains text and translation of "The law of Sunday," a legal tract concerning the observance of Sunday, probably written in the first half of the 8th century, in the editor's opinion. The text is a new edition based on five manuscripts.

Calvo, Bonifacio, *13th cent.* The poems of Bonifacio Calvo; a critical edition by William D. Horan. The Hague, Mouton, 1966. 94 p. *Studies in Italian literature,* 3. 357

Text and following prose translation of poems written in Provençal and two written in Portuguese.

Cassiodorus Senator, Flavius Magnus Aurelius, *c. 487–c. 580.* An introduction to divine and human readings, tr. with an intro. and notes by Leslie Webber Jones. New York, Columbia University Press, 1946. xvii, 233 p. *Records of civilization,* 40. 358

A translation of Institutiones divinarum et humanarum lectionum. Book I is On the Bible and its commentaries; Book II, On the seven liberal arts.

Caterina da Genova, *Saint, 1447–1510.* The life and sayings of St. Catherine of Genoa, selection tr. from Libro de la vita mirabile . . . , pub. 1551, by Paul Garvin. New York, Alba House [1964]. 139 p. 359

—— Treatise on purgatory; the dialogue, tr. by Charlotte Balfour and Helen Douglas Irvine. New York, Sheed & Ward, 1946. xv, 17–142 p. 360

This translation is from a French version of Theodore de Bussierne, 1860, but has been collated with the Italian edition of 1737 by Giovanni da Caporali. The works exist only in a redaction supposedly by Battista Venazzo, goddaughter of the saint.

Caterina da Siena, *Saint, 1347–80.* The orcherd of Syon, ed. by Phyllis Hodgson and Gabriel M. Liegey. New York, Oxford University Press for EETS, 1966. Vol. I. *Early English Text Society,* original series, 258. 361

A 15th-century translation of "Il dialogo della serafica santa Caterina da Siena," originally published by Wynken de Worde in 1519; this edition was made from that of de Worde and from three manuscript versions in English. Vol. II will contain introduction, notes, glossary.

—— [Prayers]. Aylesford (Kent), St. Albert's Press for the Dominican Sisters of the Perpetual Rosary, 1958. [16] p. 362

This translation, listed by the British National Bibliography, has not been seen.

Caucasus. *Historical sources.* "Caucasica III: the Alān capital *Magas and the Mongol campaigns," by V. Minorsky, *Bulletin of the School of Oriental and African Studies,*, 14 (52), 221–38. 363

Contains translation of excerpts from Arabic records of the Mongol campaign in the west, *c.* 1239.

—— A history of Sharvan and Darband in the 10th–11th centuries, by V. Minorsky. Cambridge [Eng.], Heffer [1958]. vii, 187, 32 p. 364

Contains translation of part of the history translated into Arabic from a Turkish version by Ahmet bin Lûtfullah Müneccimbaşi, d. 1702 (the Library of Congress erroneously lists his death date as 1072). Müneccimbaşi ("Chief astronomer") preserved a nonextant contemporary history of the region of the Caucasus now part of the Soviet Republic of Azerbaijan and along the Caspian Sea—during the Middle Ages a "pathway of migrations," according to Professor Minorsky. Professor Minorsky has also translated here excerpts from geographical works of Ibn al-Azraq al-Fariqī, b. 1121; al-Mas'ūdī, d. 956; and Ibn Rustah, Aḥmad ibn 'Umar, *fl.* 903.

—— "Münejjim Bāshī's account of Sulṭān Malik Shah's reign," by S. A. Hasan, *Islamic Studies,* 3 (December, 1964), 429–69. 365

Contains translation (pp. 445–64) of part of Müneccimbaşi's (d. 1702) translation of a contemporary record for 1072–92.

—— Studies in Caucasian history. I. New light on the Shaddādids of Ganja; II. The Shaddādids of Ani; III. The prehistory of Saladin, by V. Minorsky. London, Taylor's Foreign Press, 1953. 178, 18 p. *Cambridge Oriental series.* 366

Contains translation from Müneccimbaşi (d. 1702) of a lost contemporary text covering the years 951–1193 in the history of the Shaddādids, Moslems living in eastern Transcaucasia in Ganja and in ancient Dvin, capital of Armenia.

Cavalcanti, Guido, *d. 1300.* Guido Cavalcanti's theory of love; the Canzone d'amore and other related problems, by James E. Shaw. Toronto, University of Toronto Press, 1949. ix, 228 p. *University of Toronto Romance series,* 1. 367

Contains text and a prose translation of the Canzone.

Caxton, William, *d. 1491.* William Caxton and his critics; a critical reappraisal of Caxton's contributions to the enrichment of the English language, . . . with

CELTES, CONRADUS

Caxton's Prologue to *Eneydos* [1490] in facsimile, and rendered into present-day English by Curt F. Bühler. [Syracuse, N.Y.], Syracuse University Press [1960]. 30 p. **368**

Celtes, Conradus, *1459–1508*. Selections from Conrad Celtis, 1459–1508, ed. with a translation and commentary by Leonard Forster. Cambridge [Eng.], Cambridge University Press, 1948. xii, 122 p. **369**

Latin text and facing translation of five poems, two epigrams, and the prose Oratio in gymnasio.

Celtic literature. *Collections.* A Celtic miscellany; translations from the Celtic, by Kenneth Jackson. Cambridge, Harvard University Press; London, Routledge & Kegan Paul, 1951. 359 p. **370**

Selections in new prose translations from Celtic languages "from the beginning to the nineteenth century": Irish, Welsh, Scottish-Gaelic, Scottish-Irish, Manx, Cornish, Breton.

Cent nouvelles nouvelles. The hundred tales, tr. by Rossell H. Robbins. New York, Crown [1960]. xxvi, 390 p. **371**

A 15th-century anthology of French stories, compiled perhaps by Antoine de la Sale, the translator thinks. Another translation, entitled The Hundred Stories, by Robert B. Douglas, privately printed in 1924, has been reissued by Ace Books, 1961, 350 p. This translation was not noted in Farrar and Evans. For another translation, abridged and somewhat bowdlerized, see item 718 below.

Chalcidius, *fl. 295–357*. Calcidius on matter, his doctrine and sources; a chapter in the history of Platonism, by J. C. M. van Winden. Leiden, Brill, 1959. 256 p. *Philosophia antiqua,* 8. **372**

Contains an outline of Chalcidius' commentary on Plato's Timaeus and translation largely from the last chapter, De silva, On matter.

Chanson de Roland. The song of Roland, tr. by Frederick B. Luquiens, intro. by Nathan A. Smyth. New York, Macmillan, 1952. xxv, 101 p. **373**

—— The song of Roland, a new translation by Dorothy L. Sayers. [Harmondsworth, Eng.], Penguin Books [1957]. 206 p. **374**

—— The song of Roland; the legend that Turoldus relates, the Oxford version tr. by Laura Moore Wright. New York, Vantage Press [1960]. 156 p. **375**

—— The song of Roland, tr. by Hilda Cumings Price. London and New York, Warne Publishing Co. [1961]. 103 p. **376**

An abridged verse translation.

—— Chanson de Roland, tr. by Patricia Terry. Indianapolis, Bobbs-Merrill, 1965. xxxii, 146 p. **377**

Chaucer, Geoffrey, *d. 1400*.

COLLECTIONS

—— The portable Chaucer, ed. and tr. by Theodore Morrison. New York, Viking Press, 1949. viii, 600 p. **378**

Modernized versions of most of the Canterbury tales, Troilus and Criseyde (abr.), and a selection of the minor poems.

CANTERBURY TALES

—— The Canterbury tales, tr. into modern English by Nevill Coghill. Baltimore, Penguin Books [1952]. 528 p. 379

This translation, often reprinted, was revised in 1958. Professor Coghill's translation of The Nun's Priest's tale was published separately by A. and R. Lane [Edinburgh? 1950], 29 p.

—— The Canterbury tales, tr. into modern English prose, by R. M. Lumiansky. New York, Rinehart [1954]. xxviii, 482 p. 380

Includes the text of the Prologue and the Nun's Priest's tale.

—— Canterbury tales, ed. with an intro. by A. C. Cawley. [Rev. ed.] London, Dent; New York, Dutton [c. 1958]. xviii, 611 p. *Everyman's library.* 381

Although this is an edition rather than a translation proper, it is listed here because difficult words and lines are glossed on the page with the text.

—— The Canterbury tales, tr. into modern English prose by David Wright. London, Barrie and Rockliff [1964]. xii, 299 p. 382

—— Chaucer's Canterbury tales, interlinear translation, by Vincent F. Hopper. Great Neck, N.Y., Barron's Educational Series, 1948. 463 p. 383

Contains text and translation of the Prologue, Knight's tale, Prioress' prologue and tale, Nun's Priest's prologue, tale, and epilogue, Wife of Bath's prologue and tale, Franklin's prologue and tale.

—— Canterbury tales; Chaucer for the present-day reader, prepared by Henry H. Hitchins. London, J. Murray, 1946; enlarged ed., 1949. xi, 128 p. 384

Modernized except for about twenty often-repeated words retained in their Middle English forms; contains the Prologue, tales of the Reeve, Prioress, Nun's Priest, Pardoner, Canon's Yeoman, and Chaucer's farewell; omitted tales are briefly summarized.

—— A Chaucer reader; selections from the Canterbury tales, ed. by Charles W. Dunn. New York, Harcourt, Brace [1952]. xxxviii, 225 p. 385

Contains prose translation of the Prologue, the links of all the tales, the Reeve's tale, Clerk's tale, Canon's Yeoman's tale; also has text of the Prologue and six other tales.

—— Canterbury tales; tales of Caunterbury, ed. [and tr.] by A. Kent Hieatt and Constance Hieatt. New York, Bantam Books [1964]. xxiv, 423 p. *Bantam dual-language book.* 386

Text and facing translation of the Prologue, tales of the Knight, Wife of Bath, Miller, Merchant, Pardoner, Prioress, and Nun's Priest.

—— Translation of Chaucer's prologue with running commentary, by James A. Walker. Iowa City, Iowa Supply Co. [c. 1950]. 92 p. 387

No attempt has been made to locate all modernizations of separate Canterbury tales, but a few others are as follows: Prologue: tr. by James J. Donahue, Dubuque, Iowa, Loras College Press [1954] 23 p.; by W. J. Frank Davies and Myfanwy G. Davies, London, J. Brodie [1951?], 22 p. The Davies have also translated The Squire's tale and the tale of Sir Thopas, London, J. Brodie [1954], 24 p.

OTHER WORKS

—— [House of fame] The house of fame; a rendition into modern English verse by Marion Badwell Smith. Vancouver, B.C., Department of English,

University of British Columbia [1955]. iv, 42 leaves [reproduced from typed copy]. 388

A copy of this translation, which has not been seen, is in the Library of Congress.

—— [Troilus and Criseyde] Geoffrey Chaucer's Troilus and Criseyde, rendered into modern English prose, by R. M. Lumiansky. Columbia, University of South Carolina Press, 1952. xii, 217 p. 389

—— Troilus and Criseyde, ed. by John Warrington. London, Dent; New York, Dutton [1953]. ix, 337 p. *Everyman's library.* 390

A highly glossed edition.

—— Troilus and Criseyde, tr. into modern English by Margaret Stanley-Wrench. London, Centaur Press, 1965. 328 p. 391

This translation has not been seen.

Chelčický, Peter, *1390–1460.* "Peter Chelčický: treatises on Christianity and the social order," by Howard Kaminsky, *Studies in Medieval and Renaissance History,* I (1964), 104–79. 392

Includes text and translation. Chelčický was a follower of Jan Hus.

Chester plays. The Chester mystery plays; sixteen pageant plays from the Chester craft cycle, adapted into modern English by Maurice Hussey. London, Heinemann [c. 1957]. xxi, 160 p. 393

Translated here in somewhat abridged form are the Fall of Lucifer, Creation of man, Noah's deluge, Abraham and Isaac, the Nativity, Adoration of the shepherds, Adoration of the magi, Slaying of the innocents, Simon the leper, the Betrayal, Passion, Resurrection, and Ascension of Christ, the Antichrist, Last Judgment.

—— The Chester trilogy, rendered into somewhat more contemporary English, by Kenneth Beaudoin. [Memphis, Tenn., privately printed, 1950]. 14 p. 394

An acting version of The shepherds play, Offering of the shepherds, Adoration of the Magi. A copy of this work is in the Columbia University library.

Choeroboscus, Georgius, *fl. before 8th cent.?* Imagery of the Igor tale in the light of Byzantino-Slavic poetic theory, by Justina Besharov. Leiden, Brill, 1956. 115 p. *Studies in Russian epic tradition,* 2. 395

Contains first edition and translation of a tract on tropes and figures from the Svjatoslav codex of 1073.

Chrestien de Troyes, *12th cent.* The story of the Grail, tr. by Robert White Linker. Chapel Hill [N.C.] Book Exchange, 1952. 202 p. 396

A translation of Perceval le Galois.

—— Ywain, the knight of the lion, tr., with an intro., by Robert W. Ackerman and Frederick W. Locke. New York, Ungar [1957]. vii, 64 p. 397

Lines 3416–6526 are summarized.

Christian literature. *Collections.* Advocates of reform, from Wyclif to Erasmus, ed. by Matthew Spinka. Philadelphia, Westminster Press [1953]. 399 p. *Library of Christian classics,* 14. 398

Contents: Wycliffe, On the pastoral office, On the Eucharist, tr. Fred L. Battles; Henry (Heinrich) of Langenstein, Epistola concilii pacis, tr. James K. Cameron; John Gerson, On the unity of the church, tr. James K. Cameron; Dietrich of Niem, De modis uniendi ac reformandi ecclesiae and John Hus, On simony, tr. Matthew Spinka; and two 16th-century documents. Another work of Gerson's appeared in mimeographed form; a copy is in the Library of Congress: Gersoniana, a Latin sermon on the Immaculate Conception of the Virgin Mary, ascribed to Jean Gerson, by Max Lieberman, New York, 1951, 78 p.

—— Alexandrian Christianity; selected translations of Clement and Origen with intro. and notes by John E. L. Oulton and Henry Chadwick. Philadelphia, Westminster Press [1954]. 475 p. *Library of Christian classics,* 2. 399

Contains translations of Clement of Alexandria's Stromateis 3 and 7 (On marriage, On spiritual perfection) and of Origen's On prayer, Exhortation to martyrdom, Dialogue with Heraclides.

—— Assumption of the blessed Virgin [and other] extracts from ecclesiastical writers [compiled by John Harvey Treat]. N.p., n.d. [18??]. 400

This volume, not listed by Farrar and Evans, contains separately paged short extracts from various writers, with Latin or Greek text and parallel translations; arranged as a Christian apologetic. The source for each item is indicated. A copy of this rare work is in the Harvard University Library; it is described in the National Union Catalog, pre-1956 imprints, *s.v.* Assumption.

—— Catholicism, ed. by George Brantl. New York, Braziller, 1961. 256 p. *Great religions of modern man,* 1. 401

Contains excerpts of ritual, dogmas, commentary, and apologetic writings.

—— Christian ethics; sources of the living tradition, ed. by Waldo Beach and H. Richard Niebuhr. New York, Ronald Press, 1955. viii, 496 p. 402

A textbook of translations; pp. 100–243 contain excerpts from medieval authors, including Augustine, Benedict, Francis of Assisi, Meister Eckhart, and Thomas Aquinas.

—— The Christian reader; inspirational and devotional classics, compiled and ed. by Stanley I. Stuber. New York, Association Press [c. 1952]. xiv, 514 p. 403

Includes translations from thirty-two medieval writers, pp. 1–191.

—— Christology of the later Fathers, ed. by Edward R. Hardy, in collaboration with Cyril C. Richardson. Philadelphia, Westminster Press [1954]. 400 p. *Library of Christian classics,* 3. 404

Contains previously published translations of Athanasius, On the incarnation of the word; Gregorius Nazianzenus, The theological orations, Letters on the Apollinarian controversy; and new translations by the editors of Gregory of Nyssa, An answer to Ablabius, An address on religious instruction; and of documents relating to the Christology of the ecumenical councils.

—— The church teaches; documents of the church in English translation, by John F. Clarkson *et al.* St. Louis, Herder, 1955. xiv, 400 p. 405

A collection of documents from the Apostles' Creed to modern times, organized topically; many are old translations. Another useful work, not a translation but containing summary and paraphrase from many medieval writers (pp. 1–320) is Masterpieces of Christian literature in summary form, ed. by Frank N. Magill with Ian P. McGreal, New York, Harper and Row [c. 1963], 1193 p. The summaries have been made by thirty distinguished Protestant theologians.

CHRISTIAN LITERATURE

—— The Cistercian heritage, by Louis Bouyer, tr. from the French by Elizabeth A. Livingstone. London, Mowbray [1958]. xvi, 207 p. 406

This translation of Bouyer's La spiritualité de Cîteaux contains *passim* excerpts from several medieval Cistercians translated by various translators directly from the Latin for the present volume.

—— The coasts of the country; an anthology of prayer drawn from the early English spiritual writers, ed. by Clare Kirchberger, intro. by Godfrey Anstruther. London, Harvill Press [1952]. 266 p. 407

Selections modernized or translated by the editor, many from manuscripts never before published; instructions to abbeys as well as works of major mystics are included. Many of the excerpts appeared previously in *The Life of the Spirit*, a journal edited by Conrad Pepler.

—— The Council of Constance: the unification of the church, tr. by Louise R. Loomis, ed. by John H. Mundy and Kennerly M. Woody. New York, Columbia University Press, 1961. xiii, 562 p. *Records of civilization,* 63. 408

Contains translations of contemporary accounts of the Council, including the chronicles of Ulrich Richental, Guillaume Fillastre, and Jacob Cerretano, as well as other documents.

—— Creeds, councils, and controversies, documents illustrative of the history of the church, A.D. 337–461, ed. by James Stevenson, based upon the collection ed. by the late B. J. Kidd. London, S.P.C.K., 1966. xx, 390 p. 409

A selection and revision of Kidd's earlier work; see Farrar and Evans, item 1966.

—— Creeds of the churches; a reader in Christian doctrine from the Bible to the present, ed. by John H. Leith. Chicago, Aldine [1963] and New York, Doubleday [1963]. xiv, 589 p. 410

Excerpts from medieval creeds translated by the editor, pp. 16–61.

—— Documents illustrating papal authority, A.D. 96–454, ed. by Edward Giles. London, S.P.C.K., 1952. xiv, 344 p. 411

Many short excerpts from the "raw material" for study of the dispute as to the primacy of the Bishop of Rome, reprinted from previously published translations. See also The Papacy, a brief history, by James A. Corbett, Princeton, Van Nostrand Press [1956], 192 p., which contains translation of twelve papal documents from the medieval period.

—— Documents of the Christian church, sel., ed. [and tr.] by Henry Bettenson. London, Oxford University Press, H. Milford [1943]. xviii, 456 p. 412

The documents range from *c.* 60 A.D. to 1920; medieval works include creeds, monastic rules, writings of the church fathers. The editor is responsible for the translation but acknowledges a debt to an earlier collection, item 1361 in Farrar and Evans. The second edition (1963) contains no change in the medieval contents.

—— Early Christian creeds, by John N. D. Kelly. London and New York, Longmans, Green [c. 1950]. xi, 446 p. 413

Contains *passim* the author's translation of many creeds, usually accompanied by text.

—— The early Christian fathers; a selection from the writings of the fathers from St. Clement of Rome to St. Athanasius, ed. and tr. by Henry S. Bettenson. London and New York, Oxford University Press, 1956. vii, 424 p. 414

—— Early Christian fathers, newly ed. and tr. by Cyril C. Richardson [*et al.*], London, S.C.M. Press [1953]. 415 p. *Library of Christian classics,* 1. 415

Contains translations from Clemens I, Ignatius, Polycarp, Justin Martyr, Athenagoras, Irenaeus, the Didache, and Epistle to Diognetus by various translators, including the editor.

—— Early Christian prayers, ed. by Adalbert Hamman, tr. [from the French ed. of 1952] by Walter Mitchell. Chicago, Regnery [1961]. xiii, 320 p. **416**

Contains prayers from the Bible, early Christian writers, inscriptions, papyri, church fathers, Eastern liturgies, including Syriac and Coptic versions, Western liturgies, as well as selections from Origen and Cyprian on the Lord's prayer.

—— Early Fathers from the Philokalia, together with some writings of St. Abba Dorotheus, St. Isaac of Syria, and St. Gregory Palamas, sel. and tr. from the Russian text Dobrotolubiye by E. Kadloubovsky and G. E. H. Palmer. London, Faber & Faber [1954]. 421 p. **417**

Besides the saints named in the title, there are in this volume translations of the following: St. Anthony, St. Mark the Ascetic, St. Evagrius, St. Nilus of Syria, St. Maximus the Confessor, and the Blessed Theodore. Other selections from the Philokalia, with text and facing translation, by the same translators, appeared in Writings from the Philokalia on prayer of the heart, London, Faber & Faber, 1951, 420 p.

—— Early Latin theology; selections from Tertullian, Cyprian, Ambrose, and Jerome, tr. and ed. by Stanley L. Greenslade. Philadelphia, Westminster Press [1956]. 415 p. *Library of Christian classics,* 5. **418**

Tertullian's Against the heretics is translated, along with its source, St. Irenaeus' Adversus haereses; and Tertullian's On purity and On idolatry. Cyprian's Unity of the Catholic church is translated, as well as several of his letters. From Ambrose and Jerome, only letters are translated.

—— Early medieval theology, newly tr. and ed. by George E. McCracken in collaboration with Allen Cabaniss. Philadelphia, Westminster Press [1957]. 430 p. *Library of Christian classics,* 9. **419**

Contains selections from works written in the 5th–12th centuries by Vincent of Lérins, Paschasius Radbertus of Corbie, Ratramnus of Corbie, Remigius (bp. of Lyons), Gregory the Great, Alcuin, Claudius of Turin, Rupert of Deutz, Guibert of Nogent, Rabanus Maurus of Mainz, Ivo of Chartres, Agobard of Lyons, Theodulph of Orléans, Bede.

—— "Early Russian monasticism," by Robert P. Casey, *Orientalia Christiana Periodica,* 19 (1953), 373–423. **420**

Contains translation of excerpts from the Pecherskii Paterik, a 15th-century compilation about the history of the monastery of the caves, and from a letter of Simon, bp. of Vladimir (13th century) concerning the monks.

—— The early Syrian fathers on Genesis . . . , ed. and tr. . . . by Abraham Levene. London, Taylor's Foreign Press, 1951. 354 p. **421**

Text and translation from a Syriac manuscript on the Pentateuch in the Mingana collection; the manuscript is a compilation made about 900, representing "five centuries" of Biblical exegesis. The Syriac authors include Theodore of Mopsuestia, *c.* 350–*c.* 428, and Ephraem Syrus, 308?–373. Only the first eighteen chapters, covering about half the book of Genesis, are translated here. Included is a translation of Rabbinic material which is the source for or parallel to the Syriac-Christian.

—— Faithful witnesses, records of early Christian martyrs, sel. and ed. by Edward R. Hardy. London, Lutterworth Press, 1959; New York, Association Press [1960]. 80 p. *World Christian books,* 2d series, 31. **422**

Translation of accounts of 2d–4th-century martyrdoms from the Acta martyrum.

CHRISTIAN LITERATURE

—— The fathers of the primitive church [sel. and tr.] by Herbert Musurillo. New York, New American Library [1966]. 272 p. **423**

Contains translations of fathers from Clement of Rome to Athanasius and the First Council of Nicaea.

—— The fellowship of the saints; an anthology of Christian devotional literature, ed. by Thomas S. Kepler. New York, Abington-Cokesbury Press, 1948. 800 p. **424**

Brief excerpts, chronologically arranged, largely from previously published translations, but some translations are new for this volume. Pp. 1–254 contain medieval works. Another anthology intended for devotional use is Letters from the Saints . . . from St. Thomas Aquinas to Blessed Robert Southwell, compiled by Claude H. Williamson, London, Rockcliff [1958], x, 214 p. This work has not been seen, but according to a review it contains some twenty letters from medieval sources.

—— Gnosticism; a source book of heretical writings from the early Christian period, ed. by Robert M. Grant. New York, Harper [1961]. 254 p. **425**

Contains translation of most of the known Gnostic writing of the 1st and 2d centuries, according to the editor, excluding Mandaeans. Includes work of St. Irenaeus, Baruch by the Gnostic Justin, writings of Basilides and his son Isidore, and of Valentinus and his school, including the Gospel of truth.

—— A history of Christianity. Vol. I, Readings in the history of the early and medieval Church, ed. by Ray C. Petry. Englewood Cliffs, N.J., Prentice-Hall, 1962 [i.e., 1963]. xiv, 561 p. **426**

Excerpts from letters, liturgies, rules of worship, saints' lives, monastic rules, crusades, etc.; some newly translated by the editor for this volume.

—— The holy fire; the story of the fathers of the eastern church, by Robert Payne. New York, Harper, 1957. xii, 313 p. **427**

Contains *passim* many excerpts newly translated by the author.

—— Late medieval mysticism, ed. by Ray C. Petry. Philadelphia, Westminster Press [1957]. 424 p. *Library of Christian classics,* 13. **428**

A collection largely of previously published translations from Bernard of Clairvaux, Hugh, Richard, and Adam of St. Victor, St. Francis, St. Bonaventure, Ramon Lull, Meister Eckhart, Richard Rolle, Henry Suso, Catherine of Siena, Jan van Ruysbroek, Theologica Germanica, Nicholas of Cusa, and Catherine of Genoa.

—— The mediaeval mystics of England, ed. by Eric Colledge. New York, Scribner [1961]. 309 p. **429**

Contains excerpts from Aelred of Rievaulx (Ethelred), St. Edmund Rich (Edmund of Canterbury), Richard Rolle, the Book of Privy Counsel by the author of the Cloud of Unknowing, Walter Hilton, Julian of Norwich, and Margery Kempe. The translation and modernization seem to be by the editor.

—— A new Eusebius; documents illustrative of the history of the church to A.D. 337. Based upon the collection ed. by . . . B. J. Kidd, ed. by James Stevenson. London, S.P.C.K., 1957. xix, 427 p. **430**

This is a selection and revision of Kidd's work; see Farrar and Evans, item 1966. Some omissions and some additions appear, including translation of additional passages in the notes.

—— Niceta of Remesiana: Writings, tr. by Gerald G. Walsh; Sulpicius Severus: Writings, tr. by Bernard M. Peebles; Vincent of Lerins: Commonitories, tr. by Rudolph E. Morris; Prosper of Aquitaine: Grace and free will, tr. by J. Reginald O'Donnell. New York, Fathers of the Church, 1949. 443 p. *Fathers of the Church*, 7. **431**

—— The ordination prayers of the ancient western churches, by H. B. Porter, Jr. London, S.P.C.K., 1967. xviii, 98 p. **432**

Text and facing translation of all of the oldest extant western ordination prayers, many translated here for the first time by the author. Beginning with the prayers of the Apostolic tradition attributed to St. Hippolytus, the author has included prayers from Rome, Gaul, Spain, England through the 11th century, and from later composite rites.

—— The papacy, a brief history, by James Arthur Corbett. Princeton, N.J., Van Nostrand Press [1956], 192 pp. *Anvil books.* **433**

The first 90 pp. of this work constitute the author's brief history of the papacy; pp. 91–180 include translation of documents about the papacy, about half of them of medieval provenience.

—— Patrology, by Johannes Quasten. Westminster, Md., Newman Press, 1950–60. 3 v. **434**

Detailed summaries and many excerpts in translation from the earliest patristic writing through the Council of Chalcedon; some liturgies and hymns as well as expository writing are translated, by the author.

—— Poems of prayer, ed. by Ralph L. Woods. New York, Hawthorn Books [1962]. 287 p. **435**

Contains translations of some twenty-five medieval Christian poems and prayers.

—— The prayers of man, from primitive peoples to present times, by Alfonso M. di Nola, tr. [from Italian] by Rex Benedict, ed. by Patrick O'Connor. New York, Obolensky [1961]. 544 p. **436**

Contains translations of many medieval prayers, rites, and liturgies.

—— Readings in church history, ed. by Colman J. Barry. Westminster, Md., Newman Press, 1959–65. 3 v. V. 1, From Pentecost to the Protestant revolt. xx, 633 p. **437**

Includes translations of excerpts from the Apocrypha, the Apostolic fathers, apologists, later fathers, canons, monastic rules, letters.

—— Roman state and Christian church; a collection of legal documents to A.D. 535, [ed.] by P. R. Coleman-Norton. London, S.P.C.K., 1966. 3 v. **438**

Contains translations of 652 secular documents, including letters as well as edicts and mandates, "affecting the Christian church in the Roman Empire."

—— Sacraments and forgiveness, history and doctrinal development of penance, extreme unction, and indulgences, ed. by Paul F. Palmer. Westminster, Md., Newman Press, 1955. 410 p. *Sources of Christian theology*, 2. **439**

Translations organized topically from the church fathers, synods and councils, penance handbooks, treatises of the Scholastics; much of the translation has been made by the editor.

—— A scholastic miscellany: Anselm to Ockham, ed. and tr. by Eugene R. Fairweather. Philadelphia, Westminster Press [1956]. 457 p. *Library of Christian classics*, 10. **440**

Contains translations of excerpts from seventeen writers, 11th–13th centuries.

—— Second-century Christianity, a collection of fragments, ed. by Robert M. Grant. London, S.P.C.K., 1946. viii, 143 p. **441**

Translation by the editor of letters, sermons, exegetical and polemical works by Jews, Greeks, and the provincial churches.

—— Spirituality through the centuries; ascetics and mystics of the western church, ed. by James Walsh. London, Burns & Oates; New York, Kenedy [1964]. x, 342 p. **442**

This is a collection of modern essays, largely reprinted from *The Month,* including translation *passim* of excerpts not elsewhere translated of St. Bruno, prior of Chartreuse, 1030–1101, John Scotus Eriugena, and Caesarius of Arles.

—— Studies in Christian Caucasian history, by Cyril Toumanoff. Washington, Georgetown University Press [c. 1963]. 599 p. **443**

Contains translation *passim* (frequently in footnotes) of excerpts from various Armenian and Georgian documents; also summary and paraphrase.

—— Syriac and Arabic documents regarding legislation relative to Syrian asceticism, ed. and tr. by Arthur Vööbus. Stockholm, Etse, 1960. 226 p. *Papers of the Estonian theological society in exile,* 11. **444**

Contains twenty-three sets of monastic rules and admonitions, from the 5th–9th centuries; see review by J. B. Segal, *Bulletin of the School of Oriental and African Studies,* 1963, pp. 178–82. This work has not been seen.

—— To any Christian; letters from the saints, sel. and arr. by a Benedictine of Stanbrook. London, Burns & Oates [1964]. ix, 299 p. **445**

Some apparently new translations by the editor; mostly previously published translations from Chrysostomus, Ignatius, Jerome, Augustine, Leo the Great, Basil, Bernard of Clairvaux, Gregory the Great, Gregory VII, Anselm.

—— A treasury of early Christianity, ed. by Anne Fremantle. New York, Viking Press, 1953. xiv, 625 p. **446**

Topically arranged selections from early fathers to the 7th century, including poetry, hymns, and apologetics from martyrs and heretics, as well as fathers. Apparently largely drawn from previously published translations.

—— A treasury of Russian spirituality, ed. by Georgii P. Fedotov. New York, Sheed & Ward, 1948. xvi, 501 p. **447**

This work contains translations particularly from mystical works. Fedotov's *The Russian Religious Mind* (Cambridge, Harvard University Press, 1946–66, 2 v.) contains copious translation *passim* from many works. Vol. 1, Kievan Christianity, 10th–13th centuries, was published as a Harper Torchbook in 1960 and was reissued by Harvard with vol. 2, 1966.

—— Western asceticism, ed. [and tr.] by Owen Chadwick. Philadelphia, Westminster Press, 1958. 368 p. *Library of Christian classics,* 12. **448**

Includes translation of excerpts from the Sayings of the fathers (Verba seniorum), the Conferences of Cassian, the Rule of St. Benedict.

—— The wisdom of Catholicism, ed. by Anton C. Pegis. New York, Random House [1949]. xxix, 988 p. **449**

Contains substantial excerpts from many writers; new translations made for this volume by the editor and others include St. Anselm's Proslogion; the prologue and chs. 5–7 of St. Bonaventure's Ascent of the mind to God; part of Thomas Aquinas' Summa contra Gentiles; a letter of Petrarch.

—— The world's best orations from the earliest period to the present time, ed. by Edward A. Allen, *et al.* St. Louis, Kaiser, 1899. 10 v. **450**

Contains in alphabetical order excerpts from speeches and sermons of many medieval authors. Often reprinted with slightly varying title. This work was omitted by Farrar and Evans.

Christina of Markyate, *c. 1096–1155/66.* The life of Christina of Markyate, a twelfth-century recluse, tr. and ed. by C. H. Talbot. Oxford, Clarendon Press 1959. 193 p. **451**

Text and facing translation from Ms. Cotton Tiberius E.1. According to the Catholic Encyclopedia, Christina was also known as St. Theodora; the life is by an anonymous monk of St. Albans.

Chronicle of Morea. Crusaders as conquerors; the Chronicle of Morea, tr. . . . by Harold E. Lurier. New York, Columbia University Press, 1964. 346 p. *Records of civilization,* 69. **452**

A prose translation of a poetic chronicle of the years following the fourth crusade and the sack of Constantinople. Text based on Copenhagen Codex Havniensis 57.

Chrysostomus, Joannes, *Saint, patriarch of Constantinople, d. 407.* Baptismal instructions, tr. by Paul W. Harkins. Westminster, Md., Newman Press, 1963. 375 p. *Ancient Christian writers,* 31. **453**

Translation of Ms. 6 of monastery of Stavronikita, the full contents of which became known only in 1955; edited as Jean Chrosostome, Huit catecheses batismales inedites, by Antoine Wenger, Paris, 1957.

—— Christianity and pagan culture in the later Roman empire, together with an English translation of John Chrysostom's Address on vainglory and the right way for parents to bring up their children, by Max. L. W. Laistner. Ithaca, N.Y., Cornell University Press [1951]. vi, 145 p. **454**

—— Chrysostom and his message; a selection from the sermons of St. John Chrysostom of Antioch and Constantinople, [tr.] by Stephen Neill. London, Lutterworth Press [1962]. 80 p. **455**

Contains new translation of A Sunday homily (33d homily on Gospel of Matthew), "On the statues" (extracts from several sermons), the 7th panegyric on St. Paul, extracts from the 30th homily on the Acts of the Apostles.

—— Commentary on Saint John the apostle and evangelist; homilies [1–88], tr. by Sister Thomas Aquinas Goggin. New York, Fathers of the Church, 1957–60. 2 v. *Fathers of the Church,* 33 and 41. **456**

—— In praise of St. Paul, tr. by Thomas Halton. [Boston], St. Paul Editions, 1963. 123 p. **457**

Includes translations of all seven of Chrysostom's panegyrics on St. Paul.

—— The preaching of Chrysostom; homilies on the Sermon on the mount, ed. with an intro. by Jaroslav Pelikan. Philadelphia, Fortress Press [1967]. ix, 230 p. **458**

A selection from the Homiliae in Matthaeum, homilies 15–24. The translation is that of the Schaff edition of the *Nicene and Post-Nicene Fathers* (1886–90; see Farrar and Evans, item 428).

CHRYSOSTOMUS, JOANNES

—— The priesthood, a translation of the Peri hierosynes of St. John Chrysostom, by W. S. Jurgens. New York, Macmillan, 1955. xxv, 133 p. 459

—— Six books on the priesthood, tr. by Graham Neville. London, S.P.C.K., 1964. 160 p. 460

A translation of De sacerdotio.

SUPPOSITIOUS WORKS

—— "A discourse by St. John Chrysostom on the sinful woman in the Ṣa'īdic dialect," by Y. 'Abd al-Masīḥ, *Bulletin de la Société archéologique copte,* 15 (1958–60), 11–39. 461

Contains text and translation of a version differing greatly from the Greek and Arabic ones, according to the author.

—— "Edition with a translation of a Hypapante homily ascribed to John Chrysostom," by E. Bickersteth, *Orientalia Christiana Periodica,* 32 (1966), 53–77. 462

Translation of a homily on the presentation of Christ in the Temple; this is the first edition of the text, based on ten manuscripts.

Cid Campeador, El. The poem of the Cid: selections; a literal translation, by Leonard E. Arnaud. Great Neck, N.Y., Barron's Educational Series [c. 1953]. 28 p. 463

—— The poem of the Cid, tr. by Lesley Byrd Simpson. Berkeley, University of California Press, 1957. 139 p. 464

This prose translation is based on the Pidal text but omits the first folio missing in the Abbat manuscript and supplied by Pidal from a 13th-century prose version.

—— Poema del Cid, texto espanol de Ramon Menendez Pidal. Poems of the Cid, English verse translation by W. S. Merwin. New York, Las Americas Publishing Co. [1960]. 311 p. 465

The translation without text was published in London by Dent, 1959, xiii, 240 p.

—— The epic of the Cid, tr. with an intro. by Gerald J. Markley. Indianapolis, Bobbs-Merrill, 1961. xii, 132 p. 466

—— The poem of the Cid, a modern translation with notes by Paul Blackburn, intro. by Glen Willbern. New York, R.D.M. Corporation [c. 1966]. 155 p. *A study master publication.* 467

Clara of Assisi, *Saint, d. 1253. Legend.* The legend and writings of Saint Clare of Assisi, intro., translation, and studies by Ignatius Brady. St. Bonaventure, N.Y., Franciscan Institute, 1953. xiv, 177 p. 468

The legend is ascribed to Thomas of Celano, *fl.* 1257. Documents connected with the saint, including the bull of canonization, letters to and from Clare, her Rule and Testament, are included.

Claretus de Solencia, *14th cent.* Clareti Enigmata; the Latin riddles of Claret, ed. with intro. and notes by Frederic Peachy. Berkeley, University of California Press, 1957. 64 p. *Folklore studies,* 7. 469

Contains text and translation of a collection of riddles made in Bohemia in the late 14th century.

Claudius, *Saint, martyr; fl. 3d cent. Legend.* "Apa Claudius and the thieves," by J. Drescher, *Bulletin de la Société d'archéologie copte,* 8 (1942), 63–86. **470**

Text and translation of a story found in an encomium on Claudius delivered by Constantine, bp. of Assiut, *c.* 600.

Clemens, Romanus, *1st cent.* The epistles of St. Clement of Rome and St. Ignatius of Antioch, newly tr. and annotated by James A. Kleist. Westminster, Md., Newman Bookshop, 1946. ix, 162 p. *Ancient Christian writers,* 1. **471**

For other translations, see above, *Apostolic Fathers.*

Clemens, Titus Flavius, *Alexandrinus, c. 150–c. 212.* Christ the educator, tr. by Simon P. Wood. New York, Fathers of the Church, 1954. xxiii, 309 p. *Fathers of the Church,* 23. **472**

A translation of Paidagogos (Paedagogus).

—— Clement of Alexandria, selections from the Protreptikos, an essay and a translation by Thomas Merton. [Norfolk, Conn.], New Directions [1963]. 27 p. **473**

—— The philosophy of Clement of Alexandria, by E. F. Osborne. Cambridge, [Eng.], Cambridge University Press, 1957. xi, 205 p. **474**

Conains *passim* translation of many excerpts from Clement's writings.

Cloud of unknowing. The cloud of unknowing, a version in modern English of a fourteenth-century classic. New York, Published in association with Pendle Hill by Harper [1948]. xxvii, 146 p. **475**

This version claims to be an interpretation rather than a translation; it contains 52 of the 75 chapters, rearranged. There is a preface by Howard H. Brinton; the translation was made by an anonymous member of the Pendle Hill Community.

—— The cloud of unknowing and other treatises . . . , ed. by Justin McCann. Westminster, Md., Newman Press [1952]. xxix, 220 p. 6th rev. ed. **476**

The revised edition is based on the text of Phyllis Hodgson, Oxford University Press for the Early English Text Society, 1944. *Cf.* Farrar and Evans, item 1000. Includes The epistle of privy counseling and The translation of Denis hid divinity, *i.e.,* of Dionysius the Areopagite.

—— The cloud of unknowing, a new translation by Ira Progroff. New York. Julian Press, 1957. 243 p. **477**

—— The cloud of unknowing, tr. by Clifton Wolters. Baltimore, Penguin Books [1961]. 143 p. **478**

Codex Theodosianus. The Theodosian code and novels, and the Sirmondian constitutions, a translation by Clyde Pharr, in collaboration with Theresa S. Davidson and Mary B. Pharr, with an intro. by C. Dickerman Williams. Princeton, Princeton University Press, 1952. xxvi, 643 p. *Corpus of Roman law (Corpus juris Romani),* 1. **479**

Contains translation of laws compiled under the Roman emperors from 313 to 468, as well as of interpretations of the code up to 506.

Colet, John, *1467?–1519.* John Colet and Marsilio Ficino by Sears [R.] Jayne. London, Oxford University Press, 1963. 172 p. **480**

Contains text and facing translation of Colet's marginalia in his copy of the Epistolae of Marsilio Ficino and of some correspondence between the two men.

Colombo, Cristoforo, *1451?–1506.*

Although Farrar and Evans did not include Columbus, it has been considered necessary to refer here to the major translations, since modern scholarship views Columbus as in many ways "a man of the Middle Ages." See the commentary and bibliography in G. R. Crone, The discovery of America, New York, Weybright and Talley [c. 1969], xiv, 224 p.

—— Select documents illustrating the four voyages of Columbus, including those contained in R. H. Major's Select letters of Christopher Columbus [1847], ed. and tr. by Cecil Jane. London, Hakluyt Society, 1930–32. 2 v. **481**

—— Journal, tr. by Cecil Jane [rev. and annotated by L. A. Vigneras] with an appendix by R. A. Skelton. New York, C. N. Potter, 1960. xxiii, 227 p. **482**

—— Journals and other documents on the life and voyages of Christopher Columbus, tr. and ed. by Samuel Eliot Morison. New York, Heritage Press, 1963. xv, 417 p. **483**

Colonna, Egidio, *abp., d. 1316.* Errores philosophorum, critical text with notes and intro. by Josef Koch, tr. by John O. Riedl. Milwaukee, Marquette University Press, 1944. lix, 69 p. **484**

Text and facing translation. The author is also known as Aegidius Romanus, Giles of Rome.

—— Theorems on existence and essence (Theoremata de esse et essentia) [by] Giles of Rome, tr. with an intro. by Michael V. Murray. Milwaukee, Marquette University Press, 1952 [*i.e.*, 1953]. xiv, 112 p. *Medieval philosophical texts in translation,* 7. **485**

Columba, *Saint, of Iona, d. 597.* "A new translation of St. Columba's Altus prosator in the National Library of Ireland," by Gareth W. Dunleavy, *Éire: Ireland, a Journal of Irish Studies,* 2 (1967), no. 1, 16–26. **486**

Translation from unpublished manuscript No. 229–30.

Columban, *Saint, 543–615.* Sancti Columbani opera, ed. and tr. by G. S. M. Walker. [Dublin], Dublin Institute for Advanced Studies, 1957. xciv, 247 p. *Scriptores Latini Hiberniae,* 2. **487**

Text and facing translation of letters, sermons, rules, penitential, poems; also works ascribed to St. Columban.

—— The poems of St. Columban, tr. by Perry F. Kendig. Philadelphia [privately printed], 1949. x, 80 p. **488**

Blank verse translation of Letters to Hunald and Fedolius, Gnomic lines, Epigram against woman, Concerning the vanity and wretchedness of human life, Rowing song.

—— The prose letters of Saint Columban, translation with an intro. and commentary, by Charles B. Flaherty. Washington, Catholic University of America Press [1955]. ix, 124 p. **489**

This work has not been seen.

Constantinus VII Porphyrogenitus, *Emperor of the East, 905–959.* De administrando imperio, Greek text ed. by Gy. Moravcsik, English translation by R. J. H. Jenkins. New, rev. ed. Washington, Dumbarton Oaks Center for Byzantine Studies [distributed by J. J. Augustin, Locust Valley, N.Y.], 1967. ix, 341 p. *Corpus fontium historiae Byzantinae*, 1. **490**

The first edition, in two volumes, appeared 1949–62; vol. 1 contained the text and facing translation; vol. 2, commentary by F. Dvornik, B. Lewis, S. Runciman, *et al.* The original treatise is actually a compilation made by Contantine, who supplied linking material. Section 3 of the treatise discusses the origin and history of many nations bordering the Byzantine empire in the 10th century; the work constitutes "one of the most important historical documents surviving from medieval Byzantium," according to the editor.

Constantius II, Flavius Julius, *317–61.* "Constantius II on Flavius Philippus," by Louis J. Swift and J. H. Oliver, *American Journal of Philology,* 83 (1962), 247–64. **491**

Reconstructed text, English translation, and commentary on a letter written by Constantius to Flavius Philippus, an official in Cyprus.

Coptic texts. Bala'izah; Coptic texts from Deir el-Bala izah in Upper Egypt, ed. and tr. by Paul E. Kahle. London, Oxford University Press, 1954. 2 v. **492**

Text and translation of passages from manuscripts dating 675–775, of a miscellaneous nature; out of 370 texts, 300 are non-literary.

—— Coptic studies in honor of Walter Ewing Crum, *Bulletin of the Byzantine Institute,* 2 (1950), xi, 572 p. **493**

Several articles contain translations of excerpts of Coptic poetry and prose, including Acta Apostolorum Apocrypha, Martyrdom of St. Phocas, the dying prayer of St. Athanasius. According to a footnote, other translations appear in a work by T. Säve-Söderbergh, Studies in the Coptic Manichaean psalmbook, prosody and Mandaean parallels, Uppsala, Uppsala University, 1949. This work has not been seen.

—— Coptic ostraca from Medinet Habu, by Elizabeth Stefanski and Miriam Lichtheim. Chicago, University of Chicago Press, 1952. 50 pp., 93 pp. *Oriental Institute publications,* 71. **494**

Contains text and translation of the ostraca.

—— "A Coptic calculation manual," by J. Drescher, *Bulletin de la Société archéologie copte,* 13 (1948–49), 137–60. **495**

Text and translation of the "chief Coptic representative" of documents in the history of mathematics. The second part, translated here almost in full, deals with amounts in various measures and corresponding money values.

—— "Remarks on the interpretation of a Coptic magical text," by L. Kákosy, *Acta Orientalia Academiae Scientiarium Hungaricae,* 13 (Budapest, 1961), 325–28. **496**

Contains translation of a short 8th-century text which the author maintains is important in showing the survival of Old Egyptian pagan religion after many centuries of Christianity.

—— A short account of the Copts, by W. H. Worrell. Ann Arbor, University of Michigan Press, 1945. xii, 55 p. **497**

Contains paraphrase and translation of excerpts from many Coptic works, including the Cambyses romance, a prose account dating from perhaps the 6th century of the invasion of Egypt by Cambyses (Nebuchadnezzar); and a poem, Archilletes and Synkltikē, concerning the apocryphal acts of Andrew and Paul. Some translation also of the Coptic version of the Sayings of the fathers (Verba seniorum) which differs considerably from Greek and Syriac versions, according to the author.

—— Three Coptic legends: Hilaria, Archellites, The seven sleepers, ed. with translation and commentary by James Drescher. Le Caire, Imprimerie de l'Institut français d'archaeologie orientale, 1947. viii, 179 p. **498**

Text and translation of legends from early Christian times; texts of Greek and ancient Egyptian parallels also given.

Cornish plays. The Ordinalia, ed. and tr. by R. Morton Nance and A. S. D. Smith. Unpublished manuscript in the Royal Institution of Cornwall, Truro. **499**

This translation, along with the also unpublished "Corrections and notes to Norris' Ordinalia," furnished the basis for Halliday's translation of excerpts (see below) and for a series of publications entitled Extracts from Cornish texts in unified spelling, published in St. Ives by the Federation of Old Cornwall Societies, 1951–. The Extracts have also included selections from Bewnans Meryasek, St. Meriasek in Cornwall, a saint's legend not part of the Ordinalia. For more detailed bibliography, see Robert Longsworth, The Cornish Ordinalia, religion and dramaturgy, Cambridge, Harvard University Press, 1967.

—— The legend of the Rood, with "The three Maries" and "The death of Pilate" from the Cornish miracle plays, done into English verse . . . by Frank E. Halliday. London, Duckworth [1955]. ix, 142 p. **500**

Poetic version of excerpts from Parts 2 and 3 of the Cornish Ordinalia.

Corpus juris civilis. The elements of Roman law, with a translation of the Institutes of Justinian, by Robert W. Lee. London, Sweet & Maxwell, 1944. xxvii, 489 p. **501**

An earlier partial translation of Digest 41, parts 1 and 2, was made by Francis de Zulveta in 1922 and reprinted by the Clarendon Press, 1950, 111 p.; this was not entered in Farrar and Evans.

Courtenay, William, *abp. of Canterbury, 1381–96.* William Courtenay, archbishop of Canterbury, 1381–1396, by Joseph Dahmus. University Park, Pa., and London, Pennsylvania State University, 1966. viii, 341 p. **502**

An appendix, pp. 239–76, contains translation of works by Courtenay, including his oath of obedience to Pope Urban VI and documents relating to his quarrel with Thomas Brantingham, bishop of Exeter.

Crusades. The crusades, a documentary survey, ed. by James A. Brundage. Milwaukee, Marquette University Press, 1962. 318 p. **503**

Translations from original documentary accounts of the times woven together with narrative introductions; many previously published translations are used, but the editor has also made new ones for the volume.

—— The crusades, by Régine Pernoud, tr. by Enid McLeod. London, Martin Secker; New York, Putnams [c. 1962]. 295 p. **504**

Excerpts from many primary sources are translated with narrative links added. The original work in French, Les Croisades, appeared in 1960.

—— The crusaders, by Régine Pernoud, tr. by Enid Grant. Philadelphia, Dufour, 1964. ix, 291 p. **505**

A collection of excerpts from poems, letters, and chronicles, linked as a narrative focused on the personalities of the leaders of the crusades. There is some overlap with the material in the author's The crusades. This work appeared in 1959 as Les croisés. Apparently the translator is the same person as Enid McLeod who translated The Crusades, but I have been unable to verify this information.

—— The third crusade, an eye witness account of the campaign of Richard Coeur-de-Lion in Cyprus and the Holy Land, ed. by Kenneth Fenwick. London, Folio Society, 1958. 164 p. **506**

The original work is an Anglo-Norman poem Carmen Ambrosii by Ambroise, *fl. c.* 1196; it was translated into Latin prose perhaps by Richard, canon of Holy Trinity, London, under the title Itinerarium peregrinorum et gesta Regis Ricardi. The work was formerly ascribed to Geoffrey de Vinsauf; *cf.* Farrar and Evans, item 3774. The translation is based on that of 1848 for Bohn's Library, from the Latin version.

Cuchulain cycle. The second book of Irish myths and legends, by Eoin Neeson. A Mercier paperback [1966], distributed by the Folklore Associates, Hatboro, Pa. 128 p. **507**

A translation or retelling (no translator named) of the Red Branch cycle, a conflation of the 11th- and 15th-century versions, according to the author.

—— Longes mac n-Usnig, being The exile and death of the sons of Usnech, tr. by Thomas Kinsella from the Irish text in the Book of Leinster. [Dublin], Dolmen Press [1954]. 32 p. **508**

—— Longes mac n-Uislenn, The exile of the sons of Uislin, ed. and tr. by Vernam Hull. New York, Modern Language Association; London, Oxford University Press, 1949. 187 p. **509**

A translation of the early version, *c.* 1000.

—— Táin bó Cúailnge from the Book of Leinster, ed. and tr. by Cecile O'Rahilly. Dublin, Institute for Advanced Studies, 1967. lxi, 283 p. **510**

Text and translation.

—— [Táin bó Flidais] "Carn Fraoich soitheach na saorchlann," by James Carney, *Celtica*, 2 (1952–54), 154–94. **511**

Irish text with facing normalized Irish text and following prose translation of a poem from the Book of Uí Maine, written "at the latest in the 14th century," according to the author.

Cyprianus, *Saint, bp. of Carthage, d. 258.* De bono patientiae, tr. by M. George Edward Conway, Washington, Catholic University of America Press, 1957. xx, 193 p. *Patristic studies,* 92. **512**

Text and facing translation.

—— De opere et eleemosynis, tr. by Edward V. Rebenack. Washington, Catholic University of America Press, 1962. xviii, 162 p. *Patristic studies,* 94. **513**

Text and facing translation of "On corporal works of mercy."

—— The lapsed, The unity of the Catholic Church, tr. and annotated by Maurice Bévenot. Westminster, Md., Newman Press, 1957. 133 p. *Ancient Christian writers,* 25. **514**

—— Letters (1–81) [by] Saint Cyprian, tr. by Rose Bernard Donna. Washington, Catholic University of America Press [1965, c. 1964]. xxvi, 358 p. *Fathers of the Church*, 51. **515**

—— Nature and the vocabulary of nature in the works of St. Cyprian, by Mary Tarcisia Ball. Washington, Catholic University of America Press, 1946. xix, 303 p. *Patristic studies*, 75. **516**

Contains translation pp. 6–28 and *passim* of excerpts from several of Cyprian's works.

—— The "Our Father," a translation of the famous commentary by [S. Redmond] a priest of the Irish Jesuit Province. Dublin, Clonmore & Reynolds [1953]. 41 p. **517**

This translation has not been seen.

—— Treatises, tr. and ed. by Roy J. Deferrari, with The dress of virgins, tr. by Angela Elizabeth Keenan; Mortality, tr. by Mary Hannan Mahoney, and The good of patience, tr. by Sister George Edward Conway. New York, Fathers of the Church, 1958. 372 p. *Fathers of the Church*, 36. **518**

Contains translations of all of Cyprian's treatises except Ad Quirinum.

SPURIOUS AND DOUBTFUL WORKS

—— The Pseudo-Cyprianic "De Pascha computus," tr. with brief annotations by George Ogg. London, S.P.C.K., 1955. x, 42. **519**

According to the translator, this is the earliest extant work on the computation of Easter.

Cyprus passion cycle. The Cyprus Passion cycle, ed. and tr. by August C. Mahr. Notre Dame, Ind., University of Notre Dame Press, 1947. xvi, 225 p. *University of Notre Dame publications in medieval studies*, 9. **520**

Text and facing translation of a play ascribed by the editor to Konstantinos Euteles Anagnostes, b. 1241. According to the British Museum Catalog, this is not a true translation but a reconstruction of the play from the scenario in Codex Palatinus Graecus 367.

Cyrillus, *Saint, bp. of Jerusalem, 315?–386?* Cyril of Jerusalem and Nemesius of Emesa, ed. and tr. by William Telfer. Philadelphia, Westminster Press [1955]. 466 p. *Library of Christian classics*, 4. **521**

Contains translation of selections from Cyril's Catchetical lectures and his Letter to Constantius, and of Nemesius' On the nature of man, an essay indebted to Hippocrates.

—— St. Cyril of Jerusalem's lectures on the Christian sacraments, the Procatchesis, and the five mystagogical catecheses, ed. by Frank L. Cross. London, S.P.C.K., 1951. xliii, 84 p. **522**

Text and translation. The translation alone, by R. W. Church, appeared in 1838; *cf.* Farrar and Evans, item 1163.

Cyrillus III, *patriarch of Alexandria, fl. 1235–50.* "The canons of Cyril III ibn Laḳlaḳ, 75th patriarch of Alexandria, A.D. 1235–50," by O. H. E. Khs.-Burmester, *Bulletin de la Société archéologique copte,* 12 (1946–47), 71–136; 14 (1950–51), 113–50. **523**

Text and translation of the complete code of canon law for the Coptic church in the middle ages.

D

Dafydd ap Gwilym, *14th cent.* Selected poems, tr. by Nigel Heseltine, with a preface by Frank O'Connor. Dublin, Cuala Press, 1944. 45 p. **524**

Damascius, the Syrian, *supposed author, fl. c. 500.* Lectures on the Philebus, wrongly attributed to Olympiodorus. Text, translation, notes, and indices by L. G. Westerink. Amsterdam, North Holland Publishing Co., 1959. xxii, 149 p. **525**

Text and facing translation of a commentary on Plato.

Daniel (liturgical drama). The play of Daniel, a thirteenth-century musical drama, ed. by Noah Greenberg, tr. by J. Misrahi. New York, Oxford University Press, 1959. 111 p. **526**

The translation includes rubrics for music and stage directions. A narration by W. H. Auden supplements the translation.

Danse macabre. La danse macabré des charniers des Saints Innocents à Paris, ed. [and tr.] by Edward F. Chaney. [Manchester], University of Manchester Press, 1945. vi, 65 p. **527**

Text from a 1486 edition with prose translation.

Dante Alighieri, *1265–1321.*

COLLECTIONS

—— The portable Dante, The divine comedy, complete, tr. by Laurence Binyon, with notes from C. H. Grandgent; La vita nuova, complete, tr. by D. G. Rossetti; excerpts from the Latin prose works, ed., and with an intro., by Paolo Milano. New York, Viking Press, 1947. xlii, 662 p. **528**

—— Dante's lyric poetry [ed. and tr. from the Italian by] K. Foster and P. Boyde. Oxford, Clarendon Press, 1967. 2 v. **529**

Text and prose translation are in vol. 1; commentary, vol. 2. Two of the poems are letters addressed to Dante by Guido Cavalcanti. The text is that of Michele Barbi for the Opere, Società Dantesca Italiana.

—— Odes, tr. by H. S. Vere-Hodge. Oxford, Clarendon Press, 1963. x, 269 p. **530**

Text and facing translation of twenty-three of the Canzoni, the sestina, and the double sestina; text is that of Michele Barbi for the Opere, Società Dantesca Italiana.

SINGLE WORKS

—— [Canzoni] The heart of stone, being the four Canzoni of the "Pietra" group, done into English by Dorothy L. Sayers. Witham, Essex [Eng.], J. H. Clarke [1946]. [16] p. **531**

—— [De monarchia] Monarchy and Three political letters, translation and intro. by Donald Nicholl, and a note on the chronology of Dante's political writings by Colin Hardie. London, Weidenfield and Nicolson [1954]; New York, Noonday Press, 1954. xxi, 121 p. **532**

The letters translated are nos. 5, 6, 7 in Toynbee's edition.

DANTE ALIGHIERI

—— On world-government, or De monarchia, tr. by Herbert W. Schneider. New York, Liberal Arts Press, 1949. xiv, 61 p. **533**

The translation is somewhat abridged, omitting three chapters of Book III and part of Book II, largely historical.

—— [Divina Commedia] Dante, theologian, the Divine comedy; translation and commentary by Patrick Cummins. London and St. Louis, Herder, 1948. 604 p. **534**

A "literal" and a "spiritual" commentary line by line for the Commedia, which the editor interprets as if a version of Thomas Aquinas' Summa theologica. The translation is in *terza rima* and *endecasillabo.*

—— The Divine comedy of Dante Alighieri, tr. by John D. Sinclair. London, John Lane, 1948; New York, Oxford University Press, 1948. 3 v. **535**

Text and facing prose translation. The first two volumes appeared originally in 1939; they have been revised and the third volume added.

—— The Divine comedy, a new translation into English blank verse by Lawrence Grant White. New York, Pantheon Books, 1948. xiv, 188 p. **536**

—— La divina commedia, with an English translation by Harry M. Ayres. New York, S. F. Vanni, 1949–53. 3 v. **537**

A prose translation.

—— The Comedy of Dante Alighieri, the Florentine, tr. by Dorothy L. Sayers. Harmondsworth, [Eng.], Penguin Books [1950–63]. 3 v. **538**

A verse translation. Barbara Reynolds is co-translator of vol. 3.

—— The divine comedy, a new prose translation, with an intro. and notes by H. R. Huse. New York, Rinehart [1954]. xviii, 492 p. **539**

The prose translation is set up in tercet form, to parallel the original.

—— The divine comedy, tr. and ed. by Thomas G. Bergin. New York, Appleton-Century-Crofts [1955]. xvi, 122, 114, 112, ii p. **540**

The three parts of this verse translation were published separately 1948–54.

—— The Divine comedy, a translation in *terza rima,* with intro. and arguments, by Glen Swiggett. Sewanee, Tenn., University of the South Press, 1956. xiv, 567 p. **541**

—— The comedy of Dante Alighieri, tr. into English unrhymed hendecasyllabic verse, by Mary Prentice Lillie. San Francisco, Grabhorn Press, 1958. 3 v. **542**

—— Dante's Divine poem, written down freely into English [prose], by Clara Stillman Reed. Wilbraham, Mass. [Privately printed] [c. 1962]. vi, 312 p. **543**

—— The Divine comedy, tr. . . . into English triple rhyme, by Geoffrey L. Bickersteth. Cambridge, Harvard University Press, 1965. xliii, 795 p. **544**

This translation, facing the text, is based on the text of Manfredi Porena (Bologna, 1956) and is a revision of Bickersteth's earlier translation based on the Vandelli text, which appeared first in 1932, reprinted 1955 without text by Aberdeen University Press.

—— The divine comedy, tr. into blank verse by Louis Biancolli. New York, Washington Square Press [1966]. 3 v. **545**

Text (based on edition of E. Moore) and facing translation.

—— Il paradiso di Dante, an English version by T. W. Ramsey with a foreword by Roy Campbell. Aldington-Kent, Hand & Flower Press, 1952. x, 148 p. **546**

A poetic version.

—— The Inferno, translation in verse by John Ciardi, historical intro. by A. T. McAllister. New Brunswick, N.J., Rutgers University Press, 1954. 288 p. **547**

—— The Purgatorio . . . , tr. by Sydney Fowler Wright. Edinburgh and London, Oliver & Boyd [1954]. ix, 147 p. **548**

A poetic translation. The translator's version of the Inferno appeared in 1928.

—— The Inferno . . . , tr. . . . by Warwick Chipman, intro. and notes by Kenelm Foster. London and New York, Oxford University Press, 1961. 151 p. **549**

Translation in *terza rima,* based on text established by La società italiana.

—— The Purgatorio, a verse translation for the modern reader by John Ciardi, intro. by Archibald T. McAllister. [New York], New American Library [1961]. 350 p. **550**

—— Dante and his Comedy, by Allan Gilbert. New York, New York University Press, 1963. ix, 207 p. **551**

This monograph contains prose translation of many passages from the Commedia as well as from early commentators.

—— Dante's Hell, Inferno, tr. into English verse by Aldo Maugeri. Messina, La Sicilia [1965]. 208 p. **552**

—— Inferno, the new, annotated BBC ed., in Italian and English, ed. by Terence Tiller. New York, Schocken Books [1967, c. 1966]. 315 p. **553**

Text and facing translation by twelve translators, "an experiment in collective translation."

—— [Vita nuova] La vita nuova, tr. by Mark Musa. New Brunswick, N.J., Rutgers University Press [1957]. ix, 86 p. **554**

—— Dante's Vita nuova, tr. by Ralph Waldo Emerson, ed. and annotated by J. Chesley Matthews. Chapel Hill, University of North Carolina Press, 1960. xiii, 145 p. *University of North Carolina studies in comparative literature,* 26. **555**

Emerson's prose translation, made in 1843, was the first complete translation into English, according to the editor, but was not published until this edition appeared in the *Harvard Library Bulletin,* 11 (Nos. 2 and 3, Spring and Autumn 1957), 208–44, 346–62.

—— The new life, La vita nuova, tr. by William Anderson. Baltimore, Penguin Books [1964]. 109 p. **556**

Dastin, John, *14th cent.* "The text of John Dastin's 'Letter to Pope John XXII'," by C. H. Joston, *Ambix,* 4 (1949), 34–51. **557**

Text of two manuscripts of the letter and translation; the topic is alchemy and medicine.

Dasxurançi, Movsēs, *c. 11th cent.* The history of the Caucasian Albanians by Movses Dasxurançi, tr. by C. J. F. Dowsett. London, Oxford University Press, 1961. xx, 252 p. *London oriental series,* 8. **558**

The translation from the Armenian Patmut'ium Atuaniç is based on an edition and all manuscripts; the work is a compilation of the late 11th or early 12th century of Albanian history up to the 8th century.

Daude de Pradas, *13th cent.* The romance of Daude de Pradas called "Dels auzels cassadors," ed. with intro. by Alexander H. Schutz. Columbus, Ohio State University Press, 1945. xi, 225 p. **559**

Includes a "résumé with excerpts translated for the benefit of the non-provençalists, such as ornithologists and others concerned with the history of science." The work is a treatise on falconry aimed at amateurs.

Dawit 'Alawkay, *d. 1140.* The Penitential of David of Ganjak, ed. and tr. by C. J. F. Dowsett. Louvain, Secretariat du Corpus SCO, 1961. 2 v. *Corpus scriptorum Christianorum orientalium,* 216–17; *Scriptores Armeniaci,* 3–4. **560**

The text is in vol. 3, translation in vol. 4. According to the editor, this "Canonical advice or instructions" is similar to the Celtic and Anglo-Saxon penitentials; it not only prescribes the penalties but describes the crimes.

Dead Sea scrolls.

Although the so-called Dead Sea scrolls discovered at Qumran in Palestine in 1947 and after are pre-medieval, a few translations are listed here because of the importance of these documents for medieval studies. For an outline and bibliography, see Menahem Mansoor, The Dead Sea scrolls, a college textbook and a study guide, Grand Rapids, Mich., Eerdman's [1964].

—— The Scriptures of the Dead Sea scrolls in English translation, by T. H. Gaster. New York, Doubleday; London, Secker and Warburg, 1956. 359 p. **561**

A translation of the major scrolls. A 2d edition of 1957 adds the Aramaic Genesis Apocryphon and some hymns.

—— The Nezer and the Submission in suffering hymns from the Dead Sea scrolls, reconstructed, vocalized, and tr. with critical notes by Meir Wallenstein. Istanbul, Institut Istanbul, 1957. 47 p. **562**

—— The Thanksgiving hymns, tr. and annotated with an intro. by Menahem Mansoor. Leiden, Brill, 1961. 227 p. **563**

—— The Dead Sea scrolls in English, tr. with intro. by Géza Vermès. Baltimore, Penguin Books, 1962. 254 p. **564**

—— The Rule of Qumran and its meaning, intro., translation, and commentary, by A. R. C. Leaney. Philadelphia, Westminster Press, 1966. 310 p. **565**

Translation of the Manual of discipline.

—— The Dead Sea Psalms scroll, by J. A. Saunders. Ithaca, N.Y., Cornell University Press [1967]. xi, 174 p. **566**

Text and facing translation of a scroll first unrolled in 1961.

Demetrius XII, *patriarch of Alexandria.* "The Coptic calenderical computation and the system of epacts known as 'The epact computation,' ascribed to Abba

Demetrius, the XIIth patriarch of Alexandria," tr. by George Sobhy, *Bulletin de la Société d'archéologie copte,* 8 (1942), 169–99 [translation]; 9 (1943), 237–52 [text]. 567

De rebus bellicis. A Roman reformer and inventor, being a new text of the treatise De rebus bellicis, with a translation and interpretation by E. A. Thompson and a Latin index by Barbara Flower. Oxford, Clarendon Press, 1952. xii, 132 p. 568

Text and following translation of a "Tract on defense," written *c.* 366–75; addressed to the emperors, it offers a series of suggestions for reforming financial policy, currency, the army, law, and provincial administration; it also describes new mechanical contrivances.

Deschamps, Eustache, *c. 1340–c. 1410.* "A moral for moralists," tr. by Knox Wilson, *Philological Papers,* 15 (1966), 1–2. (Bulletin of West Virginia University.) 569

A verse translation of "Je ne finay depuis longtemps."

al-Dhahabī, *c. 1274–c. 1352.* "Adh-Dhahabī's record of the destruction of Damascus by the Mongols in 699–700/1299–1301," by Joseph Somogyi, in Ignace Goldziher Memorial Volume ed. by David S. Löwinger and Joseph Somogyi. Budapest, 1948. vii, 434, 44 p. 570

The translation, which appears on pp. 360–86, is from a work of "a hitherto unknown authority" on the Mongol invasion.

Di'bil b. 'Alī, al-Khuzā'ī, *765 or 66–860 or 61.* Di'bil b. 'Alī, the life and writings of an early 'Abbasīd poet, by Leon Zolondek. Lexington, University of Kentucky Press, 1961. 188 p. 571

Text and translation of the Book of the poets; the author's full name as given in the text is Abū 'Alī Muḥammad b. 'Alī b. Razīn al-Khuzā-i.

Dictys Cretensis. The Trojan War; the chronicles of Dictys of Crete and Dares the Phrygian, tr., with an intro. and notes, by Richard M. Frazer, Jr. Bloomington, Indiana University Press [1966]. v, 185 p. *Indiana University Greek and Latin classics.* 572

Dicuil, *fl. 825.* Dicuili Liber de mensura orbis terrae, ed. [and tr.] by James J. Tierney, with contributions by Ludwig Bieler. Dublin, Dublin Institute for Advanced Studies, 1967. vii, 135 p. *Scriptores Latini Hiberniae,* 6. 573

Text and facing translation of a geographical work.

Digenes Acritas (epic poem), *10th–11th cent.?* Digenes Akrites, ed. with an intro., translation and commentary by John Mavrogordato. Oxford, Clarendon Press; New York, Oxford University Press, 1956. lxxxiv, 273 p. 574

Text and facing translation of a Byzantine "provincial epic" about "Twyborn the Borderer." Text from five manuscripts in poetry and two others.

Dimetian code. The laws of Hywel Da, tr. by Melville Richards. Liverpool, Liverpool University Press, 1954. 154 p. 575

Contains translation of Welsh laws from the time of Howel the Good, d. 950.

Dionysius the Pseudo-Areopagite, *6th cent.* Dionysius the pseudo-Areopagite, the Ecclesiastical hierarchy, tr. and annotated by Thomas S. Campbell. Washington, Catholic University of America Press, 1955. 48 p. 576

This abstract of a dissertation contains chapters 1 and 2 of the dissertation translation of De ecclesiastica hierarchia.

—— Cosmic theology; the Ecclesiastical hierarchy of Pseudo-Denys, by Denys Rutledge. London, Routledge & Kegan Paul [1964]. xi, 212 p. 577

This is not a formal critical translation, says the author, but a "translation of practically the whole of the treatise in a running commentary."

—— A letter of private direction, by the author of the "Cloud of unknowing," rendered into modern English with an intro. by James Walsh. London, Burns & Oates [1965]. 77 p. 578

The Middle English adaptation by the author of the Cloud of unknowing of Dionysius' Mystical theology is here modernized.

Dubois, Pierre, *fl. 1300.* The recovery of the Holy Land, tr. with an intro. and notes by Walther I. Brandt. New York, Columbia University Press, 1956. xvi, 251 p. *Records of civilization,* 51. 579

Translation of proposals for recovery of the Holy Land, addressed to Edward I of England and Philip IV of France, written *c.* 1306; the proposals are for reforms in education and law on the ground that they would result in a successful crusade.

Duns, Joannes, Scotus, *1265?–1308?* Duns Scotus, philosophical writings, a selection, ed. and tr. by Allan Wolter. Edinburgh, Nelson, 1962. xxiii, 162, 162, [163]–198 p. *Nelson philosophical texts.* 580

Text and facing translation of selections from Duns Scotus' Ordinatio, his Oxford commentary on the Sentences of Peter Lombard. Part of the translation appeared earlier in the editor's article "Duns Scotus on the Necessity of Revealed Knowledge," *Franciscan Studies,* XI (1951), 231–72.

—— The De primo principio of John Duns Scotus, a rev. text and a translation by Evan Roche. St. Bonaventure, N.Y., Franciscan Institute, 1949. xvii, 153 p. *Franciscan Institute publications, philosophy series,* 5. 581

Text and facing translation, omitting the Additiones.

—— John Duns Scotus, a Treatise on God as first principle, a revised Latin text of the De primo principio tr. into English along with two related questions from an early commentary [by Duns Scotus] on the Sentences, by Allan Wolter. [Chicago], Franciscan Herald Press [1966]. xxiii, 189 p. 582

Text and facing translation.

E

Eadmer, *d. 1124?* Eadmer's History of recent events in England, Historia novorum in Anglia, tr. by . . . Geoffrey Bosanquet, foreword by R. W. Southern. London, Cresset Press, 1964. xv, 240 p. 583

Books I–IV of what is essentially a record of the public life of St. Anselm are translated.

—— Eadmer's Treatise on the Immaculate Conception, a translation and critical introduction, by the Reverend George Hingor. Washington, Catholic University of America Press [1954]. v, 57 p. **584**

This work has not been seen.

—— The life of St. Anselm, archbishop of Canterbury, ed. and tr. by R. W. Southern. London and New York, Nelson [c. 1962]. xxxvi, 171, 171, 172–79 p. **585**

Text and facing translation of Vita Anselmi.

Ecbasis captivi. Ecbasis cuiusdam captivi per tropologiam, Escape of a certain captive told in a figurative manner, an eleventh-century Latin beast epic. Intro., text, translation, commentary, and an appendix by Edwin H. Zeydel. Chapel Hill, University of North Carolina Press [1964]. 110 p. *University of North Carolina studies in the Germanic languages and literatures,* 46. **586**

Text and facing translation of a satire using animals, formerly thought to be 10th-century, according to the editor. An Aesopian story of the sick lion often ascribed to Paulus Diaconus is also translated, in an appendix.

Eckhart, Meister, *d. 1327.* The works of Meister Eckhart, [ed.] by Franz Pfeiffer, tr. by C. deB. Evans. London, John M. Watkins, 1947–52. 2 v. **587**

This reprint of the original edition of 1924 is included here because the title has been changed; see Farrar and Evans, item 1308.

—— Meister Eckhart speaks, a collection of the teachings of the famous German mystic [tr. by Elizabeth Strakosch] with an intro. by Otto Karrer. New York, Philosophical Library, 1957. 72 p. **588**

Exactly what works are included is not clear; short excerpts from several sources are translated, apparently from an intermediary modern German translation rather than from the Middle High German documents.

—— Meister Eckhart; selected treatises and sermons tr. from Latin and German, with an intro. and notes, by James M. Clark and John V. Skinner. London, Faber & Faber [1958]. 267 p. **589**

An earlier edition published by Nelson, 1957, had the title Meister Eckhart, an introduction to the study of his works with an anthology of his sermons. The works translated are selected vernacular sermons and some homilies in Latin.

—— Sermon on Beati pauperes spiritu, tr. by Raymond B. Blakney. Pawley (Vt.?), Claude Fredericks, 1960. **590**

A copy of this work has not been located. It may be a reprint of Blakney's 1941 translation; see Farrar and Evans, item 1309.

Edda Sæmundar.

Translations of separate poems of the Edda are not noted here; they are listed in the Supplement to Halldór Hermannsson's Bibliography by Jóhann S. Hannesson, *Islandica,* 37 (1955).

—— The poetic Edda, tr. by . . . Lee M. Hollander. Austin, University of Texas Press, 1962; 2d ed., rev. xxix, 343 p. **591**

The translation has been considerably revised since the edition of 1928; *cf.* Farrar and Evans, item 1317.

Edda Snorra Sturlusonar. First grammatical treatise, the earliest Germanic philology, an edition, translation, and commentary by Einar I. Haugen. Baltimore, Linguistic Society of America [1950]. 64 p. *Language monographs,* 25. **592**

Translation of part of the Edda which is a treatise on the relation of sound and letters, with modern linguistic analysis. The editor thinks that the author may have been Hallr Teitsson, 1085–1150.

Edward the Confessor, *Saint, king of England, d. 1066.* The life of Edward who rests at Westminster, attributed to a monk of St. Bertin, ed. and tr. with notes by Frank Barlow. London and New York, Nelson [c. 1962]. lxxxii, 81, 81, [82]–145 p. *Medieval texts.* **593**

Text and facing translation.

Edward II, *king of England, 1284–1327.* The life of Edward the Second, by the so-called monk of Malmesbury, ed. and tr. with intro. and notes by Noël Denholm-Young. Edinburgh and London, Nelson, [1957]. xxviii, 145, 145, 147–50 p. *Medieval texts.* **594**

Text and facing translation of a work entitled Vita Edwardi secundi monachi cuiusdam Malmesberiensis, but possibly written by John Walwayn who died before 1327, according to the editor.

Egils saga Skallagrímssonar. Egil's saga, tr. with intro. and notes, by Gwyn Jones. [Syracuse, N.Y.], published by the Syracuse University Press for the American-Scandinavian Foundation [1960]. ix, 259 p. **595**

The translator believes that this saga of *c.* 858–990 was written by Snorri Sturluson. A portion of this translation appeared in "Egill skallagrímsson in England," *Proceedings of the British Academy,* 38 (1954), 127–44.

Elisha, Vartabad, *bp., 5th cent.* The epic of St. Vardan the brave, an abr. translation of the History of Vardan and of The war of the Armenians by the Vardapet, tr. by C. F. Neumann, annotated by Vahan M. Kurkjian. New York, Diocese of the Armenian Church of North America, 1951; Delphic Press, 1952. 108 p. **596**

A partial reprint of Farrar and Evans, item 1354, originally published 1830. The present edition seems changed enough to warrant inclusion.

Encomium Emmae reginae, Richardī ducis Normannorum filiae. Encomium Emmae reginae, ed. [with an English translation] by Alistair Campbell. London, Offices of the Royal Historical Society, 1949. lxix, 108 p. *Camden third series,* 72. **597**

Text and following translation of an anonymous work written *c.* 1040–42, according to the editor. The first two parts are on the conquest of England by the Danes; the third part is in praise of Emma, wife successively of Aethelred and of Cnut.

England. *Historical sources.*

Farrar and Evans arbitrarily excluded documents on the grounds that they did not lend themselves to the organization adopted; they intended to issue a separate bibliography for documents but were unable to do so. In view of the fact that a new edition of Charles Gross' Sources and literature of English history is now in preparation, it seems unnecessary to list documents here. However, some major collections of public documents and those containing narrative sources or private documents are listed, along with collections of other historical material. For bibliography of documents, see E. L. C. Mullins, Texts and calendars, an analytical guide to serial publications, London, Offices of the Royal Historical Society, 1957, and at five-year intervals.

—— Anglo-Saxon charters, ed. and tr. by A. J. Robertson. Cambridge [Eng.], Cambridge University Press, 1939; reprint, 1956. 555 p. *Cambridge studies in legal history.* **598**

A few of the charters are of royal origin, but most are private documents; text and facing translation.

—— Anglo-Scottish relations, 1174–1328; some selected documents, ed. and tr. by Edward L. G. Stones. London and New York, Nelson [1965]. lvi, 182, 182, 185–98 p. *Medieval texts.* **599**

Text and facing translation of bulls, treaties, letters, speeches; one document is dated 1401, though the title refers to 1328 as the final date.

—— "The British Isles according to medieval Arabic authors," by D. M. Dunlop, *Islamic Quarterly,* 4 (1957), 11–28. **600**

Translation of excerpts from several medieval Arabic writers, with commentary.

—— Building in England down to 1540, a documentary history, by Louis F. Salzman. Oxford, Clarendon Press, 1952. xv, 629 p. Rev. ed., 1967. **601**

Contains translations of documents and excerpts from various writers concerning architecture.

—— Cardinal documents in British history, ed. by Robert L. Schuyler and Corinne C. Weston. Princeton, N.J., Van Nostrand [1961]. 192 p. *Anvil books.* **602**

Documents pertaining to constitutional, legal, and political history during medieval times are translated on pp. 7–51.

—— Chaucer's world, compiled by Edith Rickert, ed. by Clair C. Olson and Martin M. Crow. New York, Columbia University Press, 1948. xxi, 456 p. **603**

A collection of documents illustrating 14th-century life as well as that of Chaucer; Middle English is somewhat modernized, Old French and Latin are translated. Some of the excerpts concern wars and travels outside of England.

—— The constitutional history of England, 1216–1399, with select documents, ed. by Bertie Wilkinson. London and New York, Longmans, Green [1948–58]. 3 v. **604**

Vols. 2 and 3 appeared under the title, The constitutional history of medieval England. Documents in translation are interspersed throughout the volumes; letters and chronicles (*e.g.*, Matthew Paris, Roger of Wendover) are included as well as more strictly documentary sources.

—— A documentary history of England, vol. 1, 1066–1540, ed. by J. J. Bagley and P. B. Rowley. Harmondsworth [Eng.], Penguin Books, 1966. 269 p. **605**

Contains the Rule of St. Benedict and of St. Francis, Magna Carta (1215), charters, assizes, and statutes, and the Cosmography of John Holywood.

—— The early middle ages, 871–1216, ed. by Derek Baker. London, Hutchinson, 1966. 239 p. **606**

An anthology of excerpts from contemporary documents: chronicles, letters, saints' lives, poems, and some sagas. A second volume to cover 1216–1485 is announced here as in preparation.

ENGLAND

—— "England's earliest treatise on the law merchant, the essay on Lex mercatoris from The little red book of Bristol (circa 1280 A.D.)," [tr.] by Paul R. Teetor, *American Journal of Legal History*, 6 (1962), 178–210. **607**

Translation of the "law of the market place" as preserved in a treatise on "lawsuits and legal procedure in mercantile courts."

—— English historical documents; general editor, David C. Douglas. London, Eyre and Spottiswoode; New York, Oxford University Press, 1953– . 9 v. **608**

Vol. I, *c.* 500–1042, ed. Dorothy Whitelock, 1955; vol. II, 1042–1189, ed. David Douglas and G. W. Greenaway, 1953; vol. IV, 1327–1485, ed. A. R. Myers, 1969; vol. V, 1485–1558, ed. C. H. Williams, 1967. Vol. III, ed. Harry Rothwell (1189–1327), has not yet appeared. These volumes contain largely new translations by the editors and others of such documents as laws, charters, and wills, but they also contain translations of many narrative and literary sources, such as the Anglo-Saxon and other chronicles, letters, biographies, Old Norse sagas, poems, sermons.

—— Historical interpretation, sources of English medieval history, by John J. Bagley. Baltimore, Penguin Books [1965]. 285 p. **609**

In this description of the sources of English medieval history, many illustrative quotations are translated from patent and close rolls, archives, monastic chronicles, and letters. The translation is apparently that of the editor.

—— How they lived, an anthology of original accounts written before 1485, ed. by William O. Hassall. Oxford, Blackwell, 1962. xvi, 356 p. **610**

The accounts are arranged by topics in order to show daily life; this is intended to be a companion volume to They saw it happen; see below, item 614.

—— Royal writs in England from the Conquest to Glanvill: studies in the early history of the common law, by R. C. van Caenegem. London, B. Quaritch, 1959. 556 p. *Selden Society*, 77. **611**

Contains text and translation of nearly two hundred writs from 1066 to 1188, some published here for the first time.

—— Select cases in the court of King's Bench under Edward II [and III], ed. with intro. and translation by G. O. Sayles. London, B. Quaritch, 1936–65. 6 v. **612**

This work has text and facing translation of "select cases from the *coram rege* rolls" (Latin, Anglo-Norman), which are of major importance for the history of common law. A seventh volume covering the reigns of Richard II and of Henry IV and V is contemplated.

—— A source book of English law, by A. K. R. Kiralfy. London, Sweet & Maxwell, 1957. xx, 445 p. **613**

Contains translation of Latin and Anglo-Norman legal records from official and unofficial sources. See also The English legal system by the same author, 1st ed., 1954.

—— They saw it happen, an anthology of eye-witnesses' accounts of events in British history 55 B.C.–A.D. 1485, compiled by W. O. Hassall and E. E. Y. Hales. New York, Macmillan, 1957. xxiii, 236 p. **614**

Reprinted by Harper Torchbooks as Medieval England: as viewed by contemporaries. Contains short excerpts from chronicles, documents, saints' lives, many newly translated by the editors. Vol. 2 of this series, covering 1485–1688, ed. by C. R. N. Routh, 1956, contains translation of excerpts from travel records of 1497 and of letters about Henry VII. See also item 610 above.

—— Wheatley Records, 956–1956, tr. by William O. Hassall. [Oxford], Oxfordshire Record Society, 1956. 199 p. *Oxfordshire record society*, 37. **615**

Although other strictly local records are excluded in this bibliography, this one is included because the documents are translated in full and are of importance for the history of Oxford University.

English literature. *Collections.* Anglo-Saxon poetry, tr. by Gavin Bone. London, Oxford University Press, 1943. 79 p. **616**

Verse translations of selected short poems, including The battle of Maldon, Judith, The fates and gifts of men, Dream of the rood, Deor, The wanderer, The seafarer, The ruin, The wife's complaint, The husband's message, some riddles and gnomic verses.

—— An anthology of Old English poetry, ed. and tr. by Charles W. Kennedy. New York, Oxford University Press, 1960. 174 p. **617**

Contains translation of many short poems and excerpts from longer works; among them are The wanderer, The seafarer, Deor, The dream of the rood, The battle of Maldon, The battle of Brunanburgh, poems of Cynewulf, riddles and charms and other poems from the Exeter Book, and Beowulf.

—— The Battle of Maldon, and other Old English poems, tr. by Kevin Crossley-Holland, ed. by Bruce Mitchell. London, Macmillan; New York, St. Martin's Press, 1965. xi, 138 p. **618**

Contains translations of The battle of Maldon, Battle of Brunanburgh, Finnesburh fragment, riddles, charms, The ruin, Deor, The wife's lament, The husband's message, Caedmon's hymn, an excerpt from the Physiologus (Panther, Whale), The wanderer, The seafarer, The Brussels cross, The dream of the rood.

—— The beginnings of English literature, by William T. McNiff. New York and London, Macmillan [1961]. v, 198 p. **619**

Translations mostly from previously published sources of excerpts from Old and Middle English prose and poetry; works completely translated include The wanderer, Dream of the rood, Middle English lyrics, and Everyman.

—— Beowulf and the Grene Knight; poems of two great eras with certain contemporary pieces, newly tr. by Gordon Hall Gerould. New York, Ronald Press, 1953. **620**

This appears to be the same work as item 1412 in Farrar and Evans, but the title has been changed. I have not been able to see the two works together to determine whether the 1953 version is merely a reprint.

—— The college survey of English literature, ed. by Bartlett J. Whiting *et al.* New York, Harcourt Brace, 1942. 2 v. **621**

Vol. 1 has translation by B. J. Whiting of Beowulf, Gawain and the green knight, Ralph the collier, Sir Orfeo, as well as of selected short poems and prose works.

—— Development of the English drama, an anthology, ed. by Gerald E. Bentley. New York, Appleton-Century-Crofts, 1950. vii, 823 p. **622**

Pages 1–49 contain modernizations or translations of the Quem quaeritis trope, the Chester Deluge, Brome Abraham and Isaac, Wakefield Second shepherds' play, Everyman.

—— The earliest English poems, tr. by Michael Alexander. [Baltimore], Penguin Books [1966]. 159 p. **623**

Verse translations of Anglo-Saxon poems: excerpts from Beowulf, The ruin, Widsith, Deor, Waldere, The wanderer, The seafarer, gnomic verse, riddles, Dream of the rood, Battle of Maldon, The wife's complaint, The husband's message, Wulf and Eadwacer.

—— The earliest English poetry, a critical survey of the poetry written before the Norman conquest, with illustrative translations, by Charles W. Kennedy. London and New York, Oxford University Press, 1943. viii, 375 p. **624**

Contains translation *passim* of many illustrative poems and excerpts.

—— Early English Christian poetry, tr. into alliterative verse, with critical commentary, by Charles W. Kennedy. New York, Oxford University Press, 1952. xii, 292 p. **625**

Contains selected short poems; excerpts from Christ, Genesis, Christ and Satan, Physiologus; complete translations of Andreas, Elene, Phoenix, and Doomsday.

—— English riddles from oral tradition, by Archer Taylor. Berkeley, University of California Press, 1951. xxxi, 959 p. **626**

Contains post-medieval versions of riddles many of which are probably of medieval provenience.

—— An English song book; part songs and sacred music of the Middle Ages and Renaissance, ed. by Noah Greenberg, intro. by Joel Newman. Garden City, N.Y., Doubleday [c. 1961]. xxviii, 199 p. **627**

Prose translation of words of each song, taken from manuscript sources. Anonymous songs from the 13th–15th centuries in Latin and Middle English are translated, as well as songs by St. Godric, John Dunstable, Henry IV (?), Leonel Power, and from the liturgy. Another musical work is translated in "'The choristers' lament,'" ed. and tr. by Francis L. Utley, *Speculum,* 21 (1946), 194–202.

—— Glee-wood, passages from Middle English literature from the eleventh to the fifteenth century, tr. and arr. by Margaret A. Williams. New York, Sheed & Ward, 1949. xi, 553 p. **628**

Excerpts from prose, poetry, drama, newly translated by the editor; some translations also from Latin.

—— Havelock and Sir Orfeo, tr. into modern English by Robert Montagu. Leicester [Eng.], Ward [1954]. 118 p. **629**

This work has not been seen.

—— A history of Anglo-Latin literature, by W. F. Bolton. Princeton, Princeton University Press, 1967. V. I, 597–740. xiv, 305 p. **630**

Includes *passim* translations in footnotes of Latin excerpts cited in the text, many translated for the first time.

—— Later medieval English prose, ed. by William Matthews. New York, Appleton-Century-Crofts [1963]. 336 p. **631**

Contains somewhat modernized versions of excerpts from miscellaneous works (mostly 15th-century), including romances, letters, biographies, travel accounts, scientific treatises, and historical records.

—— Medieval English verse, tr., with an intro., by Brian Stone. Baltimore, Penguin Books [1964]. 256 p. 632

Contains translations of many short lyrics, secular and religious, and of The adulterous Falmouth squire, Sir Orfeo, Dame Siriz and the weeping bitch, and The fox and the wolf in the well.

—— Medieval English verse and prose in modernized versions, ed. by Roger S. Loomis and Rudolph Willard. New York, Appleton-Century-Crofts [1948]. xii, 557 p. 633

Contains translation by various translators of excerpts from many major works, arranged chronologically (12th–15th centuries); some have been newly done for this volume.

—— Middle English readings in translation, by Francis X. Corrigan. Boston, Christopher Publishing House [1965]. 293 p. 634

Contains translation of selections from many works.

—— The Norton anthology of English literature, general editor M. H. Abrams. New York, W. W. Norton, 1962; rev. ed., 1968. 635

Vol. I, Part I, The Middle Ages (to 1485), ed. by E. Talbot Donaldson, contains translations by Professor Donaldson of Beowulf, The wanderer, The battle of Maldon, and a selection from The land of Cockaigne; Gawain and the Green Knight by Marie Borroff; and highly glossed texts from Chaucer's Canterbury tales, Piers Plowman, The second shepherds' play, Everyman, and selected lyrics.

—— An Old-English anthology, translation of Old-English prose and verse, by F. P. Magoun, Jr. and J. A. Walker. Dubuque, Iowa, W. C. Brown, 1950. 108 p. 636

A translation of the selections in James W. Bright's An Anglo-Saxon reader, revised by James J. Hulbert, New York, Holt, 1933.

—— Poems from the Old English, tr. with intro. by Burton Raffel, foreword by Robert P. Creed. [Lincoln], University of Nebraska Press [c. 1960]. 58 p. 637

Poetic translations, some "faithful," others "impressionistic," of short lyrics, elegies, two battle poems, excerpt from Phoenix, and six riddles.

—— Poetry and prose of the Anglo-Saxons, a textbook with intro., translation, bbl. . . . by Martin Lehnert. Berlin, VEB Deutscher Verlag der Wissenschaften, 1955–56; 2d ed., Halle (Saale), M. Niemeyer, 1960. 2 v. 638

Text and translation of many poems, including charms, gnomic poems, riddles, the runic poem, elegies, religious poems, excerpts from Widsith, Fight at Finnsburg, Beowulf. The only prose translated is King Alfred's version of St. Augustine's Soliloquiae; other prose has a parallel Latin text. Vol. I includes the texts and translations; vol. II is a glossary.

—— Richard the Lion-Hearted, and other medieval English romances, tr., ed., and with an intro., by Bradford B. Broughton. New York, Dutton, 1966. 255 p. 639

Contains translations of Floire and Blancheflor, Amis and Amiloun, Richard Coeur de Lion, and, in an appendix, excerpts from contemporary historical sources.

—— Translations of Cornish, Old Welsh, Anglo-Saxon, ed. and tr. by Jane Earthy, Moelwyn Merchant, and Robert Muscutt. Exeter [Eng.] [n.p.], 1967. *Exeter books,* 5. 640

Contains translation of excerpts from the Cornish *Ordinalia,* a Welsh version of the Seven sages of Rome, and Old English poems.

—— Translations of some poems have appeared in journals: "Deor, a new verse translation," by Lloyd M. Davis, *Philological Papers* (University of West Virginia), 14 (1963), 1–5; "The OE poem 'Pharaoh,'" by L. Whitbread, *Notes and Queries,* 190 (1946), 52–54; and "Two English Frauenlieder [Eadwacer and The wife's lament]," by Kemp Malone, *Comparative Literature,* 14 (1962), 106–17; "Three Old English elegies," tr. by C. Colleer Abbott, *Durham University Journal,* 36 (1944), 76–79 [The wanderer, The ruin, The wife's complaint]. **641**

Ennodius, Magnus Felix, *Saint, bp. of Pavia, 474–521.* The life of St. Epiphanius by Ennodius, tr. by Genevieve M. Cook. Washington, Catholic University of America Press, 1942. xvii, 262 p. *Catholic University studies in medieval and Renaissance Latin language and literature,* 14. **642**

Text and facing translation, pp. 32–113, of Ennodius' Vita as well as text alone of an anonymous 10th-century Vita and record of the removal of Epiphanius' relics from Pavia to Hildesheim in the 10th century.

Enoch, *the patriarch (pseudonym), 6th cent. (?).* 3 Enoch; or the Hebrew book of Enoch, ed. and tr. for the first time, with intro., commentary, and critical notes by Hugo Odeberg. Cambridge [Eng.], Cambridge University Press, 1928. **643**

A work of uncertain provenience describing the heavenly strata through which a mystic passes before seeing the heavenly throne; omitted in Farrar and Evans.

Ephraem Syrus, *Saint, c. 306–73.* "St. Ephrem the Syrian on church unity," by Robert Murray, *Eastern Churches Quarterly,* 15 (1963), 164–76. **644**

Contains translation of excerpts from several works of Ephraem.

Epiphanius, *Saint, bp. of Constantia in Cyprus, 310–403.* "The libertine gnostic sect of the Phibionites according to Epiphanius," by S. Benko, *Vigiliae Christianae,* 21 (1967), 103–19. **645**

Contains translation of excerpts from ch. 26 of Epiphanius' Panarion, concerning the writings and practices of a Gnostic sect.

Epistle to Diognetus. Epistle to Diognetus, the Greek text with intro., translation, and notes by Henry G. Meecham. [Manchester], Manchester University Press, 1949. xii, 165 p. *Publications of the University of Manchester, theological series,* 7. **646**

Text and facing translation of a 2d-century work formerly attributed to Justinus Martyr. It is usually included in translations of the Apostolic Fathers.

Erex saga. Erex saga Artuskappa, ed. and tr. by Foster W. Blaisdell. Copenhagen, Munksgaard, 1965. lvii, 109 p. *Editiones Arnamagnaenae, series B,* 19. **647**

Icelandic text and English translation of a prose version of Chrétien's Erèc and Enide.

Eric IX Jedvardsson, *Saint, king of Sweden, d. 1160.* "St. Eric of Sweden," by J. E. Cross, *Saga-Book,* 15 (1961), 294–326. **648**

Contains translation of two Latin vitas.

Ethelred, *Saint, 1109?–1166.* Aelred of Rievaulx, De anima, ed. by C. H.

Talbot. London, Warburg Institute, 1952. 164 p. *Medieval and Renaissance Studies,* 2. **649**

Text and detailed summary of a work which seems not to have been translated elsewhere. Most editors refer to St. Ethelred as Aelred of Rievaulx, but the Library of Congress has changed its nomenclature to Ethelred.

—— Aelred of Rievaulx, a letter to his sister, from the Latin and Middle English versions, ed. by Geoffrey Webb and Adrian Walker. London, Mowbray [1957]. 64 p. *Fleur de lys series,* 11. **650**

A modernized version of the Middle English translation by "Thomas N." found in the Vernon manuscript. This is really a rule for recluses, based on the Benedictine rule as interpreted by the Cistercians in Aelred's abbey; it seems to be the first such rule in English and is quoted in the Ancren riwle, according to the editors. It was mistakenly attributed to St. Augustine by Migne.

—— Christian friendship, by Saint Ailred of Rievaulx, tr. with intro. and notes by Hugh Talbot. London, Catholic Book Club [1942]. 148 p. **651**

This is a translation of De spiritualia amicitia; *cf.* item 653.

—— The mirror of charity, the Speculum caritatis of St. Aelred of Rievaulx, tr. and arr. by Geoffrey Webb and Adrian Walker. London, Mowbray [c. 1962]. xv, 159 p. **652**

An abridged translation, omitting parts on free will and monastic observances; a résumé of the omitted parts appears in an appendix.

—— Of spiritual friendship; a translation of the De spirituali amicitia of Saint Aelred, by M. Francis Jerome. Paterson, N.J., Saint Anthony's Guild Press [1948]. 96 p. **653**

This work has not been seen.

—— On Jesus at twelve years old, by St. Aelred of Rievaulx, tr. by Geoffrey Webb and Adrian Walker. London, Mowbray [1956]. 71 p. *Fleur de lys series,* 7. **654**

—— The pastoral prayer of St. Aelred of Rievaulx, tr. by a Religious of C. S. M. V. Westminster [London], Dacre Press [1955]. 32 p. **655**

Text and translation of Oratio pastoralis. Another translation appeared in *The Way,* July, 1964, pp. 231–35.

Ethelwerd, *d. 998?* The Chronicle of Aethelweard, ed. by Alistair Campbell. London and New York, Nelson [c. 1962]. lxiii, 56, 56, [60]–69 p. **656**

Text and facing translation of a chronicle based largely on Bede and the Anglo-Saxon chronicle except for the years 893–946, which seem to have been observed by the chronicler; covers beginning of the world to 975.

Ethiopia. *History.* The glorious victories of 'Āmda Ṣeyon, king of Ethiopia, tr. by G. W. B. Huntingford. Oxford, Clarendon Press, 1965. xii, 142 p. **657**

Translation of a 17th-century Portuguese summary of an eye-witness account of events of the anti-Moslem campaign in Ethiopia in the 14th century.

Eugippius, *fl. 511.* The life of Saint Severin, tr. by Ludwig Bieler with the collaboration of Ludmilla Krestan. Washington, Catholic University of America Press [1965]. x, 139 p. *Fathers of the Church,* 55. **658**

Eusebius of Alexandria, *d. before 359, supposed author.* "An Armenian version of the homilies on the harrowing of hell," by Sirarpie Der Nersessian, *Dumbarton Oaks Papers,* 8 (1954), 201–24. **659**

Translation of an anonymous Armenian version of four homilies ascribed to Eusebius of Alexandria (also known as Eusebius of Emesa), related to the apocryphal Gospel of Nicodemus and Gospel of Bartholomew. Professor Der Nersessian published a translation of another Armenian version (written *c.* 1302) of Eusebius: "A homily on the raising of Lazarus and the harrowing of hell," pp. 219–34 in Biblical and patristical studies in memory of R. P. Casey, Freiburg, Herder, 1963.

Eusebius Pamphili, *bp. of Caesarea, 260–340.* Ecclesiastical history, tr. by Roy J. Deferrari. New York, Fathers of the Church, 1953–55 [i.e. 1953–56]. 2 v. *Fathers of the Church,* 19, 29. **660**

—— "The epistle of Eusebius to Carpianus, textual tradition and translation," by H. H. Oliver, *Novum Testamentum,* 3 (1959), 138–45. **661**

Translation of an important document about the harmony of the Gospels.

—— The essential Eusebius, sel. and newly tr., with intro. and commentary, by Colm Luibheid. New York, New American Library [1966]. 236 p. **662**

Contains translation of excerpts from the Preparation for the Gospel, Proof of the Gospel, Ecclesiastical history, Life of Constantine, Letter to the church at Caesarea.

—— The history of the Church from Christ to Constantine [by] Eusebius, tr., with an intro., by G. A. Williamson. [New York], New York University Press, 1966 [c. 1965]. 420 p.; Baltimore, Penguin Books, 1965. 429 p. **663**

Euthymius, *Saint, patriarch of Constantinople, d. 917.* "Vita S. Euthymii" [ed. and tr.] by P. Karlin-Hayter, *Byzantion,* 25, 27 (1955, 1957), 1–172, 748–71. **664**

Contains text and translation of the Vita, which was written in 921. For other materials about St. Euthymius, see above *s.v. Byzantine empire. Historical sources.*

Eutychius, *patriarch of Alexandria, 877–940.* The book of the demonstration (Kitāb al-Burhān), Parts I and II, ed. by Pierre Cachia, tr. by W. Montgomery Watt. Louvain, Secretariat CSC, 1960–61. *Corpus scriptorum Christianorum orientalium,* 192–93; 209–10; *Scriptores Arabici,* 20–21. 4 v. in 2. **665**

Text in vol. 1, translation in vol. 2, of a work usually ascribed to St. Athanasius in the manuscript tradition; *terminus ad quem,* 944. The Arabic name of the author is Sa'īd ibn al-Biṭrīq.

Everyman. The summoning of Everyman, a modernized version of the medieval morality play, ed. by Herbert W. Payne. London, Samuel French, 1947. 22 p. **666**

I have not seen this acting version of the play. Other translations are included in many anthologies of drama; see also *Miracle and mystery plays. Collections.*

Exeter book. The Advent lyrics of the Exeter book, ed. [and tr.], with intro. and notes, by Jackson J. Campbell. Princeton, Princeton University Press, 1959. ix, 137 p. **667**

Text and facing translation of a series of poems erroneously ascribed to Cynewulf as part 1 of his poem Christ, according to the editor.

—— Anglo-Saxon riddles of the Exeter book, tr. by Paull F. Baum. Durham, N.C., Duke University Press, 1963. xx, 70 p. **668**

See also "Six Anglo-Saxon riddles," tr. by Burton Raffel, *Antioch Review,* 20 (1960), 52–54, which contains translations of nos. 8, 11, 14, 22, 29, and 60.

Eyrbyggja saga. Eyrbyggja saga, tr. from the Old Icelandic by Paul Schach, intro. and verse translation by Lee M. Hollander. [Lincoln], University of Nebraska Press, 1959. xx, 140 p. **669**

The saga is ascribed to Snorri Þorgrímsson, goði, 963–1051.

Eznik of Kolp, *bp. of Bagrevand, b. c. 400.* "Eznik's résumé of Marcionite doctrine," text and translation by C. S. C. Williams, *Journal of Theological Studies,* 1945, 65–73. **670**

Armenian text and translation of Book 4, section 1, of Against the sects.

F

Fabri, Felix, *1441 or 42–150* Friar Felix at large, a fifteenth-century pilgrimage to the Holy Land, by Hilda F. M. Prescott. New Haven, Yale University Press, 1950. 254 p. **671**

Published in England under title Jerusalem journey. Contains translation of excerpts and paraphrase of Evagatorium in terram sanctum, a record of a voyage to Jerusalem and Sinai in 1483. This volume deals with the Jerusalem journey.

—— Once to Sinai; the further pilgrimage of Friar Felix Fabri, by Hilda F. M. Prescott. New York, Macmillan, 1958. 310 p. **672**

Contains translation *passim* and paraphrase of Felix's journey to Jerusalem and Sinai; this volume focuses on Sinai. Excerpts from the journeys of other pilgrims are cited to supplement Felix's account.

Faḍl-Allāh ibn Rūzbihān al-Khunjī, *surnamed* **al-Amīn,** *c. 1456–1519.* Persia in A.D. 1478–1490, an abr. translation of Fadlullah b. Ruzbihand Khunji's Tariki-i Alam-ara-yi Amini, by V. Minorsky. London, Luzac, 1957. vii, 136 p. *Royal Asiatic Society monographs,* 26. **673**

Only the "discursive rhetorical passages" are abridged.

Falakī Shirwānī, *fl. 1107–1156.* "Muḥammad Falakī-i-Shirwānī and his unique Dīwān in Madras," by Hadi Hasan, *Islamic Culture,* 24 (1950), 77–107, 145–86. **674**

Persian text and facing translation of 292 of 315 verses of Falakī discovered since the author's edition of 1929. These contain new historical information about the reign of a Shirwān king of the 12th century of whom the poem is a panegyric.

Falashas. Falasha anthology, tr. from Ethiopic sources with an intro. by Wolf Leslau. New Haven, Yale University Press, 1951. xliii, 222 p. *Yale Judaica series,* 6. **675**

The Falashas were Ethiopic Jews; their language, Ge'ez, is a dialect of Ethiopic. The work contains apocalyptic literature dating from 7th and 8th centuries to the 14th century.

al-Fārābī, *d. 950.* "Alfārābī against Philoponus," by Muhsin Madhi, *Journal of the Near East Society,* 26 (1967), 233–60. **676**

Contains translation of al-Fārābī's argument against Philoponus' (John the Grammarian's) Against Aristotle.

—— Fārābī's article on vacuum, ed. and tr. by Necati Lugal and Aydin Sayili. Ankara, Türk Tarik Kurumú Basimevi, 1951. *Türk Tarik Kurumú Yainlarindan,* 15. **677**

Text and translation of Fārābī's discussion of whether a vacuum exists in space; from a manuscript of a work previously thought to be lost.

—— "Fārābī's Canons of poetry," by Arthur J. Arberry, *Rivista degli Studi Orientali,* 17 (1938), 266–78. **678**

Contains a translation of the Treatise on the canons of the art of poetry; this translation was omitted from Farrar and Evans.

—— "Al-Fārābī's *Eisagoge,*" by D. M. Dunlop, *Islamic Quarterly,* 3 (1956), 115–38. **679**

Text and translation of "The book of Eisagoge, that is, the Introduction."

—— "Al-Fārābī's introductory Risālah on logic," by D. M. Dunlop, *Islamic Quarterly,* 3 (1957), 224–35. **680**

Text and translation.

—— "Al-Fārābī's introductory sections on logic," by D. M. Dunlop, *Islamic Quarterly,* 2 (1955), 263–82. **681**

Contains text and translation of Fuṣūl fī 't-Tauṭi'ah, Introduction to Greek philosophy, which starts with grammar and technical expressions.

—— "Al-Fārābī's paraphrase of the Categories of Aristotle," by D. M. Dunlop, *Islamic Quarterly,* 4 (1958), 168–97; 5 (1959), 21–54. **682**

Text and translation.

—— Fuṣūl al-Madanī, Aphorisms of the statesman, ed. with translation by D. M. Dunlop. Cambridge [Eng.], Cambridge University Press [1961]. 208 p. *University of Cambridge Oriental publications,* 5. **683**

Text and translation.

—— Philosophy of Plato and Aristotle, tr. with an intro. by Muhsin Mahdi. [New York], Free Press of Glencoe [1962]. 158 p. **684**

Includes translation of Taḥṣīl al-sa'ādah, The attainment of happiness, and al-Fārābī's summaries of The philosophy of Plato and The philosophy of Aristotle. These are not his detailed commentaries on the individual works of Plato and Aristotle, nor his Harmonization of the opinions of Plato and Aristotle.

—— Short commentary on Aristotle's Prior analytics, tr. from the original Arabic with intro. and notes by Nicholas Rescher. [Pittsburgh], University of Pittsburgh Press, 1963. 132 p. **685**

The editor explains that this "short commentary" or epitome is not a translation or paraphrase of Aristotle but is al-Fārābī's presentation of Aristotle's ideas for the "first level of instruction," on the subject of logic.

Farīd al-Din 'Aṭṭār, *13th cent.* The conference of the birds, Mantiq Ut-tair; a philosophical religious poem in prose [rendered into English from the literal and complete French translation of Garcin de Tassy by S. C. Nott]. London, Janus Press [1954]. viii, 147 p. **686**

De Tassy's French translation was made in 1863. The translator claims that this is the first complete translation into English.

—— Muslim saints and mystics; episodes from the Tadhkirat-al-auliya' ("Memorial of the saints"), tr. by A. J. Arberry. Chicago, University of Chicago Press [1966]. xii, 287 p. UNESCO *collection of representative works, Persian heritage series.* **687**

An abridged translation focusing on the biographical sections of each entry, omitting dicta.

—— Selections from Fariduddin 'Attar's Tadhkaratul-auliya (Memoirs of saints), Parts I and II, abr. and tr. . . . by Bankey Behari. Lahore, Ashraf [1961]. xxxi, 202 p. **688**

A translation of sixty-two of one hundred forty-two saints' lives and also an excerpt from the "Colloquy of the Birds," Manṭíq al-ṭair. I could not see this work and Arberry's at the same time and do not know to what extent they overlap.

Felix, *of Crowland, 8th cent.* Felix's life of St. Guthlac, intro., text, translation and notes by Bertram Colgrave. Cambridge [Eng.], Cambridge University Press, 1956. xv, 205 p. **689**

Text and facing translation of a life written between 730 and 740.

—— "The life of St. Guthlac of Crowland, by Felix," tr. and ed. by Charles W. Jones in Romanesque literature. Ithaca, N.Y., Cornell University Press, 1947, Vol. 1. **690**

Ferdawsī, *c. 932–1020.* "The older preface to the 'Shāh-nāma,'" tr. by V. Minorsky in Studi orientalistici in onore di Giorgio Levi della Vida, Roma, Istituto per l'Oriente, 1956, II, 159–79; reprinted in Iranica, twenty articles by V. Minorsky, Tehran, University of Tehran, 1964, pp. 260–73. **691**

The preface translated here, dated 957, is prefixed to some manuscripts of the Shāh-nāma; there are two other later prefaces in other manuscripts. The text used for this translation was established from nine manuscripts by M. Qazvīnī, 1934.

—— The epic of the kings; Shah-nama, the national epic of Persia by Ferdowsi, tr. by Reuben Levy. Chicago, University of Chicago Press; London, Routledge and Kegan Paul, 1967. xxviii, 423 p. *UNESCO collection of representative works, Persian heritage series.* **692**

A prose translation of a poetic original; the few omissions are summarized. The poem is a collection of episodes providing a continuous story of the Iranian empire from before the creation to the Arab conquest.

Ficino, Marsilio, *1433–99.* Commentary on Plato's Symposium, text and translation by Sears R. Jayne. Columbia, University of Missouri Press, 1944. 244 p. *University of Missouri studies,* 19, no. 1. **693**

Text and translation. A translation of some of the few extant letters of Ficino appeared in John Colet and Marsilio Ficino, by Sears R. Jayne, London, Oxford University Press, 1963.

—— The philosophy of Marsilio Ficino, by Paul O. Kristeller; tr. by Virginia Conant. New York, Columbia University Press, 1943. xiv, 441 p. *Columbia University studies in philosophy.* **694**

Many excerpts from Ficino's works are translated, some with text in footnotes. Professor Kristeller's work, written in German, was originally published in 1937.

Filarete, Antonio Averlino, *known as, 15th cent.* Treatise on architecture, being the treatise by Antonio di Piero Averlino, known as Filarete, tr. with an intro. and notes by John R. Spencer. New Haven, Yale University Press, 1965. 2 v. *Yale publications in the history of art,* 16. **695**

Vol. 1 contains the translation, vol. 2 a facsimile of the Italian text. The work, composed in Milan in the 1460s, describes the new architecture advocated by Filarete.

Finn mac Çumaill. "Finn's poem on May Day," by Gerard Murphy, *Ériu,* 17 (1955), 86–99. **696**

A reconstructed text, with new translation at bottom of page of Macgnimartha Finn.

—— The pursuit of Diarmid and Grainne, ed. [and tr.] by Nessa Ni Sheaghdha. Dublin, Irish Texts Society, 1967. xxxi, 148 p. **697**

Text and facing translation of a lost 10th-century tale in a 17th-century version; the scribe was Duibhgeannáin.

Fiore di Virtù. The Florentine Fior di Virtù of 1491, an English translation by Nicholas Fersin, intro. by Lessing J. Rosenwald. Washington, Published for the Library of Congress by E. Stern, 1953. xxxi, 119 p. **698**

Translation of a collection of quotations on various themes, such as love, women, vices, virtues.

Fitzneale, Richard, *bp. of London and treasurer of England, d. 1198.* The course of the exchequer by Richard, son of Nigel, treasurer of England and Bishop of London, tr. with intro. and notes by Charles Johnson. London and New York, Nelson [1950]. lxiv, 135, 135, [136]–144 p. *Medieval classics.* **699**

Text and facing translation of the Dialogus de scaccario and of the Constitutio domus regis, establishment of the royal household under Henry I.

Fitzralph, Richard, *abp. of Armagh, d. 1360.* Richard Fitzralph, commentator of the Sentences; a study in theological orthodoxy, by Gordon Leff. [Manchester, Eng.], Manchester University Press [c. 1963]. viii, 200 p. **700**

Contains much paraphrase of excerpts with the Latin text, edited from all extant manuscripts, at bottom of the page.

Fitzstephen, William, *d. 1190?* The life and death of Thomas Becket . . . based on the account of William fitzStephen his clerk, with additions from other contemporary sources, tr. and ed. by George Greenaway. [London], Folio Society, 1961. 172 p. **701**

In addition to Fitzstephen's life, this edition contains translation of excerpts from those of Herbert of Bosham and Roger, a monk of Pontigny, and from letters of John of Salisbury, Thomas à Becket, Pope Alexander III, and Gilbert Foliot. Some of the translations appeared in English historical documents, Vol. II; see above, item 608.

Flamenca. The romance of Flamenca; a Provençal poem of the thirteenth century, English verse translation by Merton J. Hubert; rev. Provençal text by Marion E. Porter. [Princeton], Princeton University Press, 1962. 456 p. **702**

According to the editor, the author may have been one Bernadet, mentioned in verse 1717.

Floire and Blancheflor (*French romance*). The romance of Floire and Blanchefleur, a French idyllic poem of the twelfth century, tr. into English verse by

Merton J. Hubert. Chapel Hill, University of North Carolina Press [1966]. 114 p. *Studies in the Romance languages and literatures*, 63. **703**

The translation is based on the so-called aristocratic version, as edited in 1956 by Margaret Pelan.

Folgore de San Gimignano, *fl. 1309–1317.* The months of the year; twelve sonnets, with a translation into English by Thomas C. Chubb. Sanbornville, N.H., Wake-Brook House [1960]. [63] p. **704**

Text and facing translation of Sonetti de' mesi.

France. *Historical sources.* Contemporary chronicles of the Hundred Years' War, from the works of Jean le Bel, Jean Froissart, and Enguerrard de Monstrelet, tr. and ed. by Peter E. Thompson. London, Folio Society, 1966. 358 p. **705**

A new translation of large excerpts dealing with the war, based on a new text established from manuscripts but not presented here. In another volume earlier documents of French history are included: The era of Charlemagne: Frankish state and society, ed. by Stewart C. Easton and Helene Wieruszowski, Princeton, Van Nostrand [1961], 192 p. Part II, "Readings," includes excerpts from Charlemagne, Gregory of Tours, Einhard, Alcuin, as well as from edicts, donations, and capitularies—many newly translated.

Francesco d'Assisi, *Saint, 1182–1226.*

For a detailed bibliography, see that of Raphael Brown in Saint Francis of Assisi, a biography, by Omar Englebert, tr. by Eve Marie Cooper; 2d English edition, Chicago, Franciscan Herald Press [1965], which notes English translations. Listed here are major new translations. No attempt has been made to list selections from these and older translations, many of which fail to acknowledge their sources.

—— A documented history of the Franciscan order, by Raphael M. Huber. Washington, Catholic University of America Press, 1944. **706**

Contains translation of the First and Second rules of the Friars Minor, pp. 605–32.

—— The little flowers of St. Francis, first complete edition, an entirely new version, tr. by Raphael Brown. Garden City, N.Y., Hanover House [c. 1958]. 357 p. **707**

Translated from Italian and Latin; adds "The considerations of the Holy Stigmata" and material from 15th-century manuscripts to the usual canon of the Fioretti.

—— The little flowers of St. Francis and other Franciscan writings, newly tr. and with an intro. by Serge Hughes. New York, New American Library; London, New English Library [c. 1964]. vii, 222 p. **708**

Adds the Second rule and the Testament to the usual canon of the Fioretti; omits the Sayings of Brother Giles and the Canticle of the creatures.

—— St. Francis of Assisi, the legends and lauds; ed., sel. and annotated by Otto Karrer; tr. by Nora Wydenbruck [Purtscher]. New York, Sheed & Ward, 1948. xvi, 302 p. **709**

Includes several lives, the Fioretti, the Laude, the Testament; the translation is from the edition of Karrer's work in German, 1945.

—— St. Francis of Assisi, his life and writings as recorded by his contemporaries; a new version of the Mirror of Perfection [and] . . . complete collection of all the known writings of the saint, tr. by Leo Sherley-Price. New York, Harper, 1959. 234 p. 710

Selections from this translation have appeared as The little flowers of Saint Francis, Baltimore, Penguin Books, 1959; and Lent with Saint Francis, London, Mowbray, and New York, Morehouse Gorham, 1958.

—— *Legend.* St. Francis of Assisi, First and second life of St. Francis, with selections from Treatise on the miracles of Blessed Francis by Thomas of Celano, tr. by Placid Hermann. Chicago, Franciscan Herald Press [c. 1963]. liv, 405 p. 711

Franciscius, Andreas, *15th cent.* Two Italian accounts of Tudor England, a journey to London in 1497, a picture of English life under Queen Mary, tr. by Cesare V. Malfatti. Barcelona [Sociedad Alcanza de Artes, graficas . . .] 1953. xvi, 103. 712

Translation of Franciscius' Latin account and of a later anonymous one in Italian, Ritratti del regno de Inghilterra.

Fredegarii chronicon. The fourth book of the chronicle of Fredegar with its continuations, ed. and tr. . . . with intro. and notes by John M. Wallace-Hadrill. New York and London, Nelson [1960]. lxvii, 121, 121, [122]–137 p. *Medieval classics.* 713

Text and facing translation of a chronicle probably compiled by at least three authors, according to the translator; it is a major source for the history of Frankish Gaul. The parts here translated comprise "an original chronicle covering the whole of the 7th and half of the 8th century." For a discussion of authorship, see Alvar Erikson, "The problem of authorship in the Chronicle of Fredegar," *Eranos,* 63 (1965), 47–76.

French literature. *Collections.* Anglo-Norman literature and its background, by M. Dominica Legge. Oxford, Clarendon Press, 1963. x, 389 p. 714

Contains many illustrative excerpts, text with prose translations.

—— Anglo-Norman political songs, ed. [and tr.] by Isabel S. T. Aspin. Oxford, Blackwell, 1953. xviii, 180 p. *Anglo-Norman texts,* 11. 715

Text and following translation of sixteen songs, all known political songs in Anglo-Norman; some of them are macaronic, in Latin, English, and Anglo-Norman.

—— Anonymous French verse, an anthology of 15th century poems collected from mss. in the British Museum, tr. and ed. by Norbert H. Wallis. London, University of London Press, 1929. lxviii, 180, 148 p. 716

Text and following verse translation of some two hundred fifty poems. This volume was omitted by Farrar and Evans.

—— Anthology of European poetry; vol. 1, From Machault to Malherbe, 13th to 17th century, ed. by Mervyn Savill, tr. by William Stirling, intro. by Marcel Arland. London, Allan Wingate [1947]. 231 p. 717

Text and facing translation of poems from Guillaume de Machault, Jean Froissart, Eustache Deschamps, Christine de Pisan, Charles d'Orléans, Oliver Basselin, and François Villon; and an anonymous poem entitled Gentilz gallans de France. Further volumes of this series have not been published.

—— Bawdy tales of the Middle Ages, tr. from the French by Robert Eglesfield. London, Tandem, 1967. 222 p. 718

Although the Library of Congress catalogues this work as a translation of a collection without a cross reference, it is in fact a somewhat abridged and bowdlerized translation of the Cent nouvelles nouvelles, *q.v.*, item 371.

—— Chanticleer, a study of the French muse, by J. G. Legge. New York, Dutton [1935]. xi, 395 p. **719**

This work, omitted in Farrar and Evans, contains translation of poems or extracts from anonymous works (including some in Provençal) and from Marie de France, Richard de Semilli of Paris, Colin Muset, Rutebeuf, Guillaume de Machault, Jean Froissart, and François Villon. For another translation from Rutebeuf, see Renart le Restorné by Edward B. Ham, Ann Arbor, University of Michigan Press, 1947, 52 pp.

—— Chivalry, by Léon Gauthier, ed. by Jacques Levron, tr. by D. C. Dunning. New York, Barnes and Noble [1965]. xxxiv, 345 p. **720**

Contains *passim* translation of some of the songs of the trouvères, the chansons de geste, and excerpts from chivalric rites.

—— Fabliaux; ribald tales from the old French, tr., with notes and afterword, by Robert Hellman and Richard O'Gorman. New York, Crowell [1965], vi, 196 p. **721**

Contains stories from Eustache d'Amiens, Rutebeuf, Garin, Gautier le Leu, Henry d'Andeli, Jean de Condé, Marie de France, Jean Bodel.

—— A few early French verses, done into English, by Charlotte H. Martin. Albany, N.Y., Argus Press, 1949. 135 p. **722**

Text and facing translation of the following poets are found on pp. 4–37: Bernart de Ventadorn, Christine de Pisan, Marie de France, Eustache Deschamps, Charles d'Orléans, François Marot.

—— Formal spring, French Renaissance poems . . ., tr. by Ralph N. Currey. New York, Oxford University Press, 1950. xxi, 159 p. **723**

Text and facing translation of poems of Guillaume de Machault, Eustace Deschamps, Christine de Pisan, Charles d'Orléans, Francois Villon, pp. 4–67.

—— French lyrics in English verse, ed. and tr. by William F. Giese, foreword by Frederick Manchester. Madison, University of Wisconsin Press [1946]. xiv, 394 p. **724**

Contains translations of six anonymous poems from the 12th and 15th centuries; two of Guillaume de Machault; one each of Jean Froissart, Eustache Deschamps, and Alain Chartier; four of Villon, and five of Charles d'Orléans.

—— In praise of love; an introduction to the love-poetry of the Renaissance, by Maurice J. Valency. New York, Macmillan, 1958. 319 p. **725**

Includes *passim* translation by the author of many Provençal poems.

—— Lays of courtly love, in verse translation, ed. and tr. by Patricia A. Terry, intro. by Charles W. Dunn. Garden City, N.Y., Anchor Books, 1963. 130 p. **726**

Contains translation of Marie de France: Laüstic, Chevrefoil, Les deus amanz, Eliduc; Jean Renart: La lai de l'ombre; and the anonymous Chastelaine de Vergi (*c.* 1250).

—— The Penguin book of French verse . . ., vol. I, to the [end of the] 15th century, ed. and tr. by Brian Woledge. Baltimore, Penguin Books, 1961. **727**

Text with prose translation at bottom of page of many short poems, excerpts from long poems. Excludes Provençal.

—— Rondels by Charles d'Orléans and other French poets, chosen and tr. by Cedric Wallis. London, Caravel Press, 1951. 728

Text and facing translations of poems by Guillaume de Machault, Eustache Deschamps, Christine de Pisan, François Villon, and Charles d'Orléans. For other poems of Charles d'Orléans, see The English poems of Charles of Orleans, ed. from the manuscript Brit. Mus. Harl. 682, by Robert Steele, London, for the Early English Text Society by the Oxford University Press. 1941–46, 2 v. *Original series,* 215, 220.

—— A treasury of French poetry, compiled and tr. by Alan Conder, with introductions by Walter de la Mare and Louis Cazamian. New York, Harper [1951]. 388 p. 729

Translation (some of poems never before translated, according to the editor), from Charles d'Orléans, François Villon, and two anonymous poems from the 15th century. First published in 1950 under the title Cassell's anthology of French poetry.

—— The tretyse of loue, ed. by John H. Fisher. London, Oxford University Press, 1951. xxxiii, 165 p. *Early English Text Society,* original series, 225. 730

A translation, probably by Caxton's successor, Wynken de Worde, *c.* 1493, of a compilation of seven treatises on love as well as of the three-part Tretyse of loue.

—— The troubadours, by Robert Briffault, tr. from the French by the author, ed. by Lawrence F. Koons. Bloomington, Indiana University Press, 1965. xvi, 296 p. 731

The translation from the French original (1945) includes translation of many Provençal lyrics as well as of a few Arabic poems.

—— The ways of love; eleven romances of medieval France, ed. by Norma L. Goodrich. [Boston], Beacon Press [1964]. 287 p. 732

Contains new translations, some abridged, of the following works: Life of Saint Alexis, complete; Marie de France, Yonec and Eliduc; The Swan knight; Robert de Boron, Story of the Grail; Aucassin and Nicolette; Jean Renart's Lai de l'ombre, all nearly complete; and, summarized or considerably abridged, Bertrand de Bar-sur-Aube's Romance of Girart de Viene, Béroul's Tristan, Chrétien's Erèc and Enide, Romance of the Châtelain de Coucy.

Froissart, Jean, *1388?–1410?* Chronicles, in Lord Berners' translation, sel., ed., and introduced by Gillian and William Anderson. Carbondale, Southern Illinois University Press [1963]. xiv, 224 p. *Centaur classics.* 733

Although this is not a new translation, it is included here because the 16th-century English has been modernized and the selections arranged by careful abridgment to make a readable, coherent story of the 14th-century relationship between France and England.

G

Galbert de Bruges, *c. 1134.* The murder of Charles the Good, count of Flanders, tr. with an intro. and notes by James B. Ross. New York, Columbia University Press, 1960. xiv, 352 p. *Records of civilization,* 61. Rev. ed., New York, Harper, 1967. 734

The diary of 1127–28 records the murder of Charles le Bon, d. 1127; the translation is based on the Latin text ed. by Henri Pirenne, Paris, 1891.

Galenus, *Arabic version.* Galeni in Hippocratis De officina medici commentariorum: versionem Arabicam quod exstat, ex codice Scorialensi et excerpta, quae

Ali ibn Ridwan ex eis sumpsit . . ., ed. and tr. into English by Malcolm Lyons. Berlin, Akademie-Verlag, 1963. 172. *Corpus medicorum Graecorum, Supplementum Orientale,* 1. 735

Arabic text and English translation of Galen's commentary on the "doctor's shop" or "surgery" of Hippocrates. The Arabic version is found in a manuscript of 1190; the work is also extant in Greek.

—— Galen, On anatomical procedures, the later books, ed. by M. C. Lyons, and B. Towers, tr. by W. L. H. Duckworth. Cambridge [Eng.], Cambridge University Press, 1962. xix, 279 p. 736

The Arabic version (9th century) is the only source for parts of this major work of Galen. The translation into Arabic was made by Ḥunain ibn Isḥāq, called Joannitus, from a Syriac version of the Greek by Ḥubaish ibn al-Ḥasan al-A'sam. Part of Book 9 and Books 10–14 are translated.

—— Galen, On medical experience, first edition of Arabic version with English translation by R. Walzer. London and New York, Oxford University Press, 1944. 164 p. 737

The Arabic version of Ḥunain ibn Isḥāq was discovered in 1931 and is the earliest known. Previous translations of parts of this work, the original of which is lost, are from a 16th-century Latin translation.

Galganus, *Saint, c. 1148–c. 1181.* "The three earliest *vitae* of St. Galganus," by Rudolph Arbesmann, in Didascaliae, Studies in honor of Anselm M. Albareda, ed. by Sesto Prete, New York, B. Rosenthal [1961], pp. 3–37. 738

Contains text and close paraphrase of the vitae from two manuscripts.

Garcia de Cisneros, *1455–1510.* The spirit of the Spanish mystics, an anthology of Spanish religious prose from the fifteenth to the seventeenth century, ed. and tr. by Kathleen Pond. London, Burns & Oates [1958]; New York, Kenedy, 1958. xi, 170 p. 739

Only one author is from the fifteenth century: García de Cisneros.

Gardīzī, Abū Sa'īd 'Abd al-Ḥayy, *fl. c. 1050.* "Gardīzī on India," by V. Minorsky, *Bulletin of the School of Oriental and African Studies* 12 (1947–48), 625–40. 740

Translation of a chapter on India from a work dedicated to a sultan who reigned 1049–53; it describes the arts, religion, customs, sects of India but gives very little geography.

Gawain and the Grene Knight. "Gawain and the Green Knight," tr. by B. J. Whiting in College survey of English literature, ed. by B. J. Whiting *et al.,* New York, Harcourt-Brace, 1948 [c. 1942]. 2 v. 741

The translation appears on pp. 114–38 of Vol. 1. A copy of the first edition has not been seen.

—— The story of Sir Gawain and the Green Knight, tr. by Maurice R. Ridley. Leicester [Eng.], E. Ward, 1944. 95 p. 742

A prose translation, somewhat abridged. Reprinted 1962 under the title Sir Gawain and the Green Knight.

—— Sir Gawain and the green knight, a prose translation with an introductory essay by Gwyn Jones. London, Golden Cockerel Press, 1952. 95 p. 743

—— Sir Gawain and the Green Knight, a fourteenth-century alliterative poem now attributed to Hugh Mascy, tr. in the original meter by Omerod Greenwood. [London], Lion and Unicorn Press [1956]. 16 [60] p. **744**

The attribution to Mascy seems not to have been accepted, though the Library of Congress records him as the supposed author for this particular volume.

—— Sir Gawain and the Green Knight, tr. by James L. Rosenberg, ed. and with an intro. by James R. Kreuzer. New York, Rinehart [1959]. lxxxiii, 86 p. **745**

—— Sir Gawain and the Green Knight, tr. with an intro. by Brian Stone. Baltimore, Penguin Books [1959]. 143 p. **746**

This translation, reprinted several times, was revised in 1964.

—— Sir Gawain and the Green Knight, a new verse translation by Marie Borroff. New York, Norton [1967]. xiii, 63 p. **747**

This translation appears also in the revised edition of the Norton anthology of English literature; see item 635 above.

Gawain-poet, *14th cent.* The complete works of the Gawain-poet, ed. and tr. by John C. Gardner. Chicago, University of Chicago Press [1965]. xiii, 347 p. **748**

Contains verse translation of Pearl, Purity, Patience, Sir Gawain and the Grene Knight, St. Erkenwald (the latter attributed to the Gawain-poet). See also item 1531 below.

Gelmírez, Diego, *abp., d. 1140.* Diego Gelmirez, first archbishop of Compostella, by Anselm G. Biggs. Washington, Catholic University of America Press, 1949. xi, 398 p. *Catholic University studies in medieval history,* n.s., 12. **749**

Contains translation of the decrees of Diego II, bishop of Santiago, for the protection of the poor, issued at the Council of Compostella, 1113.

Genizah documents.

Only translations since 1964 are included here; for previous translations, see Saul Shaked, A tentative bibliography of Geniza documents, Paris and The Hague, Mouton, 1964, 355 p. This work lists editions, translations, and works about the some 10,000 documents discovered in Cairo 75 years ago, "the most important collection of documentary evidence for ths history of Islamic lands in the Middle Ages."

—— "Genizah fragments in the Chetham's Library, Manchester," by Meir Wallenstein, *Bulletin of the John Rylands Library,* Manchester, 49 (1967), 159–77. **750**

Includes translation of four Biblical and two non-Biblical fragments—one on science, the other an elegy.

Gentile da Foligno, *d. 1348.* "A case of snake-bite from the Consilia of Gentile da Foligno," [tr.] by Lynn Thorndike, *Medical History,* 5, (1961), 90–95. **751**

Geoffrey of Monmouth, *bp. of St. Asaph, 1100?–54.* The history of the kings of Britain, tr. by Lewis Thorpe. Baltimore, Penguin Books [1966]; Magnolia, Mass., P. Smith, 1967. 373 p. **752**

The translation is based on the text of Acton Griscom, 1929.

Geoffroi de Paris, *14th cent.* . . . Six historical poems, written 1314–1318 . . ., tr. by Walter H. Storer and Charles A. Rochedieu. Chapel Hill, University of North Carolina Press, 1950. x, 92 p. *University of North Carolina studies in Romance languages and literatures,* 16. **753**

Text (based on Ms. Fr. 146 of the Bibliothèque Nationale) and facing translation.

German literature. *Collections.* German verse from the 12th to the 20th century in English translation, by John W. Thomas. Chapel Hill, University of North Carolina Press, 1963. 160 p. *University of North Carolina studies in Germanic languages and literatures,* 44. **754**

Contains seventeen poems from Dietmar von Aist, Heinrich von Morungen, Walter von der Vogelweide, Neidhart von Reuenthal, Wolfram von Eschenbach.

—— German proverbs and proverbial phrases with their English counterparts, tr. by Edmund P. Kremer. Stanford, Cal., Stanford University Press, 1955. 116 p. **755**

—— Medieval German literature, a survey, by M. O'C. Walshe. London, Routledge & Kegan Paul [1962]. xiv, 421 p. **756**

Contains *passim* text and new translations of many poems, and of excerpts from poems and from prose.

—— Medieval German lyrics, tr. by Margaret F. Richey. Edinburgh and London, Oliver and Boyd [1958]. 90 p. **757**

Contains sixty-two poems, two anonymous and others by fourteen authors. Some appeared in the translator's earlier work, The medieval German love-lyric, Oxford, Blackwell, 1943; *cf.* Farrar and Evans, 1703.

—— The Penguin book of German verse, intro. and ed. by Leonard W. Forster, with plain prose translations of each poem. Harmondsworth [Eng.], Penguin Books [1957]. xlii, 466 p. **758**

Contains text of medieval poems and translation, at bottom of page, pp. 3–63.

—— The songs of the minnesingers, ed. and tr. by Barbara G. Seagrave and Wesley Thomas. Urbana, University of Illinois Press, 1966. ix, 232 p. **759**

Modern musical transcription and English translation of a "representative selection of minnesong from the 12th to the 15th century". The volume is accompanied by a phonograph disc.

Germany. *Historical sources.* Documents of German history, ed. by Louis L. Snyder. New Brunswick, N.J., Rutgers University Press, 1958. xxiii, 619 p. **760**

Has translation of constitutions, treaties, speeches, letters, and narratives from the medieval period; some are condensed. Most of the translations were previously published elsewhere, by various translators.

—— Imperial lives and letters of the eleventh century, tr. by Theodor E. Mommsen and Karl F. Morrison . . . ed. by Robert L. Benson. New York, Columbia University Press, 1962. x, 215 p. *Records of civilization,* 67. **761**

Contains translation of three sources especially important for German history: Wipo's The deeds of Conrad II, an anonymous Life of Henry IV, and forty-two letters of Henry IV.

Gerondi, Jonah, *d. 1263.* Rabbi Jonah ben Abraham of Gerona, his life and ethical works, by A. T. Shrock. London, Goldston, 1948. 196 p. **762**

Many excerpts quoted *passim* in Hebrew with English translation, especially in Part III, "Ethical works . . . as a source for contemporary conditions."

—— Shaarei teshuvah, The gates of repentance, by Rabbeinu Yonah ben Avraham of Gerona . . ., tr. by Shrago Silverstein. Boys Town, Jerusalem,

Yaakov Feldheim, 1967; distributed by P. Feldman, New York. xxvi, 390 p. *Torah classics library.* 763

Descriptions of methods of penance and punishment to atone for transgressions.

Gershon ben Solomon, *13th cent.* Rabbi Gershon ben Shlomoh d'Arles, the Gate of heaven (Shaar ha-Shamayim), tr. and ed. by F. S. Bodenheimer. Jerusalem, Kiryath Sepher, 1953. x, 356 p. 764

Translation of Books 1 and 2 on natural history and astronomy from an encyclopedia of science written *c.* 1280.

Gertrude, *Saint, surnamed the Great, 1256–1302?* Exercises, intro., commentary, and translation by a Benedictine nun of Regina Laudis. Westminster, Md., Newman Press, 1956. 191 p. 765

Contains seven "exercises" or chapters, on baptism, investiture, spiritual espousals, monastic profession, praise of God, and preparation for death.

Gesta Francorum et aliorum Hierosolymitanorum. The first crusade, the deeds of the Franks and other Jerusalemites . . ., tr. into English for the first time by Somerset S. De Chair. [London], Golden Cockerel Press, 1945. 92 p. 766

The translator says that his text is based on a collation of the "three manuscripts now accepted as being nearest to the original."

—— The deeds of the Franks and the other pilgrims to Jerusalem, ed. [and tr.] by Rosalind Hill. [London, New York], Nelson [1962]. xlv, 103, 103, [104]–113 p. *Medieval texts.* 767

Text and facing translation of a history of the First Crusade, 1095–99, the "source from which nearly all other historians of the First Crusade have borrowed."

al-Ghazzālī, *1058–1111.* [Ayyuha l'walad] O disciple, tr. by George H. Scherer, with an intro. Beirut [Catholic Press], 1951. xxvi, 28, 20 p. *Collections des grandes oeuvres de l'UNESCO, Arabic series.* 768

A translation of this work by the same translator was issued in 1933 (*cf.* Farrar and Evans 1723), but the present edition adds a facsimile and transliteration of the Arabic text. The work, written toward the end of al-Ghazzālī's life, describes the path of Sufi mysticism.

—— [Iḥyā' 'ulūm al-dīn] The book of knowledge, being the English translation of Kitāb al 'Ilm, tr. by Nabih Amin Faris. Lahore, Ashraf [1962]. vi, 242 p. 2d ed. rev. 1966, 246 p. 769

A translation of Book 1 of the Iḥyā' 'ulūm al-dīn, al-Ghazzylī's encyclopedic work in forty books, "The revival of the religious sciences."

—— The foundations of the articles of faith, tr. by Nabih Amin Faris. Lahore, Ashraf, 1963. viii, 144 p. 770

Translation of Book 2, on acts of worship.

—— The mysteries of purity . . ., Kitāb asrār al-taharah of al-Ghazzālī's Iḥyā' 'ulūm al-dīn, tr. by Nabih A. Faris. Lahore, Ashraf, 1966. ix, 100 p. 771

This work, Book 3 of the Iḥyā', describes the daily life of Muslims *c.* A.D. 1100.

—— The mysteries of almsgiving, translation of Kitāb asrār al-zakāh, by Nabih Amin Faris. Beirut, American University Press, 1966. xii, 96 p. 772

A translation of Book 5 of the Iḥyā'.

—— Book XX of al-Ghazali's Iḥyā' 'ulūm al-dīn, ed. [and tr.] by L. Zolondek. Leiden, Brill, 1963. 76 p. 773

Book 20, The ethics of living as exemplified in the virtues of the Prophet, concerns the customs and characteristics of Mohammadenism; an appendix includes "Abstracts of material from pre-Ghazalian sources."

—— al-Ghazali's Book of fear and hope, by William McKane. Leiden, Brill, 1962. xix, 104 p. 774

A translation of Book 33 of the Iḥyā'.

—— [Min hunā na'lam] Our beginning in wisdom, tr. by Isma'il R. el Faruqi. Washington, American Council of Learned Societies, 1953. xviii, 145 p. 775

—— [Naṣiḥat al-Mulūk] Ghazali's book of counsel for kings, tr. by F. R. C. Bagley from the Persian text ed. by Jalāl Humā'ī and the Bodleian Arabic text ed. by H. D. Isaacs, with intro., notes, and biographical index. London, Oxford University Press, 1964. lxxiv, 199 p. *University of Durham publications.* 776

—— [Risāla al-qudsiyyah] "Al-Ghazali's tract on dogmatic theology," by A. L. Tibawi, *Islamic Quarterly,* 9 (1965), 65–122. 777

Contains an edition and translation of al-Ghazzālī's tract, written in Jerusalem.

—— [Risāla al-ṭayr] "al-Ghazzali's Epistle of the birds, a translation of the Risālat al-ṭayr," by Nabih Amin Faris, *Moslem World,* 34 (1944), 46–53. 778

The work is a parable on salvation by faith.

—— [Tahāfut al-falāsifah] al-Ghazali's Tahafut al falasifah (Incoherence of the philosophers), tr. with intro. by Sabih Ahmad Kamali. Lahore, Pakistan Philosophical Congress [1958]. viii, 267 p. *Pakistan philosophical congress publication, 3.* 779

Translation of a refutation of the philosophers who deny the unity of God and His divine attributes. A partial translation appears in Averroës' The incoherence of the incoherence, tr. by Simon van den Bergh, London, Luzac, 1954. See item 235 above.

SELECTIONS

—— al-Ghazali, the mystic, by Margaret Smith. London, Luzak, 1944. 247 p. 780

Quotes extensively and paraphrases, especially from Iḥyā' 'ulūm al-dīn.

—— The faith and practice of al-Ghazzali, by W. Montgomery Watt. London, Allen & Unwin [1953]. 155 p. *Ethical and religious classics of East and West,* 8. 781

Contains translation from the Munḳidh min al-ḍalāl, "Deliverance from error," an autobiographical work; and Bidayat al-Hidāyāh, "The beginning of Guidance," an introduction to the Iḥyā' 'ulūm al-dīn.

—— The concept of man in Islam, in the writings of al-Ghazali, by Ali Issa Othman. Cairo [Dar al-Maaref Publishing House], 1960. xxi, 213 p. 782

AL-GHAZZĀLĪ

Extensive translation of excerpts *passim* and in appendices, much newly translated by the author. The author suggests that in the title Tahāfut al-falāsifah, the word *tahāfut* should be translated as "recklessness," not "incoherence" or "destruction" as it is usually rendered.

—— Some moral and religious teachings of al-Ghazzali, by Syed Nawab Ali. Lahore, Ashraf [1960]. x, 170 p. **783**

Contains translations of extracts from Iḥyā' 'ulūm al-Dīn and Minhaj al-'ābidīn.

Giraldus Cambrensis, *1146?–1220?* The first version of the Topography of Ireland, tr. by John J. O'Meara. Dundalk, Dundalgan Press, 1951. 121 p. **784**

A translation of the Topographia Hibernia, written *c.* 1185.

—— "Gerald the Welshman's 'Itinerary through Wales' and 'Description of Wales,'" by Thomas Jones, *National Library of Wales Journal,* 6 (nos. 2 and 3), 1950. **785**

Abridged translation and paraphrase.

Gísla saga Súrssonar. The saga of Gisli, tr. by George Johnston with notes and an essay by Peter Foote. Toronto, University of Toronto Press, 1963; London, Dent, 1963. xiii, 146 p. **786**

Poetic translation of poetic parts; based on text of 1943.

Glanville, Ranulf de, *1130–90.* Treatise on laws and customs of England, which is known as Glanvill, ed. and tr. by G. D. G. Hall. London, Nelson in association with the Selden Society, 1965. lxx, 213 p. **787**

A translation of the Tractatus de legibus et consuetudinibus regni Anglie qui Glanvilla vocatur, from the alpha version of the text, which is included.

Gnostic treatises. Gnosticism; a source book of heretical writings from the early Christian period, ed. by Robert M. Grant. New York, Harper [1961]. 254 p. **788**

Contains translation from Greek, Latin, Syriac, and Coptic gnostic documents, 1st to 5th century. The volume was published in England by Collins under the title Gnosticism, an anthology.

Gottfried von Strassburg, *13th cent.,* "Gottfried von Strassburg's Tristan and Isolde," by C. M. Lancaster and J. G. Frank, *Poet Lore,* 49 (1943), 301–20. **789**

Translation of selected excerpts, in verse.

—— The "Tristan and Isolde" of Gottfried von Strassburg, tr. by Edwin H. Zeydel. Princeton, Princeton University Press for the University of Cincinnati, 1948. vi, 209 p. **790**

Abridged verse translation of about one third of the poem; the rest is told in prose summaries. The conclusion is summarized from Thomas of Britain, Ulrich von Türheim, and Heinrich von Freiberg.

—— Tristan, tr. entire for the first time, with the surviving fragments of the Tristran of Thomas, newly tr. with an intro. by A. T. Hatto. Baltimore, Penguin Books [1960]. 374 p. **791**

A prose translation.

Gower, John, *1325?–1408.* John Gower, moral philosopher and friend of

Chaucer, by John H. Fisher. [New York], New York University Press, 1961. viii, 378 p. 792

Contains translation of many excerpts; those from Old French have parallel text.

—— The lover's shrift, tr. by Terence Tiller. Baltimore, Penguin Books, 287 p. 793

Selections from the Confessio amantis in verse translation; omissions summarized in prose.

—— The major Latin works of John Gower: The voice of one crying, and The tripartite chronicle, an annotated translation into English with an introductory essay on the author's non-English works, by Eric W. Stockton. Seattle, University of Washington Press, 1962. vii, 503 p. 794

The chronicle focuses on Richard II, King of England, 1377–99.

Gregorius I, *Saint, the Great, pope, c. 540–604.* Dialogues, tr. by Odo J. Zimmerman. New York, Fathers of the Church, 1959. xvi, 287 p. *Fathers of the Church,* 39. 795

Book II of the Dialogues was published under the title Life and miracles of St. Benedict, tr. Odo J. Zimmerman and Benedict R. Avery, Collegeville, Minn., St. John's Abbey Press, 1949. Books I and III contain largely lives of other saints; Book IV is on the immortality of the soul.

—— The dialogues of Gregory the Great, Book II: St. Benedict, tr. by Myra L. Uhlfelder. Indianapolis, Bobbs–Merrill, 1967. xxiv, 49. 796

This book contains the Life of St. Benedict.

—— Pope Saint Gregory the Great. Parables of the Gospel [tr. by Nora Burke]. Chicago, Scepter Press [1960]. 169 p. *Spiritual classics,* 3. 797

Selections from the Homiliae in Evangelia.

—— Pastoral care, tr. and annotated by Henry Davis. Westminster, Md., Newman Press, 1950. 281 p. *Ancient Christian writers,* 11. 798

Although known by its *incipit* Pastoralis curae, Gregory referred to this work as Liber regulae pastoralis, a rule for secular priests.

—— [Legend] "An Irish translation of the Gregory legend," by Sheila Falconer, *Celtica,* 4 (1958), 52–74. 799

Text and translation of "Geineamhain Ghrigoir," "The birth of Gregory," written probably before the end of the 15th century, in prose.

Gregorius, *Saint, bp. of Nyssa, fl. 379–94.* Ascetical works, tr. by Virginia Woods Callahan. Washington, Catholic University of America Press [1967]. xxiii, 295 p. *Fathers of the Church,* 58. 800

Contains translation of On virginity, On what it means to call oneself a Christian, On perfection, On the Christian mode of life, Life of St. Macrina, On the soul and the resurrection.

—— "De professione Christiana and De perfectione, a study of the ascetical doctrine of Saint Gregory of Nyssa," by Mary Emily Keenan, *Dumbarton Oaks Papers,* 5 (1950), 169–207. 801

Contains a summary-paraphrase and translation of illustrative excerpts from the two treatises.

—— "The doctrine of St. Gregory of Nyssa on man as the image of God," by J. T. Muckle, *Medieval Studies,* 7 (1945) 55–84. **802**

Contains much translation *passim* by the author from several works of Gregory.

—— From glory to glory, texts from Gregory of Nyssa's mystical writings, selected and with an intro. by Jean Daniélou, tr. and ed. by Herbert Musurillo. New York, Scribner [1961]. xiv, 298 p. **803**

Short excerpts from several works of Gregory, arranged topically.

—— The Lord's prayer, the Beatitudes, tr. and annotated by Hilda C. Graef. Westminster, Md., Newman Press, 1954. v, 210 p. *Ancient Christian writers,* 18. **804**

Translation of two homilies.

Gregorius, *Saint, bp. of Tours, 538–94.* Gregory of Tours, selections from the minor works, tr. by William C. McDermott, intro. by John L. LaMonte. Philadelphia, University of Pennsylvania Press, 1949. xi, 109 p. *Translations and reprints from the original sources of history,* 3d series, 4. **805**

Includes the prefaces to the eight books of Gregory's Miracles; Book I of the Miracles of Blessed Martin; The lives of the Fathers (St. Gallus of Clermont and St. Gregory of Langres); Gregory's version of the Seven sleepers of Ephesus, and his The seven wonders of the world.

Gregorius de Arimono, *d. 1358.* Gregory of Rimini; tradition and innovation in fourteenth-century thought, by Gordon Leff. [Manchester], Manchester University Press [1961]. x, 245 p. **806**

Contains *passim* much close paraphrase from Gregory's Commentary on the Sentences of Peter Lombard, with the Latin text cited in footnotes; much of this work is not elsewhere translated. Professor Leff has used a newly edited text of the Commentary and collated it with many manuscripts. An article by Professor Leff also contains translation from Gregory: "Faith and Reason in the thought of Gregory of Rimini (c. 1300–1358)," *Bulletin of the John Rylands Library* (Manchester), 42 (September, 1959), 88–112.

Gregorius Nazianzenus, *Saint, fl. 380.* Funeral orations by Gregory Nazianen and Ambrose, tr. by Leo P. McCauley *et al.* New York, Fathers of the Church, 1953. xxi, 344. *Fathers of the Church,* 22. **807**

The orations of Gregorius included are: On his brother, St. Caesarius; On St. Basil the Great, bp. of Caesarea; On his sister, St. Gorgonia; On his father.

—— "The throne and the mountain: an essay on Gregory Nazianzus," by Brooks Otis, *Classical Journal,* 56 (1960–61), 146–65. **808**

Contains translation of excerpts from orations and autobiographical poems; the latter have never before been translated into English.

Gregorius Palamas, *Saint, abp. of Thessalonica, 14th cent.* A study of Gregory Palamas, by Jean Meyendorff, tr. by G. Lawrence. London, Faith Press, 1964. 245 p. **809**

The English translation of Meyendorff's French work (1959) contains translation and paraphrase of many excerpts from works of Gregory still in manuscript. A work of Gregory, On the prayer of Jesus, is said to have been translated by "Father Lazarus" (London, John Watkins, 1952), but no copy of the volume has been located.

Grigor of Akanc‘, *13th cent.* History of the nation of the Archers (the Mongols) by Grigor of Akanc‘, hitherto ascribed to Malak‘ia the monk; the Armenian text with an English translation by Robert P. Blake and Richard N. Frye, *Harvard Journal of Asiatic Studies,* 12 (1950), 269–443. **810**

Text and facing translation, from a 13th-century manuscript. Grigor is also known as Grigor Aknerli. The work was reissued separately by the Harvard University Press for the Harvard-Yenching Institute in 1954.

Grocheo, Johannes de, *fl. 1300.* Concerning music, De musica, tr. by Albert Seay. Colorado Springs, Colorado College Music Press [1967]. 42 p. **811**

Grosseteste, Robert, *bp. of Lincoln, d. 1253.* Robert Grosseteste and the origins of experimental science, 1100–1700, by A. C. Crombie. Oxford, Clarendon Press, 1953. ix, 369 p. **812**

Contains translation of extensive excerpts from Grosseteste's works, often with text in footnotes.

—— Robert Grosseteste, scholar and bishop; essays in commemoration of the seventh centenary of his death, ed. by Daniel A. P. Callus; intro. by Maurice Powicke. Oxford, Clarendon Press, 1955. xxv, 263 p. **813**

Contains a translation by A. C. Crombie of On the heat of the sun.

——, *supposed author.* "The text of Robert Grosseteste's *Questio de flexu et reflexu maris,* with an English translation," by Richard C. Dales, *Isis*, 57 (1966), 455–74. **814**

New edition from four manuscripts of a work on the tides.

Gudrun. The story of Gudrun, based on the 3rd part of the Epic of Gudrun, by E. M. Almedingen. New York, Norton [1967]. 123 p. **815**

There is no indication of the source used, nor a statement as to whether this version in English is a translation or a paraphrase.

Guigues du Chastel, *1083–1137.* Meditations of Guigo, prior of the Charterhouse, tr. by John J. Jolin. Milwaukee, Marquette University Press, 1951. 84 p. *Medieval philosophical texts in translation,* 6. **816**

The author is also known as Guigo II, general of the Carthusians, and as Guigo de Castro Novo.

—— The solitary life, a letter of Guigo, De laude solitarie vite, tr. by Thomas Merton. Worcester [Eng., Stanbrook Abbey Press], 1963. 11 p. **817**

Translation of a letter to an unknown recipient, written toward the end of Guigo's life.

Guilelmus, *abp. of Tyre, c. 1130–c. 1190.* A history of deeds done beyond the sea, by William, archbishop of Tyre, tr. and annotated by Emily Atwater Babcock and A. C. Krey. New York, Columbia University Press, 1943. 2 v. *Records of civilization,* 35. **818**

Guillaume (chanson de geste). The song of William, la chancun de Guillelme, tr. into verse by Edward N. Stone. Seattle, University of Washington Press, 1951. xvii, 109 p. **819**

Includes a translation of part of the Song of Rainoart. The song of William is part of the epic cycle of William of Orange.

Guillaume de Guilleville, *14th cent.* Prayer to the Virgin Mary by Geoffrey Chaucer, modernised by D. O. Pitches. Cherry Hinton [Eng.], privately printed, 1965. 25 p. [?] **820**

A modernization of Chaucer's translation of a passage from de Guilleville's Pélerinage de l'homme. This translation, noted by the British National Bibliography for 1965, has not been seen.

Guillaume de Lorris, *fl. 1230.* The Romance of the rose, by Guillaume de Lorris and Jean Meun, tr. into English verse by Harry W. Robbins, ed. and with an intro. by Charles W. Dunn. New York, Dutton, 1962. xxxiii, 472 p. **821**

Guillaume de Saint Thierry, *1085?–1148?* The meditations of William of St. Thierry, Meditativae orationes, tr. by a Religious of C.S.M.V. with an intro. and notes. London, Mowbray; New York, Harpers [1954]. 108 p. **822**

This translation includes the 13th Meditation not found in all manuscripts.

—— The mirror of faith by William of Saint Thierry, tr. by Geoffrey Webb and Adrian Walker. London, Mowbray [1959]. 74 p. *Fleur de lys series,* 15. **823**

—— On contemplating God, tr. by Geoffrey Webb and Adrian Walker. London, Mowbray [1955]. 41 p. *Fleur de lys series,* 6. **824**

—— On the nature and dignity of love, by William of St. Thierry, tr. by Geoffrey Webb and Adrian Walker. London, Mowbray [1956]. 64 p. *Fleur de lys series,* 10. **825**

Based on text established in 1953.

Guillaume IX, *duke of Aquitaine, 1071–1127.* The poems of William of Poitou, with an English translation by Thomas G. Bergin. [New Haven?, 1955]. 43 p. **826**

Text and facing translation of the eleven extant poems.

Gunnlaugs saga Ormstungu. The saga of Gunnlaug serpent-tongue, ed. by Peter G. Foote, tr. by Randolph Quirk. London, Nelson, 1957. xxviii, 40, 40, [41]–47. *Icelandic texts,* 1. **827**

Text and facing translation.

Guðmundar saga Arasonar. The life of Gudmund the Good, bishop of Holar, tr. by G. Turville-Petre and E. S. Olszewska. London, Viking Society for Northern Research, 1942. xxvii, 112 p. **828**

Some omissions of "annalistic and genealogical sections." This translation is from the Resensbók manuscript, *c.* 1300, earliest of three lives of Gudmund. According to the translators, the early part may be by a contemporary named Lambkar; the rest was compiled from Islendinga saga by Sturla (part of Sturlunga saga) and other works.

H

Ḥabash al-Ḥāsib. "The introductory section of Ḥabash's astronomical tables known as the 'Damascene' Zij (in Arabic text with Turkish and English translation)," by Aydin Sayili, *Ankara Universitesi Dil ve Tarih,* 13, no. 4 (1955), 133–51. **829**

The English translation appears on pp. 139–45.

Ḥāfiẓ, *14th cent.* Fifty poems of Ḥāfiẓ, texts and translation collected and made, introduced and annotated by Arthur J. Arberry. Cambridge [Eng.] Cambridge University Press, 1947. 187 p. **830**

Text and translation, pp. 83–136, by various translators, including sixteen new ones by Arberry.

—— Hafiz of Shiraz, thirty poems, tr. by Peter Avery and John Heath-Stubbs. London, John Murray; [Hollywood-by-the-Sea, Fla.], Transatlantic Arts, 1952. v, 66 p. *Wisdom of the East.* **831**

—— Poetical horoscope, or Odes of Hafiz, by 'Abbas Āryānpūr (Kāshāni). Teheran, F. Elmi Publication Institute [1965]. 134, 134, 135–46 p. **832**

Text and facing translation. The translations of 134 of the 300 to 400 known odes are in verse, accompanied by a brief prose interpretation of each poem and a glossary of the mystical significance of the terminology.

—— Hafiz, selected poems, Persian text and translation, ed. by Y. Jamshidi pur. Tehran [n.p.] 1963. 256 p. **833**

Forty-five odes with samples of the texts are translated by various translators, including A. J Arberry, Gertrude Bell, and Walter Leaf.

Ḥāfiẓ Ābrū, *d. 1430.* A Persian embassy to China, being an extract from Zubdat't tawarikh of Hafiz Abru, tr. by K. M. Maitra. Lahore, Behari Lal, Verma, 1934. 123 p. **834**

The Persian text is translated in footnotes to each page. The extract from Ḥāfiẓ Ābrū's "Cream of chronicles" is a diary kept by Shahrukh's envoy to China, 1419–22, and records details of the journey and its route, describes the countryside, cities, buildings, and wonderful objects, and notes the system of government. This work was omitted in Farrar and Evans; also, an earlier abridged translation of the extract which appeared in Astley's Collection of voyages, III, 620–32 (London, 1745–47) is not ascribed to Ḥāfiẓ Ābrū though the collection is mentioned in Farrar and Evans, item 3215.

Ḥafṣ ben Albar al-Qūṭī, *10th cent.* "Ḥafṣ b. Albar—the last of the Goths?" by D. M. Dunlop, *Journal of the Royal Asiatic Society*, 1954, 137–51. **835**

Contains translation of a versified introduction, written A.D. 989, to a translation into Arabic of the Mozarabic psalter. Ḥafṣ is identified by the author as possibly the grandson of Alvaro of Cordova, d. 861. The original Arabic text is Ms. 86 in the Biblioteca Ambrosiana, Milan.

al-Ḥākim al-Nīsabūrī, Muḥammad ibn 'Abd Allāh, *933–1014.* An introduction to the science of tradition, being al-Madkhal ilā ma'rifat al-Iklīl, by al-Ḥākim . . ., ed. with an intro., translation, and notes by James Robson. London, Royal Asiatic Society, 1953. 54, 48 p. *Oriental Translation Fund,* n.s. 39. **836**

Arabic text included. The author is also known as Ibn al-Baiyi.

Harff, Arnold, Ritter von, *1471–1505.* The pilgrimage of Arnold von Harff in the years 1496 to 1499, tr. by Malcolm Letts. London, Hakluyt Society, 1946. xxxv, 325 p. *Hakluyt Society,* 2d series, 94. **837**

A record of travel from Cologne through Italy and the Near East, France, and Spain.

al-Harizi, Judah ben Solomon, *d. 1235.* The Tahkemoni of Judah al-Harizi, an English translation by Victor E. Reichert. Jerusalem, R. H. Cohen's Press, 1965. 233 + [61] p. **838**

Contains text and translation of sixteen of the fifty-one chapters or "gates," of the Book of the battles of Judah al-Harizi. The volume contains a facsimile of the 1578 *editio princeps*.

Hartmann, von Aue, *12th cent.* Gregorius, a medieval Oedipus legend, tr. in rhyming couplets with intro. and notes by Edwin H. Zeydel, with the collaboration of Bayard Quincy Morgan. Chapel Hill, University of North Carolina Press [1955]. 143 p. *University of North Carolina studies in the Germanic languages and literatures,* 14. **839**

The translation is somewhat abridged.

—— Gregorius, the good sinner, tr. by Sheema Z. Buehne, intro. by Helen Adolf. New York, Ungar [c. 1966]. 265 p. **840**

Text and facing poetic translation of the entire poem.

—— Selections from Hartmann von Aue, tr. into English verse by Margaret Richey. Dundee [Eng.], The Cottage. 1962. 33 p. **841**

This translation has not been seen.

Ḥasan Dihlavi, *fl. 13th cent.* "The life and works of Amir Ḥasan Dihlavi," by M. I. Borah, *Journal of the Royal Asiatic Society of Bengal, Letters,* 7 (1951), 1–60. **842**

Though born in India, Dihlavi was a Sufi poet writing in Arabic; biographical material and poems are translated *passim*.

Ḥassan ibn Thābit, *d. 674, supposed author.* "The historical significance of later Anṣārī poetry, I, II," by W. 'Arafat, *Bulletin of the School of Oriental and African Studies,* 29 (1966), 1–11, 221–32. **843**

Includes translation and text of poems by later authors attributed to Ḥassan but not now considered his, according to the author.

Hebrew literature. *Collections.*

Included here are *belles lettres*; for translations of religious works in Hebrew, see *Judaism*. Though not entirely exclusive, the two categories seem necessary since in this volume, unlike that of Farrar and Evans, Talmudic and Midrashic material are included. See also *Liturgy and ritual, Jewish.*

—— "Hebrew Ms. 6 in the John Rylands Library, with special reference to two hitherto unknown poems by Yehuda Halevi," by M. Wallenstein, *Bulletin of the John Rylands Library,* Manchester, 43 (September, 1960), 243–72. **844**

Text and translation of two poems which the author attributes to Judah ha-Levi; they are extant only in this manuscript.

—— Hebrew poems from Spain, with an intro., translation, and notes by David Goldstein. London, Routledge & Kegan Paul, 1965. vii, 176 p. **845**

Includes verse translations from poets who wrote between 942 and 1298.

—— Letters of Jews through the ages, from Biblical times to the middle of the eighteenth century, ed. by Franz Kobler. London, Ararat Publishing Society, 1952. 2 v.; 2d ed., [New York], Publication of the East and West Library issued by Farrar, Straus, and Young [1953]. **846**

The second edition has the title A treasury of Jewish letters; letters from the famous and the humble. In the first edition, pp. 65–330 of Vol. I contain translation from medieval sources.

—— Memoirs of my people through a thousand years, sel. and ed. by Leo W. Schwarz. New York, Farrar and Rinehart [c. 1943]. xxvi, 597 p. **847**

A "gallery of self-portraits," autobiographical writings from six medieval authors, pp. 3–47. Writers included are Ahimaaz ben Paltiel, Moses Maimonides, Abraham Aboulafia, Judah Asheri, Menahem ben Zerah, and Isaac Abravanel.

—— A treasury of Jewish poetry, ed. by Nathan and Marynn Ausubel. New York, Crown [c. 1957]. lxxxviii, 471 p. **848**

Contains translation of selections from Jewish poets who wrote not only in Hebrew but in other languages, arranged topically; includes biographical index of authors. Largely from previously published translations, but includes some new versions by the editors.

Heiðreks Kronungs saga. The saga of King Heidrik the Wise, tr. by Christopher Tolkien. London and New York, Nelson [c. 1960]. xxxviii, 100 p. *Icelandic texts.* **849**

Text and facing translation of one of the Fornaldsögur or sagas of ancient times, not a saga of Icelanders or family saga, according to the translator. Contains three poems inserted into the prose narrative, known as Sámsey poetry. The saga is also known as Hervarar saga of Heiðreks konungs, taking its title from Hervör, the mother of Heiðrek.

Heliand. The Heliand, tr. into English from the Old Saxon, by Mariana Scott. Chapel Hill, University of North Carolina Press, 1966. x, 206. *University of North Carolina studies in the Germanic languages and literatures,* 52. **850**

An alliterative verse translation.

Heliodorus of Emesa, *fl. 3d cent.* Ethiopian story, tr. by Walter Lamb. London, Dent; New York, Dutton, 1961. xxvi, 278 p. *Everyman's library.* **851**

A translation of the story of Theagenes and Chariclea. The translator refers to earlier translations by Thomas Underdowne (1587) and Nahum Tate (1686) which are not noted in Farrar and Evans and which have not been seen.

Henricus Lettus, *13th cent.* The chronicle of Henry of Livonia, a translation with intro. and notes by James A. Brundage. Madison, University of Wisconsin Press, 1961. vii, 262 p. *Documents from medieval Latin.* **852**

The chronicle is an eyewitness account of the devastation accompanying the Christianization of the Baltic nations by German missionaries, *c.* 1180–1227.

Henryson, Robert, *1430?–1506?* A modernization of Henryson's Testament of Cresseid, with an intro. and notes by Marshall W. Stearns. Bloomington, Indiana University Press [1945]. 43 p. *Indiana University publications, humanities series,* 13. **853**

A verse translation. Another translation is in Medieval English verse and prose in modernized versions, ed. by Roger S. Loomis and Rudolph Willard, 1948; see item 633 above.

Hermannus Contractus, *1013–54.* Musica Hermanni Contracti, ed. and tr. by Leonard Ellinwood. Rochester, N.Y., University of Rochester Press, 1936. iv, 71 p. *Eastman School of Music studies,* 2. **854**

Text based on manuscript and facing translation of "the premier German music theorist of the Middle Ages," according to the editor. This translation was omitted in Farrar and Evans.

Hermes Trismegistus. "The Krater and the grail, Hermetic sources of the Parzival," by Henry and Renée Kahane and Angelina Pietrangeli. Urbana,

University of Illinois Press, 1965. xi, 218 p. *University of Illinois studies in language and literature,* 56. **855**

Contains translation of the Krater, 4th of seventeen Greek treatises in the Corpus hermeticum; the work seems to be a source for part of Wolfram von Eschenbach's Parzival.

Herod (liturgical drama). The Fleury play of Herod, ed. by Terence Bailey. Toronto, Pontifical Institute of Mediaeval Studies, 1965. 72 p. **856**

The text is given with the music and again with the English translation. The work consists of two plays, actually: The representation of Herod and The slaying of the children, both from the 12th-century manuscript known as the "Fleury playbook."

—— The play of Herod, a twelfth-century musical drama, ed. by Noah Greenberg and [tr. by] William L. Smoldon. New York, Oxford University Press, 1965. xiv, 99 p. **857**

A performing edition, with music.

Heytesbury, William, *fl. 1340.* William Heytesbury; medieval logic and the rise of mathematical physics, by Curtis Wilson. Madison, University of Wisconsin Press, 1956. xii, 219 p. *University of Wisconsin publications in medieval science,* 3. **858**

Includes paraphrase with commentary of the physical and mathematical content of Heytesbury's Regulae solvendi sophismata, Rules for solving sophisms; also paraphrase of many of Heytesbury's predecessors and followers. Based on manuscript material.

Hieronymus, *Saint, d. 420.* The homilies of Saint Jerome, tr. by Marie Liguori Ewald. Washington, Catholic University of America Press [1964–66]. 2 v. *Fathers of the Church,* 48, 57. **859**

—— Jerome's commentary on Daniel, tr. by Gleason L. Archer, Jr. Grand Rapids, Baker Book House, 1958. 189 p. **860**

—— Letters, tr. by Charles Christopher Mierow, intro. and notes by Thomas Comerford Lawler. Westminster, Md., Newman Press, 1963. vol. 1. *Ancient Christian writers,* 33 **861**

No further volumes have been issued; the translator died before this volume appeared.

—— Saint Jerome, dogmatic and polemical works, tr. by John N. Hritzu. Washington, Catholic University of America Press [1965]. xix, 410 p. *Fathers of the Church,* 53. **862**

Includes translation of On the perpetual virginity of the Blessed Mary, the Apology against the books of Rufinus, Dialogue against the Pelagians.

—— The satirical letters of St. Jerome, tr. with an intro. by Paul Carroll. Chicago, Gateway Editions [1956]. 191 p. **863**

Translation of sixteen letters "intended . . . to present the personality of the man himself."

Higden, Ranulf, *d. 1364.* The Universal chronicle of Ranulf Higden, by John Taylor. Oxford, Clarendon Press [1966]. x, 198 p. **864**

Appendix II contains a translation of selected passages of the Polychronicon, books 2 and 4.

Hilarius, *Saint, bp. of Poitiers, d. 367?* Saint Hilary of Poitiers, the Trinity, tr.

by Stephen McKenna. New York, Fathers of the Church, 1954. xix, 555 p. *Fathers of the Church*, 25 **865**

Hilton, Walter, *d. 1396.* The scale of perfection, tr. by Gerard Sitwell. Westminster, Md., Newman Press; London, Burns & Oates, 1953. xx, 316 p. *Orchard books.* **866**

According to the translator, this is a "completely modern" translation based on the Underhill text of Harleian Ms. 6579, collated with the Wynken de Worde version (1494). See Farrar and Evans, items 1957 and 1958.

—— The ladder of perfection, a new translation with intro. by Leo Sherley-Price. [Harmondsworth, Eng.] Penguin Books [1957]. xxii, 256 p. **867**

—— Of the knowledge of ourselves and of God. A fifteenth-century florilegium from the English mystics Walter Hilton and Julian of Norwich, ed. by James Walsh and Eric Colledge. London, Mowbray [1961]. xxi, 68 p. *Fleur de lys series,* 17. **868**

A modernized version of Hilton's commentary on Psalms 90 and 91 and of Juliana's Revelation of divine love, taken from a 15th-century manuscript.

Hippocrates, *Arabic version.* Kitāb tadkīr al-amrād al-hādda li-Buqrāt (Regimen in acute diseases), ed. and tr. by M. C. Lyons. Cambridge [Eng.], published for the Cambridge Middle East Centre by W. Heffer, 1966. xxxiii, 81 p. *Arabic technical and scientific texts,* 1. **869**

Text and facing translation. The Arabic version was made by either 'Īsā ibn Yahyā or Ḥunạin ibn Isḥāq, according to the editor. The purpose of the series is to show Islamic culture and the degree to which the Arab translators of Greek understood their material.

Hippolytus, *Saint, fl. 217–235.* Apostolic tradition, tr. into English with intro. and notes by Burton Scott Easton. [Hamdem, Conn.], Archon Books, 1962 [c. 1934]. [xi], 112 p. **870**

This reprint is included here (*cf.* Farrar and Evans, item 1961) in order to cross reference it to *Liturgy and ritual, Coptic church,* which was not done by Farrar and Evans. The work is partly a liturgy, with commentaries. The translation is made from a Latin version collated with Coptic and Arabic texts which are probably redactions of the Greek original.

Historia de Segundo. Secundus the silent philosopher, the Greek life of Secundus, critically ed. and restored so far as possible together with translation of the Greek and Oriental versions . . ., by Ben Edwin Perry. Ithaca, N.Y., Cornell University Press, 1964. xiv, 176, 7, 11, 74, 96 p. *Philological monographs,* 22. **871**

Medieval translation of a life written probably in the last half of the 2d century. This volume includes text and translation of a Greek version; an Armenian version from a 10th-century manuscript; an Arabic version from 15th- and 16th-century manuscripts; and fragments of a Syriac version. Latin texts and a Latin translation of an Ethiopian version are not translated into English.

Historical sources. *Collections.*

This heading is less inclusive than in Farrar and Evans. It includes historical works not classifiable under a single heading such as *France* or *Islam* but not works classifiable under headings new to this volume, *e.g., Philosophy, Science, Christian literature, Collections.*

—— Basic documents in medieval history, tr. by Norton Downs. Princeton, N.J., Van Nostrand, 1961. 189 p. *Anvil books.* **872**

Brief excerpts from some eighty documents are translated, mostly laws, codes, charters, papal bulls.

—— Church and state through the centuries, a collection of historic documents with commentaries, tr. and ed. by Sidney Z. Ehler and John B. Morrall. London, Burns & Oates [1954]. xii, 625 p. **873**

Many documents (edicts, constitutions, the Donation of Constantine) and also letters and narratives are translated for the first time into English.

—— The crisis of church and state, 1050–1300. with selected documents, by Bruce Tierney. Englewood Cliffs, N.J., Prentice-Hall, 1964. xi, 211 p. **874**

Short excerpts from relevant documents, in translation, follow each chapter; much of the translation is newly made by the author.

—— The early Middle Ages, 500–1000, ed. by Robert Brentano. [New York], Free Press [1964]. viii, 306 p. *Sources in Western civilization*, 4. **875**

—— The guilt of the Templars, by G. Legman *et al.*; prefatory note by Jacques Barzun. New York, Basic Books, 1966. xi, 308 p. **876**

Contains *passim* translation of confessions of Knights Templar, *c.* 1307; these are taken largely from modern French translations rather than directly from the documents. Contains also a translation of Pope Clement V's bull Faciens misericordiam and of the form of the questions asked the Templars, from Sir William Dugdale's Monasticon Anglicanum (1718).

—— The high Middle Ages, 1000–1300, ed. by Bryce D. Lyon. [New York], Free Press [1964]. viii, 273 p. *Sources in Western civilization*, 5. **877**

—— A history of Rome, from its origins to 529 A.D., as told by the Roman historians, ed. and tr. by Moses Hadas. Garden City, N.Y., Doubleday, 1956. 305 p. **878**

Selections from many medieval writers, linked into a consecutive narrative.

—— "The inception of the career of the Normans in Italy—legend and history," by Einar Joransen, *Speculum*, 23 (July, 1948), 353–96. **879**

Contains translation *passim* from works of Leo of Ostia, William of Apulia, Orderic Vitalis, and others; and from the Chronicle of the monastery of St. Bartholomew of Carpineto; texts included.

—— Landmarks of the western heritage, ed. by Charles W. Hollister. New York and London, Wiley [1967]. 2 v. **880**

Vol. 1, The ancient Near East to 1715, contains translations of brief excerpts from many medieval sources, literary, artistic, political, and intellectual as well as historical.

—— Medieval commerce, ed. by Howard L. Adelson. Princeton, N.J., Van Nostrand [1962]. 192 p. *Anvil books.* **881**

Contains translation of excerpts from many sources, including travel literature, letters, privileges, bulls.

—— Medieval history, a source book, ed. by Donald A. White. Homewood, Ill., Dorsey Press, 1965. ix, 575 p. **882**

Contains many fairly short excerpts arranged chronologically and topically from the 4th to the 13th century.

—— Medieval pageant, readings in medieval history, ed. by Norton Downs. Princeton, N.J., Van Nostrand, 1964. xiv, 230 p. *Princeton University series in history.* **883**

I have not seen this work, so do not know how it differs from Downs's earlier anthology, Basic documents in medieval history (see above, item 872).

—— The medieval town, ed. by John H. Mundy and Peter Riesenberg. Princeton, N.J., Van Nostrand [1958]. 192 p. *Anvil books.* **884**

Section 2, Documents, contains translation of descriptions and historical accounts as well as statutes, treaties, and economic documents.

—— Medieval trade in the Mediterranean world; illustrative documents tr. with intro. and notes, by Robert S. Lopez and Irving W. Raymond. New York, Columbia University Press, 1955. xi, 458 p. *Records of civilization*, 52. **885**

About two hundred documents from many languages are translated, dealing "with all aspects of Mediterranean commerce in the Middle Ages." Contains not only records and documents but letters of businessmen. The languages translated directly include Latin, Greek, Italian, Catalan, Old French; translation from Arabic is made through intermediary German and French versions. Most of this material appears here for the first time in English.

—— The medieval world and its transformation, 800–1650, by Gerald M. Straka. New York, McGraw-Hill, 1967. xvi, 482 p. *Western Society, institutions and ideals,* 2. **886**

Short excerpts arranged by topics (medieval society, medieval Christianity, medieval intellectual life). Mostly old translations, but contains new translation from Ekkehard of Aurach's History of the first crusade, written *c.* 1115; an ordinance of Louis IX, 1256; the charter of Rouen; and from Bernard Gui, Manual of the Inquisitor. Other works translated include Magna carta, saints' lives, chronicles.

—— The medieval world, 300–1300, ed. by Norman F. Cantor. New York, Macmillan; London, Collier, 1963. viii, 312 p. *Ideas and institutions in Western civilization,* 2. **887**

A collection of short readings in translation.

—— Men and centuries of European civilization, ed. by Louise Fargo Brown and George B. Carson, Jr. New York, Knopf, 1948. xxiii, 628 p. **888**

Selections from medieval works, largely previously published translations, appear on the first 350 pages.

—— Putnam's dark and middle ages reader; selections from the 5th to 15th centuries, ed. by Harry E. Wedeck. New York, Putnam [c. 1964]; Capricorn Books, 1965. xxii, 362 p. **889**

Short selections from many fields organized topically. Religious, historical, political, literary, and scientific works are translated many for the first time, by the editor.

—— Renaissance and Reformation, 1300–1648, ed. by Geoffrey R. Elton. London, Collier; New York, Macmillan [c. 1963]. xii, 305 p. *Ideas and institutions in Western civilization,* 3. **890**

Much new translation by the editor of short excerpts organized topically, *e.g.*, the Church in the later Middle Ages, the Hundred Years' war, the Secular state.

—— The Renaissance and the Reformation, 1300–1600, ed. by Donald Weinstein. New York, Free Press; London, Collier [1965]. viii, 310 p. *Sources in Western civilization, 6.* **891**

A collection of short excerpts from many sources.

—— Scholarly privileges in the Middle Ages; the rights, privileges, and immunities of scholars and universities at Bologna, Padua, Paris, and Oxford, ed. by Pearl Kibre. Cambridge, Mediaeval Academy of America, 1962. xvi, 446 p. *Mediaeval Academy of America publications*, 72. **892**

Although this is not a translation, it is included here because it paraphrases and summarizes many documents not elsewhere translated.

—— Sources for the history of medieval Europe from the mid-eighth to the mid-thirteenth century, ed. [and tr.] by Brian Pullan. New York, Barnes and Noble; Oxford, Blackwell, 1966. x, 277 p. **893**

Translation by the editor of brief excerpts, concerned mainly with the history of law and government and the relationship between clerical and lay power. Four parts: Carolingian empire; Church and papacy; Emperors and empire in Germany and Italy; France and Flanders.

—— Sources of medieval history, ed. by Charles T. Davis. New York, Appleton-Century-Crofts [1967]. 2 v. **894**

Contents—vol. 1. The eagle, the crescent, and the cross, c. 250–c. 1000.—vol. 2. Western awakening, c. 1000–c. 1500. V. 1 includes a section on Byzantium and Russia and on Islam. Most of the translations have been previously published, but the editor has translated excerpts from St. Columban, Widukind, Otto III, Salimbene, and Brunetto Latini.

—— XIIIth century chronicles, tr. by Placid Herrmann, with intro. and notes by Marie-Therèse Laureilhe. Chicago, Franciscan Herald Press [1961]. xvii, 302 p. **895**

Translation of chronicles dealing mostly with Franciscans in Germany, France, England. Contains chronicles of Jordanus de Yano, *fl.* 1220–62; Thomas of Eccleston, *fl.* 1250; and Salimbene degli Adamo, b. 1221 (selections only).

—— University records and life in the Middle Ages, by Lynn Thorndike. New York, Columbia University Press, 1944. xvii, 476 p. *Records of civilization*, 38. **896**

Translation of passages from the Chartularium of the University of Paris and from other university records, as well as excerpts from the works of contemporaries: John of Salisbury, Antonio, abp. of Florence, 1440–59, and Pierre DuBois. Appendix I contains the Latin text of an educational treatise De commendatione cleri, which is translated on pp. 201–35.

Hrafnkels saga Freysgoða. The saga of Hrafnkel, priest of Frey, tr. by John C. McGalliard, in World masterpieces, ed. by Maynard Mack, *et al.* New York, Norton [c. 1965], I, 764–84. **897**

Hrafns saga Sveinbjarnasonar. The saga of Hrafn Sveinbjarnarson; the life of an Icelandic physician of the thirteenth century, tr. by Anne Tjomsland. Ithaca, N.Y., Cornell University Press, 1951. xxviii, 65 p. *Islandica,* 35. **898**

An historical saga by an anonymous contemporary of Hrafn.

Hrotsvit of Gandersheim, *10th cent.*

For a complete list of translations of the separate plays, see the bibliography of printed editions and translations by Marjorie D. Barlow, pp. 57–77, in Hrotsvitha of Gandersheim: her life, times, and works, ed. by Anne L. Haight, New York, Hroswitha Club, 1965. The club has a library of Hrotsvit's works, among them a typescript translation by Janós Scholz of the version of Dulcitius found in a 16th-century Hungarian manuscript. **899**

Hugo Candidus, *fl. 1107?–1155.* The chronicle of Hugh Candidus, a monk of Peterborough, ed. by William T. Mellows, with La geste de Burch, ed. [and tr.] with an intro. by Alexander Bell. London and New York, Oxford University Press, 1949. **900**

Only La geste de Burch is translated; it is an Anglo-Norman version of the first rescension of the chronicle of Hugh Candidus. According to the editors, this chronicle is not to be confused with the Peterborough version of the Anglo-Saxon chronicle, though the two are probably based on the same materials. This work is a history of the monastery at Peterborough (Burch). For its relationship to the Anglo-Saxon chronicle, see the introduction to Rositzke's translation, item 77 above. The Latin version of The Peterborough chronicle of Hugh Candidus was translated by Charles and William T. Mellows, Peterborough, National historical, scientific, and archaeological society, 1941, xvi, 70 p. (omitted in Farrar and Evans).

Hugo of Saint Victor, *1096 or 7–1141.* Didascalicon, a medieval guide to the arts, tr. by Jerome Taylor. New York, Columbia University Press, 1961. xii, 254 p. *Records of civilization,* 64. **901**

Translation of On the study of reading, an encyclopedic guide to education in six books, three on secular study and three on study of the Scriptures. The notes include translation from the sources of the Didascalicon.

—— The divine love: the two treatises De laude caritatis and De amori sponsi ad sponsam, tr. by a Religious of C.S.M.V. London, Mowbray; New York, Morehouse-Gorham [1956]. 38 p. *Fleur de lys series,* 9. **902**

—— On the sacraments of the Christian faith (De sacramentis), English version by Roy J. Deferrari. Cambridge, Mediaeval Academy of America, 1951 xx, 486 p. *Mediaeval Academy of America publications,* 58. **903**

—— Selected spiritual writings: Noah's ark, I–IV; The soul's three ways of seeing; Of the nature of love, tr. by a Religious of C.S.M.V., intro. by Aelred Squire. New York, Harper & Row [1962]. 196 p. **904**

The soul's three ways of seeing is from Hugo's commentary on Ecclesiastes entitled De vanitate mundi.

—— Soliloquy on the earnest money of the soul, tr. from the Latin with an intro. by Kevin Herbert. Milwaukee, Marquette University Press, 1956. iv, 37 p. *Medieval philosophical texts in translation,* 9. **905**

A translation of De arrha animae, a mystical work. Another translation of this work, by F. Sherwood Taylor, appeared in 1945 under the title The soul's betrothal gift, published in London by the Dacre Press, 39 p.

Humbertis de Romanis, *1194–1277.* Treatise on preaching, tr. by the Dominican students, province of St. Joseph, ed. by Walter M. Conlon. Westminster, Md., Newman Press, 1951; London, Blackfriars, 1955. xiii, 161 p. **906**

A translation of Liber de eruditione praedicationis.

Hus, Jan, *1369–1415.* John Hus' concept of the Church, by Matthew Spinka. Princeton, Princeton University Press, 1966. ix, 432 p. **907**

Extensive translation *passim* from Hus's sermons (written in Latin, preached in Czech) and other works. For translation of some letters of Hus and the record of his trial, see below, *Petr z Mladenovic,* d. 1451, item 1556.

Hymns. *Collections.* Eastern Orthodox hymnal, tr. by Fan Stylian Noli. Boston, Albanian Orthodox Church in America [1951?]. ix, 187 p. **908**

The hymns are translated from Old Slavonic and Greek; the volume contains a translation also of the plainsong for the liturgy.

—— The hymns of the Dominican missal and breviary, ed. with intro. and notes by Aquinas Byrnes. London and St. Louis, Herder, 1943. xi, 694 p. **909**

Text and facing translation of one hundred eighty-nine hymns of the Roman and Dominican rites; eighty-three of the Dominican rite are not in the Roman, fifty-three of Dominican have a different text from the Roman.

—— The medieval Latin hymn, by Ruth Ellis Messenger. Washington, Capital Press [c. 1953]. x, 138 p. **910**

Contains a section of "Illustrative hymns," pp. 83–112, text and translation in double columns; the translations are by various translators, including some newly done for this volume. An earlier work of the author, Latin hymns of the Middle Ages, New York, Hymn Society of America, 1948, 16 p., has not been seen.

—— The oldest Christian hymn-book, intro. and translation by Michael Mar-Yosip and Martin Sprengling. [Temple, Texas, Gresham's, 1948.] viii, 92 p. **911**

Translation from Syriac of the so-called Odes of Solomon, written around 100. The translation is based on that of A. Mingana in Woodbrooke studies, Christian documents in Syriac, Arabic, and Garshūni (Cambridge, 1928).

I

Iamblichus of Chalcis, *d. 330.* An Egyptian initiation, by Iamblichus, a neo-Platonist of the 4th century, tr. from the original mss. by P. Christian, tr. from the French mss. by Genevieve S. Astley. Denver, E. L. Bloom, 1965 (originally published 1901). xi, 64 p. **912**

Translation of a ritual resembling that of the Masons, of very ancient provenience. "P. Christian" is probably a pseudonym, according to the Library of Congress, and the "original mss." are not further identified. Translation of excerpts from Iamblichus appear in a work edited by Frederick C. Grant: Hellenistic Religions, the age of syncretism, New York, Liberal Arts Press, 1953, 196 p. This work includes also translation from rites and creeds from various Hellenistic cults, as well as excerpts from Plotinus, Proclus, and Sallustius' Concerning the gods and the universe.

Ibn ʻAbd al-Ẓāhir, Muḥyī al-Dīn, *1223–92.* Baybars I of Egypt, by Syedah Fatima Sadeque. Dacca, Pakistan, Oxford University Press [1956–]. vol. 1, xix, 379 p. **913**

Contains an English translation of The life of the founder of the Mamluk dynasty in Egypt by his confidential secretary, pp. 75–239, with Arabic text. The present volume covers the years of Baybars' reign to 1265; subsequent ones presumably would continue until 1277, but no further volumes have been seen.

Ibn Abī Sarḥ, *9th cent.* "The Kitāb Ar-Rumūz of Ibn Abī Sarḥ," tr. and annotated by James A. Bellamy, *Journal of the American Oriental Society,* 81 (1961), 224–46. **914**

Translated from a unique manuscript copied 1131 of a work written *c.* 877–8, according to the editor; it is a compendium on superstitions, drawn from 8th- and 9th-century sources.

Ibn Abū Hajala, *1325–75.* "A chess maqāma in the John Rylands library," by James Robson, *Bulletin of the John Rylands Library,* Manchester, 36 (1953–54), 111–27. **915**

Contains text and translation of a work on chess.

Ibn al-'Adīm, Kamāl al-Dīn 'Umar ibn Aḥmad, *1192–1262.* "Biography of Rāṣid al-Dīn Sinān (fl. 1162–93) as Grand Master of the Assassins in Syria, in the rescension of Yūnīnī, d. 1326, entitled Dayl Mir'āt al-zamān," tr. by Bernard Lewis, *Arabica,* 13 (1966), 225–67. **916**

Text and translation. See also Professor Lewis' essay "Three Biographies from Kamāl ad-Dīn" in Mélanges Fuad Köprülü, Istanbul, Osman Yalçin Matbassi, 1953 (*Ankara Universite, Dil ve Tarih,* 60), pp. 325–44. The texts of three biographies of the Assassins in Syria in the 12th century are published here for the first time, along with summaries of their content; the biographical excerpts are important for knowledge of Rāshid ad-Dīn, who is the "Old Man of the Mountain" of western chronicles.

—— "The prophecies of Bābā the Harrānian," by Franz Rosenthal, pp. 220–32 in A locust's leg, studies in honor of Seyyed H. Taqizadeh [ed. by W. B. Henning and E. Yarshatar]. London, Lund, 1962. **917**

Contains a translation of Ibn al-'Adīm's Arabic version of geographical excerpts from Bābā. Harrān, a city in northern Mesopotamia, was called Hellenopolis by the Fathers of the Church.

Ibn al-Ahmar, *10th cent.* "'Abd al-Raḥman al-Nāṣir's accession to the throne, a contemporary account," by S. M. Imamuddin, *Islamic Studies,* 1, no. 3 (September, 1962), 105–15. **918**

Contains an account of the years 912–30 from the only contemporary account of the accession of 'Abd al-Raḥman, III, Caliph of Cordova, 891–961.

Ibn Aknīn, Joseph, *12th cent.* "Classical and Arabic material in Ibn Aqnīn's 'Hygiene of the soul,'" by A. S. Halkin, *Proceedings of the American Academy for Jewish Research,* 14 (1944), 25–147. **919**

Contains translation of the aphorisms of the Ṭibb-al-nufūs, an ethical work with frequent citations of Plato and Galen.

Ibn al-'Arābi, *1165–1240.* The philosophy of Ibn 'Arabi, by Rom Landau. New York, Macmillan [1959]. 126 p. *Ethical and religious classics of East and West,* 22. **920**

Contains selections taken from previous translations of Bezels of Divine wisdom, Meccan revelations, and the collection of mystical odes.

—— "Ibn al-Arabī's Shajarat al-Kawn," by Arthur Jeffery, *Studia Islamica,* 10 (1959), 43–77; 11 (1959), 113–60. **921**

Translation of a work dealing with the Muslim doctrine of Muhammad as logos; starts with cosmology, creation of the world.

Ibn al-Athīr, *11th cent.* "Münejjim Bashi's account of Sultan Malik Shāh's reign," by S. A. Hasan, *Islamic Studies,* 3, no. 4. (December, 1964), 429–69. **922**

Münejjim's account of the years 1072–92, written in the 17th century, borrows verbatim from Ibn al-Athīr's contemporary account, which is no longer extant.

Ibn al-Azraq al-Farīqi, Aḥmad ibn Yūsuf, *b. 1121.* "Caucasia in the history of Mayyā fāriqīn," by V. Minorsky, *Bulletin of the School of Oriental and African Studies,* 13 (1949–51), 27–35. **923**

Translation of excerpts about the Caucasus in Ibn al-Azraq's chronicle of a small town situated on one of the tributaries of the Tigris, in Armenia; Ibn al-Azraq was employed by the Georgian King Dimitri I (1125–56).

Ibn Bābawayh, Muḥammad ibn 'Alī, *d. 991 or 992.* A Shi'ite creed, a translation of Risālatu'l-i-'tiqādāt of Muḥammad b. 'Alī Ibn Bābawayhi al-Qummī, known as Shaykh Ṣadūq, by Asaf A. A. Fyzee. London and New York, Oxford University Press, 1942. xiii, 144 p. *Islamic research association series,* 9. **924**

Ibn Barūn, Abū Ibrāhīm Iṣhāk, *11th and 12th cents.* Ibn Barun's Arabic works on Hebrew grammar and lexicography, by Pinchas Wechter. Philadelphia, Dropsie College, 1964. xvi, 235 p. **925**

Translation of the Arabic parts (definitions) of the grammar sections of a Book of comparison between the Hebrew and Arabic languages. The Hebrew words being defined are printed in Hebrew characters.

Ibn Baṭūṭa, *1304–77.* The Reḥla (India, Maldive Islands, and Ceylon), translation and commentary by Mahdi Husain. Baroda, Oriental Institute, 1953. lxxvii, 300, 16 p. *Gaekwad's Oriental series,* 122. **926**

Translation of a portion of the second part of the Reḥla.

—— Travels, A.D. 1325–1354, tr. with revisions and notes from the Arabic text ed. by C. Defrémery and B. R. Sanguinetti, by Hamilton A. R. Gibb. Cambridge, [Eng.], Published for the Hakluyt Society at the University Press, 1958, 1962. *Hakluyt Society,* 2d series, 110, 117. **927**

This is the first attempt at a complete translation of the Travels and according to a review in the *Journal of the Royal Asiatic Society,* 1959, p. 62, will be completed in four volumes. This is not the same translation as that of Sir Hamilton Gibb in 1929; *cf.* Farrar and Evans, item 2823. The Library of Congress formerly listed the author as Muḥammad ibn 'Abd Allāh, called Ibn Baṭūṭa.

Ibn Buṣrā, *after 12th cent.* "Four famous muwaṣṣahs from Ibn Buṣrā's anthology," by S. M. Stern, *al-Andalus,* 23 (1958), 339–69. **928**

Contains Arabic text and following prose translation of four poems from a collection of 11th- and 12th-century poems discovered in 1950; the compiler, Ibn Buṣrā, is otherwise unknown.

Ibn Durayd, Muḥammad ibn al-Hasan, *837 or 838–933.* Al-Maqṣūra of Ibn Durayd, tr. by Mohammad Ebrahim Dar. Bombay, 1946. *Arab culture series,* 1. **929**

This work, discarded by the Library of Congress, has not been seen.

Ibn al-Farīd, 'Umar ibn 'Alī, *c. 1181–1235.* Mystical poems, tr. and annotated by A. J. Arberry. Dublin, Walker, 1956. 130 p. *Chester Beatty monographs,* 6. **930**

Fourteen odes contained in the Chester Beatty manuscript which establishes a different corpus for Ibn al-Farīd.

—— The poem of the way, tr. . . . by A. J. Arberry. London, Walker, 1952. 88 p. *Chester Beatty monographs*, 5. **931**

A verse translation of Naẓm as-sulūk, also known as at-Tā'īyat al-kubrā (The greater ode in T') because of its monorhyme on -ti. This is the first complete translation of the poem, three fourths of which was translated by R. A. Nicholson (*cf.* Farrar and Evans, item 3725); Arberry translated part of it in his volume Sufism (1951). This translation is based on the Chester Beatty manuscript, written before 1292, which antedates all others.

Ibn al-Firkāh, *1262–1329*. Palestine—Mohammedan Holy Land, by Charles D. Matthews. New Haven, Yale University Press, 1949. xxx, 176 p. **932**

Contains a translation of Ibn al-Firkāh's Kitab Bā'ithan-Nufūs ilā Ziyārat al-Quds al-Mahrūs, the Book of arousing souls to visit Jerusalem's holy walls, based on a Yale manuscript of 1477 collated with all other manuscripts. The work is a compilation from earlier works of devotion, for the guidance of Moslem pilgrims in Palestine. The author's full name is Burhān ad-Dīn ibn al-Firkāh al-Fazāri, according to the translator.

Ibn Gabirol, Solomon ben Judah, *c. 1021–c. 1058*. Fountain of life, tr. [by Alfred B. Jacob] from Clemens Baeumker's edition of the Latin version of Johannes Hispanus and Dominicus Gundissalinus, published in *Beiträge zur Geschichte der Philosophie des Mittelalters,* Münster, 1892–1895. Philadelphia [Dropsie College], 1954. 296 p. **933**

This translation (lithographed) is the first complete English translation of a work originally written in Arabic; the work, a dialogue between teacher and pupil, is divided into five essays which attempt to answer the ultimate question, Why was man created? Johannes Hispanus is also known as Ibn Daud; the Latin version of the lost Arabic original was made in the 12th century.

—— The fountain of life, Fons vitae, by Solomon ibn Gabirol (Avicebron). Specially abridged edition, tr. by Harry E. Wedeck, intro. by Theodore E. James. New York, Philosophical Library [c. 1962]. 133 p. **934**

This translation is an excerpt from the 3d tractate.

—— The kingly crown, tr. by Bernard Lewis. London, Vallentine-Mitchell [1961]. 92 p. **935**

A new translation of a poem previously translated by Israel Zangwill; see Farrar and Evans, item 2067.

Ibn Ḥazm, 'Ali ibn Aḥmad, *994–1064*. The Ring of the dove by Ibn Hazm, a treatise on the art and practice of Arab love, tr. by A. J. Arberry. London, Luzac, 1953. 288 p. **936**

A translation in prose and verse.

Ibn Hishām, 'Abd al-Malik, *d. 834*. The life of Muhammad, a translation of Isḥāq's Sīrat rasūl Allāh, with intro. and notes by A. Guillaume. London and New York, Oxford University Press, 1955. xlvii, 813 p. **937**

An English translation of Ibn Hishām's version of the Life of Muḥammad by Ibn Iṣhāk, d. *c.* 768, whose work is otherwise not extant. The translator says that the translation is complete except for the omission of genealogical formulae. The translation includes Ibn Hishām's notes, and some other relevant documents. In a later work (New light on the life of Muhammad, Manchester University Press, 1960, 59 p.) Professor Guillaume gives a summary and paraphrase of the parts of a newly discovered manuscript relevant to Muḥammad; the manuscript contains a report of Ibn Isḥāk's lectures which supplements Ibn Hishām's.

—— The life of Muhammed, apostle of Allah, by Ibn Ishaq, ed. by Michael Edwardes, tr. by Edward Rehatsek. London, The Folio Society, 1964. 177 p. **938**

An abridgment of the first known English translation, here published for the first time, though Edward Rehatsek died in 1891.

Ibn al-Imām, Abū 'l-Ḥasan, *12th cent.* "Ibn Al-Imām, the disciple of Ibn Bajjah," by Muhammad S. Hasan al-Ma'Sumī, *Islamic Quarterly,* 5 (1960), 120–8. **939**

Contains text and translation of brief excerpts.

Ibn Jamī', *12th cent.* "Ibn Jamī' on the skeleton," by C. Rabin, in Science, Medicine, and History, Essays on the evolution of scientific thought and medical practice, written in honour of Charles Singer, ed. by E. Ashworth Underwood. London, Oxford University Press, 1953. 2 v. **940**

Vol. 1, pp. 177–202, contains text and translation of an Oxford manuscript of Hibatallah ibn Zain Ibn Jamī', the Jew, physician to Sultan Saladin of Egypt (1138–93).

—— "Sultan Saladin's physician on the transmission of Greek medicine to the Arabs," by Max Meyerhof, *Bulletin of the History of Medicine,* 18 (1945), 169–78. **941**

Contains translation of the first part of Ch. 2 of the treatise "An epistle to Saladin on the revival of the art of healing."

Ibn Jubayr, Muḥammad ibn Aḥmad, *1145–1217.* The Travels of Ibn Jubayr, being the chronicle of a medieval Spanish Moor concerning his journey to the Egypt of Saladin, the holy cities of Arabia, Baghdad, the city of the Caliphs, the Latin kingdom of Jerusalem and the Norman kingdom of Sicily, tr. by R. J. C. Broadhurst. London, Jonathan Cape, 1952. 430 p. **942**

Record of a journey undertaken 1183–85.

Ibn al-Kalbi, Hishām, *d. 819 or 821.* The book of idols, tr. with intro. and notes by Nabih Amin Faris. Princeton, Princeton University Press, 1952. xii, 59 p. *Princeton Oriental studies,* 14. **943**

Translation of a history of the adoption of idols from the time of Ishmael, son of Abraham, legendary ancestor of the Moslems.

Ibn Kammūnah, Sa'd ibn Manṣūr, *13th cent.* "Ibn Kammūna's Treatise on the immortality of the soul," by Leon Nemoy, in Ignace Goldziher memorial volume, ed. by David Samuel Löwinger, *et al.* Jerusalem [Rubin Mass], 1958. 2 v. **944**

Vol. 2, pp. 83–99, contains a translation of the treatise.

Ibn Khaldūn, *1332–1406.* Ibn Khaldūn and Tamerlane, their historic meeting in Damascus, A.D. 1401 (803 A.H.), a study based on Arabic manuscripts of Ibn Khaldun's "Autobiography," with a translation into English and a commentary, by Walter J. Fischel. Berkeley, University of California Press, 1952. x, 149 p. **945**

This is a translation of the last three chapters of Ibn Khaldūn's autobiography.

—— [Muqaddimah] An Arab philosophy of history, selections from the Prolegomena of Ibn Khaldun of Tunis, tr. by Charles Issawi. London, John Murray; Forest Hills, N.Y., Transatlantic Arts [1950]. xiii, 190 p. **946**

According to Issawi, Ibn Khaldūn is the "greatest historian of the Middle Ages."

—— The Muqaddimah, an introduction to history, tr. by Franz Rosenthal. [New York], Pantheon Books [1958]. 3 v. *Bollingen series*, 43. **947**

The Muqaddimah, or Prolegomena, "consists of Ibn Khaldūn's original preface and Book I of his universal history," according to N. J. Dawood, editor of an abridgment of Rosenthal's translation, published in 1967 in London by Routledge and Kegan Paul. The last chapter of the Rosenthal translation contains Ibn Khaldūn's collection of contemporary Arabic poetry.

—— An analytical study of the sociological thought of Ibn Khaldun, by Muhammad 'Abd al-Mun'im Nūr. Cairo [n.p.], 1960. xvii, 278 p. **948**

Includes translation of sections of the Prolegomena.

Ibn Māsawaih, 'Abū Zakariyya' Yuhannā, *d. 857.* "Ibn Māsawaih and his Treatise on simple aromatic substances," by Martin Levey, *Journal of the History of Medicine,* 16 (1961), 394–410. **949**

This pharmacological work, found in a manuscript dated 1563, is translated on pp. 397–409.

Ibn Miskawaih, Aḥmad ibn Muḥammad, *d. 1030.* Islam and Christian theology, by James W. Sweetman. London and Redhill, Lutterworth Press, 1945–67. 4 v. **950**

Part I, vol. 1, contains a translation of Ibn Miskawaih's "Shorter theology," al-Fawz ul aṣghar. In the other volumes, there is a good deal of translation *passim* from both Islamic and Christian writers, *e.g.,* Averroës and Ramon Lúll. Dr. Sweetman did not live to complete this work. Excerpts from al-Fawz al Aṣghar on botany are translated by Muhammad Hamidullah in an article "Dinwariy's Encyclopedia Botanica," pp. 195–206 in Mélanges Fuad Köprülü, Istanbul, Osman Yalçin Matbaasi, 1953. *Ankara Universite, Dil ve Tarih,* 60.

—— An unpublished treatise of Miskawaih on justice, or Risāla fī māhiyat al-'adl li Miskawaih, ed. with notes, annotations, English translation, and an intro. by M. S. Khan. Leiden, Brill, 1964. 38 p. **951**

Text followed by translation, from a unique manuscript. According to the editor, Brockelmann, who never saw the manuscript, mistakenly assigned it to 'Abdul 'Aziz 'Izzat or 'Addur Raḥmān Badawī.

Ibn al-Muthannā, Aḥmad, *10th cent.* Ibn al-Muthannâ's commentary on the astronomical tables of al-Khwârizmî, two Hebrew versions, ed. and tr., with an astronomical commentary by Bernard R. Goldstein. New Haven, Yale University Press, 1967. x, 408 p. *Yale studies in the history of science and medicine,* 2 **952**

The texts of both versions and translations of them are included. One of the Hebrew versions the editor thinks may have been written by Abraham ibn Ezra (d. 1167). The Arabic original is not extant.

Ibn al-Nadīm, Muḥammad ibn Isḥāq, *fl. 987.* "The Arabic literature on alchemy according to an-Nadīm (A.D. 987), a translation of the tenth discourse of The book of the catalogue (al-Fihrist)," by J. W. Fück, *Ambix,* 4 (1951), 81–144. **953**

IBN AL-NAFĪS

This chapter of Ibn al-Nadīm's work deals with pre-Islamic and contemporary practitioners of alchemy. The translation is based on the two earliest manuscripts.

Ibn al-Nafīs, 'Alī ibn Abī al-Ḥazm, *1210 or 11–1288.* "A mediaeval Arabic treatise on vivisection," by M. J. L. Young, *Abr-Nahram,* 3 (1961–62), 37–44. **954**

Contains translation of the treatise, pp. 38–43.

—— "A study of Ibn Nafis," by E. Edward Bittar, *Bulletin of the History of Medicine,* 29 (1955), 352–68, 429–47. **955**

Contains translation of biographical information by Ibn Usaybia, b. 1203, and others and of Ibn Naīs' commentary on the anatomy of the Canon of Avicenna; the sections on the heart and lungs from the commentary are completely translated, pp. 430–40.

Ibn Qudāmah, 'Abd Allāh ibn Aḥmad, *1147–1223.* Ibn Qudāma's Censure of speculative theology, an edition and translation of Ibn Qudāma's "Tahrīm an-nazar fī kutub ahl al-kalām," with intro. and notes . . . by George Makdisi. London, for Gibb Memorial Series by Luzac, 1962. xxvi, 55, 74. *Gibb memorial series,* n.s. 23. **956**

Ibn Qutayba, 'Abd Allāh ibn Muslim, *828–89?* The natural history section from a ninth-century "Book of useful knowledge," the Uyûn al-Akhbâr of Ibn Qutayba, tr. by L. Kopf; ed. by F. S. Bodenheimer and L. Kopf. Paris, Académie internationale d'histoire des sciences; Leiden, Brill, 1949. viii, 87 p. *Collection de travaux de l'Académie internationale,* 4. **957**

This is a translation of chapters 10–34 of Book 4, "Things of nature and blameworthy traits of character in man." The first two books of the work were translated by Joseph Horowitz, who died before completing the translation; see Farrar and Evans, item 2077. According to the present editors, the work is merely a compilation, with no original contribution by Ibn Qutayba; but it indicates the state of zoological knowledge of the time. The Library of Congress formerly transliterated the author's name as Ibn Ḳutaibah.

Ibn al-Rūmī, *836–c. 896.* Life and works of Ibn er Rûmî, by Rhuvon Guest. London, Luzac, 1944. 143 p. **958**

Contains many excerpts from works by and about Ibn al-Rūmī, including translation from his otherwise unpublished Dīwān, pp. 61–71.

Ibn Sa'd, Muḥammad, *c. 784–845.* Kitāb al-ṭabaqāt al-kabīr, English translation by S. Moinul Haq, assisted by H. K. Ghazanfar. Karachi, Pakistan Historical Society [1967]. *Pakistan Historical Society,* 46. **959**

According to the Encyclopedia of Islam, this "Book of the Classes" gives data on some 4,250 persons who had played a role as narrators or transmitters of traditions about the Prophet Muḥammad. The work has not been seen.

Ibn Sa'īd, 'Alī ibn Mūsā, *called* **al-Maghribī,** *13th cent.* Moorish poetry. a translation [by] A. J. Arberry of the Pennants, an anthology compiled in 1243, by the Andalusian Ibn Sa'id. Cambridge [Eng.], Cambridge University Press 1953. xix, 198 p. **960**

Two groups of poems are translated: those by poets of Moslem Spain, those of North Africa and Sicily. Ibn Sa'īd was the compiler; he should not be confused with Sā'id ibn Aḥmad al-Andalusī d. 1070, under whose name the Library of Congress for a time erroneously listed the work.

Ibn aṣ-Sā'igh al-'Antarī, *d. 1174*. "The Dīwān attributed to Ibn Bajjah (Avempace)," by D. M. Dunlop, *Bulletin of the School of Oriental and African Studies*, 14 (1952), 463–77. 961

Translation *passim* of material in a Dīwān which the author says is falsely ascribed to Ibn Bajjah, who shared the appellation "Ibn aṣ-Sā'igh" (son of the goldsmith) with the actual author, identified above.

Ibn al-Salāh, Aḥmad ibn Muḥammad, *1090–1153*. Galen and the syllogism, by Nicholas Rescher. Pittsburgh, University of Pittsburgh Press, 1966. 93 p. 962

Contains text and translation of the treatise "On the fourth figure of the categorical syllogism," Maqālah fī 'l-shakl al-rābi'. . . . This first of Ibn al-Salāh's treatises to be edited and studied is important, according to the editor, not only *per se* but for the bibliographical notes it contains about works no longer extant.

Ibn Ṣaṣrā, Muḥammad ibn Muḥammad, *fl. 1384–97*. A chronicle of Damascus, 1389–1397, by Muḥammad ibn Muḥammad ibn Ṣaṣrā, the unique Bodleian Library manuscript of al-Durra al-Mudī'a fī l-Dawla al-Zāhirīya (Laud or. MS 112) tr., ed., and annotated by William M. Brinner. Berkeley, University of California Press, 1963. 2 v. 963

Vol. 1 contains the English translation, vol. 2 the Arabic text.

Ibn Taghrībirdī, Abū al-Mahāsin Yūsuf, *1411–70*. History of Egypt, 1382–1469 A.D., tr. . . . by William Popper. Berkeley, University of California Press, 1954–60. 9 v. *University of California publications in semitic philology*, 13–21. 964

Ibn Taghrībirdī's work covers the period A.D. 641–1469. Professor Popper translated the portions most nearly contemporary with the author. Apparently he did not live to complete the final volume, an index, which has never appeared. A portion of Professor Popper's translation, covering the years 1441–50, was edited by Walter J. Fischel and published as History of Egypt, New Haven, American Oriental Society, 1967. v, 60 p.

Ibn Ṭāhir al-Baghdādī, 'Abd al-Qāhir, *d. 1037*. "The logical basis of early Kalām," by W. Montgomery Watt, *Islamic Quarterly*, 6 (1961), 3–10; 7 (1963), 31–39. 965

Contains a translation of the first chapter of al-Baghdādī's Kitāb Usūl ad-Dīn.

Ibn Taymīyyah, Aḥmad ibn 'Abd al-Halīm, *1263–1328*. Ibn Taimiyya on public and private law in Islam, or public policy in Islamic jurisprudence, tr. . . . by Omar A. Farrukh. Beirut, Khayats [1966]. 195 p. 966

A translation of al-Sīyasah al-Sharīyah fī islāh al-ra'ī wa-al-ra'īyah, based on a text edited in 1961.

Ibn al-Ṭiqtaqā, Muḥammad ibn 'Alī, *b. c. 1262*. Al-Fakhri On the systems of government and the Moslem dynasties, composed by Muhammad son of Ali son of Tabataba . . ., tr. by C. E. J. Whitting. London, Luzac, 1947. 326 p. 967

A complete translation except for the index.

Ibn al-Ukhuwwa, Muḥammad ibn Muḥammad al-Qurashī al-Shāf'ī, *d. 1329*. "14th Century Muslim medicine and the Ḥisba," by Martin Levey, *Medical History*, 7 (1963), 176–82. 968

Contains translation of a short treatise prescribing the qualifications and duties of physicians, bone-setters, etc.

Ibn Umail, *fl. 10th cent.* "The sayings of Hermes quoted in the Mā' al-waraqī of Ibn Umail," by H. E. Stapleton *et al., Ambix,* 3 (April, 1949), 69–90. **969**

The work of Ibn Umail from which the translation is made is his commentary on his poem concerning alchemy.

Ibn Waḥshīyah, Aḥmad ibn 'Alī, *9th cent.* Medieval Arabic toxicology, The book on poisons of Ibn Waḥshīya and its relation to early Indian and Greek texts [by] Martin Levey. Philadelphia, American Philosophical Society, 1966. 130 p. *Transactions of the American Philosophical Society,* n.s., v. 56, pt. 7. **970**

Contains a translation of Kitāb al-sumūm. An earlier article by Levey with excerpts from the Book of poisons was "Chemistry in the Kitāb al-Sumūm (Book of Poisons) by Ibn Waḥsīya," *Chymia,* 9 (1964), 33–45.

Ibn Zur'a, Abū 'Alī 'Isā b. Isḥaq, *942–1008.* "A tenth-century Arab-Christian Apologia for logic," by Nicholas Rescher, *Islamic Studies,* 2 (March, 1963), 1–16. **971**

Text and translation of a work by a Nestorian Christian living in Baghdad.

Ibrāhīm ibn 'Awn, *before 13th cent.?* "Judaeo-Christian materials in an Arabic Jewish treatise," by Shlomo Pines, *Proceedings of the American Academy for Jewish Research,* 35 (1967), 187–217. **972**

Contains translation of many excerpts from a Jewish treatise preserved in an Arabic version by Ibrāhīm ibn 'Awn, who lived before the 13th century. The polemic against Christianity shows parallels to works of Ibn Ḥazm (11th century) and Abd al-Jabbār (10th century); the original may have come from an early Judaeo-Christian sect.

Icelandic literature. *Collections.* Eirik the Red, and other Icelandic sagas, ed. and tr. by Gwyn Jones. London and New York, Oxford University Press, 1961. xvi, 318 p. *World's classics,* 582. **973**

In addition to Eiriks þáttr Rauða, this volume contains new translations, complete except for omission of some genealogical material, of the following sagas: Hrafnkels saga Freysgóða; Gunnlaugs saga Ormstungu; Hænsna-Þóris saga; Vapnfirðinga saga; Þorsteins þáttr stangarhöggs; Þiðranda þáttr siðu-Hallssonar; Auðunar þáttr Vestfirzka; Hrólfs saga Kraka.

—— Graded readings and exercises in Old Icelandic, by Kenneth G. Chapman. Berkeley, University of California Press, 1964. 72 p. **974**

Some selections have complete translation, others have partial translation.

—— A history of Norwegian literature, by Harald Beyer, tr. and ed. by Einar Haugen. New York, New York University Press, 1956. 370 p. **975**

Excerpts from medieval texts are translated *passim,* some by the editor, some by others.

—— Icelandic Christian classics, The lay of the sun, The lily, The passion-hymns, The millenial hymn, tr. in whole or part by C. V. Pilcher. Melbourne, Oxford University Press, 1950. xi, 60 p. **976**

The first two works in this collection are of medieval provenience.

—— The Icelandic family saga, an analytic reading, by Theodore M. Andersson. Cambridge, Harvard University Press, 1967. x, 315 p. **977**

This work is not a translation proper but contains synopses of twenty-four sagas, several of which have never been translated into English.

—— Late medieval Icelandic romances, ed. by Agnete Loth. Copenhagen, Munksgaard, 1962–65. 5 v. **978**

Text and running resumés on same page; the resumés are fairly full and most of these romances have not been elsewhere translated. The translations were done for the various volumes by Gillian F. Jensen and J. B. Dodsworth. Contents are as follows: Vol. 1, Victors saga ok Bláuus, Valdimars saga, Ectors saga; Vol 2, Saulus Saga ok Nikanors, Sigurðar saga þogla; Vol. 3, Jarlmanns saga ok Hermanns, Adonias saga, Sigurðar saga Fóts; Vol. 4, Vilhjalms saga sjóds, Vilmundar saga Viðutan; Vol. 5, Nitida saga, Sigrgarðs saga Frœkna, Sigrgarðs saga ok Volbrands, Sigurðar saga Turnara, Hrings saga ok Tryggva.

—— The Northmen talk; a choice of tales from Iceland, tr. and with an intro. by Jacqueline Simpson. Foreword by Eric Linklater. London, Phoenix House; Madison, University of Wisconsin Press, 1965. xxix, 290 p. **979**

Includes translation of selected Eddic lays and ballads in verse, selected sagas and chronicles in prose.

—— A pageant of old Scandinavia, ed. by Henry Goddard Leach. Princeton, Princeton University Press for the American-Scandinavian Foundation, 1946. xv, 350 p. **980**

An anthology of short excerpts by various translators from both prose and poetry, arranged topically: gods, heroes, places. Contains complete translation of the following: Auðunar þáttr vestfirzka, Brands þáttr örva, Islendings sögufróða, Ivars þáttr Ingimundarsonar, Stufs saga, Þorsteins þáttr stangarhöggs; also Darraðarljóð and Sonatorrek.

—— The sagas of Kormák and the Sworn brothers, tr. from the old Icelandic, and ed. by Lee M. Hollander, with intro. and notes. Princeton, Princeton University Press for the American-Scandinavian Foundation, 1949. xi, 217 p. **981**

Contains translation of Kormáks saga and Fóstbrœðra saga.

—— The skalds, a selection of their poems, with intro. and notes by Lee M. Hollander. Princeton, Princeton University Press for the American-Scandinavian Foundation, 1945. viii p., 216 p. **982**

Contains selections from thirteen leading skalds, up to the mid-11th century, with relevant passages from the sagas in which the skaldic verses appear.

—— Three Icelandic sagas: Gunnlaugs saga Ormstungu, tr. by M. H. Scargill; Bandamana saga [and] Droplaugarsona saga, tr. by Margaret Schlauch. Princeton, Princeton University Press for the American-Scandinavian Foundation, 1950. 150 p. **983**

—— The trumpet of Nordland and other masterpieces of Norwegian poetry from the period 1250–1700, ed. and tr. by Theodore Jorgenson. Northfield, Minn., St. Olaf College Press [c. 1954]. 208 p. **984**

The medieval works, which exist only in post-medieval form, are some ballads, including The lily, and the Dream vision of Olav Aasteson.

—— Translations in periodicals of short pieces include: "The Old Norse homily on the dedication," by G. Turville-Peter, *Medieval Studies,* 11 (1949), 206–18, which contains a translation of Kirkjudagsmál, an exposition of architectural symbolism, from a manuscript dated 1150; and "A Northern Orpheus," by Hallberg Hallmundson, *American Scandinavian Review,* 50 (1962), 267–71, which contains a translation of Gautakvæði, a folk ballad from the late Middle Ages, according to the translator. **985**

al-Idrīsī, *c. 1100–1166.* India and the neighboring territories in the Kitāb nuzhat al-mushtāq fī'khtirāq al-'āfāq of al-Sharīf al-Idrīsī, a translation with commentary of the passages relating to India, Pakistan, Ceylon . . ., by S. Maqbul Ahmad, with a foreword by V. Minorsky. Leiden, Brill, 1960. xii, 181 p. *Publications of the DeGoeje fund,* 20. **986**

This work, the editor's thesis at Oxford, was first published in 1954 by Muslim University of Aligarh, the Department of Arabic and Islamic Studies.

Imitatio Christi.

In addition to the new translations listed here, two translations have not been seen: one by Betty I. Knott, (London, Collins, 1963), listed by the British National Bibliography; and one by the Brooklyn Confraternity of the Precious Blood (Brooklyn [1954]), listed by the National Union Catalog of the Library of Congress.

According to the National Union Catalog, the translation of the present Everyman's library version (No. 484) is a new anonymous 20th-century translation, replacing the previous translation in this series; see Farrar and Evans, item 2108.

987

—— The imitation of Christ [by] Thomas à Kempis, a modern version based on the English translation made by Richard Whitford around the year 1530, ed., with intro. by Harold C. Gardiner. New York and London, Harper [c. 1943], xxv, 261 p.; Garden City, N.Y., Image Books [1955]. 236 p. **988**

A modernized text of Whitford's translation, based on a new critical edition made for the Early English Text Society in 1941, the first edition since the 16th century to go back to the original edition of 1530.

—— The imitation of Christ, by Thomas a Kempis, the full text of the autograph manuscript of A.D. 1441 translated into modern English by Edgar Daplyn. London, Latimer House, 1949; New York, Sheed & Ward, 1950. 184 p. **989**

—— The Imitation of Christ by Gerard Zerbolt of Zutphen, teacher of Thomas à Kempis, tr. for the first time and ed. by Albert Hyma. Grand Rapids, Mich., Eerdmans, 1950. 116 p. **990**

The editor claims that Book I (the first twenty-five chapters) of the Imitatio was written by Gerard rather than Thomas. I have not seen this work to determine in what respects it differs from the accepted version of the Imitatio, which was also edited by Hyma; see Farrar and Evans, item 2132.

—— The imitation of Christ, tr. by T. S. Kepler. Cleveland, World Publishing Co. [c. 1952]. 287 p. **991**

—— Of the imitation of Christ, in four books by Thomas à Kempis, tr. by Justin McCann. Westminster, Md., Newman Press; London, Burns & Oates, [1952]. xvi, 262 p. **992**

—— The Imitation of Christ, tr. by Leo Sherley-Price. Harmondsworth [Eng.], Penguin Books [1952]. 214 p. **993**

The publishers claim that this is the first unabridged edition in English.

—— The imitation of Christ, a new translation, with an intro., by George F. Maine, foreword by L. M. J. Delaisse. London and Glasgow, Collins [1959]. 280 p. **994**

—— The imitation of Christ, by Thomas à Kempis, tr. by Ronald Knox and Michael Oakley. New York, Sheed & Ward [1960, c. 1959]. 217 p. **995**

This translation, begun by Knox, was completed by Oakley.

—— The Imitation of Christ, Imitatio Christi, translated from Latin into modern English by Aloysius Croft and Harry F. Bolton. Milwaukee, Bruce Publishing Co. [1962]. xiii, 257 p. **996**

A new translation; the Treatise on Holy Communion is made Book 4 instead of Book 3.

—— The imitation of Christ, in four books, by Thomas à Kempis, tr. by the Daughters of St. Paul [Boston], St. Paul Editions [1962]. 445 p. **997**

Innocentius III, *pope, 1160–1216.* Selected letters of Pope Innocent III concerning England (1198–1216), ed. by C. R. Cheney and W. H. Semple. London and New York, Nelson [1953]. xliii, 227, 227, [228]–248 p. *Medieval texts.* **998**

The editor has chosen letters which "illustrate . . . aspects of government and diplomacy . . ., judicial and administrative activity," omitting those of merely historical interest. Eighty-seven out of a total of some six hundred letters have been included, text and facing translation.

—— Two views of man: Pope Innocent III On the misery of man; Giannozzo Manetti On the dignity of man, tr. with an intro. by Bernard Murchland. New York, Ungar [1966]. xxi, 103 p. **999**

Books 1 and 2 of Innocent's De miseria humane conditiones and Book 4 of Manetti's work are translated.

Ireland, *Historical sources.* Irish historical documents, 1172–1922, ed. by Edmund Curtis and Robert B. McDowell. London, Methuen [1943]; reprinted New York, Barnes and Noble [1968]. 331 p. **1000**

Section 1, From the Norman conquest to the Tudor period, contains documents of both secular and ecclesiastical law, up to 1460; the Magna carta Hiberniae is included.

—— Miscellaneous Irish annals, A.D. 1114–1437, ed. and tr. by Seamus O Hinnse. Dublin, Institute for Advanced Studies, 1947. xix, 222 p. **1001**

Text and facing translation of Carthaigh's Book, A.D. 1114–1437; Rawlinson Ms. B. 488, 1237–1314 and 1392–1407. The Norman invasion of England is described.

—— "Cert Rig Caisil: The right of the King of Cashel," tr. by Vernam Hull, *Medieval Studies,* 11 (1949), 233–38. **1002**

Other translations of brief works or excerpts from them, important because of early provenience or difficulty of the text, appear frequently in the journals *Celtica, Ériu, Journal of Celtic Studies;* English translations also appear in *Etudes celtiques.*

Irenaeus, *Saint, bp. of Lyons, d. c. 202.* Proof of the apostolic preaching, tr. and annotated by Joseph P. Smith. Westminster, Md., Newman Press, 1952. viii, 233 p. *Ancient Christian writers,* 16. **1003**

This early Christian apologetic, a "manual of theology," is translated from an Armenian version found in a 13th-century manuscript; the Armenian was translated from the Greek original, now lost, in the 6th century.

IRISH LITERATURE

Irish literature. *Collections.*

See also *Cuchulain cycle, Finn mac Cumaill,* and *Mythological cycle, Irish.* Many translations too brief to be noted here are to be found in the journals *Celtica, Ériu, Journal of Celtic Studies,* and *Etudes celtiques.*

1004

—— Ancient Irish lyrics, VIIIth century–XIIth century, tr. by Molloy Carson. Belfast, Emerald Press, 1955. 31 p. **1005**

The translator says that these are "verse redactions rather than translations in the true meaning of the term."

—— An anthology of Irish literature, ed. by David H. Greene. New York, Modern Library [1954]. 602 p. **1006**

A collection of previously published translations; each poem is dated and its translator named. Part I, early Irish lyrics; Part II, myth, saga and romance; Part III, the bardic tradition: court poetry. Pages 3–217 contain medieval poems.

—— Anthology of Irish verse, the poetry of Ireland from mythological times to the present, by Padraic Colum. New York, Liveright [1948]. xiv, 425 p. **1007**

Previously published translations of poems, many medieval, arranged topically. The book was originally published in 1922 but does not appear in Farrar and Evans; poems added since the first edition appear at the end of the volume.

—— Collection of Irish riddles, by Vernam Hull and Archer Taylor. Berkeley, University of California Press, 1955. xiv, 129 p. *Folklore studies,* 6. **1008**

Contains translation only.

—— Early Irish literature, by Myles Dillon. Chicago, University of Chicago Press [c. 1948]. xix, 192 p. **1009**

Contains paraphrase and translation of many excerpts illustrative of Irish saga and poetry.

—— Early Irish literature, by Eleanor Knott [and] Gerard Murphy, with an intro. by James Carney. New York, Barnes & Noble; London, Routledge & Kegan Paul, 1966. vii, 205 p. **1010**

Much translation *passim* in the introduction and the essays by Knott and Murphy.

—— Early Irish lyrics, eighth to twelfth century, ed. with translation, notes, and glossary by Gerard Murphy. Oxford, Clarendon Press, 1956. 315 p. **1011**

Text and facing translations from Old and Middle Irish, both monastic and secular lyrics.

—— Early Irish poetry, ed. by James Carney. [Dublin], published for Radio Eirann by the Mercier Press [1965]; distributed by Folklore Associates, Hatboro, Pa. 99 p. **1012**

Has translation *passim* by the authors of the following essays which appear in the book [The Thomas Davis Lectures]: Early Irish poetry, by Myles Dillon; Latin poetry in Ireland, by Francis J. Byrne; Poems of Blathmac, son of Cú Brettan, by James Carney; The metrical Dindshenchas, by Máirín O Daly; The religious epic, by David Greene; and Giolla Brighde Mac Con Midhe, by Anne O'Sullivan.

—— The first book of Irish myths and legends, tr. by Eoin Neeson. Cork, Mercier Press, 1965. 126p. [Distributed by Hatboro, Pa., Folklore Associates.] **1013**

Contents: The fate of the children of Tuireann, The wooing of Etain, The combat at the ford, Deirdre and the sons of Usna. Another volume in this series by the same editor and publisher, The second book of Irish myths and legends, 1966, 128 p., contains The children of Lir, Diarmuid and Graine, and The sickbed of Cuchulain.

—— A golden treasury of Irish poetry, A.D. 600 to 1200, ed. and tr. by David Greene and Frank O'Connor [i.e., Michael F. O'Donovan]. London, Macmillan, 1967. x, 214 p. **1014**

Normalized Irish text and prose translation, usually on same or facing page, of fifty-four poems.

——Ireland, harbinger of the Middle Ages, by Ludwig Bieler; Eng. translation by Ludwig Bieler. New York and London, Oxford University Press, 1963. viii, 148 p. **1015**

A translation by the author of the German edition, Irland, Wegweiser des Mittelalters, 1961. Contains *passim* translations from original sources for the 7th–9th centuries; some are translated by the author, some previously published. Several poems from Sedulius Scottus, 9th century, are included.

—— Irish classical poetry, commonly called Bardic poetry, by Eleanor Knott. Dublin, O Lochlain, 1957. 82 p. 2d ed., 1960, 93 p. **1016**

Includes translation by the author of some thirty-five poems or excerpts; text with prose translation.

—— Irish sagas and folk-tales retold by Eileen O'Faolain. London, Oxford University Press, 1954. 245 p. **1017**

Includes sections "In the time of Cuchullin" and "In the time of Finn and Fianna"; paraphrase rather than translation.

—— The Irish tradition, by Robin Flower. Oxford, Clarendon Press, 1947. 173 p. **1018**

Has *passim* translation by the author of excerpts from both prose and poetry; the book is a collection of earlier lectures and works of Professor Flower.

—— Kings, lords, and commons, an anthology from the Irish, tr. by Frank O'Connor [*i.e.*, Michael F. O'Donovan]. New York, Knopf, 1959. xiii, 167 p. **1019**

Two sections: Saints and soldiers, A.D. 600–A.D. 1200; Lords and scholars, A.D. 1200–A.D. 1700.

—— The little monasteries, poems translated from the Irish by Frank O'Connor [*i.e.*, Michael F. O'Donovan]. Dublin, Dolmen Press; London, Oxford University Press, 1963. 43 p. **1020**

All but four of the poems translated are medieval; some are revisions of O'Connor's previous translations.

—— Medieval Irish lyrics, sel. and tr. by James Carney. Berkeley, University of California Press, 1967. xxxii, 103 p. **1021**

Text and facing translation of poems from both Latin and Gaelic.

—— More poems from the Irish, tr. by the Earl of Longford. Dublin, Hodges, Figgis; Oxford, Blackwell, 1945. 64 p. **1022**

Contains translation of twelve poems from medieval times. Two other volumes by Lord Longford [Edward A. H. Pakenham] have not been seen: Poems from the Irish, Dublin, Hodges,

Figgis, 1944, x, 76 p.; The dove in the castle, a collection of poems from the Irish, Dublin, Hodges, Figgis, 1946, 217 p.

—— One thousand years of Irish poetry, the Gaelic and Anglo-Irish poets from pagan times to the present, ed. by Kathleen Hoagland. New York, Devin-Adair Co., 1947. liv, 830 p. **1023**

A collection from previously published translations; poetry to the end of the 15th century, pp. 1–138.

—— "A poem of prophecies," by Eleanor Knott, *Ériu,* 18 (1958), 55–84. **1024**

The work translated is a compilation of two documents written perhaps *c.* 1150 from the late 14th-century manuscript, the Book of Hy Many.

—— Poems & translations, by Thomas Kinsella. New York, Atheneum, 1961. 89 p. **1025**

Contains translations of the Thirty-three triads, Breastplate of St. Patrick, excerpts from Longes Mac nUsnig, pp. 70–89. The translation of the Thirty-three triads was first published in 1955 by Dolmen Press, Dublin, as the fourth part of the Dolmen Chapbook, and reprinted separately in 1957.

—— Poems from the Irish, a selection of early and medieval Irish poetry, tr. into literal English and then reconstructed into verse in English, by Eoin Neeson. Cork, Mercier Press [1967]. 143 p. **1026**

—— The portable Irish reader, sel. and ed. by Diarmuid Russell. New York, Viking Press, 1946. xxx, 670 p. **1027**

This is an anthology largely of Anglo-Irish works but contains old translations of the Cattle Raid of Cooley (abridged), Bricriu's Feast from the Cuchulain cycle, and a few poems of medieval provenience.

—— "Some early devotional verse in Irish," by Brián Ó Cuív, *Ériu,* 19 (1962), 1–24. **1028**

Contains text with translation at bottom of the page of medieval poems some of which exist only in the 17th-century manuscript Brussels 20978–9.

—— "Some Irish charms," by R. I. Best, *Ériu,* 16 (1952), 27–32. **1029**

Charms in Latin and Irish, text and following translation; from a 15th–16th century manuscript.

—— "Studies in early Irish satire," by Howard Meroney, *Journal of Celtic Studies,* 1 (1949–50), 199–226; 2 (1953), 59–130. **1030**

Contains text, translation, and discussion of two satires, one perhaps by Fingen mac Flaind, 9th century?

—— "Two Old Irish poems," ed. and tr. by James Carney, *Ériu,* 18 (1958), 1–43. **1031**

Old Irish and facing translation of a version of the Gospel of Thomas and a poem on the Virgin Mary, from Gaelic Ms. 50 in the National Library of Ireland; they date from the 7th or 8th century. These poems were included in Professor Carney's The poems of Blathmac, 1964; see item 310 above.

Isaac, *Saint, presbyter of Antioch, 5th cent.* "Isaac of Antioch's homily against the Jews," by S. Kazan, *Oriens Christianus,* 45 (1961), 30–53. **1032**

Text and translation in double columns, from Syriac. In vols. 46, 47, and 49 of *Oriens Christianus,* articles commenting on this homily contain translation of extracts from other Syriac anti-Jewish writers. Professor Kazan places Isaac in the first half of the 4th century instead of using the accepted 5th century date based on internal evidence of works ascribed to Isaac.

Isaac [ben Solomon] Israeli, *c. 832–c. 932.* A neoplatonic philosopher of the early tenth century, his works tr. with comments and an outline of his philosophy, by A. Altman and S. M. Stern. London, Oxford University Press, 1958. xxiii, 226 p. *Scripta Judaica,* 1. 1033

Translation from Latin, Hebrew, and Arabic manuscripts of the Book of definitions, the Book of substances, the Book on spirit and soul; and excerpts from the Book on the elements. The translation of the Book on the elements, with Hebrew text, appeared in the *Journal of Jewish Studies,* 7 (1956), tr. by A. Altman.

Isaac Judaeus, *880?–932*? "Guide for physicians (Musar harofim) by Isaac Judaeus," tr. from the Hebrew with an intro. by Saul Jarcho, *Bulletin of Medical History,* 15 (1944), 180–88. 1034

Īshō'bar Nūn, *c. 743–828.* The selected questions of Ishō bar Nūn on the Pentateuch, ed. and tr. from ms. Cambridge Add. 2017 with a study of the relationship of Ishō 'Dādh of Merv, Theodore bar Kōnī and Ishō bar Nūn on Genesis, by Ernest G. Clark. Leiden, Brill, 1962. 187, [28] p. *Studia post-Biblica,* 5. 1035

Facsimile of the Syriac and translation.

Isidorus, *Saint, bp. of Seville, d. 636.* Isidore of Seville's History of the kings of the Goths, Vandals, and Suevi, tr. by Guido Donini and Gordon B. Ford, Jr. Leiden, Brill, 1966. viii, 46 p. 1036

The first English translation, according to the translators, of Historia Gothorum, Vandalorum et Suevorum.

—— Isidore of Seville, the medical writings, tr. by William D. Sharpe. Philadelphia, American Philosophical Society, 1964. 75 p. *Transactions of the American Philosophical Society,* n.s., v. 54, pt. 2. 1037

Translation of Liber XI, De homine et portentis, and Liber IV, De medicini, of the Etymologiae.

—— "The letters of St. Isidore of Seville," tr. by Gordon B. Ford, Jr., *Nuovo Didaskaleion,* 16 (1966), No. 1, 1–49. 1038

Contains translation of fourteen letters written between 620 and 636, twelve by Isidore and two by Bishop Braulio of Saragossa; the fourteenth letter is a brief preface to Isidore's *Etymologies,* the composition of which is discussed elsewhere in the letters.

Isidorus, *cardinal of Thessalonica, d. 1463.* "Isidore's encyclical letter from Buda," by J. Gill, pp. 1–8, in Miscellanea in honorem Cardinalis Isidori, 1463–1963, Romae, Sumptibus PP., Basilianorum, 1963. 1039

Contains a translation from an Old Russian version of a letter the Greek original of which has been lost.

Islam. *Historical sources.* Documents from Islamic chanceries, first series . . ., ed. by S. M. Stern. Oxford, Cassirer [1965]. 254 p. *Oriental studies,* 3. 1040

Essays by several authors, three of which contain translation from medieval sources: Two Ayyūbid decrees from Sinai, by S. M. Stern; A Mamlūk commercial treaty concluded with the Republic of Florence, 894/1489, by J. Wansbrough; Seven Ottoman documents from the reign of Meḥemmed II [*c.* 1471–78], by V. L. Ménage.

ISLAM

—— Fāṭimid decrees; original documents from the Fāṭimid chancery by S. M. Stern. London, Faber & Faber [1964]. 188 p. **1041**

Contains facsimile text, transliteration, and translation of ten decrees, among the few Islamic archival works surviving. The documents concern Coptic monks, Karaite and Rabbanite Jews, the monks of Mt. Sinai; the manuscripts were found at Mt. Sinai. Some of Professor Stern's translations of Fāṭimid documents appeared earlier in Studi orientalistici in onore di Giorgio Levi della Vida, Roma, Istituto per l'oriente, 1956, I, 529–38; and *Bulletin of the School of Oriental and African Studies,* 23 (1960), 439–55.

—— Medieval Muslim government in Barbary until the sixth century of the Hijra, by J. F. P. Hopkins. London, Luzac, 1958. xxv, 169 p. **1042**

Contains *passim* translation of brief excerpts from many works and detailed explanation of legal and governmental terms.

—— "Petitions of the Ayyūbid period," by S. M. Stern, *Bulletin of the School of Oriental and African Studies,* 26 (1964), 1–32. **1043**

Text and translation of all petitions from this period (13th century) known to the author; they include one from Italian merchants and two from the monks of Mt. Sinai.

—— "Petitions from the Mamlūk period: notes on the Mamlūk documents from Sinai," by S. M. Stern, *Bulletin of the School of Oriental and African Studies,* 29 (1966), 233–76. **1044**

Contains text and translation of seven petitions not previously published.

—— "Venice and Florence in the Mamluk Commercial Privileges," by John Wansbrough, *Bulletin of the School of Oriental and African Studies,* 28 (1965), 483–523. **1045**

Contains texts and translations of two documents, one in Italian, one in Arabic, of commercial privileges granted by the Mamluk sultan in 1497.

Islamic literature. *Collections.*

This heading is rather a catch-all; it parallels *Christian literature, Collections* and *Judaism, Collections* in including religious works (none of these categories appeared in Farrar and Evans). But since Islam was not only a religion but a culture, under this category are subsumed collections of literary, historical, and philosophical works from Islamic sources, written in both Arabic and Persian. See also *Arabic literature* and *Persian literature.* Purely documentary material is found under *Islam. Historical sources.*

1046

—— Anthology of Islamic literature, from the rise of Islam to modern times, ed. by James Kritzeck. New York, Holt, Rinehart, and Winston [1964]. vii, 379 p. **1047**

More than two thirds of the selections are medieval.

—— Aspects of Islamic civilization, as depicted in the original texts, by A. J. Arberry. New York, A.S. Barnes [c. 1964]. 408 p. **1048**

All but fifty pages of this anthology contain translations, many newly done for this volume, from medieval works from the 6th century on.

—— "A Christian mission to Muslim Spain in the 11th century," by D. M. Dunlop, *al-Andalus,* 17 (1952), 259–310. **1049**

Contains translation of correspondence between an anonymous monk and al-Muqtadir b. Hūd, ruler of Saragossa (1046–81); the reply constitutes a polemical defense of Islam. The Arabic text is included.

—— Free will and predestination in early Islam, by W. Montgomery Watt. London, Luzac, 1948. x, 181 p. **1050**

Extensive excerpts in translation from Abū Ḥanīfa al-Nu'man b. Thabit, d. 767; al-Ṭaḥāwī, Abū Dja'far, b. 853–4; and al-Ash'ari.

—— Haft bab, or seven chapters, ed. in the original Persian and tr. into English by W. Ivanow. Bombay, Ismaili Society, 1959. 27, 85, 68 p. *Ismaili Society*, Series A, 10. **1051**

This work exists only in the version of an author identified by Ivanow as Quhistānī, Abū Isḥāq, early 16th century; but Ivanow claims that the work has often been ascribed to Nāṣir ibn Khusraw. The Encyclopedia of Islam does not so ascribe it and makes no reference to Quhistānī nor do the National Union Catalog of the Library of Congress and the British Museum Catalog. Widener Library of Harvard University, which has a copy of the book, lists it under Quhistānī. Since the Ismā'īlīya documents have long been secret, the work may well be of much earlier provenience than the 16th century.

—— A history of Muslim historiography, by Franz Rosenthal. Leiden, Brill, 1952. vii, 558 p. **1052**

Part II has translation into English of Arabic treatises on history, two of them written before 1500: a "short work on historiography," by Muḥammad ibn Sulaimān, Muḥyī-ad-dīn al Kāfiyajī, written 1463; and "The open denunciation of the adverse critics of the historians," by al-Sakhāwī, Muḥammad ibn 'Abd al-Raḥman, 1427 or 28–1497.

—— "Husain and his followers," by M. A. Haldar Khan, *Muslim Review*, 37–38 (1950–51). **1053**

In a five-part article, many excerpts are translated from the writings of Muhammad's followers.

—— An introduction to Islamic cosmological doctrines; conceptions of nature and methods used for its study by the Ikhwan al-Safa, al-Biruni, and Ibn Sina, by Seyyed Hossein Nasr. Cambridge, Harvard University Press, 1964. xxi, 312 p. **1054**

Contains paraphrase and translation *passim* with Arabic and Persian texts frequently cited in footnotes of works on nature by various writers, including the three mentioned in the title.

—— Islam, ed. by John Alden Williams. New York, Braziller; London, Prentice-Hall, 1961. 256 p. *Great religions of modern man.* **1055**

Contains excerpts from Islamic religious writings, recently translated or newly translated for this volume. Among the authors newly translated are Ibn Qudāmah and al-Bukhāri.

—— Islam: Muhammad and his religion, ed. with an intro. by Arthur Jeffery. New York, Liberal Arts Press [1958]. xviii, 252 p. **1056**

An anthology of selections from the Koran, the traditions, and legends, "made with the help of a practicing Muslim."

—— "Islamic eschatology, I, II, III, and IV," by John MacDonald, *Islamic Studies*, 3 (1964), 285–308, 485–519; 4 (1965), 55–102, 137–79. **1057**

In a series of articles, the author has included text and translation from an unpublished collection of traditions, including those of Abū Layth Samarqandī, d. 983, known as Imām al-Hudā, according to the Encyclopedia of Islam, 2d edition.

—— Islamic literature, an introductory history with selections, by Najib Ullah. New York, Washington Square Press, 1963. 441 p. **1058**

Mostly new translations by the author; most of the selections are medieval.

—— Ismaili tradition concerning the rise of the Fatimids, by W. Ivanow. London and New York, published for the Islamic research association by the Oxford University Press, 1942. xxii, 337, [113] p. *Islamic research association series,* 10. **1059**

A history of the Shi'ite movement, previously a "jealously guarded secret," this work includes translations, pp. 157–313, from historical and esoteric documents relevant to the history of the Faṭimid caliphate, ranging from the 10th to the 12th century.

—— Materials on Muslim education in the Middle Ages, by A. S. Tritton. London, Luzac, 1957. xii, 201 p. **1060**

Contains *passim* translation and paraphrase from many sources.

—— Muhammad's people, a tale by anthology; the religion and politics, poetry and violence, science, ribaldry and finance, of the Muslims from the age of ignorance before Islam and the mission of Gods prophet to sophistication in the eleventh century; a mosaic translation by Eric Schroeder. [Portland, Me., The Bond Wheelwright Co. 1965]. xviii, 838 p. **1061**

The translator says he has translated with the aid of previous translations and reference to the Arabic texts. His sources are indicated in an Appendix, but it is difficult to identify the portions in the text itself.

—— The Muslim creed, its genesis and historical development, by A. J. Wensinck. Cambridge [Eng.], Cambridge University Press, 1932. vii, 304 p. **1062**

Though not included by Farrar and Evans, this work contains translation of the Fikh Akbar I and II, of the waṣīya (testament) of Abū Hanīfa, and of creeds, commentaries, and catechisms of al-Ash'arī, al-Baghdādī, and al-Shāfi'ī.

—— Muslim devotions, a study of prayer manuals in common use, by Constance C. Padwick. London, S.P.C.K., 1961. xxix, 313 p. **1063**

Contains *passim* translation from modern prayer books inspired by and often quoting famous religious leaders of the medieval period.

—— Muslim education in medieval times, by Bayard Dodge. Washington, Middle East Institute, 1962. 119 p. **1064**

Contains translation *passim* and in appendices summary-paraphrase of the "dogmas of al-Ash-'arī" and works of al-Shāfi'ī.

—— Muslim theology, by A. Tritton. [London], Published for the Royal Asiatic Society by Luzac, 1947. 218 p. *Royal Asiatic Society publications,* 23. **1065**

A collection of material in translation from various sources, arranged to form a coherent whole.

—— The order of Assasins, the struggle of the early Nizân Ismailis against the Islamic world, by Marshall G. S. Hodgson. The Hague, Mouton, 1955. xi, 352 p. **1066**

Translation in appendices of the Haft-Bab ("Seven chapters," written largely in Persian) of al-Ḥasan ibn al-Sabbah (d. 1124), and of al-Ḥasan's doctrine in the translation of al-Shahrastānī, Abū al-Fatḥ Muḥammad, 1086–1153. The Ismā'īlīya sect flourished in Egypt in the 12th century.

—— A reader on Islam, passages from standard Arabic writings . . ., ed. [and tr.] by Arthur Jeffery. 678 p. The Hague, Mouton, 1962; New York, Humanities Press, 1963. *Columbia University publications in Near and Middle East studies,* series A, 2. **1067**

New translation of selections from the Koran, traditions, canon law, the life of Muhammad, creeds, confessions, a catechism, prayers and liturgies, and from Sufi writings.

—— Readings from the mystics of Islam, translations from the Arabic and Persian, together with a short account of the history and doctrines of Sufism . . ., by Margaret Smith. London, Luzac, 1950. 144 p. **1068**

This work is supplemented by the same author's The Sufi path of love; see below, item 1071. It contains translation, mostly newly done by the author, of short excerpts from many authors, arranged chronologically, from the 8th to the 19th century; most of the selections are from medieval works, pp. 8–125.

—— Revelation and reason in Islam, by A. J. Arberry. London, Allen & Unwin; New York, Macmillan [1957]. 122 p. *The Forwood lectures, University of Liverpool,* 1956. **1069**

Contains translation *passim* of excerpts from works not elsewhere translated.

—— Studies in early Persian Isma'ilism, by Vladimir A. Ivanov. Bombay, Isma'ili Society, 1948; 2d ed., 1955. **1070**

Contains excerpts in translations from various works, including that of Ibn Hawshab al-Kūfī, *fl.* 880.

—— The Sufi path of love, an anthology of Sufism, compiled by Margaret Smith. London, Luzac, 1954. 154 p. **1071**

Brief selections from some fifty medieval Sufi writers, prose and poetry, by various translators; arranged chronologically around topics. This work supplements Readings from the mystics of Islam by Margaret Smith; see item 1068.

—— Sufism, an account of the mystics of Islam, by A. J. Arberry. London, Allen & Unwin [1950]. 141 p. *Ethical and religious classics of East and West,* 2 **1072**

Contains selected short translations from the Koran and many mystics, 8th–13th centuries; the translations are by Arberry and others.

Italian literature. *Collections.* Dante and the legend of Rome, by Nancy Lenkeith. London, Warburg Institute, 1952. ix, 184 p. *Medieval and Renaissance studies,* Supplement 2. **1073**

Contains *passim* text and translation of many passages from works of Dante and others about Rome.

—— The Italian Renaissance, ed. by Werner L. Gundersheimer. Englewood Cliffs, N. J., Prentice-Hall [c. 1965]. vii, 184 p. **1074**

Contains translation of works from the 14th and 15th centuries by Coluccio Salutati, Petrus Paulus Vergerius, Vespasiano da Bisticci, Lorenzo Valla, Pope Pius II, Pico della Mirandola, and Frencesco Matarazzo.

—— The lover's martyrdom . . ., translations from Dante, Guarini, Tasso, and Marino, with original texts, by Iain Fletcher. Swinford [Eng.], Fantasy Press, 1957. 25 p. **1075**

ITALIAN LITERATURE

The only medieval works translated are Dante's canzone "Amor, de che convien pur ch'io mi doglia" and two madrigals of Guarini; text and facing translation.

—— Lyric poetry of the Italian Renaissance; an anthology with verse translation, ed. by Levi R. Lind, with an intro. by Thomas G. Bergin. New Haven, Yale University Press, 1954. xxvii, 334 p. **1076**

Text and facing translation of poems up to the end of the 16th century; many are new translations by the editor.

—— Pageant of Europe; sources and selections from the Renaissance to the present day, ed. by Raymond P. Stearns. New York, Harcourt, Brace & World, 1947; rev. ed. [1961]. 1072 p. **1077**

Includes from the medieval period excerpts from Petrarch, Boccaccio, Vespasiano da Bisticci, and Dante, largely from old translations.

—— The Penguin book of Italian verse, with plain prose translations of each poem, ed. by George R. Kay. [Harmondsworth, Eng.], Penguin Books [1958]. 424 p. **1078**

Text with prose translation at bottom of page for works of twenty-four medieval authors, pp. 1–154.

—— Prose and poetry of the continental Renaissance in translation, ed. by Harold H. Blanchard. New York, Longmans, Green, 1949; 2d ed., 1955. 1084 p. **1079**

Includes forty-three canzoniere, Life of solitude, and three letters of Petrarch; Boccaccio's Il Filostrato and selections from the Decameron.

—— Renaissance and Baroque lyrics; an anthology of translations from the Italian, French, and Spanish, ed. by Harold Priest. [n.p.], Northwestern University Press [c. 1962]. 288 p. **1080**

The only translation from medieval works is from Italian: excerpts from Petrarch, Boccaccio, Lorenzo de' Medici, Angelo Poliziano appear on pp. 1–27.

—— A Renaissance treasury . . ., ed. by Hiram Hayden and John Charles Nelson. Garden City, N.Y., Doubleday, 1953. 432 p. **1081**

Contains previously published translations of selections from Petrarch, Boccaccio, Lorenzo de' Medici, Pico della Mirandola, Angelo Poliziano, and Girolamo Savonarola.

—— Selections from Italian poetry, ed. by A. Michael De Luca and William Giuliano, with a foreword by Thomas G. Bergin. New York, Harvey House, 1966. 128 p. **1082**

Text and facing translation of poems of St. Francis, Dante, Petrarch, Boccaccio, Lorenzo de' Medici, and Angelo Poliziano; the translations are largely from previously published works.

—— Wit and wisdom of the Italian Renaissance, ed. and tr. by Charles Speroni. Berkeley, University of California Press, 1964. 317 p. **1083**

Translation from the Latin and Italian writings of Poggio Bracciolini, Ludovico Carbone, Angelo Poliziano, Niccolò Angèli dal Bùcine, Leonardo da Vinci, Giovanni Pontano, and Piovano Arlotto [Arlotto Mainardi], as well as from some 16th-century writers. The genre is largely "facetiae," humorous anecdotes.

Italy. *Historical Sources.* The Spanish college at Bologna in the fourteenth century, ed. and tr. by Berthe M. Marti. Philadelphia, University of Pennsylvania Press, 1966. 393 p. **1084**

Text and facing translation of the statutes of the Spanish college.

J

Jacme d'Agramont, *d. 1349.* "Regiment de preservacio a epidemia o pestilencia e mortaldats; epistola de maestre Jacme d'Agramont . . .," tr. into English by M. L. Duran-Reynals and C.-E. A. Winslow, *Bulletin of the History of Medicine,* 23 (1949), 57–89. **1085**

An article by the same authors describing the manuscript here translated is found in the *Bulletin of the History of Medicine,* 22 (1948), 747–65: "Jacme d'Agramont and the first of the plague tractates."

Jacopo Ragona, *15th cent.* "Jacopo Ragona and his Rules for artificial memory," by Michael P. Sheridan, *Manuscripta,* 4 (1960), 131–47. **1086**

Includes a translation of an abridged text of the Rules.

Jalāl al-Dīn Rūmī, Mawlānā, *1207–1273.* Discourses of Rumi, tr. by Arthur J. Arberry. London, John Murray [c. 1962]. ix, 276 p. **1087**

Translation based on text edited in 1952, of four discourses, in both Arabic and Persian.

—— The life and work of Muhammad Jalal al-Din al-Rumi, by Afzal Iqbal. Lahore, Institute of Islamic Culture, 1956; 2d ed., rev., 1964. xv, 196 p. **1088**

Contains *passim* new translations by the author of many of Rumi's poems.

—— Makhzah al-Asrār, the treasury of mysteries, tr. by Ghulam Husayn Darab. London, Probsthain, 1945. 258 p. *Probsthain oriental ser.,* 27. **1089**

—— The Rubā'īyāt of Jalāl al-Dīn Rūmī, selections tr. into English verse, by A. J. Arberry. London, Emery Walker, 1949. xxviii, 209 p. **1090**

Contains translation of 360 quatrains "of what appeared to be the best" of the 1,980 quatrains in the Chester Beatty Manuscript; the text used is newly edited.

—— Rumi the Persian; rebirth in creativity and love, by A. Reza Arasteh, with a preface by Erich Fromm. Lahore, Ashraf [1965]. xx, 200 p. **1091**

Contains *passim* extensive quotations from Rumi, some from old translations, some apparently new by the author.

—— Rumi, poet and mystic, 1207–1273, selections from his writings tr. with intro. and notes by Reynold A. Nicholson. London, Allen & Unwin [1950]. 190 p. *Ethical and religious classics of East and West,* 1. **1092**

The translation was made in 1898 by Nicholson; but this reprint includes the text, with translation facing. *Cf.* Farrar and Evans, item 2215.

—— Sun of Tabriz, a lyrical introduction to higher metaphysics, selected poems, tr. by Colin Garbett. Cape Town, South Africa, Beerman, 1956. xiii, 77 p. **1093**

JALĀL AL-DĪN RŪMĪ

—— Tales from the Masnavi, [by] A. J. Arberry. London, Allen and Unwin [1961]. 300 p. UNESCO *collection of representative works, Persian series.* **1094**

Contains a hundred selections, one half the total.

—— More tales from the Masnavi, [by] A. J. Arberry. London, Allen and Unwin [1963]. 252 p. UNESCO *collection of representative works, Persian series.* **1095**

Contains another hundred tales.

Jāmī, *1414–1492.* FitzGerald's Salaman and Absal, a study by A. J. Arberry. Cambridge [Eng.], Cambridge University Press, 1956. vii, 205 p. *University of Cambridge Oriental publications,* 2. **1096**

Contains FitzGerald's first and last versions in verse, plus a literal prose translation by Arberry.

Jan van Ruysbroek, *1293–1381.* The Chastising of God's children and the Treatise of perfection of the sons of God, ed. from the mss. by Joyce Bazire and Eric Colledge. Oxford, Blackwell, 1957. x, 359 p. **1097**

An edition of Middle English translations, the first printed by Wynken de Worde, 1490, the second, printed here for the first time. Though the translations are from the early fifteenth century, they seem readable enough to list here.

—— The seven steps of the ladder of spiritual love, tr. from Flemish by F. Sherwood Taylor, with an intro. by Joseph Bolland. London, Dacre Press [1944]. viii, 63 p. **1098**

—— The spiritual espousals, tr. from the Dutch with an intro. by Eric Colledge. New York, Harper [1953]. 195 p. *Classics of the contemplative life.* **1099**

al-Jarsīfī, 'Umar ibn 'Uthman, *fl. 1250–1300?* "Al-Jarsīfī on the Ḥisba," by G. M. Wickens, *Islamic Quarterly,* 3 (1956), 176–87. **1100**

Translation of a Spanish-Arabic manual. For suggested revisions to this translation see "Observations on the text and translation of al-Jarsīfī's treatise on 'Hisba,'" by J. Derek Latham, *Journal of Semitic Studies,* 5 (1960), 124–43.

Jean de Meun, *d. 1305?* The Romance of the Rose, by Guillaume de Lorris and Jean Meun, tr. into English verse by Harry W. Robbins, ed. and with an intro., by Charles W. Dunn. New York, Dutton, 1962. xxxiii, 472 p. **1101**

Jeanne d'Arc, *Saint, 1412–1431.* The first biography of Joan of Arc, with the chronicle record of a contemporary account, tr. and annotated by Daniel Rankin and Claire Quintal. [Pittsburgh], University of Pittsburgh Press [1964]. xi, 155 p. **1102**

The biography is translated from an anonymous work written before 1515, the editor thinks, preserved as Ms. Fr. 518 in the Municipal Library at Orléans. The chronicle is the so-called Chronicle of Cordeliers, Bibliothèque Nationale Ms. 23018. This translation omits the letters in the chronicle and the records of the trials of Joan, but includes the epilog of letters of Henry VI.

—— Joan of Arc by herself and her witnesses, by Régine Pernoud., tr. by Edward Hyams. London, Macdonald & Co., 1964; New York, Stein and Day [1966]. 287 p. **1103**

The English translation is from the modern French version by Régine Pernoud, who constructed a narrative of Joan's life, condemnation, and rehabilitation trial from original documents, with interspersed commentary.

—— The trial of Joan of Arc, being the verbatim report of the proceedings from the Orléans Ms., tr. by W. S. Scott. London, Folio Society [1956]. 173 p. **1104**

The report of the rehabilitation trial of 1456 is omitted, but the compilation of chronicles on Joan's life and the report of the trial of 1431 are included. This translation and the one of Rankin and Quintal noted above thus overlap in that they both include the first part of the Orléans manuscript.

Jerome of Moravia, *fl. 1375.* "Two XIII century treatises on modal rhythm and the discant," by Janet Knapp, *Journal of Music Theory,* 6 (1962), 200–16. **1105**

Contains a translation of Jerome's Discantus positio vulgaris.

Jerome of Prague, *c. 1365–1416.* "The death of Jerome of Prague: divergent views," by Renée Neu Watkins, *Speculum,* 42 (1967), 104–29. **1106**

Contains in an appendix translation of a letter of Poggio Bracciolini (30 May 1416), a passage from an anonymous chronicler (Peter of Mladoňovice, the author suggests), and a comment of Theodore of Vrie on the Council of Constance.

Jews. *Historical sources.* Corpus papyrorum Judaicarum, ed. by Victor A. Tcherikover and Alexander Fuks. Cambridge, published for the Magnes Press, Hebrew University, by Harvard University Press, 1957–64. 3 v. **1107**

Vol. 3 has text and translation of documents concerning Jews in Egypt during late Roman and Byzantine periods, 1st to 7th century.

—— Jewish self-government in the middle ages, by L. Finkelstein, with a foreword by Alexander Marx. New York, P. Feldheim [1964]. 2d ed., xxviii, 390 p. **1108**

Text and translation of various documents, including ordinances, appear on pp. 109–382. The first edition, published by the Jewish Theological Seminary of America in 1924, was omitted in Farrar and Evans; this is merely a reprint, rather than a new edition.

—— The Jews in medieval Germany, a study of their legal and social status, by Guido Kisch. Chicago, University of Chicago Press [1949]. xv, 655 p. **1109**

Contains *passim* translation of many short excerpts from medieval German, Roman, and canon law.

—— The Marranos of Spain, from the late XIVth to the early XVIth century, according to contemporary Hebrew sources, by Benzion Netanyahu. New York, American Academy for Jewish Research, 1966. vii, 254 p. **1110**

Contains *passim* translation and paraphrase of Hebrew works otherwise not translated: exegesis, polemic, and responsa literature from Joseph Albo, Solomon Alami, Isaac Arama, Isaac Caro, among others.

—— "Relations between Jewish and Christian courts in the Middle Ages," by Guido Kisch, *Historia Judaica,* 21 (1959), 81–108. **1111**

Contains translation of excerpts from German law in a rare document of 1093 about the jurisdiction of the courts.

Jihān-Shāh, *sultan, 1438–67.* "Jihan-Shah Qara-Qoyunlu and his poetry," by V. Minorsky, *Bulletin of the School of Oriental and African Studies,* 16 (1954), 271–97. **1112**

Text and translation of eight poems in Persian and Turkish, as well as of biographical and critical material. The author, known as al-Ḥaqīqī, is also called Abul-Hamid, according to Professor Minorsky.

Joannes, *monk of Cluny, fl. 945.* St. Odo of Cluny, being the life of St. Odo of Cluny by John of Salerno, and the life of St. Gerard of Aurillac by St. Odo, tr. by Gerard Sitwell. London and New York, Sheed & Ward [1958]. xxix, 186 p. **1113**

Joannes Climacus, *Saint, c. 525–600.* The illustration of the Heavenly ladder of John Climacus, by John Rupert Martin. Princeton, Princeton University Press, 1954. vii, 198 p. **1114**

Has text, translation, and description of the illustrations for the Penitential canon, a hymn in honor of the "holy criminals" described in Ch. 5 of the Heavenly ladder, pp. 128–49.

—— St. John Climacus, the ladder of divine ascent, tr. by Archimandrite Lazarus Moore with an intro. by M. Heppell. London, Faber and Faber [1959]. 270 p. *Classics of the contemplative life.* **1115**

The translation includes five prefatory items from the Greek text. The translator says that the previous translation by Father Robert (Farrar and Evans, item 2262) "is often a paraphrase."

Joannes, *of Damascus, Saint, d. c. 754.* Writings [The fount of knowledge, etc.] tr. by Frederic H. Chase, Jr. New York, Fathers of the Church, 1958. l, 426 p. *Fathers of the Church,* 37. **1116**

Contains translations of The fount of knowledge, On heresies, The orthodox faith.

Joannes, *of Hildesheim, d. 1375.* The story of the Three Kings: Melchior, Balthasar, and Jaspar, which originally was written by John of Hildesheim in the fourteenth century and is now retold by Margaret B. Freeman. New York, Metropolitan Museum of Art, 1955. 80 p. **1117**

The translator has used two Middle English texts as the basis of her version, with additions from Latin and German versions, the total rearranged to form a coherent story. The two Middle English texts were edited in the Early English Text Society series by Carl Horstman.

Jocelin de Brakelond, *fl. 1200.* The chronicle of Jocelin of Brakelond concerning the acts of Samson, abbot of the monastery of St. Edmund, tr. by H. E. Butler. Edinburgh, Nelson [1949]; New York, Oxford University Press, 1949. xxviii, 139, 139 [140]–167 p. *Medieval classics.* **1118**

Text and facing translation.

Johannes XXI, *pope, d. 1277.* The Summulae logicales of Peter of Spain [ed. and tr. by] Joseph P. Mullally. Notre Dame, Ind., University of Notre Dame Press, 1945. civ, 172 p. *University of Notre Dame publications in medieval studies,* 8. **1119**

Text and facing translation of the seventh (last) tract only, De proprietatibus terminorum or "logica moderna."

Johannes de Tepla, *c. 1350–1414?* Death and the plowman; or, The Bohemian plowman; a disputatious and consolatory dialogue about death from the year 1400, tr. from the modern German version of Alois Bernt, by Ernest N. Kirrmann. Chapel Hill, University of North Carolina Press [1958]. xviii, 40 p. *University of North Carolina studies in the Germanic languages and literatures, 22.* **1120**

—— The plowman from Bohemia, by Johannes von Saaz, tr. by Alexander and Elizabeth Henderson, intro. by Reinhold Schneider. New York, Ungar [c. 1966]. 117 p. **1121**

Text and facing translation. The author is also known as Jan Zatecky; the Library of Congress prefers *Johannes de Tepla.*

Johannes Mercurius Corrigiensis, *15th cent.* "An hermetic plague-tract by Johannes Mercurius Corrigiensis: text, translation, and bio-bibliography of the author," by W. B. McDaniel 2d, *Transactions and Studies of the College of Physicians of Philadelphia,* 9 (1941–42), 96–111; 217–25. **1122**

The first part of this article contains text and facing translation of a description of the plague and its cure. The author suggests that Corrigiensis may be a fictional character to whom the work is ascribed; it may actually be by Lodovicus Enoch Lazarellus, b. 1450.

John of Salisbury, *bp of Chartres, d. 1180.* Historia Pontificalis, memoirs of the Papal court, tr. with an intro. and notes by Marjorie Chibnall. London, Nelson [1956]. l, 109 p. *Medieval texts.* **1123**

Text and facing translation of a work by the "most accomplished Latin stylist of the twelfth century," according to the translator.

—— Letters, ed. by W. J. Millor, tr. by H. E. Butler, rev. by C. N. L. Brooke. London, Nelson, [1955–]. *Medieval texts.* **1124**

Vol. 1 contains letters nos. 1–135, written 1153–61 when the author was secretary to Archbishop Theobald of Bec. No further volumes have appeared, the translator having died before this volume was fully complete.

—— The metalogicon, a twelfth-century defense of the verbal and logical arts of the trivium, tr. with an intro. and notes by Daniel D. McGarry. Berkeley, University of California Press, 1955. xxvii, 305 p. **1125**

Joinville, Jean, *sire de, 1224?–1317?* Chronicles of the crusades, ed. and tr. by Margaret Renée Bryers. Baltimore, Penguin Books [1963]. 362 p. **1126**

Contains the Life of St. Louis by Joinville and Villehardouin's Conquest of Constantinople; these are records of the fourth and seventh crusades, neither of which reached Jerusalem.

—— The life of St. Louis, tr. by René Hague from the text ed. by Natalis de Wailly. New York, Sheed & Ward, 1955. 306 p. **1127**

A memoir of the seventh crusade, with special emphasis on Louis IX, King of France, d. 1270; an appendix contains translation of various documents associated with Louis: letters and his epitaph.

Jómsvíkinga saga. The saga of the Jómsvíkings, tr. by Lee M. Hollander. Austin, University of Texas Press, 1955. 116 p. **1128**

This is an historical saga, according to Professor Hollander, written about two centuries after the Jómsvíkings were crushed by the Danes in 986.

—— The saga of the Jomsvikings, tr. with intro., notes, and appendices, by

JORDAN OF SAXONY

Norman F. Blake. London and New York, Nelson [1962]. xxviii, 44, 44, [45]–56 p. *Icelandic texts.* **1129**

Text and facing translation.

Jordan of Saxony, *d. 1237.* Love among the saints, the letters of Blessed Jordan of Saxony to Blessed Diana of Andalò, tr. by Kathleen Pond. London, Bloomsbury Publishing Co., 1958. vii, 139 p. **1130**

Contains translation of fifty letters to Diana plus fragments of two letters to an unknown nun about the death of Henry, Prior of Cologne. The ascription of the letters to Johannes von Quedlinberg, d. 1380, is erroneous.

—— To heaven with Diana, a study of Jordan of Saxony and Diana d'Andalo, with a translation of the letters of Jordan, by Gerald Vann. New York, Pantheon Books; London, Collins, 1960. 158 p. **1131**

Six "other letters" of Jordan are contained in an appendix, in addition to the letters to Diana.

Josephus, Flavius, *37–95?* Josephus. London, Heinemann; New York, Putnam, 1926–65. 9 v. *Loeb classics.* **1132**

Vol. 1–4 were translated by H. St. J. Thackeray, vol. 5 by Thackeray and R. Marcus, vols. 6–8 by R. Marcus, and vol. 9 by L. H. Feldman. Contents are: vol. 1, The life; Against Apion; vols. 2–3, The Jewish War; vols. 4–9, Jewish antiquities. Selections from this translation, ed. by Moses I. Finley, were published by Washington Square Press, New York, 1965, xxxvi, 347 p. Another translation of The Jewish war was made by G. A. Williamson, Baltimore, Penguin Books, 1959, 411 p. Another selection made by Nahum N. Glatzer entitled Jerusalem and Rome, the writings of Josephus, was published by Meridian Books in 1960, 320 p.

Joveynī, ʻAlā al-Dīn ʻAṭā Malek, *1226–1283.* The history of the World-Conqueror, by ʻAla-ad-Din ʻAta-Malik Juvaini, tr. from the text of Mirza Muhammad Qazvini by John Andrew Boyle. Cambridge, Harvard University Press, 1958. 2 v. UNESCO *collection of representative works, Persian series.* **1133**

Translation of an eyewitness account of the Mongols in Persia after the death of Jenghis Khan.

Judah, ha-Levi, *12th cent.* Jehuda Halevi, Kazari, the book of proof and argument, abridged edition by Isaak Heinemann. Oxford, Phaidon Press, 1947. 147 p. *East and West Library, Philosophica Judaica.* **1134**

The editor says he has based his translation on that of Hirschfeld (see Farrar and Evans, item 2304) but refers to "my translations of the Arabic text," apparently into German? The preface, introduction, and commentary were translated from German by Mrs. Hebe R. Mayer-Bentwick. Four poems translated by Nina Salaman (*cf.* Farrar and Evans, item 2305) are also included.

Judaism. *Collections.*

See also *Hebrew literature. Collections; Midrash; Mishnah; Talmud; Liturgy and Ritual, Jewish.*

Basic sources of the Judaeo-Christian tradition, ed. by Fred Berthold *et al.* Englewood Cliffs, N.J., Prentice-Hall, 1962. xi, 444 p. **1135**

Contains translation of The manual of discipline from the Dead Sea Scrolls, excerpts from the Talmud and Moses ben Maimon's Thirteen principles, as well as of many medieval Christian documents.

—— Conscience on trial, three public disputations between Christians and Jews in the thirteenth and fifteenth centuries, tr. by Morris Braude. New York, Exposition Press [1952]. 1136

Includes the 13th-century disputations of Rabbi Yechiel of Paris *vs.* Nicholas Donin and of Moses ben Nachmann (Nachmanides) *vs.* Pablo Christiani; and the 15th-century Tortosa disputation of Spanish rabbis and Antipope Benedict XIII (Pedro de Luna) *vs.* Geronimo de Santa Fé.

—— Days of awe, being a treasury of traditions, legends, and learned commentaries concerning Rosh ha-Shanah, Yom Kippur, and the days between, culled from three hundred volumes . . . by Samuel J. Agnon, [ed. by Nahum N. Glatzer, tr. by Maurice T. Galpert]. New York, Schocken Books [1948]. 300 p. 1137

An abridged version of Agnon's Yamim noraim.

—— "The dietary laws of the Damascus covenant in relation to those of the Karaites," by Norman Golb, *The Journal of Jewish Studies,* 8 (1957), 51–69. 1138

Contains translation of the laws, pp. 58–69.

—— Encyclopedia of Biblical interpretation, a millennial anthology, by Menachem Mendel Kasher, tr. under the editorship of Harry Freedman. New York, American Biblical Encylopedia Society [1953–67]. 7 v. 1139

This is a translation of part of the Torah Shelemah (35 v.), which contains all known Jewish commentary on the Bible from the 6th to the 16th centuries.

—— Faith and knowledge, the Jew in the medieval world, ed. and intro. by Nahum N. Glatzer. Boston, Beacon Press, 1963. xx, 227 p. 1140

Selections by various translators, revised by the editor, from several authors including Judah ha-Levi, Judah the Pious (12th or 13th century, Germany), Moses ben Maimon.

—— "Four unpublished poems in Rylands Hebrew Ms. 6—one by Abraham (Ibn Ezra?)" by M. Wallenstein, *Bulletin of the John Rylands Library,* Manchester, 44 (January, 1962), 238–44. 1141

Hebrew text and translation, with commentary, of four sacred poems.

—— The great Jewish books and their influence on history, ed. by Samuel Caplan and Harold U. Ribalow, intro. by Ludwig Lewisohn. New York, Horizon Press, 1952; London, Vision Press, 1963. 351 p. 1142

An anthology of translations and commentary; selections from the Talmud, prayerbook, the Zohar, Rashi (Solomon ben Isaac), Maimonides, and Judah ha-Levi, from the medieval period.

—— Hebraic literature; translations from the Talmud, midrashim, and Kabbala, ed. and tr. by Maurice H. Harris. New York, Tudor Publishing Co. 1946. 1143

This work has not been seen.

—— In time and eternity, a Jewish reader, ed. by Nahum N. Glatzer. New York, Schocken Books, 1946. 255 p. 1144

The translation was done largely by Olga Marx, according to the introduction. A later volume by the same editor, The rest is commentary (Boston, Beacon Press, 1961, 271 p.), contains somewhat longer excerpts than In time and eternity, from post-Biblical Jewish documents.

—— Jewish gnosticism, Merkabah mysticism, and Talmudic tradition, by Gershom G. Scholem. New York, Jewish Theological Seminary of America, 1960. 120 p. **1145**

Contains translation *passim* of works of uncertain date, 3d–6th centuries, including hymns of the Greater Hekhaloth.

—— Jewish religious polemic of early and later centuries, a study of documents here rendered in English by Oliver Shaw Rankin. Edinburgh, Edinburgh University Press, 1956. viii, 256 p. *Edinburgh University publications in language and literature*, 9. **1146**

Contains translation of the Chronicle of Moses, dating from perhaps the 2d century, Rankin thinks, but compiled between the 6th and 13th centuries; "Memoir of the Book of Nizzachon of Rabbi Lipman," a poem of the early 15th century; the Debate of Rabbi Moses ben Nachman, 1195–1270, rabbi of Gerona, and Fra Paulo (Pablo Christiani).

—— Judaism, ed. by Arthur Hertzberg. New York, Braziller, 1961. 256 p. *Great religions of modern man.* **1147**

Short excerpts with commentary, arranged topically, from rabbinic commentaries, letters of Maimonides and others; some of the translation is new for this volume.

—— Judaism and Islam, Biblical and Talmudic backgrounds of the Koran and its commentaries, by Abraham I. Katsch. New York, New York University Press, 1954. xxv, 265 p. **1148**

Contains Suras II and III of the Koran in Palmer's translation (see Farrar and Evans, item 2372) with translation by the author of the Rabbinic sources for them. The work was reprinted as Judaism and the Koran, New York, Barnes, 1962.

—— Karaite anthology, excerpts from the early literature, tr. from Arabic, and Hebrew sources, with notes by Leon Nemoy. New Haven, Yale University Press, 1952. xxvi, 412 p. *Yale Judaica series*, 7. **1149**

Translation (text not included) of works written by Karaites, a sect of Iraqui Jews who rejected the orthodox Rabbinate interpretation of the Talmud. The selections include chronicles, travel literature, excerpts from liturgy, Biblical commentary, poetry. By the 10th century, the Karaites had spread to Jerusalem, Spain, the Caucasus, Egypt.

—— Karaites in Byzantium, the formative years, 970–1100, by Zvi Ankori. New York, Columbia University Press; Jerusalem, Weizman Science Press, 1959. xiii, 546 p. **1150**

Contains *passim* translation of Karaite commentary, particularly by Tobias ben Eliezer of Castoria and Thessalonica and Tobias ben Moses (11th century).

—— The last trial on the legends and lore of the command to Abraham to offer Isaac as a sacrifice: the Akedah, by Shalom Spiegel, tr. from Hebrew by Judah Goldin. Philadelphia, Jewish Publication Society of America [c. 1967]. xxvi, 162 p. **1151**

A study of the legend, with translation of midrash and of medieval poems on it; includes a translation in full of the poem Akedah by Ephraim ben Jacob of Bonn, 12th century.

—— Major trends in Jewish mysticism, by Gershom G. Scholem. New York, Schocken Books [c. 1946]. xiv, 454 p. **1152**

Contains *passim* in text and notes translation and paraphrase of many works, often directly from manuscripts. Later editions (1954, 1961) have some additions to both text and bibliography.

—— The Passover anthology, ed. by Philip Goodman. Philadelphia, Jewish Publication Society of America [*c.* 1961]. 496 p. **1153**

Chapters on the Passover in medieval Jewish literature and in Jewish law contain translations from many Jewish writers.

—— A Rabbinic anthology, sel. and arr. with comments and introductions by C. G. Montifiore and H. Loewe. London, Macmillan, 1938. cviii, 853 p. **1154**

This anthology has been often reprinted, most recently by the World Publishing Company of Cleveland, 1963. It was not listed in Farrar and Evans.

—— The Talmudic anthology, tales and teachings of the rabbis, sel. and ed. by Louis I. Newman and Samuel Spitz. [New York], Behrman [c. 1945]. xxxiv, 570 p. **1155**

Topically arranged excerpts from Talmud, midrash, Zohar; many selections are newly translated by the editors.

—— A treasury of responsa, ed. by Solomon B. Freehof. Philadelphia, Jewish Publication Society of America, 1963 [c. 1962]. 313 p. **1156**

Anthology of translations from writings on Jewish law in answer to questions put to the gaonim. Pages 1–96 contain material from the 10th to the 16th century.

—— The wisdom of Israel, ed. by Lewis Browne. New York, Random House [1945]. xxxii, 748 p. **1157**

Translation of excerpts from mishnah, gemara, midrash, and from many authors. A revised edition was published in London by Michael Joseph, 1955, 596 p.; the original volume was reprinted by Modern Library in 1956.

Juliana, *anchoret, 1343–1443.* Juliana of Norwich: an introductory appreciation and an interpretative anthology, by P. Franklin Chambers. London, Gollancz, 1955. 224 p. **1158**

Excerpts from Juliana's works are rearranged and translated by the author.

—— Lent with Mother Julian, readings from her "Revelations of divine love," ed. by Leo Sherley-Price. London, Mowbray; New York, Morehouse-Barlow, 1962. 69 p. **1159**

I have been unable to locate a copy of this work in the United States to determine whether the editor is also the translator. The reference was obtained from the British National Bibliography, but the book is not listed by the British Museum or the Library of Congress.

—— The revelations of divine love of Julian of Norwich, tr. by James Walsh. New York, Harper [c. 1961]. xix, 210 p. **1160**

This is a translation of the so-called longer version, based on a collation of the Paris and Sloane manuscripts.

Julianus Pomerius, *fl. 497.* The contemplative life, tr. by Mary Josephine Suelzer. Westminster, Md., Newman Press, 1947. 220 p. **1161**

A translation of De vita contemplativa, ascribed to Prosper of Aquitaine until the 17th century, according to the translator.

al-Junayd ibn Muḥammad, Abū al-Qāsim, *d. 910?* "The doctrine of al-Junayd, analytical study of the doctrine of al-Junayd based on his letters," by Ali Abdel-Kader, *Islamic Quarterly,* 1 (1954), 167–77. **1162**

Contains extensive translation of excerpts from the letters. Another article by the same translator in the same volume, pp. 219–28, "Al-Junayd's theory of Fanā," contains translation from a risāla on fanā, oblivion.

—— Hindu and Muslim mysticism, by R. C. Zaehner. London, University of London Athlone Press, 1960. 234 p. **1163**

Contains on pp. 218–24 a translation of part of al-Junayd's Kitāb al-Fanā.

—— The life, personality, and writings of al-Junayd, a study of a third/ninth century mystic, ed. and tr. by Ali Hassan Abdel-Kader. London, Luzac, 1962. xviii, 183, 64 p. *Gibb memorial series,* n.s. 22. **1164**

Translation and text of the Rasā'il or "Sayings" of al-Junayd, as well as letters. Some of this translation appeared earlier in *Islamic Quarterly,* 1 (1954), 71–89.

Justinus, *Martyr, Saint, d. 165.* Saint Justin Martyr: The first apology, the second apology, dialogue with Trypho, exhortation to the Greeks, discourse to the Greeks, the monarchy, or the rule of God, by Thomas B. Falls. Washington, Catholic University of America Press [1948]. 486 p. *Fathers of the Church,* 6. **1165**

The first three works mentioned in the title are considered genuine works of Justin, according to the editor; the Exhortation to the Greeks, Discourse to the Greeks, and The monarchy, or Rule of God, are attributed to him but possibly erroneously. The translation seems to have been made from an intermediary Latin translation rather than directly from the Greek.

—— Selections from Justinus Martyr's Dialogue with Trypho, ed. and tr. by Richard P. C. Hanson. London, United Society for Christian Literature [1963]; New York, Association Press [1964]. 80 p. *World Christian books,* 3d series, 49. **1166**

A new translation of an apologetical work seeking to convert Trypho, a Jew, to Christianity.

K

Kalevala. Kalevala, a prose translation from the Finnish by A. K. Johnson. Hancock, Mich., The Book Concern, 1950. 278 p. **1167**

An abridged translation.

—— The Kalevala, or poems of the Kaleva district, compiled by Elias Lönnrot, a prose translation with foreword and appendices by Francis P. Magoun, Jr. Cambridge, Harvard University Press, 1963. xxiv, 410 p. **1168**

A translation of the 1849 longer version.

al-Kāshī, Jamshīd ibn Mas'ūd, *d. c. 1436.* The extraction of the n-th root in the sexagesimal notation, tr. by Abdul-Kader Dakhel, ed. by Wasfi Hijab and E. S. Kennedy. Beirut, American University [1960]. 42 p. *Sources and studies in the history of the exact sciences,* 2. **1170**

Facsimile text and facing translation of ch. 5 of Treatise 3 of "The Key to Arithmetic," Miftāḥ al-Ḥisāb.

—— Ghiyath al-Din al-Kashi's letter on Ulugh Bey and the scientific activity in Samarquand, by Aydin Sayili. Ankara, Türk Tarik Kurumu Basimevi, 1960. 115 p. *Publication of the Turkish Historical Association,* ser. 7, no. 49. **1171**

Persian text translated into English and Turkish, with analysis in Turkish of al-Kāshī's letter to his father about the scientific activity in Samarquand organized and patronized by Ulugh Bey; the letter was written *c.* 1420 at the time of the construction of a new observatory.

—— "Al-Kashi's Treatise on astronomical observational instruments," by E. S. Kennedy, *Journal of the Near East Society,* 20 (1961), 98–108. 1172

Contains Persian text and translation of a short treatise on medieval observatory equipment.

—— "A letter of Jamshīd al-Kāshī to his father," tr. by E. S. Kennedy, *Orientalia,* 29 (1960), 191–213. 1173

A translation of the same letter as above. This translation was reprinted with the subtitle "Scientific research and personalities at a fifteenth century court," Rome, Pontificium Institutum Biblicum, 1960.

—— "A medieval interpolation scheme using second order differences," by E. S. Kennedy, pp. 117–20 in A Locust's Leg, studies in honor of S. H. Taqizadeh, ed. by W. B. Henning and E. Yarshater. London, Humphries, 1962. 1174

Translation of a method of solving an astronomical problem.

—— The planetary equatorium of Jamshīd Ghiyāth al-Dīn al-Kāshī (d. 1429): an edition of the anonymous Persian manuscript 75 ⟨44b⟩ in the Garrett Collection at Princeton University; being a description of two computing instruments, the plate of heavens and the plate of conjunction, with translation and commentary by E. S. Kennedy. Princeton, Princeton University Press, 1960. xv, 267 p. *Princeton Oriental studies,* 18. 1175

Facsimile text and facing translation of a Persian redaction of al-Kāshī's Arabic text Nuzhat al-ḥād'iq, "A fruit garden stroll," written 1416.

Kaykāvūs ibn Iskandar ibn Qābūs, 'Unṣur al-Ma'ālī, *1021 or 1022–1098 or 1099.* A mirror for princes, the Qābūs nāma, by Kai Kā'ūs ibn Iskandar, Prince of Gurgān, tr. from the Persian by Reuben Levy. New York, Dutton [1951]. xxi, 265 p. 1176

The translation is based on Levy's edition of the text for the Gibb Memorial Series, 1951. The work represents not only precepts for the education of princes but Islamic ethics.

Khāqānī, Afẓal al-Dīn Shirrānī, *c. 1126–1198 or 1199.* "Khāqānī and Andronicus Comnenus," by V. Minorsky, *Bulletin of the School of Oriental and African Studies,* 11 (1945), 550–78; reprinted in Iranica, twenty articles by V. Minorsky, Tehran [University of Tehran Press], 1964, 120–50. 1177

Contains a translation of his "Christian" ode addressed to Andronicus, a satirical poem addressed to a Christian ruler in which the poet really avers his fidelity to Islam.

al-Khaṭīb al-Tibrīzī, Muḥammad ibn 'Abd, *fl. 1336.* Mishkāt-ul-Maṣābīḥ, English translation with explanatory notes by James Robson. Lahore, Ashraf [1960–65]. 4 v. in 5. 1178

A commentary on the hadith, traditions of Islam collected by al-Baghawī (d. *c.* 1120) and revised by al-Khaṭīb. Contains more than two thousand traditions, with indication of their sources. Farrar and Evans enter this author as Muḥammad ibn 'Abd Allāh al-Khaṭīb.

al-Khayyāt, Abū al-Ḥusayn ibn Uthmān. Kitāb al-Intiṣar, by al-Khayyāt, tr. by Albīr N. Nādir. Beyrouth, Editions les lettres orientales, 1957. 175, 156 p. **1179**

Text and English translation of a "refutation of a refutation," the only surviving book of the Mu'tazila, a heretical Islamic sect, according to the translator.

al-Khwārizmī, Muḥammad ibn Aḥmad, *fl. c. 976.* "The logic chapter of Muḥammad ibn Aḥmad al-Kwārizimī's encyclopedia, Keys to science (c. 980)," by Nicholas Rescher, *Archiv für Geschichte der Philosophie,* 44 (1962), 62–74. **1180**

A translation of the 2d chapter of the 2d part of the work, valuable for definitions of Aristotelian logical terms.

—— "The science of music in the Mafātīḥ al-'ulūm," by Henry G. Farmer, *Transactions of the Glasgow Oriental Society,* 17 (1957–58), 1–9. **1181**

A translation of Part II, Section 7, from a tenth-century encyclopedia containing definitions of musical terms.

Al-Khwārizmī, Muḥammad ibn Musa, *fl. c. 840.* The astronomical tables of al-Khwarizmi, translation with commentary of the Latin version ed. by H. Suter . . . by O. Neugebauer. Copenhagen, Munksgaard, 1962. 247 p. *Historisk-filosofiske skrifter, Det koneglige Danske videnskabernes Selskab,* 4, no. 2. **1182**

The Arabic original having been lost, the translation is made from the Latin version of Adelard of Bath, based on the Arabic of al-Majrītī, *fl.* 1000.

Kimchi, David, *1160–1235.* David Kimchi's Hebrew grammar (Mikhol), ed. by William Chomsky. New York, Bloch, 1952. xxxiv, 427 p. **1183**

Part I of this work was published in 1933; see Farrar and Evans, item 2363. That part plus the rest of the work is now translated.

al-Kindī, *d. c. 873.* "Al-Kindī on the 'Ēthos' of rhythm, colour, and perfume," by Henry G. Farmer, *Transactions of the Glasgow Oriental Society,* 16 (1955–56), 29–38. **1184**

Contains translation of a treatise concerning the Informative Parts of music.

—— "Al-Kindī's Epistle on the concentric structure of the universe," by Haig Khatchadourian and Nicholas Rescher, *Isis,* 56 (1965), 190–95. **1185**

First translation into any European language of a short treatise first edited in 1953.

—— "Al-Kindī's Epistle on the finitude of the universe," by Nicholas Rescher and Haig Khatchadourian, *Isis,* 56 (1965), 426–33. **1186**

—— "Al-Kindī's Treatise on the distinctiveness of the celestial sphere," by Nicholas Rescher and Haig Khatchadourian, *Islamic Studies,* 4 (1965), 45–54. **1187**

Translation of a work parallel to Aristotle's De caelo in which al-Kindī attempts to demonstrate that there is a fifth substance which makes up the outer heavens.

—— "Al-Kindī's Treatise on the intellect," by Richard J. M. McCarthy, *Islamic Studies,* 3 (1964), 119–49. **1188**

Text and "tentative" translation of the treatise and of other relevant passages from al-Kindī.

—— The medical formulary or Aqrābādhīn, ed. and tr. by Martin Levey.

Madison, University of Wisconsin Press, 1966. xiii, 410 p. *University of Wisconsin publications in medieval science,* 7. **1189**

Facsimile text and facing translation of a newly discovered list or register of drugs; the translator aims at "clarification . . . of the medical and technical aspects of the work," and includes indices of words in the work in thirty-four languages plus Greek and Latin, giving a synonymic list of Arabic *materia medica.* Excerpts from Ibn Waḥsh'īya (*fl.* before 912) and from Abū'l Faḍl Dā'ūd b.a. al-Bayān al Isrā'īlī (*b.* 1161) are also translated and the editor states that he intends soon to issue complete translations from these authors. Some translation appeared earlier in *Chymia,* 8 (1962), 11–20.

—— Al-Kindī, the philosopher of the Arabs, by George N. Atiyeh. Rawalpindi [Pakistan], Islamic Research Institute, 1966. **1190**

Appendices II and III contain translation by A. S. B. Ansari of "The sayings of al-Kindi" and "On the intellect." The full name of the al-Kindī who died *c.* 873 is Yakub ibn Ishāk. The only al-Kindī referred to in Farrar and Evans is 'Abd al-Masīḥ ibn Isḥāk, al-Kindī, 10th century (items 12 and 13). It would appear that these items should have been ascribed to the 9th-century al-Kindī, who was a philosopher and scientist; at any rate, all of the works listed here are of 9th century provenience.

Kitāb fī bayān faḍl. Arab archery, an Arabic manuscript of about A.D. 1500, "A book on the excellence of the bow and arrow," and the description thereof, tr. and ed. by Nabih Amin Faris and Robert P. Elmer. Princeton, Princeton University Press, 1945. xi, 182 p. **1191**

Translation of Kitāb fī bayān faḍl, Ms. 793 in the Descriptive catalog of the Garrett Collection of Arabic manuscripts in the Princeton University Library.

Koran. The Holy Quran with English translation and commentary, ed. by Malik Ghulām Farīd [tr. by Maulavi Shir 'Alī]. Rabwah, W. Pakistan [M. Mas'ud Ahmad], 1947–63. 3 v. **1192**

Text and facing translation. A second edition which began appearing in 1964 apparently has no text; a copy has not been seen. The place and publisher vary with different volumes.

—— The holy Qur'an, Arabic text, translation and commentary, by Maulana Muhammad Ali. Lahore, Ahmadiyyah Anjuman, 1951. lxxvi, 1254 p. **1193**

This fourth edition (originally published 1917; *cf.* Farrar and Evans, item 2375) is said by the translator to contain extensive revisions; it includes the text and translation in double columns. A third revised edition without the text appeared in 1948. Without comparison to earlier editions it is impossible to tell when the revisions occurred; this may be merely a reprint of a pre- 1942 revision.

—— The Koran, a new translation, by N. J. Dawood. [Harmondsworth, Eng.], Penguin Books [1956]. 428 p. **1194**

The chapters have been rearranged but the traditional chapter numbers have been included.

—— The Koran interpreted, by Arthur J. Arberry. London, Allen & Unwin; New York, Macmillan, 1955. 2 v. London, Oxford University Press, 1964. xiii, 674. *World's classics.* **1195**

Arberry has used the term "interpreted" as less offensive to Moslems than "translated," but his work is in our terms a complete translation, in a rhythmical prose which attempts to reproduce the style as well as the sense of the original. The introduction reviews the history of English versions of the Koran.

SELECTIONS

—— A book of Quranic laws; an exhaustive treatise with full Quranic text, compiled by Muhammad V. Merchant. Lahore, Ashraf [1947]. vi, 232 p. **1196**

Laws from the Koran arranged topically, Doctrine of God, Prayers, Fasts, etc.

—— The short Koran, designed for easy reading, ed. by George M. Lamsa. Chicago, Ziff-Davis Publishing Co. [1949]. xx, 377 p. **1197**

An arrangement in topical order, based on the George Sales translation (1891).

—— The holy Koran, an introduction with selections, by Arthur J. Arberry. New York, Macmillan; London, Allen & Unwin [1953]. 141 p. *Ethical and religious classics of East and West,* 9. **1198**

About one sixth of the Koran is translated; the selections present Koranic teaching on the nature of God and evidence of his existence, some of the personal experiences of Muhammad, and accounts of the experience of earlier prophets. *Cf.* Arberry's complete translation above.

—— The Koran, selected suras, tr. by Arthur Jeffery. New York, Limited Editions Club, 1958. 231 p. **1199**

This volume has not been seen.

—— The students Koran, ed. [and tr.?] by Hashim Amir Ali. New York, Asia Publishing House [c. 1961]. xxx, 154 p. **1200**

Contains the earliest twenty-five suras, according to a chronological plan. There is no indication as to whether this is a new translation or not.

Kormáks saga. The sagas of Kormák and The sworn brothers, tr. with intro. and notes by Lee M. Hollander. Princeton, Princeton University Press, 1949. xi, 217 p. **1201**

Translation of Kormáksaga and of Þorgeir and Þormód suari brœðr; both are biographic sagas, written by skalds, according to the translator.

Kritoboulos, *15th cent.* History of Mehmed the Conqueror, tr. from the Greek by Charles T. Riggs. Princeton, Princeton University Press, 1954. ix, 222 p. **1202**

Translation of a chronicle covering from the Turkish point of view the reign of Muḥammad II, Sultan of Turkey, for the years 1451–68; essentially a history of Constantinople for this time.

Kūshyar ibn Labbān, *10th cent.* Principles of Hindu reckoning, a translation with intro. and notes . . . by Martin Levey and Marvin Petruck. Madison, University of Wisconsin Press, 1965. xi, 114 p. *University of Wisconsin publications in medieval science,* 8. **1203**

Facsimile text and facing translation of Kitāb fī uṣūl ḥisāb al-hind, "one of the most important of Arabic arithmetical treatises," according to the editor; it shows not only Arabic transmission but Arabic contributions. The text is that of the only extant Arabic manuscript compared with a Hebrew translation of it by Shālōm ben Joseph 'Anābī, 15th century.

L

Labīd ibn Rabī'a, *d. c. 661.* "A prose translation of the *Mo'allqah of Labīd* by William Wright," by Ursula Schedler, *Journal of Semitic Studies,* 6 (1961), 97–104. **1204**

This translation of one of the seven poems in the Mu'allaqat was discovered recently in a book which had belonged to Professor Wright, Professor of Arabic at Cambridge, 1870–89. See also item 1404 below.

Lacnunga. Anglo-Saxon magic and medicine, illustrated specially from the semi-pagan text "Lacnunga," by J. H. G. Grattan and Charles Singer. London and New York, Oxford University Press, 1952. xii, 234 p. *Publications of the Wellcome Historical Medical Museum,* n.s., 3. **1205**

Lacnunga is edited from Ms. Harley 585, British Museum. Text in Latin and Anglo-Saxon, facing translation.

—— Anglo-Saxon magic, ed. [and tr.] by Godfrid Storms. The Hague, Nijhoff, 1948. xiii, 336 p. **1206**

Part II contains text and facing translations of eighty-six charms from Lacnunga and Laece boc and other manuscripts, newly edited here. The first English translation of Lacnunga and Laece boc (1864–66) has been reissued with an introduction by Charles Singer by the Holland Press, London, 1961, in 3 v.; *cf.* Farrar and Evans, items 2391 and 2395.

Lactantius, Lucius Caecilius Firmianus, *d. c. 325.* The divine institutes, books I–VII, tr. by Mary Francis McDonald. Washington, Catholic University of America Press [1964]. xxv, 561 p. *Fathers of the Church,* 49. **1207**

—— Lactantius' Epitome of the Divine Institutes, ed. and tr. with a commentary by E. H. Blakeney. London, S.P.C.K., 1950. xiv, 175 p. **1208**

Text and translation of Lactantius' own summary of the Divinae institutiones.

—— Minor works, tr. by Mary F. McDonald. Washington, Catholic University of America Press, 1965. x, 248 p. *Fathers of the Church,* 54. **1209**

Contains translation of The workmanship of God, The wrath of God, The deaths of the persecutors, The phoenix, and two works attributed to Lactantius: On the motions of the soul and a poem On the passion of our Lord.

Lanfranc, *abp. of Canterbury, 1005?–1089.* The monastic constitutions, tr. with intro. and notes by David Knowles. London and New York, Nelson [1951]. xl, 149, 149, [150]–157 p. *Medieval classics.* **1210**

Text and facing translation of Decreta Lanfranchi, a rule for "novices according to the custom of the Church of Canterbury," based on the Cluniac rule.

Langland, William, *1330?–1400?* The book concerning Piers the Plowman, tr. . . . by Donald and Rachel Attwater. London, Dent; New York, Dutton [1957]. xv, 208 p. *Everyman's library.* **1211**

An alliterative verse translation; includes the translation of the B version published by Donald Attwater in 1930 (*cf.* Farrar and Evans, item 2408) plus The Vision of Do-well, Do-Better and Do-Best, tr. by Rachel Attwater.

—— Piers the Ploughman, tr. into modern English with an intro. by J. F. Goodridge. [Harmondsworth, Eng.] Penguin Books, [1959]. 365 p. *Penguin classics,* L87. **1212**

A translation in prose of the B text.

—— Visions from Piers Plowman, taken from the poems of William Langland

and tr. into modern English by Nevill Coghill. London, Phoenix House [1949]. 143 p. **1213**

Alliterative verse translation of excerpts from the B text.

Laxdœla saga. The Laxdœla saga, tr. by A. Margaret Arent. Seattle, University of Washington Press [1964]. xlii, 210 p. **1214**

This 13th-century saga is both a regional and a family saga, according to the translator.

Leabhar gabhála. Lebor gabála Érenn, the Book of the taking of Ireland, Part V, ed. and tr. by R. A. S. MacAlister. Dublin, for the Irish Texts Society, 1956. *Irish Texts Society*, 44. **1215**

The first four parts appeared in 1938–41; *cf.* Farrar and Evans, item 2432.

Leabhar méig. The Book of Magauran, Leabhar méig Shamhradháin, ed. [and tr.] by Lambert McKenna. Dublin, Institute for Advanced Studies, 1947. xxvi, 470 p. **1216**

Text and prose translation of a work copied by Ruaidhrí Ó Cianáin, d. 1387. The work contains bardic poems on the Brian family and is the earliest example of a duanaire, an official family book, according to the editor.

Leabhar na g-cert. Lebor na Cert, the Book of rights, ed. [and tr.] by Myles Dillon. Dublin, for the Irish Texts Society, 1962. xxv, 194 p. *Irish Texts Society*, 46. **1217**

Text and prose translation of poems about the rights of Irish kings, usually in terms of tributes and stipends. A compilation, probably from the mid-11th century, the work includes a poem on the Norse of Dublin and one on tabus and lucky things. The text is based on four manuscripts.

Leo I, *Saint, the Great, pope, d. 461.* Letters, tr. by Edmund Hunt. New York, Fathers of the Church, 1957. 312 p. *Fathers of the Church*, 34. **1218**

Leo VI, *the Wise, emperor, reigned 886–912. Legend.* "The legend of Leo the Wise," by Cyril Mango, *Recueil des travaux de l'Académie Serbe des Sciences*, 65, *Institut d'Études Byzantines*, 6 [Zbornik Radova 65] (1960), 59–93. **1219**

Contains translation *passim* of the Leonine oracles and related works, written in the 13th century or earlier; the oracles concern the fate of the Byzantine empire and of Constantinople.

Leonardo da Vinci, *1452–1519.* The fables of Leonardo da Vinci. [Norfolk, Va.], Vincent Torre at the Ink-Well Press, 1953. Unpaged. **1220**

No translator's name is given for the fourteen fables translated. A copy of this rare work is in the New York Public Library.

—— Leonardo the anatomist, by Elmer Belt, M.D. Lawrence, University of Kansas Press, 1955. 76 p. **1221**

Has translation of excerpts *passim.*

—— Leonardo da Vinci on the human body: the anatomical, physiological, and embryological drawings of Leonardo da Vinci, with translations, emendations, and a biographical intro., by Charles D. O'Malley and J. B. de C. M. Saunders. New York, H. Schuman [1952]. 506 p. **1222**

Leonardo's notes to his sketches and the texts appearing on the drawings are translated; the whole is organized according to anatomical systems.

—— Leonardo da Vinci on movement of the heart and blood, by Kenneth David Keele, foreword by Charles Singer. London, Harvey & Blythe, 1952. xviii, 142 p. **1223**

Passages from Leonardo on these topics culled from manuscripts are translated with running commentary by a physician.

—— [Trattato della pittura] Treatise on painting (Codex urbinas latinus 1270), tr. and annotated by A. Philip McMahon, with an intro. by Ludwig H. Heydenreich. Princeton, Princeton University Press, 1956. 2 v. **1224**

Vol. 1, translation; Vol. 2, facsimile. The text, discovered in 1810, is a compilation by Francesco Melzi of notes from the original manuscripts of Leonardo, according to the Library of Congress. The 1802 translation by Rigaud (*cf.* Farrar and Evans, item 2452) was based on another manuscript; an abridged version of it, with introduction by Alfred Werner, was published in 1957 by the Philosophical Library, New York, with the title The art of painting.

—— Leonardo da Vinci on painting, a lost book (Libro A) reassembled from the Codex Vaticanus Urbinas 1270 and from the Codex Leicester by Carlo Pedritti, with a chronology of Leonardo's "Treatise on Painting." Foreword by Sir Kenneth Clark. Berkeley, University of California Press, 1964. xvi, 301 p. **1225**

Text and translation in double columns. The editor thinks that the Treatise was written between 1508 and 1515 by Leonardo.

—— Paragone, a comparison of the arts, intro. and tr. by Irma A. Richter. London and New York, Oxford University Press [1949]. xi, 112 p. **1226**

Text and facing translation of the first chapter of Leonardo's so-called Treatise on painting; the text is the Codex urbinas latinus 1270 of the Vatican. The name Paragone is a modern one commonly given to the chapter, according to the editor. The present translation is reprinted from J. P. Richter's edition of the Literary works of Leonardo da Vinci; *cf.* Farrar and Evans, item 2448.

—— Philosophical diary, tr. and with an intro. by Wade Baskin. New York, Philosophical Library [1959]. [viii], 87 p. **1227**

Selections from Leonardo's notebooks and other works are newly translated from manuscripts and arranged to show Leonardo as "student and philosopher" (part 1) and "moralist and writer" (part 2).

Lesbos, *chronicle of.* "The short chronicle of Lesbos, 1355–1428," ed. and tr. by G. T. Dennis, *Lesbiaca,* 5 (1965), 1–24. **1228**

This work has not been seen.

Levi ben Gershon, *1288–1344.* The commentary of Levi ben Gerson (Gersonides) on the book of Job, tr. with an intro. and notes by Abraham L. Lassen. New York, Bloch, 1946. xxi, 266 p. **1229**

Lev z Rožmitálu a z Blatné, *c. 1425–1485.* The travels of Leo of Rozmital through Germany, Flanders, England, France, Spain, Portugal, and Italy, 1465–1467, ed. and tr. by Malcolm Letts. Cambridge [Eng.], Published for the Hakluyt Society at the University Press, 1957. xv, 196 p. *Hakluyt Society,* 2d. series, 108. **1230**

Translation of Gabriel Tetzel's German record of the journey, supplemented by translation of passages from Václav Šašek z Bířkova's record, a Latin version of the original Czech.

Lex Burgundionum. The Burgundian code: Liber constitutionum sive lex Gundobada, Constitutiones extravagantes, ed. and tr. by Katherine Fischer. Philadelphia, University of Pennsylvania Press, 1949. xiii, 106 p. *Translations and reprints from the original sources of history,* 3d series, 5. **1231**

The code of King Gundobad (reigned 474–516) and the "Additional enactments" are edited and translated here.

Libanius, *4th cent.* A history of Antioch in Syria, from Seleucus to the Arab conquest, by Glanville Downey. Princeton, Princeton University Press, 1961. xvii, 752 p. **1232**

Contains translation of Libanius' Oration 5, Artemis, and Oration 10, On the Plethron, a building in Antioch. A condensed version of this work, Ancient Antioch, Princeton University Press, 1963, does not include the translation. See also another translation by Professor Downey: "Libanius' Oration in praise of Antioch (Oration XI)," in *Proceedings of the American Philosophical Society,* 103 (1959), 652–86.

—— Libanius' Autobiography (Oration I), the Greek text ed. with intro., translation, and notes by A. F. Norman. London, for University of Hull by Oxford University Press, 1965. xxxiii, 244 p. **1233**

According to the introduction, Libanius was born in 314; the autobiography is based on his Oration of 374 with addenda dated up to 394. Text and facing translation.

—— "Libanius, On the silence of Socrates, a first translation and an interpretation," [tr.] by Michael Crosby and [interpretation by] William M. Calder III, in *Greek, Roman, and Byzantine Studies,* 3 (1960), 186–96. **1234**

A pretended plea of Socrates to be allowed to speak.

Liber consuetudinum Imperii Romaniae. Feudal institutions as revealed in the assizes of Romania, the law code of Frankish Greece, translation of the text of the assizes with a commentary on feudal institutions in Greece and in medieval Europe, by Peter W. Topping. Philadelphia, University of Pennsylvania Press, 1949. x, 192 p. *Translations and reprints from the original sources of history,* 3d series, 3. **1235**

A translation (pp. 15–99) of the Book of customs of the "Empire of Romania," which was in the Middle Ages the principality of Achaia or Morea; according to the editor, this is a "very representative compilation of feudal customs from the later Middle Ages, . . . especially full on matters of private law."

Literature. *Collections.*

This heading parallels *Medieval literature. Collections* in Farrar and Evans. See also such headings as *English literature, Hebrew literature, Christian literature.* In addition to the anthologies listed here, translations of single poems appear in many periodicals; see especially *Poet Lore,* vols. 49–62 (1943–67).

1236

—— The ancient world, 800 B.C.–A.D. 800, ed. by Richard J. Burke. New York, McGraw-Hill, 1967. *Western society, institutions and ideals,* 1. **1237**

Includes translation of many medieval works or excerpts from them, mostly from previously published translations; literary, historical, and religious works are included.

—— An anthology of medieval lyrics, ed. by Angel Flores. New York, Modern Library [c. 1962]. 472 p. **1238**

New translations especially for this volume by various translators; the contents include poems from Provence, France, Italy, the Iberian peninsula (including Arabic and Hebrew), and Germany.

—— An anthology of world literature, rev. ed. by Philo M. Buck, Jr., assisted by Hazel S. Alberson. New York, Macmillan, 1945 [c. 1940]. 1,148 p. **1239**

The revised edition adds translations of lyric poetry to the medieval section of the 1934 first edition, pp. 393–504.

—— Aphrodite's garland, five ancient love poems, tr. by John Heath-Stubbs. Saint Ives, Latin Press, 1951. 32 p. *Crescendo poetry series,* 2. **1240**

The medieval works translated are Pervigilium Veneris and Venantius Fortunatus, To the Lady Radegunde. This work has not been seen.

—— Asia through Asian eyes . . . , compiled by Baldoon Dhingra, with a foreword by K. M. Panikkar. Rutland, Vt., C. E. Tuttle Co. [1959]. 295 p. **1241**

Largely old translations of excerpts from many medieval Arabic and Persian sources (among others), arranged topically; anecdotes, poetry, proverbs are included.

—— A book of Latin quotations with English translations, compiled by Norbert Guterman. Garden City, N.Y., Doubleday [1966]. vi, 433 p. **1242**

Text and facing translation of quotations, from a line to several pages long, including many 3d–6th century writers.

—— Classics of western thought: middle ages, Renaissance, and Reformation, ed. by Karl F. Thompson. New York, Harcourt, Brace, & World [c. 1964]. xi, 345 p. **1243**

Brief excerpts from medieval works, old translations, pp. 1–193. Among the works excerpted are the Rule of St. Benedict, Imitatio Christi, Chanson de Roland, Chrétien's Lancelot, lyric poetry, and selections from Thomas Aquinas, Dante, Chaucer.

—— Confucious to Cummings, an anthology of poetry, ed. by Ezra Pound and Marcella Spann. New York, New Directions [1964]. xxii, 353 p. **1244**

Contains translation by Pound and others of medieval works, mostly Latin, pp. 66–119.

—— A day and a night in Venice and other poems from the Italian, French, and German, tr., printed, and published by Arthur Davidson. London, 1953. 96 p. **1245**

Contains translation from Cavalcanti, Dante, Petrarch, Boccacio, Poliziano, Villon, Froissart, D'Orléans, and Deschamps, one poem by each except for ten by Villon. All the German poems (mentioned in title) are from modern sources.

—— Death and life in the tenth century, by Eleanor S. Duckett. Ann Arbor, University of Michigan Press [1967]. x, 359 p. **1246**

Contains translation *passim,* pp. 219–80, of Latin sequences, short poems from various languages, excerpts from drama, including Hrosvit's Dulcitius and her preface and the tropes of Notker.

—— Double ballade of dead ladies and other poems, tr. from the Italian, French, and German by Arthur Davidson. London [privately printed, 1955]. 48 p. **1247**

The translations in this volume do not duplicate those in Davidson's other collections; this one includes four poems from Villon, nine from D'Orléans, two from Jean de la Taille, one from Froissart, four from Petrarch, one from Dante. All of the German works are post-medieval.

—— The early English and Celtic lyric, by P. L. Henry. London, Allen & Unwin [1966]; New York, Barnes and Noble [1967]. 244 p. *A publication of The Institute of Irish Studies, Queen's University, Belfast.* **1248**

Contains *passim* translation of many poems from Old English, Irish, and Welsh and of prose background material, *e.g.,* voyages, saints' lives, gnomic sayings.

—— Eos, an inquiry into the theme of lovers' meetings and partings in poetry, ed. by Arthur T. Hatto. The Hague, Mouton, 1965. 854 p. **1249**

An anthology of dawn songs from world-wide sources; texts and prose translation on same page. Included are Hebrew poems translated by J. B. Segal; Arabic by Bernard Lewis and S. M. Stern; Provençal and Old French by B. Woledge; Persian, Latin, Welsh, Icelandic, Mozarabic, Galician, Castilian, Italian, German, Flemish, and Old Czech by various translators.

—— Epics of the western world, [tr. and summarized by] Arthur E. Hutson and Patricia McCoy. Philadelphia, Lippincott [1954]. 512 p. **1250**

Contains translation of abridged versions of Beowulf, Chanson de Roland, Nibelungenlied, the Cid, and Dante's Commedia.

—— Erotic poetry . . . , ed. by William Cole, foreword by Stephen Spender. [New York], Random House, 1963. liv, 501 p. **1251**

Contains translation of eight medieval works: two poems by Villon, one each by Beatriz de Dia, Francesco da Barberini, Guillaume de Poitiers, Abu Nuas (8th century), Walther von der Vogelweide, and an excerpt from Jean Ruiz.

—— "French and Latin poems on manners and meals in the olden time, from mss. in the Imperial library at Paris, the British Museum, London, etc.," ed. and tr. by F. J. Furnivall in Manners and meals in olden time, Part II. London, Early English Text Society, [1868]. *Early English Text Society,* original series, 32. **1252**

A translation of Part I of this work is listed in Farrar and Evans, item 1434; it contains modernizations by Edith Rickert of 15th-century English works on meals and manners. Farrar and Evans listed this work under *English literature* and failed to note that Part II of the original contained translations of similar works in French and Latin.

—— The Goliard poets, medieval songs and satires in new verse translations by George F. Whicher. Philadelphia, Lippincott (distributors for New Directions), 1949. 303 p. **1253**

Text and facing translation of seventy-five of the Carmina Burana. Five of the poems appeared in *Poet Lore,* 49 (1943), 165–76.

—— The heritage of European literature, ed. by Edward H. Weatherly *et al.* Boston, Ginn and Co., 1948. 2 v. **1254**

Vol. 1, Greece, Rome, the Middle Ages, contains fairly liberal selections from many medieval works, among them the Lay of Hildebrand, translated by Edwin H. Zeydel.

—— Latin poetry in verse translation, from the beginnings to the Renaissance, ed. by Levi R. Lind. Boston, Houghton Mifflin [1957]. 438 p. **1255**

Short selections from medieval poets are translated on pp. 313–88.

—— The limits of art; poetry and prose chosen by ancient and modern critics, ed. by Huntington Cairns. [New York], Pantheon Books [1948]. xliv, 1,473 p. *Bollingen series,* 12. **1256**

Includes text and translation of brief selections, many medieval, from works judged by critics to be perfect or nearly so.

—— The literary riddle before 1600, by Archer Taylor. Berkeley, University of California Press, 1948. 131 p. **1257**

Contains English translation of many early riddles, including Hebrew and Arabic versions.

—— Literature of Western Civilization, sel. and ed. by Louis G. Locke, John P. Kirby, and M. R. Porter. New York, Ronald Press, 1952. 2 v. **1258**

Vol. 1 contains Laurence Binyon's translation of Dante's Inferno, cantos 1–15, corrected for this edition; and old translations of the Chanson de Roland and episodes from the Nibelungenlied.

—— A little treasury of world poetry, translations from the great poets of other languages, 2600 B.C. to 1950 A.D., ed. with an intro. by Hubert Creekmore. New York, Scribner's, 1952. xl, 904 p. **1259**

Contains translations, some recent, of poems from many medieval sources, organized by languages, including the Western vernaculars, Latin, Hebrew, Arabic, and Persian.

—— Lyrics of the Middle Ages, ed. by Hubert Creekmore. New York, Grove Press [1959]. 278 p. **1260**

Contains translations from many languages, some new for this volume, divided into four main groups: classical, Romance, Gaelic, Germanic, from 500 to 1400. Portuguese poems are among those translated for the first time into English.

—— Masterworks of world literature, ed. by E. M. Everett, Calvin S. Brown, and John C. Wade. New York, Dryden Press [1947]. 2 v. **1261**

Vol. 1, Homer to Cervantes, has not been seen.

—— Medieval age, ed. by Angel Flores. [New York, Dell, 1963]. 606 p. **1262**

Contains many new translations of poetry and prose from all Western Europe by such translators as Thomas C. Chubb, Angel Flores, Jack Lindsay, Mario Pei, Burton Raffel.

—— Medieval and Tudor drama, plays from the tenth century through Elizabethan times, ed. with intro. and modernizations by John Gassner. New York, Bantam [1963]. 457 p. **1263**

Contains new translation by Mary M. Butler of Hrotswitha's Dulcitius and Paphnutius and four Latin tropes; eleven Middle English mysteries and Everyman modernized by the editor and the Cornish Death of Pilate adapted by the editor from the translation of E. Norris (1859).

—— Medieval epics. New York, Random House [c. 1963]. 590 p. *Modern library.* **1264**

Contains Beowulf, translated by William Alfred; Chanson de Roland, translated by W. S. Merwin; Nibelungenlied, translated by Helen W. Mustard; Poem of the Cid, translated by W. S. Merwin.

—— Medieval Latin and the rise of European love-lyric, by Peter Dronke. Oxford, Clarendon Press, 1965–66. 2 v. **1265**

Vol. 1 is a study, Vol. 2 an anthology of medieval Latin love poetry, text and prose translation, organized by type—lyrics, sequences, conductus, Leonine verse. Some poems are translated in Vol. 1; all are newly edited from manuscript, some for the first time.

—— Medieval literature in translation, ed. by Charles Williams Jones. New York, Longmans, Green, 1950. xx, 1004 p. **1266**

This anthology of prose and poetry by various translators, including the editor, excludes Middle English but otherwise is comprehensive. It has been often reprinted.

—— The medieval myths, ed. by Norma L. Goodrich. New York, New American Library; London, New English Library [c. 1961]. 222 p. **1267**

Various translators, including the editor; contents: abridged versions of Beowulf, Chanson de Roland, Berta of Hungary (version of Adenes li Rois), Nibelungenlied, the Cid; Peredur from the Mabinogion; and Prince Igor (Slovo o polku Igoreve).

—— Medieval romances, ed. by Roger Sherman Loomis and Laura Hibbard Loomis. New York, Random House [c. 1957]. xi, 424 p. *Modern library.* **1268**

Various translators, including the editors; contents (many in abridged form): Chrétien's Perceval, Gottfried von Strassburg's Tristan and Isolt, The Youth of Alexander the Great, Aucussin and Nicolete, Havelock the Dane, Sir Orfeo, Gawain and the Green Knight, Malory's Book of Balin.

—— Musa pervagans; being translations with original texts of selected lyric poetry over two thousand years from divers languages, ed. by Herbert T. Sorley. Aberdeen, Aberdeen University Press, 1953. 206 p. **1269**

Contains text and facing verse translation of eight poems by Ibn Zaidun, five by Adam of St. Victor, three verses of the Dies irae, here attributed to Thomas of Celano.

—— Neo-Latin literature and the pastoral, by W. Leonard Grant. Chapel Hill, University of North Carolina Press [1965]. x, 434 p. **1270**

Contains *passim* new verse translation by the editor of pastorals of Matteo Maria Boiardo, Count of Scandiano (1441–94); Antonio Mario, fl. 1450; Baptista Mantuanus (1448–1516); and Giacopo Sannazaro (*c.* 1456–1530).

—— One thousand and one poems of mankind: memorable short poems from the world's chief literatures, ed. by Henry W. Wells, with a foreword by Clifton Fadiman. Atlanta, Tupper & Love [c. 1953]. 448 p. **1271**

Includes translations (mostly previously published) of many medieval poems from Persian, Arabic, Middle English, Italian, Latin; arranged topically, with an index of authors and languages.

—— The other world according to descriptions in medieval literature, by Howard R. Patch. Cambridge, Harvard University Press, 1950. ix, 386 p. *Smith college studies in modern languages,* n.s., 1. **1272**

Contains throughout (especially in early chapters) extensive paraphrase, summary, and illustrative quotations in translation of visions, journeys to paradise, and similar works.

—— The palace of pleasure; an anthology of the novella, medieval and Renaissance tales, 13th–16th century, ed. by Maurice Valency and Harry Levtow. New York, Capricorn Books [1960]. 277 p. **1273**

Contains translations, many new for this volume, from anonymous authors and from Marie de France, Boccaccio, Franco Sachetti, Giovanni Fiorentino, Masuccio Salernitano, Poggio Bracciolini, Lorenzo de' Medici, Sabadino degli Arienti, Luigi da Porto.

—— The Penguin book of Latin verse, with plain prose translations of each poem by Fred Brittain. [Hardmondsworth, Eng.], Penguin Books [1962]. 380 p. **1274**

Latin text with prose translation on same page; includes secular and religious verse from 6th–15th centuries (and later): Boethius' O stelli feri conditor orbis, hymns, sequences, selections from Carmina Burana.

—— The Penguin book of modern verse translation, ed. by George Steiner. [Harmondsworth, Eng.], Penguin books [1966]. 332 p. **1275**

Contains translations of medieval poems by poets from Swinburne to the present; includes, among others, Vladimir Nabokov's translation of Prince Igor's campaign (Slovo o polku Igoreve); Kenneth Rexroth's from the Carmina Burana; and W. S. Merwin, from Spanish.

—— The portable medieval reader, ed. and with an intro., by James Bruce Ross and Mary Martin McLaughlin. New York, Viking Press, 1949. xiv, 690 p. *Viking portable library*, 46. **1276**

This anthology contains translations by various translators (some new for the volume) from historical as well as literary works; the selections are either short works or brief excerpts from longer ones. Among the works newly translated by the editors and Henry F. Schwarz are excerpts from German historical documents, Geoffrey le Baker, Hugh of St. Victor, Bernard Gui, Gui de Chauliac, and Nicholas Cusanus.

—— Serbo-Croatian heroic songs, by Milman Parry and [tr. by] Albert Bates Lord, foreword by John H. Finley and Roman Jakobson, intro. by A. Belic. Cambridge, Harvard University Press, 1953–54. 2 v. **1277**

Vol. 1, translations, vol. 2, texts of modern versions of tales, many aspects of which are parallel to medieval ones. Though not strictly a medieval work, this collection undoubtedly represents medieval tradition, surely as much as the Kalevala; Parry and Lord's conclusions about the technique of oral composition have been the basis of widespread discussion of the technique of medieval poetic composition.

—— The sources of the Faust tradition, from Simon Magus to Lessing, by Philip M. Palmer and Robert P. Moore. New York, Oxford University Press, 1936; reprinted Haskell House, 1965; Octagon Books, 1966. vi, 300 p. **1278**

This work, omitted by Farrar and Evans, contains versions in translation of the Magus legend by Simon Magus, Cyprian of Antioch, Theophilus of Adana; the last two works have been newly translated by the authors, the Cyprian from a Greek version and Theophilus from the Latin version of Paulus Diaconus. Some authorities consider Theophilus himself a legendary figure.

—— Translations by Ezra Pound, ed. with an intro. by Hugh Kenner. Norfolk, Conn., New Directions, 1963. 448 p. **1279**

A collection of Pound's translations from Guido Cavalcanti, Arnaut Daniel, Bertrand de Born, Charles d'Orléans, Francesco d'Assisi, Bernart de Ventadorn; and The seafarer. These have all been previously published (*cf.* Farrar and Evans, items 833, 2195, 3762) but not collected. Includes text and facing translation. Though the 1963 edition is labeled "enlarged," the 1954 edition includes all of the medieval works.

—— A treasury of Asian literature, ed. by John D. Yohannan. New York, John Day Co. [c. 1956]. 487 p. **1280**

Includes selections, largely from old translations, of Arabic and Persian works organized by genre—story, drama, poetry, scripture.

—— The troubadours, tr. from the French by Robert Briffault, ed. by Lawrence F. Koons. Bloomington, Indiana University Press, 1965. xvi, 296 p. **1281**

Briffault has translated his own French work, Les troubadours et le sentiment romanesque, Paris, 1945. It contains *passim* translations from many poems in Provençal, some in Arabic, from various translators in addition to the author and the editor.

—— An uninhibited treasury of erotic poetry, ed. by Louis Untermeyer. New York, Dial Press, 1963. 580 p. **1282**

Contains translation of medieval works on pp. 86–154, including four poems by Villon and selections from the Carmina burana.

—— Vagabond verse; secular Latin poems of the Middle Ages, tr., with an intro. and commentary, by Edwin H. Zeydel. Detroit, Wayne State University Press, 1966. 307 p. **1283**

Includes translations, arranged topically, from Archipoeta, Hugh of Orléans, Walter of Châtillon, the Carmina Burana, and the Cambridge Songs.

—— The Works of John Millington Synge (no editor named). Dublin, Maunsel, 1910. 4 v. **1284**

Contains prose translations, Vol. 2, pp. 231–50, of poems of Petrarch, Villon, and Walter von der Vogelweide. Another edition of Synge, the Collected works, ed. by Robin Skelton, London, Oxford University Press, 1962, contains these and translations of two more poems, Vol. 1, Part 3, pp. 79–102.

—— The world in literature, ed. by George K. Anderson and Robert Warnock. Chicago, Scott Foresman, 1950–51. **1285**

This often reprinted anthology varies from two to four volumes; one section, Centuries of transition: Christendom, Islam, and the Middle Ages, contains translations from many medieval works, including the Greek anthology.

—— World masterpieces, gen. ed. Maynard Mack; New York, Norton [1956]; rev. ed., 1965. 2 v. **1286**

Vol. I, Part II, Masterpieces of the Middle Ages, ed. by John C. McGalliard. Contains old translation of many medieval works and new translation of Hrafnkels saga Freysgoða by John C. McGalliard and a modernization of Everyman by E. Talbot Donaldson (also found in the Norton Anthology of English Literature).

Lithuanian literature. *Collections.* The green oak, selected Lithuanian poetry, ed. [and tr.] by Algirdas Landsbergis and Clark Mills. New York, Voyages Press, 1962. 117 p. **1287**

Pages 25–49 contain translation from "some 1000-year old dainos" or folk-songs.

Liturgy and ritual

For other translations, see the British Museum Catalog *s. v.* Liturgies.

COLLECTIONS

—— Eastern Catholic worship, by Donald Attwater. London, Duckett; New York, Devin-Adair, 1945. xviii, 224 p. **1288**

Contains translation of the eucharistic liturgies of the Byzantine, Armenian, Alexandrian (Coptic), Antiochene (Ethiopic), Maronite, Chaldean (East Syrian), and Malabar rites, as well as the Roman mass. The introduction states that the translation first appeared in the author's

Oratre Fratres, Collegeville, Indiana, St. John's Abbey, but I have been unable to locate a copy of this work or to determine whether it is the same as Attwater's 1931 volume, Prayers from the Eastern Liturgies; see Farrar and Evans, item 2478.

—— Eastern liturgies, by Irenée-Henri Dalmais, tr. from French by D. Attwater. New York, Hawthorne Books, 1966. *Twentieth Century Encyclopedia of Catholicism.* **1289**

A translation of Les liturgies d'Orient, Paris, Librairie Fayand, 1959; contains translation of "the most important formulas of each liturgy."

—— The eucharistic liturgies of the eastern churches, by Nikolaus Liesel, tr. by David Heimann. Collegeville, Minn., Liturgical Press [c. 1963]. 310 p. **1290**

A translation from a German work which describes the liturgies and contains translations of the spoken parts.

—— The rites of eastern Christendom, by Archdale A. King. Rome, Catholic Book Agency, 1947–48; London, Burns & Oates, 1950. 2 v. **1291**

Contains description of and extensive quotations in translation from Syrian, Maronite, Syro-Malankra-Coptic, Ethiopic, Byzantine, Syro-Malabar, and Armenian rites.

—— Studies of the Syrian liturgies, by Humphrey W. Codrington. London, G. E. J. Coldwell [pref. 1952]. 90 p. **1292**

Contains description and translation of the Syrian, Marionite, Chaldean, and Malabar liturgies for the eucharist, the mass of the catchecumens, and the Divine Office. The work originally appeared in the *Eastern Churches Quarterly,* 1936–37, but was not noted by Farrar and Evans. Much of the translation is directly from unpublished manuscripts.

ARMENIAN CHURCH

—— A collection of prayers from the ancient Armenian book of office and divine liturgy, compiled and tr. by Terenig Poladian. New York, Delphic Press, 1943. 193 p. **1293**

Text and facing translation of liturgical and private prayers, litanies, and the devotions of St. Nerses Shnorhali, d. 1173.

COPTIC CHURCH

—— "The baptismal rite of the Coptic church (a critical study)," by O. H. E. Khs.-Burmester, *Bulletin de la société d'archéologie copte,* 11 (1945), 27–84. **1294**

Includes text and translation of the rite in double columns; text of the Greek rite is also given for comparison. This rite dates from pre-451, the author thinks.

—— "The Canon of the resurrection," by Y. 'Abd al-Masīḥ, *Bulletin de la société d'archéologie copte,* 14 (1950–51), 23–35. **1295**

Contains Greek, Arabic, Coptic texts and translation of hymn to be recited for Easter.

—— "The Coptic-Greek-Arabic Holy Week lectionary of Scetis," by O. H. E. Khs.-Burmester, *Bulletin de la société d'archeologie copte,* 16 (1961–62), 83–137; 17 (1963–64), 35–56; and 18 (1965–66), 23–50. **1296**

Contains text and translation of a trilingual lectionary and other documents from Scetis, from a 13th- or 14th-century manuscript.

LITURGY AND RITUAL

—— The Egyptian or Coptic church, a detailed description of her liturgical services and the rites and ceremonies observed in the administration of her sacraments, by O. H. E. Khs.-Burmester. Cairo, Societé d'archéologie copte, 1967. xii, 419 p. *Textes et documents.* **1297**

This work, a summary, revision, and extension of the author's series of articles on Coptic liturgy, contains translations of hymns and prayers (some abridged) and of all rubrics; many are translated directly from manuscript for the first time. The articles appeared in *Eastern Churches Quarterly,* 10–16 (1953–59); these are in addition to the articles cited in this bibliography from the *Bulletin de la société d'archéologie copte.*

—— "Doxologies in the Coptic Church, unedited Boḥairic doxologies," by Yassā 'Abd al-Masīḥ, *Bulletin de la société d'archéologie copte,* 8 (1942), 31–61; 11 (1945), 95–158. **1298**

Text and translation of doxologies for special saints' days. An earlier article by the same author on edited doxologies, with translation, appeared in the same journal, 4 (1938), 97–113; 5 (1939), 175–91; 6 (1940), 19–76; it was not included in Farrar and Evans.

—— "A historical survey of the convents for women in Egypt," by Iris Habib el-Masri, *Bulletin de la société d'archéologie copte,* 14 (1950–51), 63–111. **1299**

Contains text and translation of ordination rites of nuns.

—— The liturgy of the Ethiopian church, tr. by Marcos Daoud, Addis Ababa, 1954. **1300**

I have not seen this translation, which was mentioned by O. H. E. Khs.-Burmester in his article "The Anaphorae of the Ethiopic Church," *Eastern Churches Quarterly,* 13 (1959), 13–42.

—— "An offertory-consecratory prayer in the Greek and Coptic liturgy of St. Mark," by O. H. E. Khs.-Burmester, *Bulletin de la société d'archéologie copte,* 17 (1963–64), 23–33. **1301**

—— The rite of consecration of the Patriarch of Alexandria (text according to Ms. 253 Lit. Coptic Museum), tr. by O. H. E. Khs.-Burmester. Cairo, Société d'archéologie copte, 1960. 100 p. *Textes et documents.* **1302**

Translations from Coptic and Arabic; includes translation of appendices containing rubrics from other manuscripts.

EASTERN ORTHODOX CHURCH

—— "The 'Akathistos,' a study in Byzantine hymnography," by Egon Wellesz, *Dumbarton Oaks Papers,* 9 (1956), 143–74. **1303**

Has text and translation of excerpts from a hymn in honor of the Virgin Mary. Professor Wellesz thinks that the author may have been one Romanos, *fl.* during the reign of Justinian.

—— Byzantine liturgy, complete text with music, in English, ed. by A. P. Mohrachev and Frederick J. Saato. New York, Fordham University, 1964. 36 p. **1304**

—— The Byzantine liturgy, a new English translation of the liturgies of St. John Chrysostom and St. Basil the Great [by Clement C. Englert]. London, Duckett; New York, Fordham Russian Center [1953]. 78 p. **1305**

This translation has not been seen.

—— A Christian Palestinian Syriac horologion (Berlin Ms. Or. Oct. 1019), ed. [and tr.] by Matthew Black. Cambridge [Eng.], Cambridge University Press, 1954. x, 457 p. *Cambridge texts and studies, contributions to Biblical and Patristic literature,* n.s. **1306**

Text and translation of a complete Malkite (Melchite) service book, which was translated from Greek into Palestinian Syriac (with some passages in the Karshuni dialect); the Syriac contains some two hundred hymns from the Greek service book, with some hymns and prayers not in modern Greek service books. According to the editor, the Malkites were the "only branch of Syrian Christianity which fully embraced the dogmatic formula of Chalcedon."

—— The divine liturgy of St. John Chrysostom, Patriarch of Constantinople, ed. by Archbishop Benjamin of Pittsburgh. New York [Rossiya Publishing Co.], 1948. 4th ed. 320 p. **1307**

Russian text and tracing translation. I have been unable to locate any reference to an earlier edition.

—— Eastern rite prayers to the Mother of God, tr. and ed. by John H. Ryder. New York, Fordham University Russian Center, 1955. 46 p. **1308**

Contains eight prayers translated from the Byzantine rite for the Greater Feasts of the Mother of God.

—— Gospel lectionary of the Eastern Orthodox Church, tr. by Fan S. Noli. Boston, Albanian Orthodox Church in America, 1956. 543 p. **1309**

Translation from Greek of the lessons as arranged for the church year.

—— The great canon: a poem of Saint Andrew of Crete, recited during some of the Lenten offices of the Eastern Orthodox Church, tr. by Derwas J. Chitty. London, Fellowship of St. Alban and St. Sergius, 1957; 2d ed., 1966. 47 p. **1310**

—— The Greek Orthodox liturgy of S. John Chrysostom, arranged for use in English by Stephen A. Hurlbut. Washington, St. Albans Press, 1942. 13 pp. **1311**

This version is a translation of the "simpler form of the 8th century."

—— Liturgy and catechism of the Eastern Orthodox Church, in Albanian and English, tr. by Bishop F. S. Noli. Boston, Albanian Orthodox Church in America, 1955. 235 p. **1312**

Contains Preparation for the liturgy, the Liturgy of St. John Chrysostom, short catechism. A longer version of the catechism (not seen) by the same translator and from the same publisher appeared in 1954, according to the introduction here; it contains translation of two hymns as well as the catechism.

—— The liturgy of St. John Chrysostom, Ruthenian form, historical background, intro. and commentary by Basil Shereghy. Collegeville, Minn., Liturgical Press [1961]. 64 p. **1313**

Contains translations of the liturgy.

—— A manual of Eastern Orthodox prayers (A collection of prayers taken from the Euchologion of the Orthodox Church), [tr. by Charles P. L. Dennis and Margaret C. Dampier]. London, S.P.C.K., 1945. xiv, 113 p. **1314**

This translation has not been seen; a copy is in the British Museum.

—— The order for celebration of vespers, matins, and the divine liturgy, according to the Ruthenian rescension, a translation of "Ordo celebrationis vesperarum, matutini, et divinae liturgiae, iuxta rescensionem Ruthenorum," published by the Sacred Congregation for the Eastern Church, Rome, 1944, by Matthew A. Berko. Washington, 1958. 122 p. **1315**

This translation has not been seen.

—— Prayerbook and hymnology of the holy eastern orthodox church rendered in Greek, English, and English phonetics, by H. P. Hatzopoulos. New York, Minos, 1962. 208 p. **1316**

This work has not been seen.

—— Three liturgies of the Eastern Orthodox Church, tr. by Fan S. Noli. Boston, Albanian Orthodox Church in America, 1955. 344 p. **1317**

The translation is made from the Greek prayerbook, Mega euchologion, Athens, 1902, and contains the liturgies of St. John Chrysostom, St. Basil, and the Presanctified sacraments.

NESTORIAN OR EAST SYRIAN CHURCH

—— Assyrian apostolic church prayer, hymn, and liturgical service book, compiled and tr. into English by Peter Barsoum. [Worcester, Mass., P. Barsoum], 1957. xiv, 80 p. **1318**

Text in Syriac and English, according to the Oriental Catalog of the New York Public Library. I have not seen this work.

SYRIAN RITE

—— The holy Mass according to the Syrian rite of Antioch, with Anaphora of the Twelve Apostles, tr. by Joseph Redlinger. Jacksonville, Fla. [A. C. Shashy] 1955. 50 p. **1319**

Translation from a Syriac dialect of Aramaic of Kthobo Dkhourobo.

WEST SYRIAN OR JACOBITE CHURCH

—— The Mar Thoma Syrian liturgy, tr. by George K. Chacko. New York, Morehouse-Gorham, 1956. vii, 19 p. **1320**

MANDAEANS

See *Mandaean texts* for writings and rituals of this sect, a branch of the Nasorean; according to E. S. Drower, *Nasorean* means *priest, Mandaean* means *layman.* The Mandaeans are the only surviving Gnostic sect, now fast disappearing; see E. S. Drower, The Secret Adam, a study of Nasoraean Gnosis. Oxford, Clarendon Press, 1960.

1321

JEWISH

This category was not included in Farrar and Evans, but because of recent recognition of the close connection between Jewish and early Christian writings (neither medieval, according to our definition, but the latter included in Farrar and Evans), it was felt advisable to note here the main translations of Jewish ritual, which has much accretion from the medieval period, including many hymns. For a discussion and translation of illustrative portions, see Jewish prayer and worship: an introduction for Christians, by William W. Simpson, New York, Seabury Press, 1967, 128 p. This work includes a bibliography of recent translations of special prayerbooks, not noted here.

—— The book of prayer and order of Service according to the custom of the Spanish and Portuguese Jews, with an English translation based principally on the work of the late D. A. da Sola, ed. and rev. by Moses Gaster. London, Henry Fraude, 1901–7. 6 v. **1322**

This is a revised edition of the standard translation of the Sephardic rite; according to Simpson (see above), the main difference in this and the Ashkenazic rite is that this version contains more hymns, mostly medieval.

—— The daily prayer book, ed. and tr. by Philip Birnbaum. [New York, Hebrew Publishing Co.], 1949. xxiii, 790 p. **1323**

Text and facing translation, newly done. In another work, the weekday prayers of the synagogue service are translated: Seder R. Amram Gaon; Hebrew text with critical apparatus, translation with notes and intro. by David Hedegard, Lund, Lindstedt [1951], 201 p. plus Hebrew text. This is the oldest Jewish prayerbook, compiled by Rabbi Amram, d. 875. The translation is based on the new critical edition of the manuscripts of the 15th and 16th centuries.

—— The standard prayer book, authorized English translation by Simeon Singer. New York, Bloch Publishing Co., 1958. 469, 470 p. **1324**

This is a reprint of the Authorized daily prayer book, which appeared originally in 1880 and has had many reprints and editions. This is the Ashkenazi or "German" rite; text and facing translation.

—— Haggadah for Passover, copied and illustrated by Ben Shahn, with a translation, intro. and historical notes by Cecil Roth. Boston, Little, Brown, 1965. xix, 133 p. **1325**

Text and facing translation.

—— The language of faith, ed. by Nahum N. Glatzer, tr. by Jacob Sloan and Olga Marx. New York, Schocken, 1947. **1326**

Contains text and facing translation of fifty-one prayers originally in Hebrew, Aramaic, and Yiddish.

Llywarch Hen, *496?–646?, supposed author.* The saga of Llywarch the old, a reconstruction, by Glyn Jones, with the verse interludes tr. by T. J. Morgan and an intro. by Ifor Williams. London, Golden Cockerel Press, 1955. 37 p. **1327**

From the dramatic interludes extant, the author has reconstructed the prose saga; the interludes are translated, with some rearrangement of lines. The work was prepared for broadcast on the BBC. The text is in the Red Book of Hergest; the author believes that it is not the work of Hen but is a 9th-century composition.

Louis I, *le Pieux, emperor, king of the Franks, 778–840.* Son of Charlemagne, a contemporary life of Louis the Pious, tr. with intro. and notes by Allen Cabaniss. [Syracuse, N.Y.], Syracuse University Press [1961]. 182 p. **1328**

Translation based on the Momumenta Germaniae historica and Migne's Patrologiae editions of Vita Hludowici imperatoris, ascribed to the so-called Astronomus, *fl.* 814–840, a member of the court; the editor says that the work is anonymous.

Lucena, Vasco Fernandes de, *d. 1499, supposed author.* The obedience of a king of Portugal, ed. and tr. by Francis M. Rogers. Minneapolis, University of Minnesota Press, 1958. 120 p. **1329**

Facsimile text and facing translation of an oration delivered at the "obedience" of John II, King of Portugal, to Pope Innocent VIII, in 1485.

Ludolphus de Saxonia, *d. 1378.* The Vita Christi of Ludolphus the Carthusian, by Mary I. Bodenstedt. Washington, Catholic University of America Press, 1944. viii, 160 p. *Catholic University studies in medieval and Renaissance Latin language and literature,* 16. **1330**

This monograph contains an analysis of the entire vita, only part of which has ever been translated (see Farrar and Evans, item 2581), and contains translation of some excerpts about prayer.

Ludus de Antechristo (*liturgical drama*). The play of Antichrist, tr. with an intro. by John Wright. Toronto, Pontifical Institute of Mediaeval Studies, 1967. 110 p. **1331**

The translation is from a Latin text in Karl Young's The drama of the medieval church.

Lupus Servatus, *abbot of Ferrières, 805–c. 862.* The letters of Lupus of Ferrières, tr. and intro. by Graydon W. Regenos. The Hague, Nijhoff, 1966. xii, 160 p. **1332**

One hundred and thirty letters, from the Monumenta Historica Germanica; four are addressed to Einhard, the biographer of Charlemagne.

Luxorius, *6th cent.* A Latin poet among the vandals, by Morris Rosenblum, together with a text of the poems and an English translation. New York, Columbia University Press, 1961. xvi, 310 p. *Records of civilization,* 62. **1333**

Text and facing prose translation of all the extant poems, which are in the Latin Anthology; they are largely epigrammatic.

M

Mabinogion. The Mabinogion, tr. by Gwyn Jones and Thomas Jones. London, J. M. Dent; New York, E. P. Dutton [1949]. xxxiii, 282 p. *Everyman's library.* **1334**

This translation, which takes the place of the Guest translation in Everyman's library, first appeared in 1948 in London, Golden Cockerel Press Edition de luxe. It is based on the White book of Rhydderch, with omissions supplied from the Red book of Hergest.

Macrobius, Ambrosius Aurelius Theodosius, *fl. c. 400.* Commentary on the dream of Scipio, tr. with intro. and commentary by William H. Stahl. New York, Columbia University Press, 1952. xi, 278 p. *Records of civilization,* 48. **1335**

Includes a translation of Scipio's dream, by Cicero, as well as translation of Macrobius' commentary.

Magna carta.

Translations of Magna carta were not included by Farrar and Evans, probably because they expected to issue a separate volume on documents. Since that volume never materialized, it was thought wise to include major documents here. For a complete text and translation of Magna carta, as well as a bibliography of "original versions, printed editions, and commentary" up to 1905, see William Sharp McKechnie, Magna Carta, a commentary on the Great Charter of King John. Glasgow, 1905; 2d ed. 1914; reprinted New York, Burt Franklin, 1958. xvii, 530 p. McKechnie's text furnished the basis for a volume of translations by Noël Denham-Young published in 1938 by Guyon House Press, London; it included the charters of Henry I (1100), Stephen (1135), Henry III (1154), the unknown charter of liberties (1214), the charter of the forest (1217), and the great charters of 1215 and 1225.

—— Magna carta, by J. C. Holt. Cambridge [Eng.], Cambridge University Press, 1965. xv, 378 p. 1336

In an appendix contains translation of the 1215 version, facing the text, with facsimile of some pages.

—— Magna carta, legend and legacy, by William F. Swindler. Indianapolis, Bobbs-Merrill, [1965]. xi, 379 p. 1337

Part 2 contains translation of both the 1215 Concordia inter Regem Johannen et barones and the 1225 Carta de libertatibus Regis Henrici III.

Makrembolites, Alexios, *fl. 1350?* "Alexios Makrembolites and his 'Dialogue between the rich and the poor,'" by Ihor Ševčenko, *Recueil des travaux de l'Académie Serbe des Sciences,* 65, *Institut d'Études Byzantines,* 6. [*Zbornik Radova,* 65] (1960), 187–228. 1338

Text and translation from a very obscure Greek writer; an unusual document for the time.

Malory, Sir Thomas, *15th cent.* The works of Sir Thomas Malory, ed. by Eugène Vinaver. Oxford, Clarendon Press, 1947; 2d ed. 1967. 3 v.; (text alone), London, Oxford University Press, 1959. xviii, 919 p. 1339

A new edition based on the Winchester manuscript discovered in 1934. There have been many editions of parts of Malory's work, based largely on the Caxton text; these are readily available and are not noted here.

Mandaean texts.

Although no Mandaean documents from the medieval period survive, E. S. Drower (Lady Stevens) has collected later manuscripts and has recorded oral traditions of a gnostic sect still surviving but with few practitioners; she considers the documents to be of 1st or 2d century provenience surviving with practically no change in later times. See her The secret Adam, a study of Nasoraean gnosis, Oxford, Clarendon Press, 1960, which contains *passim* translation of representative documents, as well as a discussion and bibliography. See also Eric Segelberg, Maṣbūtā, Studies in the ritual of the Mandaean baptism, Uppsala [Almqvist & Wiksells], 1958, which contains *passim* translation of many terms and a discussion of Mandaean studies.

—— Alf trisar šuialia, the thousand and twelve questions, a Mandaean text, ed. in transliteration and translation by E. S. Drower. Berlin, Akademie-Verlag, 1960. 300 p, plus 63 p. facsimile text in pocket. *Deutsche Akademie der Wissenschaften zur Berlin, Institut für Orientforschung,* 32. 1340

A dialog, commentary on ritual.

—— The ascension of the apostle and the heavenly book, by George Widengren. Uppsala, University of Uppsala, 1950. 117 p. *Universitets Årsskrift,* 7. 1341

Contains translation and text (in footnotes) of passages from Mandaean writing about ascension and its relation to the giving of a Book, parallel to Muhammad's.

—— The book of the zodiac (Sfar Malwasig), tr. by E. S. Drower. London, Royal Asiatic Society, 1949. 218, [145] p. *Oriental trust fund,* 36. 1342

MANDAEAN TEXTS

Facsimile text and translation of a work whose main subjects are astrology and omens; probably a translation from an Arabic or Persian version of a Babylonian work. The volume contains "no trace of Mandaic ideas or religion," according to Lady Stevens, though it is written in Mandaic, a dialect of Persian surviving almost solely among the gnostic sect.

—— The canonical prayerbook of the Mandaeans, tr. by E. S. Drower. Leiden, Brill, 1959. Unpaged. **1343**

I have not seen a copy of this work, but, according to the catalog of Widener Library of Harvard University, it includes a facsimile reproduction of the manuscript as well as a translation. The Harvard copy seems to have been lost.

—— The coronation of the great Šišlam, being a description of the rite of coronation of a Mandaean priest. . . , tr. from two mss. . . . by E. S. Drower. Leiden, Brill, 1962. xviii, 48 p. **1344**

Contains a facsimile, transliteration, and translation of the text.

—— Diwan abatur, or progress through the purgatories, text with translation, notes, and appendices, by E. S. Drower. Città del Vaticano, Biblioteca Apostolica Vaticani, 1950. vi, 45 p.; foldout facsimile, with illustrations. *Studi e testi,* 151. **1345**

Translation of a work describing the progress of the soul after death through the seven planetary spheres.

—— The Haran Gawaita and the Baptism of Hibil-Ziwa; the Mandaic text . . . with translation, notes, and commentary, by E. S. Drower. Città del Vaticano, Biblioteca Apostolica Vaticana, 1953. xi, 96 p. *Studi e testi,* 176. **1346**

The Mandaean facsimile text is a folded insert. The "Haran-Gawaita" is a place, the "inner Haran," involved in the liturgy of baptism. Some hymns are included in the ritual. According to J. B. Segal in a review, *Bulletin of the School of Oriental and African Studies,* 18 (1956), 373–75, the work was probably written down toward the end of the 12th century.

—— "A Mandaean book of black magic," transliterated and translated by E. S. Drower, *Journal of the Royal Asiatic Society,* 1943, 149–80. **1347**

—— "Mandaean Polemic," by E. S. Drower, *Bulletin of the School of Oriental and African Studies,* 25 (1962), 438–48. **1348**

Has translation *passim* from Mandaean documents of anti-Jewish, anti-Christian, and anti-Muslim polemic.

—— Mandaic incantation texts, by Edwin M. Yamauchi. New Haven, American Oriental Society, 1967. ix, 422 p. *American Oriental series,* 49. **1349**

Text and translation of thirty-three incantations from bowls dating *c.* 600.

—— "Pišra ḏ-Šamtra, a phylactery of rue," by E. S. Drower, *Orientalia,* 15 (1946), 324–46. **1350**

A charm against disease, from a 19th-century manuscript.

—— Sarh ā̱. quabin ā̱ Sislam Rba, explanatory comment on the marriage ceremony of the great Šišlam, text transliterated and tr. by E. S. Drower, *Biblica et Orientalia,* 12 (1950), 108 p. **1351**

The final section is an astrological appendix to the rite.

Mandeville, Sir John, *14th cent.*

For a complete bibliography of manuscripts and of editions in every language, see Josephine W. Bennett, The rediscovery of Sir John Mandeville, New York, Modern Language Association of America, 1954. Professor Bennett considers a real Sir John Mandeville to have been the author of the Travels, as does Malcolm Letts in Sir John Mandeville, 1949.

—— Mandeville's Travels, ed. by M. C. Seymour. Oxford, Clarendon Press, 1967. xxi, 303 p. **1352**

A slightly modernized text of the Cotton manuscript, a conflation of *c.* 1400.

—— Sir John Mandeville, Travels, texts and translations by Malcolm Letts. London, Hakluyt Society, 1953. 2 v. *Hakluyt Society*, 2d series, 101–2. **1353**

Contains the text of a hitherto unpublished English translation of one of the Latin versions (1442), as well as a translation of Von Diemeringen's German version, of the Latin vulgate version (Strassburg, 1484), and of extracts from Prester John's letter.

Manetti, Giannazzo, *1396–1459.* Two views of man: Pope Innocent III On the misery of man; Giannozzo Manetti On the dignity of man, tr. with an intro. by Bernard Murchland. New York, Ungar [1966]. xx, 103 p. **1354**

Books 1 and 2 of Innocent's work are translated; Book 4 of Manetti's.

Mani (Manes, Manichaeus), *215–6–274?, supposed author.* "The Book of the giants," by W. B. Henning, *Bulletin of the School of Oriental and African Studies,* 11 (1943–46), 52–74. **1355**

Contains translation of versions in several languages (Greek, Syriac, Persian, Sogdian, Arabic) of a work ascribed to Mani.

Mansūr ibn Ba'ra, *fl. 1218–38.* "Extracts from the technical manual on the Ayyūbid mint in Cairo," by A. S. Ehrenkreutz, *Bulletin of the School of Oriental and African Studies,* 15 (1953), 423–47. **1356**

Text, translation, and commentary of the technical parts of a previously unpublished treatise on the Egyptian mint, written 1218–38, according to the author, who does not accept Brockelman's dating. The author's interest was primarily in the technological aspects of coinage.

Manzio, Aldo Pio, *1449 or 1450–1515.* Aldus Manutius and his Thesaurus cornucopiae of 1496 . . . , tr. by Antje Lemke, intro. by Donald P. Bean. [Syracuse, N.Y.], Syracuse University Press [c. 1958]. 14 [17] p. **1357**

Translation of the prologue in which Aldus announces his plans to publish the works of Aristotle and other Greek authors.

Marinus, *of Flavia Neapolis, fl. 5th cent.* The philosophy of Proclus, the final phase of ancient thought, by Laurence J. Rosán. New York, Cosmos, 1949. ix, 271 p. **1358**

Contains translation of Marinus' Vita Procli, as well as of many illustrative excerpts from Proclus, with Greek text in appendix.

Marsilius of Padua, *d. 1342?* Marsilius of Padua, the Defender of peace, tr. by Alan Gewirth. New York, Columbia University Press, 1951–56. 2 v. *Records of civilization,* 46. **1359**

Vol. 1 is a study entitled Marsilius of Padua and medieval political philosophy; vol. 2 is a translation of Defensor pacis.

Martinez de Toledo, Alfonso, *1398?–1466.* Little sermons on sin; the archpriest of Talavera, tr. by Lesley Byrd Simpson. Berkeley, University of California Press, 1959. viii, 200 p. **1360**

The translation omits the treatise on astrology at the end of El arcipreste de Talavera (also known as El corbacho, The scourge).

al-Marwāzī, *fl. 1056–1120.* "Marvazi on the Byzantines," by V. Minorsky in Mélanges H. Grégoire. Brussels, University of Brussels, 1950. 2 v. *Annuaire de l'institut de philologie et d'histoire orientales et slaves,* 10. **1361**

Contains Arabic text and translation, vol. 2, pp. 455–69.

Mary, Virgin. An eighth-century treatise on the Assumption of Our Lady, tr. from the Latin [with an introduction] by Ernest Graf. [Buckfast], Buckfast Abbey, 1950. 23 p. **1362**

I have not seen a copy of this work, which is described in the British Museum Catalog.

—— A voice said Ave!, tr. by Charles Dollen. Boston, St. Pauls Editions, 1963. 229 p. **1363**

Contains selected passages in translation from writings of church fathers, doctors, and other theologians about the Virgin.

Marzubān-nāma. The tales of Marzuban, tr. from the Persian by Reuben Levy. Bloomington, Indiana University Press, 1959. 254 p. UNESCO *collection of representative works, Persian series.* **1364**

These fables, similar to those in the Kalīla wa-Dimna and the Arabian nights, are here translated for the first time into any European language. Though attributed to Marzubān ibn Rustam ibn Sharwīn, *fl.* 1000?, they may have existed for four hundred years before being compiled in the 13th century by Sa'd al-Dīn al-Warāwīnī, according to the Encyclopedia of Islam.

Maximus Confessor, *Saint, c. 580–662.* The ascetic life. The four centuries on charity, tr. and annotated by Polycarp Sherwood. Westminster, Md., Newman Press, 1955. viii, 284 p. *Ancient Christian writers,* 21. **1365**

The "centuries" are one hundred sententiae; both works are in dialog form.

—— The earlier Ambigua of St. Maximus the Confessor, by Polycarp Sherwood. *Studie Anselmiania,* 36, 1955. 235 p. **1366**

Contains detailed summary of the Ambigua, Part 1, as well as translation of lengthy excerpts; the work consists of scholia on the writings of Gregory Nazianzen. Another monograph, Microcosm and mediator, the theological anthropology of Maximus the Confessor, by Lars Thunberg (Lund, Gleerup, 1965; xii, 500 p.), contains paraphrase from many of Maximus' untranslated works.

al-Maynaqī, Abū Firās ibn Jaushan, *fl. 1324?* Ash-Shâfiya (The healer), an Ismâ'ilî poem attributed to Shihâb ad-Dîn Abû Firâs, ed. and tr. with intro. and commentary by Sami Nassib Makarem. Beirut, American University of Beirut, 1966. 260 p. *American University Oriental series,* 48. **1367**

Text and facing prose translation of a work unknown to Islamic scholarship, according to the editor; it is a comprehensive account of Ismaili beliefs. W. Ivanow considers the author to have lived in the 16th century, but Makarem believes him to have lived in the late 13th and early 14th centuries. Since the work is a compilation, it is difficult to assign authorship; I have accepted the designation of the Widener Library of Harvard University and the dates from Brockelman.

Mechthild, *of Magdeburg, c. 1212–c. 1282.* The revelations of Mechthild of Magdeburg; or the flowing light of the Godhead, tr. by Lucy Menzies. London and New York, Longmans, Green [1953]. xxxvii, 263 p. **1368**

Somewhat abridged; omissions of a few chapters, some paragraphs are indicated.

Melito, *Saint, bp. of Sardis, 2d cent.* "Peri Pascha in a Georgian version," by J. Neville Birdsall, *Le Muséon,* 80 (1967), 121–38. **1369**

Text and translation of a homily on the passion originally in Greek, translated into Georgian and found in a manuscript of the 10th or 11th century.

Mennas, *Saint, Egyptian martyr, d. c. 295.* "Acrostical St. Menas-Hymn in Sahidic," by Søren Giversen, *Acta Orientalia,* 23 (1958), 19–32. **1370**

Text in Sahidic, a dialect of Coptic, with facing translation of a liturgical hymn from an 11th-century manuscript. This saint, whose name seems to be spelled more often *Menas,* should not be confused with Mennas, patriarch of Constantinople, born in Alexandria *c.* 500.

—— *Legend.* Apa Mena, a selection of Coptic texts relating to St. Menas, ed. with tr. and commentary, by James Drescher. Le Caire, Société d'archéologie Copte, 1946. xxxvi, 186 p. *Textes et documents.* **1371**

Coptic texts based on three manuscripts discovered in 1910 at Hamouli, are translated; contains the martyrdom, miracles, encomium (attributed to John, Abp. of Alexandria), further miracles, and the antiphon. A translation from an Ethiopic text of the life of St. Mennas and a summary of the nineteen miracles performed by him appeared in "The Coptic frescoes of Saint Menas at Medinet Habu," by Donald N. Wilber, *Art Bulletin,* 22 (1940), 86–103.

Merswin, Rulman, *1307–82.* Mystical writings, ed. and interpreted by Thomas S. Kepler. Philadelphia, Westminster Press [1960]. 143 p. **1372**

Contains a translation of Merswin's Vier anfangende Jahre (The four beginning years) and Das Buch von der neuen Felsen (The book of the nine rocks).

Mesrop Mashtots, *Saint, c. 361–441.* The life of Mashtots . . . written in the 5th century by Koriun, tr. and ed. by B. Norhadian [or Norehad]. New York [n.p.], 1964. **1373**

This Armenian text and English translation of a biography of the inventor of the Armenian alphabet was listed in Blackwell's Catalog No. 843.2520A, but no copy has been located.

Methodius, *Saint, bp. of Olympus, d. c. 311.* The symposium; a treatise on chastity, tr. and annotated by Herbert A. Musurillo. Westminster, Md., Newman Press, 1958. vi, 249 p. *Ancient Christian writers,* 27. **1374**

The translation has been made from manuscript but the text is not included here. Methodius is also known as Eubulius, according to the translator.

Mézières, Philippe de, *1327?–1405.* Description of the Festum praesentationis Beatae Mariae, a fourteenth-century prompt book, tr. and introduced by Albert B. Weiner. [New Haven, A. Kner, 1958.] 85 p. **1375**

Translation of description of characters, costumes, etc., and of a sermon to accompany a play in praise of the Virgin Mary first performed in 1372.

Midrash Tehillim. The Midrash on Psalms, tr. from the Hebrew and Aramaic by William G. Braude. New Haven, Yale University Press, 1959. 2 v. *Yale Judaica series,* 13. **1376**

The Midrash represents accretions from the 3d through 13th centuries, though Professor Braude thinks that the "overwhelming body of material . . . goes back to the Talmudic period."

Mirror of simple souls.

The "unknown M. N." referred to in Farrar and Evans, item 2772, as the author of the Mirror of simple souls has been identified as Margaret Porette by Romana Guarnieri, "Lo Specchio delle anime semplia . . . ," *Osservatore Romano,* June 16, 1946. 1377

Misʿar ibn Muhalhil Abū Dulaf, *10th cent.* Abū Dulaf Miʿsar ibn Muhalhil's travels in Iran (circa A.D. 950), ed. and tr. by Vladimir Minorsky. Cairo, University Press, 1955. 136, 31 p. 1378

Text and translation of a record of journeys in Central Asia; contains considerable material on mining and mineralogy and archaeology, as well as the geographical material.

Mishle Sendabar. Tales of Sendebar, Mishle Sinbad, an edition and translation of the Hebrew version of the Seven Sages based on unpublished manuscripts, ed. by Morris Epstein. Philadelphia, Jewish Publication Society of America, 1967. ix, 410 p. *Judaica, texts and translations,* 1st series, 2. 1379

One of the Eastern versions of a group of popular tales known collectively as the Book of Sindibad or the Seven Sages; Sendebar is known in Arabic as Bidpai. This is not the same story as that of Sindbad in the Arabian Nights. Professor Epstein includes a detailed discussion of the relationship of this Hebrew version, the seven other Oriental versions, and the numerous occidental versions.

Mishnah. The Mishnah, tr. . . . by Herbert Danby. London, Oxford University Press, 1933; often reprinted, including 1967. 1380

This is the first complete translation of the Mishnah into English. In footnote 4, the author enumerates previous translations of parts of the Mishnah. Although this material was not included in Farrar and Evans, it has seemed advisable to note the main translation of a source important, like the apocrypha of the New Testament and the works of the apostolic fathers, in describing the first and second centuries of the Christian era. Partial translations will be noted only when they contain variants and commentary from the medieval period.

—— Mishnahyoth, ed. and tr. by Philip Blackman. London, Mishna Press, 1952–57. 7 v. 1381

Text and facing translation of the entire Mishnah, including in an appendix the Tosephta, commentaries of the 5th and 6th centuries.

—— The Mishnah . . . , text with commentary of R. Obadiah Bertinoro, translation, intro., and new commentary in English by Jacob D. Herzog. New York, Bloch, 1947. 190 p. 1382

This translation of the first three tractates of the Mishnah contains the commentary of Obediah Yareh ben Abraham Bertinoro, d. *c.* 1500.

—— Horayot. Mishnah Horayoth, its history and exposition; notes by P. R. Weis, text and translation by Edward Robertson. [Manchester, Eng.], Manchester University Press [1952]. xxxvii, 111 p. 1383

The Horayot or "Instructions" are part 10 of the Fourth Division, Nezikin or "Damages." Variants of this tract found in later commentators are included. Text and translation.

Moses ben Joshua, *of Narbonne, 14th cent.* "Moses Narboni's 'Epistle on Shi'ur Qomā,' a critical edition of the Hebrew text with an intro. and translation," by Alexander Altmann, pp. 225–88 in Jewish medieval and renaissance studies, ed. by Alexander Altmann, Cambridge, Harvard University Press, 1967. **1384**

According to the editor, the Shi'ur Qomā is "The Measure of the Divine Body," a mystical anthropomorphic work of early Judaism reacted to by all major Jewish writers.

Moses ben Maimon, *1135–1204.* [Al-Fadhalye] Treatise on poisons and their antidotes, ed. by Suessman Muntner. Philadelphia, Lippincott [1966]. xxxviii, 77 [59] p. *The medical writings of Moses Maimonides,* 2. **1385**

Facsimile text and translation of a work written in Arabic in Hebrew characters. The Arabic title of the work is derived from the name of the official for whom it was written; according to the editor, it has the "character of a medical treatise dealing with public health under government supervision."

—— [Fī 'l-jima] Maimonides on sexual intercourse, tr. and ed. by Morris Gorlin. Brooklyn, N.Y., Rambash [c. 1961]. 128 p. *Medical historical studies of medieval Jewish medical works,* 1. **1386**

The translation from Arabic is based on an intermediary translation into German by Ismar Lipshutz. In addition to Maimonides' treatise, a longer spurious work On sexual intercourse, probably written during the 14th century, is included; in appendices are translations of excerpts from Maimonides' medical aphorisms, based on Galen, and of other sources used by Maimonides.

—— [Fī tadbīr al-ṣiḥḥah] The preservation of youth, essays on health, tr. by Hirsch L. Gordon. New York, Philosophical Library [1958]. 92 p. **1387**

—— Two treatises on the regimen of health . . . , tr. from Arabic and ed. in accordance with the Hebrew and Latin versions by Ariel Bar-Sela, Hebbel E. Hoff, and Elias Faris. Philadelphia, American Philosophical Society, 1964. 50 p. *Transactions of the American Philosophical Society,* n.s., v. 54, pt. 4. **1388**

Translation of the Regimen of health and the Treatise on accidents, from a text based on fourteen manuscripts and a printed edition (text not furnished here).

—— ['Iggarot] "Maimonides' letter to Joseph B. Jehudah—a literary forgery," by J. L. Teicher, *Journal of Jewish Studies,* 1 (1948), 35–54. **1389**

Excerpts from the letter are translated.

—— ['Iggarot Teman] Epistle to Yemen, Arabic original and the three Hebrew versions, ed. by Abraham S. Halkin, English translation by Boaz Cohen. New York, American Academy for Jewish Research, 1952. xx, 111 p. *Louis M. and Minnie Epstein Series.* **1390**

Text and translation of a letter dealing with forced conversions and advice to a Jewish community on how to react to persecution.

—— [Mishneh Torah] The Code of Maimonides, gen. ed. Julian Obermann [d. 1956], Leon Nemoy. New Haven, Yale University Press, 1949–. *Yale Judaica Series,* 2–5, 8–9, 11–12, 14–16. **1391**

Eventually the complete fourteen books of Mishneh Torah will be translated in this series. The volumes appear in the order of completion by the translators; so far the following have appeared: Book XIII, The book of civil laws, tr. Jacob J. Rabinowitz, Series No. 2; Book XIV, The book of judges, tr. Abraham M. Hershman, Series No. 3; Book IX, The book of offerings, tr. Herbert Danby, Series No. 4; Book XII, The book of acquisition, tr. Isaac Klein, Series No. 5; Book X, The book of cleanness, tr. Herbert Danby, Series No. 8; Book XI, The book of torts, tr. Hyman Klein, Series No. 9; Book III, Treatise 8, Sanctification of the new moon, tr. by Solomon Gandz, Series No. 11; Book VIII, The book of temple service, tr. Mendell Lewitts, Series No. 12; Book III, The book of seasons, tr. Solomon Gandz and Hyman Klein, Series No. 14; Book VI, The book of asservations, tr. B. D. Klien [*sic*], Series No. 15; Book V, The book of holiness, tr. Louis I. Rabinowitz and Philip Grossman, Series No. 16. Maimonides wrote this work in Hebrew and the translations are directly from his text, newly edited for each volume but not furnished.

—— The degrees of Jewish benevolence, by Moses ben Maimon and Israel ibn al-Nakawa, intro. and translation by Abraham Cronbach. New York, Society for Jewish Bibliophiles, 1964. 57 p. **1392**

Hebrew text and facing translation of part of the Mishneh Torah.

—— The Mishneh Torah by Maimonides, Book II, The book of adoration, ed. according to the Bodleian (Oxford) Codes, with an English translation by Moses Hyamson, the Talmudical references and Hebrew footnotes by Chaim M. Brecher. Jerusalem, Boys Town, 1962. 2 v. **1393**

Book I, translated by Moses Hyamson, appeared in 1937; see Farrar and Evans, item 2800. It was reprinted when Vol. 2 appeared; together the two volumes are part of the Torah Classics Library. Hebrew text and facing translation.

—— Mishneh Torah, ed. and tr. by Philip Birnbaum. New York, Hebrew Publishing Co. [1967]. lxxxiii, 336 p. **1394**

Hebrew text, facing translation of selections from the Mishneh Torah. The text without translation was first published in 1944.

—— [Morek nebukim (Arabic: Dalālat al-hā'irīn)] The guide of the perplexed, abr. translation by Chaim Rabin, intro. by Julius Guttman. New York, Farrar, Straus; London, East and West Library, 1952. x, 233 p. *Philosophica Judaica.* **1395**

—— The guide of the perplexed, tr. with an intro. and notes by Shlomo Pines, with an introductory essay by Leo Strauss. [Chicago], University of Chicago Press [1963]. cxxxiv, 658 p. **1396**

—— [Responsa] Maimonides on listening to music, from the Responsa of Moses ben Maimon, texts ed. with translation and commentary by Henry George Farmer. Bearsden, Hinrichsen, 1941. 21 p. *Medieval Jewish tracts on music,* 1. **1397**

—— [Sefer ha-mitzvoh] The commandments: Sefer ha-mitzvoth of Maimonides; tr. from the Hebrew with foreword, notes, glossary, appendices, and indices by Charles B. Chavel. London and New York, Soncino Press [1967]. 2 v. **1398**

The Hebrew version is that of Joseph Kafaḥ, 1958; the original is in Arabic. Vol. II, originally published in 1940, was translated from a medieval Hebrew version; it has been revised in the light of Kafaḥ's version. *Cf.* Farrar and Evans, item 2804.

—— [Sefer ha-qazereth] Treatise on asthma, ed. by Suessman Muntner. Philadelphia, Lippincott [1963]. xxiv, 115 p. *The medical writings of Moses Maimonides,* 1. **1399**

This translation is from a modern Hebrew version of the Arabic and Latin ones, according to the editor. Maimonides' psychosomatic treatment of asthma is strikingly modern.

—— [Sharḥ fuṣūl Abiqrāt] "Maimonides' interpretation of the first aphorism of Hippocrates," by Ariel Bar-Sela and Hebbel E. Hoff, *Bulletin of the History of Medicine,* 37 (1963), 347–54. 1400

Contains translation of Maimonides' commentary on the version of Hippocrates' aphorism translated into Arabic by Ḥunain ibn Ishaq (Joannitus).

SELECTIONS

—— The world of Moses Maimonides, with selections from his writings by Jacob Samuel Minkin. New York, T. Yoseloff [1957]. 448 p. 1401

Moses ben Nahman, *c. 1195–c. 1270.* The commentary of Nahmanides on Genesis, chapters 1–6[8]; intro., critical text, translation and notes by Jacob Newman. Leiden, Brill, 1960. 19, 20–95, 20–95, xxv. *Pretoria Oriental series,* 4. 1402

Text and facing translation (first into any language, the editor says) of a mystical and kabbalistic interpretation.

—— Ramban, his life and teachings, by Charles B. Chavel. New York, Feldheim [c. 1960]. 128 p. 1403

Contains *passim* translation from Nahmanides' poems, letters, Biblical commentary, disputation with Pablo Christiani. The Dispute with Pablo Christiani is also translated in Conscience on Trial, ed. Morris Braude, New York, Exposition Press, 1952, and in Jewish religious polemic of early and later Centuries, ed. by Oliver S. Rankin, Edinburgh, University Press, 1956.

al-Mu'allaqāt. The seven odes; the first chapter in Arabic literature [by] A. J. Arberry. London, Allen & Unwin; New York, Macmillan [1957]. 258 p. 1404

Contains translation of 6th-century Arabic poems, among the few pre-Islamic works extant in Arabic. The Mu'allaqāt are called the "Suspended Poems" because they were suspended in the temple at Mecca; the work is also known as the "Golden Odes." A lengthy selection from Arberry's translation appears in Masterpieces of the Orient, ed. George L. Anderson, New York, Norton, 1961. For another translation of one of the odes, see item 1204 above.

Müller, Johannes, *Regiomontanus, 1436–76.* Regiomontanus On triangles, De triangulis omnimodis . . . tr. by Barnabas Hughes, with an intro. and notes. Madison, University of Wisconsin Press, 1967. vii, 298 p. 1405

Text and facing translation.

Muḥammad, *the prophet.* The living thoughts of the prophet Muhammad, presented by Muhammad Ali. London, Cassell [1947]. xi, 142 p. 1406

Contains selections from the Koran and the hadith (traditions), with commentary interspersed.

—— "The medicine of the Prophet," by Cyril Elgood, *Medical History,* 6 (1962), 146–53. 1407

Contains translation of excerpts from various medieval versions of the Ṭibb-ul-Nabbī, reports of Muhammad's sayings in the 7th century about medicine.

—— New light on the life of Muhammad, by Alfred Guillaume. [Manchester,

Eng.], Manchester University Press [1960]. 59 p. *Journal of Semitic studies, monograph* 1. **1408**

Contains a summary and paraphrase of excerpts about Muhammad in a manuscript discovered in 1932; the manuscript is a report of Ibn Iṣḥāḳ's lectures and contains material omitted by Ibn Hishām (*q.v.*, item 937 above).

—— The orations of Muhammad the prophet of Islam, compiled and tr. from Arabic into English by M. U. Akbar. Lahore, Ashraf [1954]. xix, 109 p. **1409**

English-Arabic in double columns. The orations have been collected from various sources. Translations of some pre-Islamic orations are included to show the form of the oration.

—— Prayers of Muhammed, the messenger of God . . . , a collection of prayers from the Holy Quran and the traditions of Muhammed . . . tr. by Abdul Hamid Farid with a foreword by . . . W. Q. Lash, Bishop of Bombay. Karachi, Karkhana Tijarat Kutub, 1959. 308 p. **1410**

Text and translation on same page. Part I contains prayers from the Koran, Part II from the Hizb al-Maqbul, daily prayers of Moslems.

—— The sayings of Prophet Muhammad, ed. by M. Amin. Lahore, Lion Press, 1960. 110 p. **1411**

The translator is not specified in the edition seen; this may well be the same work listed by Farrar and Evans, item 2820, but it was impossible to compare it with that work. The preface here is dated 1945; the Widener catalog at Harvard University lists what seems to be a reprint in 1963.

—— Thus spake prophet Muhammad, compiled by M. Hafiz Syed. Mylapore, Sri Ramakrishna Math, 1962. x, 102 p. **1412**

The translator is not specified.

Muḥammad ibn Mu'ādh, Abū 'Abd Allāh al-Yajjānī, *fl. 1080*. Euclid's conception of ratio and his definition of proportional magnitudes as criticized by Arabian commentators, including the text . . . and translation of the commentary on ratio of Abū 'Abd Allāh Muḥammad ibn Mu'ādh, al-Djajjānī, by Edward B. Plooij. Rotterdam, Van Heugel, 1950. 71 p. **1413**

Includes translation of Euclid's first seven definitions and commentary by a mathematician from Seville.

Muḥammad ibn 'Umar, al-Rāzī, *1149 or 50–1210*. A study of Fakhr al-Din Razi and his Controversies in Transoxiana, by Fathalla Kholeif. Beyrouth, Far al-Machreq, 1966. xvi, 226, 70 p. **1414**

Includes text and translation of the Controversies in Transoxiana, which are al-Rāzī's own resumés of philosophical arguments already engaged in; involves a commentary on the Koran.

Muḥammad ibn Zakarīya, Abū Bakr, al-Rāzī, *d. c. 923*. "Rhazes on the philosophic life," by Arthur J. Arberry, *Asiatic Review*, 45 (1949), 703–13. **1415**

Translation of an apologia pro vita sua.

—— The "Spiritual physick" of Rhazes, tr. by A. J. Arberry. London, John Murray; [Forest Hills, N.Y.], Transatlantic Arts [1950]. 115 p. *Wisdom of the East.* **1416**

According to Professor Arberry, this is the first translation into any modern language; some excerpts from Rhazes' Autobiography are also translated.

al-Mu'izz ibn Bādīs, Emir of Ifrīqiyah, *1008–62.* Medieval Arabic book-making and its relation to early chemistry and pharmacology, by Martin Levey. Philadelphia, American Philosophical Society, 1962. 79 p. *Transactions of the American Philosophical Society,* n.s., v. 52, pt. 4. **1417**

Chiefly a translation of 'Umdat al-Kuttāb wa-'uddat dhawī al-alkāb. The translator has traced the technical terms and names of materials used in the earliest literature available.

Musaeus, *5th or 6th cent.* Hero & Leander, tr. by F. L. Lucas. London, C. Sandford, 1949. 47 p. **1418**

This translation has not been seen.

Music.

For a more complete bibliography, see "Music theory in translation, a bibliography," by James Coover, *Journal of Music Theory,* 3 (1959), 70–95.

—— "The adventures of an English minstrel and his varlet," by Bertram Schofield, *Musical Quarterly,* 35 (1949), 361–76. **1419**

Contains translation of "Confession of an English minstrel who was executed in Paris in the year of grace 1384," from British Museum Ms. Egerton 3509.

—— "Another look at the Montpellier Organum treatise," by Fred Blum, *Musica Disciplina,* 13 (1959), 15–24. **1420**

Contains an English translation of the treatise and of musical examples of its theory. The treatise dates from the early 12th century but describes an 11th-century style, according to the author.

—— Byzantine sacred music, by Constantine Cavarnos. Belmont, Mass., Institute for Byzantine and Modern Greek Studies [c. 1956]. 31 p. **1421**

In addition to translation of the canons, this work contains excerpts from the Greek fathers on music and its manner of presentation.

—— Historical anthology of music, by A. T. Davison and Willi Apel. Cambridge, Harvard University Press, 1946–50; rev. ed., 1949, 1966. 2 v. **1422**

Chs. 2 and 3, Early and late medieval music, and Chs. 4 and 5, The Fifteenth century, have music and texts followed by prose translation of the texts from many languages.

—— Masterpieces of music before 1750, an anthology of musical examples from Gregorian chant to J. S. Bach, compiled and ed. by Carl Parrish and John F. Ohl. New York, Norton, 1951. x, 235 p. **1423**

All-non-English texts other than liturgical Latin have been translated into English in the songs, with music; liturgical texts are translated at the head of the texts. In addition to anonymous liturgical music, the work includes songs of an anonymous trouvère, of Neidhart von Reuenthal, Gilles Binchois, Guillaume Dufay, Johannes Ockeghem, Jacob Obrecht, Josquin des Prez.

—— Medieval carols, ed. by John Stevens. London, 1952. 145 p. *Musica Britannica, a national collection of music:* 4. **1424**

15th-century Latin carols are translated; Middle English ones have been modernized in spelling.

—— "Musical compositions in Renaissance intarsia," by Gustave Reese, *Medieval and Renaissance Studies,* 2 (1966), 74–97. **1425**

Contains translation of two 15th-century songs, "J'ay pris amours en ma devise," and Johannes

Ockeghem's "Prenz sur moi vostre exemple amoureux," and a 12th-century Christmas hymn, "Verbo caro factum est."

—— The new Oxford history of music. Vol. II, Early medieval music up to 1300, ed. by Anselm Hughes, London and New York, Oxford University Press, 1954, xviii, 434 p; Vol. III, Ars nova and the Renaissance, 1300–1540, ed. by Anselm Hughes and Gerald Abraham, New York and London, Oxford University Press, 1960. **1426**

Both volumes contain text and prose translation of the words for many examples of both liturgical and secular music, from many languages, as well as translation of excerpts from musical theorists and commentators.

—— "The song captions in the Kitāb al-Aghāni al-Kabīr," by George Henry Farmer, *Transactions of the Glasgow University Oriental Society,* 15 (1953–54), pp. 1–10. **1427**

From the captions in a 10th-century compilation, by Abū al-Faraj al-Iṣfahānī, Professor Farmar deduces the modes.

—— Source readings in music history, ed. by Oliver Strunk. New York, Norton, 1950. xxi, 919 p. **1428**

Contains translation of many medieval treatises, including those by anonymous writers, Franco of Cologne, Cassiodorus, Guido Aretinus, Jacques de Liege, Johannes de Muris, Marchettus de Padua, Odo of Cluny, Ramos de Pareja, Joannes Tinctoris.

Mustansir bi'l-lah, Jalāl al-Dīn, *15th cent.* Pandiyat-i-jawanmardi, or Advices of manliness, ed. in the original Persian and tr. . . . by W. Ivanow. Leiden, Brill, 1953. 19, 97, 102 p. *Ismaili Society,* series A, 6. **1429**

A collection of religious and moral maxims ascribed to Mustansir but compiled by an anonymous follower.

al-Mutanabbī, Abū al-Tayyib Aḥmad, *915 or 916–965.* Poems of al-Mutanabbi, tr. by A. J. Arberry. Cambridge [Eng.] and New York, Cambridge University Press, 1966. vi, 155 p. **1430**

Text and facing translation of twenty-six poems, largely about heroes, by, in Arberry's opinion, "the greatest of all Arabic poets."

Mxit'ar Goš, *c. 1130–1213.* "The Albanian chronicle of Mxit'ar Goš," by C. J. F. Dowsett, *Bulletin of the School of Oriental and African Studies,* 21 (1958), 472–90. **1431**

A translation from Armenian of a work dealing with events *c.* 1130–62 in Armenia and Albania, by a contemporary.

Mystery and miracle plays.

The revival in the 1950s and 1960s of performances of the English plays has led to new modernized acting versions, not all of which have been published, by such directors as Jean Claudius and Peter Jackson. In addition to collections listed here, see also the individual cycles, Chester, York, Towneley, the Cornish Ordinalia, etc.

—— An anthology of English drama before Shakespeare . . . , ed. by Robert B. Heilman. New York, Rinehart [c. 1952]. xvii, 405 p. **1432**

Contains from the Middle Ages: Ludus Coventriae (N-towne) Betrayal; York Crucifixion, Wakefield (Towneley) Noah and Second shepherds' play; Everyman.

—— Everyman and medieval mystery plays, ed. by Arthur C. Cawley. New York, Dutton [c. 1959]. xxi, 266 p. *Everyman's library* **1433**

Strictly speaking, these are not translations, except of the Cornish trilogy, the Death of Pilate; but difficult words in the text are glossed at the right and many passages translated at the bottom of the page. Included are six plays from the York cycle, two from N-Towne, Chester, and Towneley, and the Brome Abraham and Isaac, as well as the Cornish Trilogy and Everyman. The translation of the Cornish plays has been extensively revised in the second edition, 1959. Professor Cawley also published a modernized version of the Wakefield (Towneley) Second shepherds' play, *Yorkshire Dialect Society Transactions,* 8, part 50 (1950), pp. 8–28.

—— Fourteen plays for the Church, ed. by Robert Schenkkan and Kai Jurgensen. New Brunswick, N.J., Rutgers University Press, 1948. xii, 268 p. **1434**

Six plays are modernizations of Middle English: one each from York and the Brome manuscript, two each from Wakefield (Towneley) and Coventry. Four plays are from a French manuscript of Latin: Herod and the Kings, St. Nicholas and the Scholars, the Fleury Sepulchre play, Journey to Emmaeus; others translated are The King of Glory, from a Klosterneuberg manuscript, in German and Latin; the Redentin Easter Play, and Hilarius' Raising of Lazarus.

—— Medieval mysteries, moralities, and interludes, ed. by Vincent F. Hopper and Gerald B. Lahey. Woodbury, N.Y., Barron's Educational Series [c. 1962]. 299 p. **1435**

Contains from the Middle Ages modernizations of the Brome Abraham and Isaac, Wakefield (Towneley) Second shepherds' play, the Castle of Perseverance, Everyman.

—— Miracle plays, seven medieval plays for modern players, adapted by Anne B. Malcolmson. London, Constable [c. 1959]; Boston, Houghton Mifflin, 1959. xii, 142 p. **1436**

Contains modernizations of the Chester Noah, Brome Abraham and Isaac, York Nativity, Wakefield (Towneley) Second shepherds' play, Coventry Herod and the Magi; and translation from Hilarius' Tres clerici and the Ludus super Iconia Sancti Nicolai.

—— The Redemption: a play of the life of Christ adapted from the medieval mystery cycles of York, Towneley, Chester, the Ludus Coventriae, and the Coventry Corpus Christi plays, by Gordon Honeycombe. London, Methuen, 1964. 108 p. **1437**

The play was produced in England, with music, under title The Miracles.

—— Seven miracle plays, ed. by Alexander Franklin. [London and New York], Oxford University Press, 1963. 158 p. **1438**

Rather loose adaptation and abridgment of some parts, but translation into modern verse acting versions of the Towneley Cain and Abel, Chester Noah's Flood, Brome Abraham and Isaac, Chester Shepherds and King Herod, York Three kings, Norwich Adam and Eve.

—— Three medieval plays, ed. by John P. Allen. London, Heinemann, 1953. xi, 43, 40, 54 p. **1439**

Contains new versions of the Coventry Nativity and of Everyman, and a translation of Master Pierre Pathelin, a 15th-century French play.

—— A treasury of the theatre, ed. by John Gassner. New York, Simon & Schuster [c. 1951], 3d ed. [c. 1967]. **1440**

All three editions contain the Brome Abraham and Isaac, the Towneley Second shepherds' play, Everyman; the 3d edition adds Hrotsvitha's Paphnutius, translated by M. M. Butler, and the Cornish Death of Pilate, adapted by Gassner.

MYSTERY AND MIRACLE PLAYS

—— Twenty-one medieval mystery and morality plays, ed. by E. Martin Browne. Cleveland, World Publishing Co. [1958]. 317 p. *Religious drama*, 2. **1441**

Contains twelve plays from the York cycle; the Chester Noah's Flood; Brome Sacrifice of Isaac; Wakefield Shepherds' play; Hegge Parliament of heaven, Annunciation, and Woman taken in Adultery; Coventry Herod; the two David plays and excerpts from the Three Maries from the Cornish cycle; and Everyman.

Mysticism. *Collections.*

For other mystical writings, see under headings *Islamic literature* for Sufism, *Judaism* for Hebrew mystical writings, and individual writers; see index *s.v. Mysticism.*

—— Anthology of mysticism, ed. by Paul de Jaegher, tr. by Donald Attwater and others. Westminster, Md., Newman Press, 1950. viii, 281 p. **1442**

Contains translations from St. Angela of Foligno, Jan Ruysbroek, Henry Suso, Richard Rolle, John Tauler, Juliana of Norwich, the Cloud of unknowing, St. Catherine of Siena, Walter Hilton, and St. Catherine of Genoa.

—— The mystics of Spain, by E. Allison Peers. London, Allen & Unwin [1951]. 130 p. **1443**

From medieval writers, contains translation of only a few excerpts from Ramón Lull, pp. 41–45, and Garcia de Cisneros, pp. 46–48.

—— The soul afire, revelations of the mystics, by Carol North Valhope [pseud. of Olga Marx], ed. by H. A. Reinhold. New York, Pantheon Books [1944]. xxiii, 413 pp. **1444**

Has translations, many new for this volume, of excerpts from mystical writings from Plato to modern times; organized by topics. Many medieval works are included, especially from the German mystics.

—— Varieties of mystic experience, an anthology and interpretation, by Elmer O'Brien. New York, Holt, Rinehart, and Winston, 1964. x, 321 p. **1445**

Includes excerpts from previously published translations of Christian and Islamic mystics.

Mythological cycle, Irish. The cycle of the kings, by Myles Dillon. London and New York, Oxford University Press, 1946. 124 p. **1446**

Although these are retellings rather than translations, they are included here because many of the tales have not been translated previously, according to a review by Kenneth Jackson in *Speculum,* 1948, p. 119.

N

al-Narshakhī, Muḥammad ibn Ja'far, *d. 959.* The history of Bukhara, tr. from a Persian abridgment of the Arabic original by Narshakhī, [ed. and tr. by] Richard N. Frye. Cambridge, Mediaeval Academy of America, 1954. xx, 178 p. *Mediaeval Academy of America publications,* 61. **1447**

The Persian translation was made in 1128 from the Arabic of 943 or 944, contemporary with the events recorded.

Nāṣir li-'l-Ḥaqq, al-Ḥasan, *d. 917.* "A Zaydī manual of Ḥisbah of the 3rd Century (H)," ed. and tr. by Robert Serjeant, *Revista degli Studia Orientali,* 28 (1953), 1–10. **1448**

Contains detailed outline of the contents of "one of the earliest known texts" specifying application of traditions to daily behaviour.

Nāṣir ibn Khusraw, Mu'īn Abū-Mu'īn, *1003–88.* Six chapters or Shish fasl, also called Rawshana'i-nama, Persian text ed. and tr. by W. Ivanow. Leiden, Brill, 1949. xii, 111, 47 p. *Ismaili Society,* series B, 6. **1449**

An Ismaili work on the nature of the soul and its relation to God. Newly discovered evidence indicates a considerably earlier date of birth for Nāṣir ibn Khusraw than was previously accepted.

——, *supposed author.* "The Sa'ādatanāmeh attributed to Nāṣir-i Khusrau," by G. M. Wickens, *Islamic Quarterly,* 2 (1955), 117–32, 206–21. **1450**

Translation of a Persian poem on how to be happy, "Book of felicity." Unlike other works attributed to Nāṣir, this contains no Ismaili doctrines, according to the translator. Another article by Wickens also contains translation, *passim*: "The Chronology of Nāṣir-i Khusrau's Safarnāma," *Islamic Quarterly,* 4 (1957), 67–77.

Naṣr al-Dīn, kwājah, *13th or 14th cent.* The exploits of the incomparable Mulla Nasrudin by Idries Shah. London, Cape, 1966. 158 p. **1451**

The work gives no indication of the source used or the extent of paraphrase.

—— More tales of Mullah Nasir-ud-Din, Persian wit, wisdom, and folly, by Eric Daenecke. New York, Exposition Press [1961]. 72 p. Vol. 2. **1452**

One hundred tales are included here. Vol. 1 has not been located.

—— Once the Hodja, tr. by Alice G. Kelsey. New York, Longmans, Green, 1943. xii, 170 p. **1453**

A collection of oral tales, retold; a version of The Turkish jester. Strictly speaking, these belong to the category of fairy stories, where the Library of Congress classifies them; but tradition assigns them medieval provenience.

—— Tales of the Hodja, retold by Charles Downing. New York, Henry Z. Walck, 1965 [c. 1964]. 98 p. **1454**

Nathan ben Joel Palquera, *13th cent.* "Naṭhan ben Joel and his Ẓori HaÇuf," by Mordecai B. Etziony, *Bulletin of the History of Medicine,* 37 (1963), 257–78. **1455**

Contains translation of a portion of the third treatise of the second part of Nathan's work, a section on "Balsam for the body."

Neckam, Alexander, *1157–1217.* Daily living in the twelfth century, based on the observations of Alexander Neckam in London and Paris, by Urban Tigner Holmes, Jr. Madison, University of Wisconsin Press, 1952. ix, 337 p. **1456**

An "almost complete" translation of De nominibus utensilium, with commentary interspersed, to show Alexander as if on a journey from England to Paris; includes translation of excerpts from other contemporary and later sources.

Neidhart von Reuental, *13th cent.* The songs of Neidhart von Reuental; 17 summer and winter songs set to their original melodies with translation and a musical and metrical canon, by A. T. Hatto and R. J. Taylor. [Manchester], Manchester University Press [1958]. xi, 112 p. **1457**

Nemesius, *bp. of Emesa, 4th or 5th cent.* Cyril of Jerusalem and Nemesius of

Emesa, ed. and tr. by William Telfer. Philadelphia, Westminster Press [1955]. 466 p. *Library of Christian classics*, 4. **1458**

Contains a translation of Nemesius' On the nature of man, an essay indebted to Hippocrates, pp. 224–453.

Netherlands literature. *Collections.* Coming after, an anthology of poetry from the Low Countries, ed. by A. J. Barnouw. New Brunswick, N. J., Rutgers University Press, 1948. xx, 348 p. **1459**

Medieval works translated on pp. 3–61 include selections from John, Duke of Brabant; Hadewijch; Willem's Reynard the Fox; Jacob von Maerlant; Anthonis de Roovere; and some ballads and devotional songs from 1300–1500.

— Medieval Netherlands religious literature, tr. by Eric Colledge. Leyden and London, Heinemann; New York, London House and Maxwell, 1965. 226 p. *Bibliotheca Neerlandica*, 2. **1460**

Contains translation of works by Beatrice of Nazareth (*c.* 1200–68); Hadewijch of Antwerp; Jan Ruysbroek; and a poem, Beatrice, from a manuscript of 1375.

—— Reynard the fox and other medieval Netherlands secular literature, ed. by Eric Colledge, tr. by Adriaan J. Barnouw and Eric Colledge. Leyden, Sijthoff; London, Heinemann; New York, London House and Maxwell, 1967. 226 p. **1461**

Contains translation of Reynard the Fox; Lancelot of Denmark and Say that Again (dramas from the Hulthem Manuscript); Charles and Elegast, attributed to Peter Vostaert; and two episodes from Walewein: the fight with the dragon, the king of faerie's castle.

Nibelungenlied. The Nibelungenlied, a new translation by A. T. Hatto. Baltimore, Penguin Books [1965, c. 1964]. 403 p. **1462**

A prose translation.

—— The Nibelungenlied, tr. with an intro. and notes by D. G. Mowatt. London, Dent; New York, Dutton [1963, c. 1962]. xiv, 225 p. *Everyman's library.* **1463**

Although this volume has the same number in the Everyman library (312), it is a new prose translation based on a text of 1956, replacing the translation of Margery Armour.

—— The Song of the Nibelungs, a verse translation from the Middle High German by Frank G. Ryder. Detroit, Wayne State University Press, 1962. xiv, 421 p. **1464**

This translation is in a verse form approximating that of the original; it is based largely on Ms. B.

Niccolò da Poggibonsi, *fl. 1345.* A voyage beyond the seas (1346–1350), tr. by T. Bellorini and E. Hoade. . . . Jerusalem, Franciscan Press, 1945. xlviii, 143 p. *Publications of the Studium Biblicum Franciscanum.* 2. **1465**

A translation of Libro d'oltramare, record of a journey from Venice to Cyprus, Jerusalem, Syria, Bagdad, Sinai, and Egypt by a Franciscan who describes in detail many churches and religious customs. Vol. I of this series is a new edition of the text upon which this translation is based.

Nicephorus, *patriarch of Constantinople, d. 828.* The patriarch Nicephorus of Constantinople; ecclesiastical policy and image worship in the Byzantine empire, by Paul J. Alexander. Oxford, Clarendon Press, 1958. xii, 287 p. **1466**

Contains a summary and paraphrase of "Refutatio et eversio," pp. 242–62. An earlier article by Professor Alexander contains a translation also of the florilegium which Nicephorus was refuting: "The iconoclastic Council of St. Sophia," *Dumbarton Oaks Papers*, 7 (1953), 35–66. The Council occurred in 815.

Nicolas de Lyre, *1270–1349*. Rashi and the Christian scholars, by Herman Hailperin. Pittsburgh, University of Pittsburgh Press [1963]. xvii, 379 p. **1467**

Has extensive translation of excerpts from Nicolas' biblical commentary, Postilla litteralis super totam Bibliam, as well as some translation of the commentary on the Pentateuch by Rashi (Solomon ben Isaac, 1040–1105).

Nicolaus Cusanus, *cardinal, 1401–64*. Of learned ignorance by Nicolas Cusanus, tr. by Germain Heron, intro. by D. J. B. Hawkins. New Haven, Yale University Press; London, Routledge & Kegan Paul, 1954. xxviii, 174 p. **1468**

—— Unity and reform; selected writings, ed. by John Patrick Dolan. [Notre Dame, Ind.], University of Notre Dame Press [c. 1962]. viii, 260 p. **1469**

Selections, some newly translated by the editor, are from De docta ignorantia, De sapientia, De visione Dei, De pace fidei, De staticis experimentis. In another work, a summary and extensive quotations from an otherwise untranslated work of Nicolaus appear: The political ideas of Nicholaus of Cusa, with special reference to his De concordantia Catholica, by Morimichi Watanabe, Geneva, Libraire Droz, 1963, 214 p.

Nicolaus Damascenus, *b. 40* B.C. Nicolaus Damascenus on the philosophy of Aristotle, fragments of the first books, tr. from the Syriac by H. J. D. Lulofs. Leiden, Brill, 1965. xi, 174 p. *Philosophia antiqua,* 13. **1470**

Text and facing translation of an anonymous Syriac translation from the original Greek.

Nicolaus de Autricuria, *fl. 14th cent*. Nicolaus of Autrecourt, a study in fourteenth-century thought, by Julius Rudolph Weinberg. Princeton, N.J., Princeton University Press for the University of Cincinnati, 1948. ix, 242 p. **1471**

Translation *passim* and paraphrase of the fragmentary works of Nicolaus which constitute a refutation of Aristotle.

Nider, Johannes, *c. 1380–1438*. On the contracts of merchants, tr. by Charles H. Reeves, ed. by Ronald B. Shuman. Norman, University of Oklahoma Press [c. 1966]. xiii, 77 p. **1472**

The work is a moral guide to buying and selling.

Nikolaos I, Mystikos, *Saint, patriarch of Constantinople, 852–925*. "Three documents concerning the tetragamy," by Romilly J. H. Jenkins, *Dumbarton Oaks Papers,* 16 (1962), 231–41. **1473**

Text and translation of three letters of Nikolaos concerning the marriage in 906 of Leo VI, the Wise, Emperor of the East.

Nikolaos Mesaritēs, *b. 1163 or 1164*. Description of the church of the Holy Apostles at Constantinople, ed. and tr. by Glanville Downey. Philadelphia, American Philosophical Society, 1957. *Transactions of the American Philosophical Society,* n.s. v. 47, pt. 6, pp. 855–924. **1474**

Translation and text.

Nikolaus, *von Dresden, d. c. 1416*. The old color and the new; selected works contrasting the primitive church and the Roman church [by] Nicholas of Dresden, ed., annotated and tr. by Howard Kaminsky [and others]. Philadelphia, American Philosophical Society, 1965. 93 p. *Transactions of the American Philosophical Society,* n.s., v. 55, pt. 1. 1475

Text and translation in double columns of Tabule veteris et novi coloris, The tables of the old and new color; and of Consuetudo et ritus primitive ecclesie et moderne, Customs and rites of the primitive and modern churches. These works were once attributed to John Hus but now Nicholas' authorship is certain, according to the editor.

Nikulus Bergsson of Munkathvera, *d. 1159–60.* "The pilgrim-diary of Nikulus of Munkathvera: the road to Rome," by Francis P. Magoun, Jr., *Medieval Studies,* 6 (1944), 314–54. 1476

Has text and translation (pp. 347–50) of an Icelandic record of a journey made in 1154 which indicates routes, stopping places, and time.

Niẓām al-Mulk, *1018–1092.* The book of government; or, Rules for kings: the Siyāsatnāma or Siyar al-mulūk, tr. from the Persian by Hubert Darke. New Haven, Yale University Press, 1960. xi, 259 p. *Rare masterpieces of philosophy and science.* UNESCO *collection of representative works, Persian series.* 1477

Niẓāmī Ganjavī, *1141–1203.* An English translation of Gulshan-i-Ma'ani, . . . by K. M. Maitra. Lahore, Punjab University, 1934. 1478

Selections from the Haf Paikar, a collection of seven stories. This translation was not listed by Farrar and Evans; a copy is in the British Museum but has not been seen.

—— Makhzanol Asrār, the treasury of mysteries of Nezāmī of Ganjeh, tr. . . . by Gholām Hosein Dārāb. London, Probsthain, 1945. xvi, 258 p. 1479

Translation of the Makhzan al-asrār, a poem appealing for religious and governmental reforms, with exemplary stories. Excerpts from other works of Niẓāmī are translated in the introductory essay.

Njála. Njál's saga, tr. with intro. and notes by Carl F. Bayerschmidt and Lee M. Hollander. [New York], New York University Press for the American-Scandinavian Foundation, 1955. xii, 390 p. 1480

The translation is based on the 1908 text of F. Jónsson, though checked against the new text of Einár O. Sveinsson, 1954.

—— Njal's saga, tr. with an intro. by Magnus Magnusson and Hermann Pálsson. Baltimore, Penguin Books, [1960]. 375 p. 1481

The translation is based on the 1954 edition of Einár O. Sveinsson.

Nonnus Panopolitanus, *5th cent., supposed author.* "The Armenian and Syriac versions of the Ps-Nonnus mythological scholia," by Sebastian Brock, *Le Muséon,* 79 (1966), 401–28. 1482

Translation of parts of the Syriac version of the scholia to Gregory of Naziazen's orations, attributed to Nonnus of Panopolis. The author expects to publish a complete edition and translation soon.

al-Nu'man, Abū Ḥanīfa, *d. 974.* Selections from Qazi Noaman's Kitab-ul-himma fi adabi ataba-ul-a'emma or Code of conduct for the followers of the Imam, tr. into English by Jawad Muscati and A. M. Moulvi. Karachi, Ismaila Association of West Pakistan, 1950. ii, 135 p. 1483

Contains a code of ethics outlining duties to the Imam and to fellows, from a "classic of Ismā'īlī literature." A translation of part of another work of al-Nu'man, "The pillars of wisdom," appeared in an unpublished Columbia University thesis by Gerard G. Salinger, Ann Arbor, University Microfilms No. 8256, 1956.

O

Ockham, William, *d. c. 1349.* Ockham, philosophical writings, a selection, ed. and tr. by Philotheus Boehner. [Edinburgh and New York], Nelson [1957]. lix, 147, 147, [148]–154 p. **1484**

Text and facing translation of selections of Ockham's works on logic, physics, and theology, as well as political writings on his break with the papacy. The English translation only of this was published by the Bobbs-Merrill Company, Indianapolis, 1964, lix, 167 p.

Odo, *Saint, abbot of Cluny, c. 879–942.* Saint Odo of Cluny, being the life of St. Odo of Cluny by John of Salerno, and the life of St. Gerard of Aurillac by St. Odo, ed. and tr. by Gerard Sitwell. London and New York, Sheed & Ward, [1958]. xxix, 186 p. **1485**

Odo de Deuil, *abbot of Saint Denis, d. c. 1162.* De profectione Ludovici VII in orientem, ed., with an English translation by Virginia Gingerick Berry. New York, Columbia University Press, 1948. xliv, 154 p. *Records of civilization*, 42. **1486**

Text and facing translation of a history of the second crusade, 1147–49, led by Louis VII, King of France.

Oliverus, *bp. of Paderborn, d. 1227.* The capture of Damietta, tr. by John J. Gavigan. Philadelphia, University of Pennsylvania Press; London, Oxford University Press, 1948. ix. 112 p. *Translations and reprints from the original sources of history*, 3d series, 2. **1487**

Translation of a firsthand account of the fifth crusade.

Olympiodorus the Younger of Alexandria, *6th cent.* Anonymous prolegomena to Platonic philosophy, intro., text, translation, and indices by L. G. Westerink. Amsterdam, North Holland Publishing Co., 1962. lii, 69 p. **1488**

Text and facing translation of a neoplatonic work ascribed to Olympiodorus.

'Omar Khayyām, *d. 1123.* [Rubáiyát].

During the 1940s and 50s, three new manuscripts of the Rubáiyát have been discovered, two hundred years closer to the author than others previously known; they indicate that 'Omar was undoubtedly the author of many of the quatrains that have been thought to be later additions, as was noted in Farrar and Evans. See A. J. Arberry, "Omar Again," *Bulletin of the School of Oriental and African Studies,* 14 (1952), 413–19; and in the same journal, pp. 207–8, a review of Arberry's translation of the Chester Beatty manuscript version of the Rubáiyát. The translations which follow are listed chronologically in order to show their relationship to the new manuscripts.

—— The unknown Omar Khayyam, seventy-nine quatrains, tr. by Yusuf Khan. West Worthing [Eng.], Fantasma Press, 1947. 12 p. **1489**

This work, a copy of which is in the British Museum, has not been seen.

—— The Rubaiyat of Omar Khayyam, ed. from a newly discovered ms. dated

658 (1259–60) in the possession of A. Chester Beatty, Esq., by A. J. Arberry, with comparative English versions of Edward Fitzgerald, E. H. Whinfield, and the editor. London, E. Walker, 1949. vii, 172 p. **1490**

For each quatrain, the Persian text and the three English versions are given on the same page.

—— The Rubaiyat, a new version based upon recent discoveries by A. J. Arberry. London, Murray; New Haven, Yale University Press, 1952. 159 p. **1491**

This version translated by Arberry is based on the newly discovered Cambridge manuscript dated 604 (1207), 75 years after Omar's death. It contains 172 quatrains; see pp. 151–59 for a chart comparing quatrains of various manuscripts and editions.

—— The Rubaiyat. A new version by Horace Thorner. London, Brookside Press [c. 1955]. 55 p. **1492**

The translator explains that his work is "based upon" Fitzgerald's fifth edition and upon the French translation of J. B. Nicolas, 1867; but he does not make clear whether or not he has translated from Persian or from intermediary translations; he does say "I have made use of texts not known to Fitzgerald, as well as those he knew."

—— The romance of the Rubaiyat, by A. J. Arberry: Edward Fitzgerald's first edition, reprinted with intro. and notes. London, Allen & Unwin; New York, Macmillan, 1959. 245 p. **1493**

The reprint is noted here because Arberry evaluates it in the light of the newly discovered manuscripts.

—— From a Persian garden: new quatrains of Omar Khayyam; renderings [by] Isak David du Plessis, based on the Arberry version of the Teheran ms. Capetown, H. Timmins, 1959; 2d ed., 1960. London, Bailey, 1960. 149 p. **1494**

Seventy quatrains not in the Fitzgerald versions. The author states that he has no knowledge of Persian; therefore he must refer in the title to Arberry's English version of the "Teheran manuscript," but he does not specify the date of the manuscript.

—— The Rubaiyat, a new selection . . . rendered into English verse by John Charles Edward Bowen, with a literal translation by A. J. Arberry. London, Unicorn Press, 1961. xv, 136 p. **1495**

Contains text and translation of sixty quatrains from the Cambridge and Chester Beatty manuscripts.

—— "Omar Khayyam and Fitzgerald," by F. R. C. Bagley, *Durham University Journal,* 59, n.s. 28 (1966), 81–93. **1496**

Contains author's translation of some stanzas not translated by Fitzgerald.

—— The original Rubaiyat of Omar Khayyam, a new translation by Robert Graves and Omar Ali-Shah. London, Cassell, 1967. 86 p. **1497**

Contains verse translations of 111 quatrains from the Cambridge manuscript, under the supervision of Omar Ali-Shah, a Sufi poet whose family owns the manuscript and who made a literal translation of it. The editors maintain that the poem is really a Sufic document, not a hedonistic one.

—— "A paper of Omar Khayyam," by A. Amir-Moéz, *Scripta Mathematica,* 26 (1961), 323–37. **1498**

Translation of titleless paper on mathematics by 'Omar.

Oresme, Nicolas, *bp., d. 1382.* An abstract of Nicolas Orême's Treatise on the breadths of forms, by Charles G. Wallis. Annapolis, St. John's Bookstore, 1941. 23 p. *Great books of the St. John's program.* **1499**

This is a summary and paraphrase of a treatise printed in 1468.

—— The De moneta of Nicholas Oresme, and English Mint documents, tr. with intro. and notes by Charles Johnson. London and New York, Nelson [1956]. xli, 96, 96, 97–114 p. *Medieval texts.* **1500**

Text and facing translation of Oresme's treatise and of documents relating to the recoinages of 1247, 1279, 1300 and to the gold coinage of Edward III.

—— De proportionibus proportionum, and Ad pauca respicientes [by] Nicole Oresme, ed. with intro., English translation and critical notes by Edward Grant. Madison, University of Wisconsin Press, 1966. xxii, 466 p. *University of Wisconsin publications in medieval science, 9.* **1501**

The first work is on ratios, the second about circular motion. The editor maintains that these are "essentially original treatises" rather than redactions of others' works.

—— Maistre Nicole Oresme: le livre de yconomique d'Aristote, tr. by Albert D. Menut. Philadelphia, American Philosophical Society, 1957. *Transactions of the American Philosophical Society,* n.s., 47 (1957), 783–853. **1502**

Oresme translated a Latin version of the pseudo-Aristotelian "Economics," rearranging it and interpolating commentary; the present translation is from Oresme's Old French into English.

—— Nicole Oresme and the astrologers, a study of his Livre de divinacions . . ., by G. W. Coopland. Liverpool, University Press; Cambridge, Harvard University Press, 1952. vii, 221 p. **1503**

Contains Old French text and facing translation of Oresme's Livre de divinacions and the text of his Tractatus contra judicarios astronomos.

—— "Part I of Nicole Oresme's Algorismus proportionum," by Edward Grant, *Isis,* 56 (1965), 327–41. **1504**

Annotated translation based on author's edition from thirteen manuscripts of a treatise which is the "first known attempt to present operational rules for multiplication and division."

—— Quaestiones super Geometriam Euclidis, ed. and tr. by Hubertus L. L. Busard. Leiden, Brill, 1961. xiv, 179 p. **1505**

Text and translation of Oresme's twenty-one questions dealing with various mathematical concepts; the editor says that Oresme's version of Euclid is a paraphrase rather than a translation.

Orientus, *bp. of Auch, 5th cent.* Orientii Commonitorium, a commentary with an intro. and translation by Mildred D. Tobin. Washington, Catholic University of America Press, 1945. 143 p. *Patristic studies,* 74. **1506**

Text and facing translation of Orientus' exhortation to a Christian mode of life.

Origenes, *d. c. 253.* Prayer; Exhortation to martyrdom, tr. by John J. O'Meara. London, Longmans, Green; Westminster, Md., Newman Press, 1954. 253 p. *Ancient Christian writers,* 19. **1507**

—— Contra Celsum, tr. with an intro. and notes by Henry Chadwick. Cambridge [Eng.], Cambridge University Press, 1953. xl, 530 p. **1508**

ORIGENES

According to the translator, this work represents the "culmination of the whole apologetic movement of the second and third centuries."

—— The Song of songs: commentary and homilies, tr. and annotated by R. P. Lawson. Westminster, Md., Newman Press, 1957. 385 p. *Ancient Christian writers,* 26. **1509**

The English translation has been made from the Latin versions by Rufinus (Commentary) and St. Jerome (homilies).

—— Treatise on prayer, translation and notes . . . by Eric George Jay. London, S.P.C.K., 1954. x, 237 p. **1510**

A translation of Peri euches appears on pp. 79–219.

Orosius, Paulus, *fl. c. 417.* The seven books of history against the pagans, tr. by Roy J. Deferrari. Washington, Catholic University of America Press [1964]. xxi, 422 p. *Fathers of the Church,* 50. **1511**

The work is also known as Orosius' Apology; in it Orosius argues that history supports Christian views.

Ossianic poems. Duanaire Finn, the book of the lays of Fionn, Part III, containing notes to all the poems, glossary, indices, etc., by Gerard Murphy. Dublin, Educational Company of Ireland, 1953. 190 p. *Irish Texts Society,* 43. **1512**

For text and translation, *cf.* Farrar and Evans, item 3032. Part III contains corrigenda for Parts I and II.

Otto, *bp. of Freising, d. 1158.* The deeds of Frederik Barbarossa, by Otto of Freising and his continuator Rahewin, tr. by Charles C. Mierow, aided by Richard Emery. New York, Columbia University Press; London, Oxford University Press, 1953. xi, 366 p. *Records of civilization,* 49. **1513**

Otto's chronicle covers the years 1075–1158; Rahewin (d. 1177), continued through 1160, with a "few jottings" for 1161 and 1169.

Owl and the nightingale. *Middle English poem.* The owl and the nightingale, tr. by Graydon Eggers, with a foreword by Paull F. Baum. [Durham, N.C.], Duke University Press, 1955. xvii, 62. **1514**

P

Paccioli, Luca, *d. c. 1514.* Paciolo on accounting, tr. and ed. by R. Gene Brown, intro. by Alvin R. Jennings. New York, McGraw-Hill, 1963. xviii, 144 p. **1515**

Facsimile text and translation of the Particularis de computis et scripturis, Details of accounting and recording, a treatise on bookkeeping from Paccioli's Summa de Arithmetica . . . . According to the editor, Paccioli's work introduced double-entry bookkeeping, and his Summa was "the most widely read mathematical work in the whole of Italy."

Palladius, *successively bp. of Helenopolis and of Aspona, d. c. 430.* Palladius: the Lausiac history, tr. and annotated by Robert T. Meyer. Westminster, Md., Newman Press, 1965. vii, 265 p. *Ancient Christian writers,* 34. **1516**

The Lausiac history deals with Egyptian monasticism.

Pamphilus, Maurilianus, *12th cent., supposed author.* "Pamphilus, De amore," an intro. and translation by Thomas Jay Garbáty, *Chaucer Review,* 2 (1967), 108–34. **1517**

Translation of an Art of love written around 1200.

Paris e Viana. Paris and Vienne, tr. . . . by William Caxton, ed. by MacEdward Leach. London and New York, published for the Early English Text Society by the Oxford University Press, 1957. xxxi, 120 p. *Early English Text Society,* original series, 234. **1518**

According to the editor, Caxton translated from a French version apparently based on a lost Provençal version written in the late 14th century.

Paschasius Radbertus, *Saint, abbot of Corbie, d. c. 860.* Charlemagne's cousins; contemporary lives of Adalard and Wala, tr. with intro. and notes, by Allen Cabaniss. [Syracuse, N.Y.], Syracuse University Press [1967]. vii, 266 p. **1519**

Translation of Vita sancti Adalhardi and Vita Walae seu Epitaphium Arsenii, both of which record life in a ninth-century monastery. The Vita Walae is a dialogue.

Paston letters. The Paston letters, ed. by John Warrington. New York, Dutton; London, Dent [1956]. 2 v. *Everyman's library* **1520**

This edition in Everyman's library replaces the earlier one listed by Farrar and Evans, item 3066; based on the Fenn edition and the 1894 Gairdner edition, it includes selections "which best reveal characters, customs, manners." Spelling and punctuation have been modernized.

—— Paston letters, sel. and ed. by Norman Davis; critical comment by Horace Walpole, Virginia Woolf, and others. Oxford, Clarendon Press, 1958. xii, 288 p. **1521**

According to a review in the *Durham University Journal,* 52 (1959–60), p. 44, by A. I. Doyle, this is not only the "first proper edition . . . in fifty years but also . . . first to be wholly transcribed from the originals since Fenn's editio princeps." The selection is intended to illustrate Paston family history rather than political history, according to the editor, who is preparing a text of the complete Paston letters for the Early English Text Society. A more modernized and somewhat different selection by the editor appeared as The Paston Letters, a selection in modern spelling, London, Oxford University Press, 1963 (*World's Classics*).

Patrick, Saint, *373?–463?.* The Breastplate of Saint Patrick, here tr. into English by Thomas Kinsella. [Dublin, Dolmen Press, 1954]. [11] p. Reprinted 1957; new ed. 1961. **1522**

A translation of Luireach Phádruig, or Lorica, also known as The deer's cry. Another translation, entitled Luireach Phádruig, St. Patrick's breastplate, translated by Whitley Stokes, Cecil Frances Alexander, and Emily Hickey, was published in London by the Catholic Truth Society sometime in the 20th century; it is probably a reprint or modification of Stokes's translation: see Farrar and Evans, item 3080.

—— St. Patrick's writings, a modern translation, by Arnold Marsh. Dundalk, Dundalgan Press, 1961. 28 p. **1523**

This work, which has not been seen, contains the Confessio and the Letter to the soldiers of Coroticus.

—— The works of St. Patrick and St. Secundinus, "Hymn on St. Patrick," tr. and annotated by Ludwig Bieler. London, Longmans, Green; Westminster, Md., Newman Press, 1953. v. 121 p. *Ancient Christian writers,* 17. **1524**

St. Patrick's extant works include two complete letters, fragments of others, a set of rules for ecclesiastical discipline. Secundinus' hymn Audite omnes is a biography of the saint. The translation is based on Bieler's text, published separately in 1950.

Patrick, *bp. of Dublin, d. 1085, supposed author.* The writings of Bishop Patrick, 1074–1084, ed. and tr. by Aubrey Gwynn. Dublin, Institute for Advanced Studies, 1955. 147 p. *Scriptores Latini Hiberniae,* 1. **1525**

Translation of four poems: The wonders of Ireland, On the human condition, On the frailty of life, Allegorical poem; and one prose work, On the three mansions of the soul, which has a verse prologue, Perge carina. According to the editor, the prose work was translated by "R.S." [Robert Southwell?] in the 16th century; this translation is not noted by Farrar and Evans and has not been seen. The works here translated are ascribed to Patrick for the first time in this edition.

Paulinus, *Saint, bp. of Nola, 353–431.* Letters of St. Paulinus of Nola, tr. and annotated by P. G. Walsh. Westminster, Md., Newman Press, 1966–67. 2 v. *Ancient Christian writers,* 35–36. **1526**

Vol. 1 contains letters 1–22, Vol. 2, 23–51.

Paulus Diaconus Emeritensis, *fl. 633–38?, supposed author.* The Vitas Sanctorum Patrum Emeretensium, tr. by Joseph N. Garvin; text and translation with an intro. and commentary. Washington, Catholic University of America Press, 1946. vii, 567 p. *Catholic University studies in medieval and Renaissance Latin language and literature,* 19. **1527**

Text and facing translation of a collection of biographical anecdotes about persons who lived in Spain in the late 6th and early 7th centuries; intended by the author to support the validity of Gregory the Great's dialogues relating saints' lives.

Pearl. *Middle English poem.* The pearl, mediaeval text with a literal translation and interpretation by Mary Vincent Hillman. [Convent Station, N.J.], College of Saint Elizabeth Press [1961]. xiii, 175 p. **1528**

A prose translation.

—— The pearl, medieval text and notes . . ., with verse translation by Sara deFord [and others]. New York, Appleton-Century-Crofts [1967]. x, 109 p. **1529**

Text and facing translation.

—— The Pearl, newly tr. by John F. Crawford and Andrew Hoyem, including Middle English text, printed interlinearly from the British Museum ms. Cotton Nero A.x. . . . San Francisco, Grabhorn-Hoyem, 1967. 130 p. **1530**

This translation has not been seen.

—— The Pearl-poet: his complete works, tr. by Margaret Williams. New York, Random House [1967]. viii, 348 p. **1531**

A fairly literal verse translation of Pearl, Patience, Cleanness, Gawain and the Grene Knight, St. Erkenwald. See also item 748 above.

Peckham, John, *abp. of Canterbury, d. 1292.* "The Perspectiva communis of

John Pecham," tr. by David C. Lindberg, *Archives Internationales d'Histoire des Sciences,* 18 (1965), 37–53. **1532**

Summary paraphrase and translation of excerpts, with text in footnotes, from a work on optics very influential in the Middle Ages and after, according to the translator. A complete edition and translation, based on the translator's thesis (Indiana, 1965), has been announced as forthcoming by the University of Wisconsin Press.

Peguilhan, Aimeric de, *d. c. 1255.* The poems of Aimeric de Peguilhan, ed. by William P. Shephard and Frank M. Chambers. Evanston, Ill., Northwestern University Press, 1950. vi, 254 p. *Northwestern University studies in humanities,* 24. **1533**

Text and following prose translation of Provençal poems; includes a brief Vida of Aimeric.

Peirol d'Auvergne, *fl. 1210.* Peirol, troubadour of Auvergne, by S. C. Aston. Cambridge [Eng.], Cambridge University Press, 1953. vii, 190 p. **1534**

Contains anthology of Peirol's works with text and for most of the poems a prose translation.

Penitentials. The Irish penitentials, ed. by Ludwig Bieler, with an appendix by D. A. Binchy. Dublin, Dublin Institute for Advanced Studies, 1963. x, 367 p. *Scriptores Latini Hiberniae,* 5. **1535**

Includes text and facing translation of Latin penitentials and synods and canon law, Welsh and Irish; and translation only by D. A. Binchy of the Old-Irish penitential table of commutations. The latter was published also in *Ériu,* 19 (1962), 47–72. It is based on a newly discovered manuscript of a work formerly entitled De arreis; *cf.* Farrar and Evans, item 3107.

Perceval. *Prose romance.* The romance of Perceval in prose: a translation of the E manuscript of the Didot Perceval by Dell Skeels. Seattle, University of Washington Press, 1961. x, 98 p. *University of Washington publications in language and literature,* 15. **1536**

Includes as "prologue" the conclusion of the prose Merlin. Ascribed by some scholars to Robert de Boron, 13th century.

Persian literature. *Collections.* Ancient Iranian literature, tr. by Maneckji N. Dhalla. Karachi [Dhalla], 1949. 229 p. **1537**

Selections from the Avesta, Pahlavi, and Pazend periods (ending in 900) of largely religious writings, with some liturgical works.

—— Classical Persian literature, by Arthur J. Arberry. New York, Macmillan [1958]. 464 p. **1538**

Contains much translation *passim* of illustrative material, most of it translated by the author; the work covers material written through the 15th century.

—— Court poets of Iran and India, an anthology of wit and verse, tr. by Rustamji Pestonjī Masānī. Bombay, The New Book Company [1938]. xiv, 202 p. **1539**

Text and translation of short excerpts, with commentary; many of the selections are medieval. Omitted in Farrar and Evans.

—— Immortal rose, an anthology of Persian lyrics, tr. by A. J. Arberry. London, Luzac, 1948. viii, 174 p. **1540**

Translation of poems of Sanā'ī, Farīd al-Dīn 'Aṭṭār, Jalāl al-Dīn Rūmī, Sa'dī, Hāfiz, and Jāmī. Professor Arberry translated two other medieval poems in "Three Persian poems," *Iran, Journal of the British Institute of Persian Studies,* 2 (1964), 1–12, from Ḥāfiẓ and Athīr-i Akhsīkatī. The article illustrates the problems of translating Persian poetry.

—— The Kūfic inscriptions in Persian verses in the court of the royal palace of Mas'ud III at Ghazni, by Alessio Bombaci. Rome, Istituto Italiano per il Medio ed Estremo Oriente, 1966. xv, 68 p. **1541**

Contains text and translation (pp. 11–15) of a recently unearthed inscription of 1099–1115, significant at this time because it is in Persian rather than Arabic and also because it is evidence of the use of inscriptions architecturally.

—— The legacy of Persia, ed. by A. J. Arberry. Oxford, Clarendon Press, 1953. xvi, 421 p. **1542**

This is a collection of essays about Persia, two of which contain translation *passim* of illustrative excerpts: H. W. Bailey, "The Persian language," and A. J. Arberry, "Persian literature."

—— Persian-English proverbs, together with idioms, phrases, glossarial notes, mother stories, etc. [ed. by] Sulaiman Hayyim. Tehran, Beroukhim, 1956. 10, 750, 62 p. **1543**

Persian text and translation.

—— Persian poems, an anthology of verse translations, ed. by A. J. Arberry. London, Dent; New York, Dutton [1954]. xvi, 239 p. *Everyman's library.* **1544**

Contains translation from some fifteen poets from the medieval period.

—— "Persian poetical manuscripts from the time of Rūdakī," by W. B. Henning, pp. 89–104 in A locust's leg, studies in honor of S. H. Taqizadeh, ed. by W. B. Henning and E. Yarshater. London, Lund, 1962. **1545**

Transliteration and translation of two 10th-century manuscripts written in a non-Persian alphabet at the "very beginning of Persian literature." One work is a complaint by a *vita anima* against its forgetful companions.

—— Persian proverbs, by Laurence P. Elwell-Sutton. London, Murray [1954]. 103 p. *Wisdom of the East.* **1546**

Many of the proverbial stories, some Aesopian, are of medieval provenience.

—— Poems from the Persian, tr. by John Charles Edward Bowen. Oxford, Blackwell, 1948. x, 105 p. Often reprinted. **1547**

Contains translation in verse of fifty poems, all but one medieval, from eleven authors.

—— Shiraz; Persian city of saints and poets, by Arthur J. Arberry. Norman, University of Oklahoma Press [1960]. xv, 177 p. **1548**

Contains *passim* translation by Arberry of poems from Ibn Khafif, Ruzbihan, Sa'dī, and Ḥāfiẓ, much of it apparently new for this volume.

—— "Sogdian tales," by W. B. Henning, *Bulletin of the School of Oriental and African Studies,* 11 (1943–46), 465–87. **1549**

Has text and translation of fragmentary stories taken from Manichaean manuscripts, illustrating the role of Manichaeans in transmitting tales from East to West and vice versa. Sogdian is a dialect of Persian.

—— "Some early documents in Persian, I," by V. Minorsky, *Journal of the Royal Asiatic Society,* 1942, 181–94; 1943, 86–99. **1550**

Contains texts and translation of some of the few extant documents "having a personal character" before 1220; the second section contains translation of documents discovered at Bāmiyān.

Pervigilium Veneris. Catullus, Tibullus, and Pervigilium Veneris. Pervigilium Veneris tr. by J. W. Mackail. Cambridge, Harvard University Press, 1962. xiv, 379 p. *Loeb classics.* **1551**

Text and facing translation. The verse translation of Thomas Parnell is found in The Latin poets, ed. Francis R. B. Godolphin, New York, Modern Library, 1949, pp. 599–604.

—— The vigil of Venus, tr. by F. L. Lucas. London, Golden Cockerel Press [1939]. 27 p. **1552**

This translation, not listed by Farrar and Evans, was reprinted in Aphrodite, the Homeric hymn to Aphrodite and the Pervigilium Veneris, Cambridge [Eng.], Cambridge University Press, 1948. 53 p.

—— The vigil of Venus, tr. by Allen Tate. [Cummington, Mass.], Cummington Press [c. 1943]. 28 p. **1553**

Text and poetic translation.

—— The Vigil of Venus, done into English by Lewis Gielgud. London, Muller, [1952]. 49 p. **1554**

Text and translation.

—— "The night-watch of Venus," tr. by Miriam Allen de Ford, *Poet Lore,* 62 (1967), 5–8. **1555**

Petr z Mladenovic, *d. 1451.* John Hus at the Council of Constance [by Peter of Mladoňovice] tr. from the Latin and the Czech with notes and intro. by Matthew Spinka. New York, Columbia University Press, 1965 [*i.e.*, 1966]. 327 p. *Records of civilization*, 73. **1556**

Translation of eyewitness account of Hus's trial, Relatio de . . . Hus causa, as well as of Hus's letters from Constance and other documents relevant to Peter's account.

Petrarca, Francesco, *1304–74.* Petrarch and his world, by Morris Bishop. Bloomington, Indiana University Press, 1963. 399 p. **1557**

Contains much translation *passim,* largely by the author, of excerpts from Petrarch's works.

—— [De remediis utruisque fortune] Petrarch: four dialogues for scholars, ed. and tr. by Conrad Rawski. Cleveland, Press of Western Reserve University [1966]. 204 p. **1558**

Contains On the abundance of books, On the fame of writers, On the master's degree, On various academic titles, text and facing translation from De remediis utriusque fortune. An appendix contains translations of three letters by Petrarch.

—— [De sui ipsius et multorum ignorantia] Of his own ignorance and that of many others, tr. by Hans Nachod, pp. 47–133, in The Renaissance philosophy of man, ed. by Ernst Cassirer and Paul O. Kristeller *et al.* Chicago, University of Chicago Press, 1948. **1559**

—— [Epistolae] "The devil and Francis Petrarch," by John E. Wrigley, *Library Chronicle of the University of Pennsylvania,* 33 (1967), 75–96. **1560**

Contains text and translation of "A letter sent to Pope Clement VI."

—— Letters, sel. and tr. by Morris Bishop . . . Bloomington, Indiana University Press [1966]. xi, 306 p. **1561**

Includes Epistle to posterity, selections from Letters on familiar matters, Miscellaneous letters, Letters of riper years. Some of the letters are complete, others abridged; most have never before been translated.

—— Petrarch at Vaucluse, letters in verse and prose, tr. by Ernest Hatch Wilkins. Chicago, University of Chicago Press, 1958. xi, 215 p. **1562**

Translation in verse and prose of a selected fifty letters linked by commentary.

—— [Rime] Anthology of German songs and lyrics, with specimens of French songs and Italian sonnets . . ., tr. and published by Arthur Davidson. London [privately printed, 1948?]. 152 p. **1563**

The only medieval work included is translation of twelve sonnets of Petrarch.

—— Rhymes, a selection of translations compiled by Thomas G. Bergin. Edinburgh, Oliver and Boyd [1955]. xi, 62 p. **1564**

Contains translation by Bergin, Morris Bishop, *et al.,* arranged in two groups: In Laura's lifetime, After Laura's death.

—— . . . Sonnets & songs, tr. by Anna Maria Armi [pseud.], intro. by Theodor E. Mommsen. [New York], Pantheon [1946]. xlii, 521 p. **1565**

Text and facing translation of the complete canzonieri. *Armi* is a pseudonym for *Ascoli.*

—— The sonnets of Petrarch, in the original Italian, together with English translations sel. and ed. with an intro. by Thomas G. Bergin. New York, Heritage Press [1966]. xviii, 369 p. **1566**

Translations of all the sonnets, by various translators including the editor.

—— Selected sonnets, odes, and letters by Petrarch, ed. by Thomas G. Bergin. New York, Appleton-Century-Crofts [c. 1966]. xix, 137 p. **1567**

Contains the Letter to posterity, three metrical letters, and about one hundred sonnets and odes, selected largely from the editor's previous editions; see above.

—— Petrarch's Testament, ed. and tr. by Theodor E. Mommsen. Ithaca, N.Y., Cornell University Press [1957]. viii, 93 p. **1568**

Text and facing translation, based on editio princeps of 1499 or 1500.

—— Triumphs, tr. by Ernest Hatch Wilkins. [Chicago], University of Chicago Press [1962]. ix, 112 p. **1569**

These six poems were written over a long period of time and do not in a sense constitute one poem; Love and Chastity were complete by 1340–44, Death and Fame were written after the death of Laura, and Time and Eternity toward the end of Petrarch's life.

Petrus Chrysologus, *Saint, bp of Ravenna, 406–450?* Saint Peter Chrysologus, selected sermons; and Saint Valerian, homilies, tr. by George E. Ganss. New York, Fathers of the Church, 1953. viii, 454 p. *Fathers of the Church,* 17. **1570**

Philip the Arab, *emperor, 244–49.* "The anonymous Enconium of Philip the Arab," by Louis J. Swift, *Greek, Roman, and Byzantine Studies,* 7 (1966), 267–89. **1571**

Contains translation of an oration perhaps written in the 3d century, but the date is uncertain.

Philippe de Vitry, *1291–1361.* "Philippe de Vitry's Ars nova, a translation," by Leon Plantinga, *Journal of Music Theory*, 5 (1961), 204–20. **1572**

The author points out that the work contains material "plundered from various earlier sources."

Philo Judaeus, *d. c. 50.*

Although Philo is not a medieval author and was not included by Farrar and Evans, it has been thought wise to list the main translation of his work here because of the importance of his method of scriptural exegesis for later Christian and Jewish exegesis. For a full bibliography up to 1938, see Howard L. Goodhart and Erwin R. Goodenough, The politics of Philo Judaeus . . . and general bibliography of Philo, New Haven, Yale University Press; London, Oxford University Press, 1938. xii, 348 p. For a discussion of his influence on the Church Fathers see Harry A. Wolfson, Philo, foundations of religious philosophy in Judaism, Christianity, and Islam, Cambridge, Harvard University Press, 1947, 2 v., and its reviews.

—— Works. Cambridge, Harvard University Press, 1929–53. *Loeb classics.* 12 v. **1573**

Vols. I-IV, tr. F. H. Colson and G. H. Whitaker; vols. VI-IX, tr. F. H. Colson; Vol. X, by F. H. Colson, index by J. W. Earp. Two supplementary volumes contain translation from an Armenian version of the Greek text by Ralph Marcus.

Philosophy. *Collections.* The age of belief; the medieval philosophers, selected, with intro. and interpretive commentary by Anne Fremantle. [New York], New American Library; Boston, Houghton Mifflin [1955; c. 1954]. 218 p. **1574**

Contains brief selections from old translations of Greek, Latin, Arabic, and Hebrew works; included here because of its breadth of selection.

—— "Byzantine political ideas in Kievan Russia," by Francis Dvornik, *Dumbarton Oaks Papers,* 9 (1956), 76–121. **1575**

Contains translation of many illustrative quotations from Byzantine documents translated into Slavonic and from other Slavonic documents, sermons, chronicles, to show ideas of kingship and of relationship between church and state.

—— Early medieval philosophy, by George B. Burch. New York, King's Crown Press, 1951. vii, 151 p. **1576**

Contains summary and paraphrase of some of Isaac of Stella's sermons and his Treatise on the soul, not elsewhere translated; from John Scotus Erigena, The division of nature; and selections from St. Anselm, Peter Abelard, and St. Bernard of Clairvaux.

—— Forerunners of the Reformation; the shape of late medieval thought, illustrated by key documents, ed. by Heiko A. Oberman, tr. by Paul L. Nyhus. New York, Holt, Rinehart and Winston [1966]. x, 333 p. **1577**

Documents from the following medieval writers are included: John Brevicoxa, *fl.* late 14th cent.; Jacob Hoeck, d. 1509; Johan Wessel Gansfort, 1419–89; Robert Holcott, d. 1349; Thomas Bradwardine, d. 1349; Gabriel Biel, sermon preached 1460; Johann von Staupitz, 15th century; Jan Hus, d. 1415; Pope Pius II, d. 1464; Thomas de Vio, Cajetan, d. 1534.

—— Greek and Roman philosophy after Aristotle, ed. by Jason L. Saunders. New York, The Free Press of Glencoe; London, Collier-Macmillan [1966]. x, 371 p. **1578**

Contains previously translated excerpts from Philo Judaeus, Justinus Martyr, Minucius Felix, Clement of Alexandria, Origenes, Tertullianus.

—— Historical selections in the philosophy of religion, ed. by Ninian Smart. London, S.C.M. Press, 1967. 510 p. **1579**

Previously published translations of selections from St. Augustine, Pseudo-Dyonisius, St. Anselm, and Thomas Aquinas, pp. 31–84.

—— A history of Muslim philosophy, ed. and intro. by M. M. Sharif. Wiesbaden, Otto Harrassowitz, 1963–66. 2 v. **1580**

A collection of essays by modern authors, many of whom have translated excerpts from the works discussed.

—— The intellectual tradition of the west, readings in the history of ideas. Vol. 1, Hesiod to Calvin, ed. by Morton Donner *et al.* [New York], Scott Foresman [1967]. xi, 634 p. **1581**

Pages 204–432 contain fairly long excerpts from fifteen medieval authors, largely previously published translations.

—— Medieval philosophy; selected readings from Augustine to Buridan, ed. by Herman Shapiro. New York, Modern Library [1964]. xiv, 547 p. **1583**

Contains translations mostly of complete short works; many have been previously published but the following translations are new for this volume: selections from Albertus Magnus, Peter of Spain, Siger of Brabant, and Nicolaus of Autrecourt, translated by J. P. Mullally and E. A. Moody; John Scotus Eriugena and Giles of Rome (Egidio Colonna) translated by the editor.

—— Medieval political ideas, ed. by Ewart Lewis. New York, Knopf, 1954. 2 v. **1584**

An anthology of excerpts, newly translated, from "the investiture struggle . . . through the 15th century."

—— Medieval political philosophy: a sourcebook, ed. by Ralph Lerner and Muhsin Mahdi, with the collaboration of Ernest L. Fortin. [New York], Free Press of Glencoe [1963]. xii, 532 p. **1585**

Many of the translations are the first in English; whole books or sections, rather than small excerpts, have been selected from Christian, Judaic, and Islamic writers. Includes translation of Thomas Acquinas' commentary on the Politics of Aristotle, pp. 297–334.

—— Philosophic classics, basic texts sel. and ed. with prefaces by Walter A. Kaufmann. Englewood Cliffs, N.J., Prentice-Hall, 1961. 2 v. **1586**

Brief excerpts from several writers. Vol. 1, Thales to St. Thomas; Vol. 2, Bacon to Kant.

——"Philosophical predecessors and contemporaries of Ibn Bajjah," by D. M. Dunlop, *Islamic Quarterly*, 2, no. 2 (1955), 100–16. **1587**

Translation from several Arabic authors *passim*, 10th century and earlier. Ibn Bajjah is also known as Avempace.

—— Philosophies of art and beauty, readings in aesthetic form from Plato to Heidegger, ed. by Albert Hofstadter and Richard Kuhns. New York, Modern Library [c. 1964]. xix, 701 p. **1588**

Medieval works translated include St. Augustine, De ordine and De musica; Marsilio Ficino, selections from Commentary on Plato's Symposium.

—— Philosophy in the Middle Ages; the Christian, Islamic, and Jewish traditions, ed. by Arthur Hyman [and] James J. Walsh. New York, Harper & Row [1967]. vii, 747 p. **1589**

Some recent translations, most previously published, of fairly long selections organized by tradition (Christian, Islamic, Jewish) and chronology; includes works on ethics, politics, epistemology, metaphysics, natural theology, mostly from major authors.

—— Philosophy in the West; readings in ancient and medieval philosophy, [ed. by] Joseph Katz and Rudolph H. Weingartner, with new translations by John Wellmuth and John Wilkinson. New York, Harcourt Brace [1965]. xxv, 589 p. **1590**

Part 6, Philosophy in the Middle Ages, contains excerpts from St. Anselm, Roger Bacon, Thomas Aquinas, St. Bonaventure, John Duns Scotus, Walter Burley, William of Ockham, and Pietro Pomponazzi.

—— Political thought in medieval Islam, an introductory outline, by Erwin I. J. Rosenthal. Cambridge [Eng.], Cambridge University Press, 1958. xi, 323 p. **1591**

Contains paraphrase and summary of many works not otherwise translated into English, from twelve authors.

—— Reincarnation, an East-West anthology . . ., compiled and ed. by Joseph Head and S. L. Cranston. New York, Julian Press, 1961. x, 341 p. **1592**

Translation from early Christian, Egyptian, Islamic, and Judaic writers of very brief selections or poems.

—— Renaissance philosophy, selected readings tr. by Arturo B. Fallico and Hermann Shapiro. New York, Random House, 1967–. Vol. 1, The Italian philosophers. **1593**

Includes the following selections from medieval writers: selections from Book I of Petrarch's De remediis; Alberti's Intercoenales; Lorenzo Valla's De libero arbitrio; preface and Book IV of Manetti's De dignitate et excellentia hominis; Pico della Mirandola's Letter to Ermalao Barbaro; and Oration on the Dignity of Man; Marsilio Ficino's De sole, abridged. All these translations are by the editors.

—— The Renaissance philosophy of man, ed. by Ernst Cassirer, Paul Oskar Kristeller [and] John Herman Randall, Jr., in collaboration with Hans Nachod [and others.] Chicago, University of Chicago Press [1948]. viii, 404 p. **1594**

Contents: Francesco Petrarca: A self-portrait, The ascent of Mont Ventoux, On his own ignorance and that of many others, A disapproval of an unreasonable use of the discipline of dialectic, An Averroist visits Petrarca, Petrarca's aversion to Arab science, A request to take up the fight against Averroes; Lorenzo Valla: Dialogue on free will; Marsilio Ficino: Five questions concerning the mind; Giovanni Pico della Mirandola: Oration on the dignity of man.

—— "The second tract on Insolubilia found in Paris, B. N. Lat. 16617, an edition of the text with an analysis of its contents," by H. A. G. Braakhuis, *Vivarium*, 5 (1967), 111–45. **1595**

Contains outline and paraphrase of a late 12th-century or early 13th-century work, the second of two on the same subject in the manuscript.

—— Social and political thought in Byzantium from Justinian I to the last Palaeologus, passages from Byzantine writers and documents, tr. with an intro. and notes by Ernest Barker. Oxford, Clarendon Press, 1957. 239 p. **1596**

Translation of excerpts from legal documents, administrative records, literary works; the emphasis is on thought rather than institutions, from 6th to 15th century. Other documents up to the end of the 4th century are translated in another work of Professor Barker: From Alexander to Constantine, passages and documents illustrating the history of social and political ideas 336 B.C.–A.D. 337 (Oxford, Clarendon Press, 1956, xxiv, 505 p).

—— Studies in Arabic philosophy, by Nicholas Rescher. [Pittsburgh], University of Pittsburgh Press [1967]. **1597**

Contains translation largely of logical works of al-Kindī, Yaḥyā ibn ʻAdī, Ibn al-Ṣalāḥ, and Ibn al-ʻAssāl.

—— Three Jewish philosophers. Philo: Selections, ed. by Hans Lewy. Saadya Gaon: Book of doctrines and beliefs, ed. by Alexander Altmann. Jehuda Halevi: Kuzari, ed. by Isaak Heinemann. New York, Meridian Books [1960]. 112, 190, 147 p. **1598**

The works by Saadiah ben Joseph (d. 942) and Judah ha-Levi (12th century) are somewhat abridged.

—— Treasury of philosophy, ed. by Dagobert Runes. New York, Philosophical Library, 1955. xxv, 1,280 p. **1599**

Includes translation of short excerpts from many medieval sources, arranged alphabetically by author.

Philoxenus, *bp. of Hierapolis, d. 523.* . . . A letter of Philoxenus of Mabbug sent to a novice, ed. and tr. by Gunnar Olinder. Göteborg, Elanders boktryckeri aktiebolag, 1941. vii, 20 p. *Götesborgs högskola, Årskrift,* 47, 1941, 21. **1600**

Syriac text followed by translation of a letter glorifying the ascetic life.

Photius I, *Saint, patriarch of Constaninople, c. 820–c. 891.* The homilies of Photius, patriarch of Constantinople, tr. by Cryil Mango. Cambridge, Harvard University Press, 1958. xii, 327 p. **1601**

Translation of eighteen homilies written 858–67 and 877–86. This translation is extensively quoted in Francis Dvornik, "The Patriarch Photius and iconoclasm," *Dumbarton Oaks Papers,* 7 (1953), 69–97; Dvornik saw the work in manuscript.

Physiologus. The very ancient book of beasts, plants, & stones, tr. from Greek and other languages by Francis J. Carmody. San Francisco, Book Club of California, 1953. 75 p. **1602**

The original Greek text of the 2d century has been lost; the present translation is from a later Greek version and from Latin, Arabic, Syriac, Armenian, and Ethiopic versions.

Pico della Mirandola, Giovanni, *1463–94.* Of being and unity (De ente et uno), tr. by Victor Michael Hamm. Milwaukee, Marquette University Press, 1943. 34 p. *Medieval philosophical texts in translation,* 3. **1603**

—— Oration on the dignity of man, tr. by Robert Caponigri. Chicago, Regnery [1956]. xii, 40 p. **1604**

For another translation, see item 1594 above.

—— On the dignity of man, tr. by Charles G. Wallis; On being and the one, tr. by Paul J. W. Miller; Heptaplus, tr. by Douglas Carmichael. Indianapolis, Bobbs–Merrill, 1965. xxxiii, 174 p. **1605**

Wallis' translation of On the dignity of man appeared in *View Magazine*, 4 (1944), fall, pp. 88–90, 100–1; winter, pp. 134–35, 146–51, and is said to have been published by St. John's College, Annapolis, in 1940, but I have found no copy of this publication. Pico's On being is an attempt to reconcile Plato and Aristotle, according to the translator. The Heptaplus is "Septiform narration of the six days of creation."

Pietro Damiani, *Saint, 1007?–72.* St. Peter Damian, his teaching on the spiritual life, by Owen J. Blum. Washington, Catholic University of America Press, 1947. viii, 224 p. *Catholic University studies in medieval history*, 10. **1606**

Contains *passim* translation of many illustrative excerpts.

—— St. Peter Damian, selected writings on the spiritual life, tr. with an intro. by Patricia McNulty. London, Faber & Faber; New York, Harpers, 1959. 187 p. **1607**

Contains translation of selected sermons and three treatises: The book of 'The Lord be with you'; On the perfection of monks; Concerning true happiness and wisdom.

Pisan, Christine de, *1364–c. 1430.* L'Oroyson Nostre Dame, prayer to Our Lady, tr. by Jean Misrahi and Margaret Marks. New York, Kurt H. Volk, [c. 1953]. 24 p. **1608**

Text and translation in parallel columns. See also item 328 above. Bonet's work is the source for books 3 and 4 of Cristine's Book of fayttes of armes; *cf.* Farrar and Evans, item 3193.

Pitti, Buonaccorso, *1354–c. 1431.* Two memoirs of Renaissance Florence; the diaries of Buonaccorso Pitti and Gregorio Dati, tr. by Julia Martines, ed. by Gene Brucker. New York, Harper & Row [1967]. 141 p. **1609**

Both works have been abridged.

Pius II, *Pope, 1405–64.* De gestis Concilii Basiliensis commentariorum: libri II, ed. and tr. by Denys Hay and W. K. Smith. Oxford, Clarendon Press, 1967. xxxviii, 268 p. *Oxford medieval texts.* **1610**

Text and facing translation of books 1 and 2 of Pius' work. With this volume the series formerly known as *Nelson's medieval texts* has been taken over by the Oxford Press. (Pius' secular name is Aeneas Silvius Piccolomini.)

—— "From the Piccolomini papers," by Avery D. Andrews, *University of Pennsylvania Library Chronicle,* 26 (1960), 17–29. **1611**

Has facsimile text and translation of a document of 1432 apparently related to Aeneas' friendship with Kaspar Schlick, chancellor of the Holy Roman Empire.

—— Memoirs of a Renaissance Pope; the commentaries of Pius II, an abridgement, tr. by Florence A. Gragg, ed. with intro. by Leona C. Gabel. New York, Putnam [1959]; London, Allen & Unwin, 1960. 381 p. **1612**

This translation originally appeared in the *Smith college studies in history*, vols. 22, 25, 30, and 35 (1937–57); it has been abridged by the authors for this edition. *Cf.* Farrar and Evans, item 3198.

Placita Corone. Placita corone, or La Corone Pledee devant justices, ed. with intro., notes, and translation by J. M. Kaye. London, Selden Society, 1966. xxxix, 42 p. *Selden Society,* supplementary series, 4. **1613**

Contains text and facing translation of a treatise on law probably written *c.* 1274, perhaps by one Robert Carpenter; it gives an account of how felony is handled in court. The text of a somewhat different Latin version is also included.

Platina, Bartolomeo, *1421–81*. De honesta voluptate; the first dated cookery book: Venice, L. de Aguila [*i.e.*, Aquila] 1475 [tr. by Elizabeth Buermann Andrews. St. Louis?], Mallinckrodt Chemical Works [1967]. *Mallinckrodt collection of food classics*, 5. **1614**

Text and facing translation of a work including ten books of recipes; Book 1 has directions for activities such as choosing a place to live, bodily exercise, tarrying with a woman, and an explanation of the four humours, as well as descriptions of fruits and herbs.

Poeta Saxo. The Saxon poet's Life of Charles the Great, tr. by Mary E. McKinney. New York, Pageant Press [1956]. vii, 118 p. **1615**

Translation of a poetic combination of annals based on Einhard's annals and a vita based on Einhard's vita of Charlemagne.

Poggio Bracciolini, *1380–1459*. Diodorus Siculus, The bibliotheca historica, tr. by John Skelton, ed. by F. M. Salter and H. L. R. Edwards. London, published for the Early English Text Society by Oxford University Press, 1956–57. 2 v. *Early English Text Society*, original series, 233, 239. **1616**

This is the first edition of a 16th-century English translation of the 1449 Latin version by Poggio of the Greek text of Diodorus Siculus, *fl.* 1st cent. B.C. The Greek version was translated by C. H. Oldfather for the Loeb Classics, 1933–47.

—— India recognita, the Indies rediscovered, in which are included the Travels of Nicolò de Conti, in Travellers in disguise, narratives of eastern thought, English translation by John W. Jones, revised by Lincoln D. Hammond. Cambridge, Harvard University Press, 1963. xxxii, 239 p. **1617**

Poggio's India recognita was first published, separately from his Historia de varietate fortunae of which it is Book 4, in 1492. The translation by Jones appeared originally in India in the 15th century, ed. by R. H. Major, London, 1857, for the Hakluyt Society. Farrar and Evans listed this translation under Conti (item 1037) but failed to list it under Poggio, who wrote down the story of Conti's travels. The present edition includes a 16th-century travel work by Lodovic di Varthema.

Polish literature. *Collections*. Five centuries of Polish poetry, 1450–1950, an anthology with intro. and notes by Jerzy Peterkjewicz and Burns Singer. London, Secker & Warburg, 1960. 154 p. **1618**

Includes verse translation of three anonymous medieval poems, one a Lament of our Lady under the cross.

Polo, Marco, *1254–1323?* The travels of Marco Polo, tr. with an intro. by Ronald Latham. [Harmondsworth, Eng.], Penguin Books [1958]. xxix, 350 p. **1619**

A new translation based on manuscripts F and Z, 14th-century French and 15th-century Latin, respectively.

Pomerius, Julianus, *fl. 498*. The contemplative life, tr. and annotated by Mary

Josephine Suelzer. Westminster, Md., Newman Press, 1947. vi, 220 p. *Ancient Christian writers*, 4. **1620**

A translation of a work formerly ascribed to Prosper of Aquitaine; Julianus' only surviving work.

Povest' vremennykh let. The Russian primary chronicle, Laurentian text, tr. by Samuel H. Cross and Olgerd P. Sherbowitz-Wetzer. Cambridge, Mediaeval Academy of America, 1953. xi, 313 p. *Mediaeval Academy of America publications*, 60. **1621**

An enlargement and revision of the Cross translation of 1930 (see Farrar and Evans, item 3341) by Sherbowitz-Wetzer.

Praepositinus Cremonensis, *d. c. 1210, supposed author.* Summa contra haereticos, tr. by Joseph N. Garvin and James A. Corbett. Notre Dame, Ind., University of Notre Dame Press, 1958. lviii, 302 p. **1622**

This work contains text and a detailed summary (not a translation), pp. xxviii–xl, of a work which seems not to have been elsewhere translated.

Prester John. Prester John, the letter and the legend, by Vsevolod Slessarev. Minneapolis, University of Minnesota Press [c. 1959]. 127 p. **1623**

Facsimile text of the published French version, compared with manuscripts, Hebrew translation and Latin version; and translation of a letter reputedly written in 1165.

Priscus of Panium, *5th cent.* A history of the later Roman Empire. . . ., by John B. Bury. London and New York, Macmillan, 1889. 2 v., often reprinted. **1624**

Contains a translation from Greek of Priscus' account of an embassy to the court of Attila. This translation was not listed in Farrar and Evans.

Proclus, Lycius, *surnamed* **Diadochus,** *d. 485.* The philosophy of Proclus, the final phase of ancient thought, by Laurence J. Rosan. New York, Cosmos, 1949. ix, 271 p. **1625**

Many excerpts are translated in footnotes, with the Greek text in an appendix; Marinus' Vita Procli is also translated.

—— Proclus, Alcibiades I, a translation and commentary by William O. Neill. The Hague, Nijhoff, 1965. ix, 247 p. **1626**

A translation of Proclus' Commentary on the Alcibiades I of Plato; the commentary served Proclus as a "basis for a brief but comprehensive survey of later neoplatonism." Another work of Proclus, the Institutio theologica, was translated in 1933 as The elements of theology, by E. R. Dodds; *cf.* Farrar and Evans, item 3241. A second edition of this work (Oxford, 1963) contains only minor changes.

—— Proclus Commentarium in Parmenidem, ed. by Raymond Klibansky and [tr. by] Charlotta Labowski. London, Warburg Institute, 1953. xlii, 139 p. *Plato Latinus*, 3. **1627**

Text and facing translation of the last part of the seventh book of Proclus' Commentary on Plato's Parmenides. The editorial apparatus of this book is in Latin.

Procopius of Caesarea, *d. c. 565.* History of the wars, Secret history, and Buildings, newly tr., ed., abr., and with an intro. by Averil Cameron. New York, Washington Square Press, 1967. xlii, 351 p. **1628**

PROCOPIUS OF CAESAREA

—— Secret history, tr. by Richard T. Atwater; foreword by Arthur E. R. Boak. Ann Arbor, University of Michigan Press [1961]. xvi, 150 p. **1629**

Procopius records the history of the court of Justinian I, Emperor of the Byzantine empire, 527–565.

—— The secret history, tr. with an intro. by G. A. Williamson. Baltimore, Penguin Books [1966]. 204 p. **1630**

Prosper, Tiro, Aquitanus, *Saint, 390?–465.* Carmen de ingratis . . ., tr. by Charles T. Huegelmeyer. Washington, Catholic University of America Press, 1962. xx, 262 p. *Patristic studies,* 95. **1631**

Text and facing prose translation.

—— Defense of St. Augustine, tr. and annotated by P. de Letter. Westminster, Md., Newman Press, 1963. v, 248 p. *Ancient Christian writers,* 32. **1632**

SPURIOUS AND DOUBTFUL WORKS

—— The call of all nations, tr. and annotated by P. de Letter. Westminster, Md., Newman Press, 1952. 234 p. *Ancient Christian writers,* 14. **1633**

The De vocatione omnium gentium has also been attributed to St. Ambrose and to Pope Leo the Great. Another work attributed to Prosper appeared as Epistula ad Demetriadem de vera humilitate, a critical text and translation with intro. and commentary by Kathryn Clare Krabbe, Washington, Catholic University of America Press, 1965, 346 p., *Patristic studies,* 97.

—— The Carmen de providentia dei, tr. by Michael P. McHugh. Washington, Catholic University of America Press, 1964. xxiv, 462 p. *Patristic studies,* 98. **1634**

Text and facing translation.

Prudentius Clemens, Aurelius, *348–c. 405.* . . . Poems, tr. by M. Clement Eagan. Washington, Catholic University of America Press, 1962–1965. 2 v. *Fathers of the Church,* 43, 52. **1635**

Vol. 1 contains translation of Hymns for every day (Liber cathemerinon); the Martyrs' crowns (Liber peristephanon); vol. 2, apologetic and didactic poems, including the Psychomachia. The translation is in blank verse, with an attempt to reproduce the classical metres.

—— The poems of Prudentius, tr. by H. J. Thompson. Cambridge, Harvard University Press; London, Heinemann, 1949–53. 2 v. **1636**

Text and facing prose translation of complete works, based on 1926 edition of text.

Psellus, Michael Konstantinus, *1018–1100.* Fourteen Byzantine rulers; the Chronographia, tr., with an intro., by E. R. A. Sewter. [Rev. ed.] Baltimore, Penguin Books [1966]. 396 p. **1637**

This translation was first published under the title The chronographia of Michael Psellus, New Haven, Yale University Press, 1953, 323 p. Psellus gives an eyewitness account of the last few rulers; the total period covered is 976–1078.

Ptolemaeus, Arabic version. The Arabic version of Ptolemy's Planetary hypotheses, by Bernard R. Goldstein. Philadelphia, American Philosophical Society, 1967. *Transactions of the American Philosophical Society,* n.s., v. 57, pt. 4 (June, 1967), 55 p. **1638**

Text and translation of an Arabic version from 10th- and 13th-century manuscripts; the Greek original is lost.

Pūr-i Bahā, *13th cent.* "Pūr-i Bahā's 'Mongol' ode," by V. Minorsky, *Bulletin of the School of Oriental and African Studies,* 18 (1956), 261–78. **1639**

Persian text and English translation of a poem satirizing Turkish and Mongolian terms new when the poem was written, *c.* 1270.

—— "Pūr-i Bahā and his poems," by V. Minorsky, in Charisteria, ed. by J. Rypka, Prague, 1956, pp. 186–201; reprinted in Iranica. Twenty articles by V. Minorsky, Tehran, University of Tehran, 1964, pp. 292–305. **1640**

Selections from newly discovered manuscript sources; the poems, ostensibly panegyrics, are satirical, according to Professor Minorsky.

Q

Qāitbay, *sultan of Egypt, 15th cent.* "A Mamluk letter of 877/1473," by John Wansbrough, *Bulletin of the School of Oriental and African Studies,* 24 (1961), 200–13. **1641**

Translation of the Arabic original and a contemporary Italian translation of a letter from the Sultan to Doge Nicolò Trano of Venice; interesting historically and as an example of medieval translation.

al-Qāsim ibn Sallām al-Harawī, *d. 837–8?* "An 'Abbāsid Secretary-Poet who was interested in animals," by K. A. Fariq, *Islamic Culture,* 24 (1950), 261–70. **1642**

Has translation of a poem on a topic rare in Arabic poetry, elegies of animals. The poet's grandfather was also known as al-Qāsim and wrote poetry; he flourished 105–25 A.H., whereas this al-Qāsim flourished 170–218 A.H.

al-Qazwīnī, Rādī al-Dīn Aḥmad, *1117–94, supposed compiler.* A twelfth-century reading list, a chapter in Arabic bibliography, by A. J. Arberry. London, Emery Walker, 1951. 27 p. *Chester Beatty monographs,* 2. **1643**

A list of 117 books, many not extant and otherwise unknown; Arberry translates Rādī al-Dīn's notes on the source from which he received each of the books listed.

al-Qirqisānī, Ya'kūb ibn Isḥak, *10th cent.* "A tenth-century criticism of the doctrine of the logos (John I, 1)," by Leon Nemoy, *Journal of Biblical Literature,* 57 (1938), 411–20; 59 (1940), 159–68; 64 (1945), 515–29. **1644**

Translation of extracts from Kitāb al-Anwār, Book of lights, Discourse III, involving Karaite criticism of Christian doctrine.

Qudāmah ibn Ja'far, al-Kātib, al-Baghdādī, *d. 922?* Qudāma b. Ja'far's Kitāb al-kharāj, part 7, and excerpts from Abū Yūsuf's Kitāb al-kharāj, tr. with intro. and notes by A. Ben-Shemesh. Leiden, Brill, 1965. vii, 146 p. **1645**

This is vol. 2 of the translator's Taxation in Islam; vol. 1 contains a translation from Yaḥya ibn Adam, *q.v.,* item 1973. Photostats of the texts are included; both works are considerably abridged.

Queste del Saint Graal, la. Lorgaireacht an tSoidhigh Naomhtha, an early modern Irish translation of The quest of the Holy Grail, ed. with English translation by Sheila Falconer. Dublin, Dublin Institute for Advanced Studies, 1953. xcix, 394 p. **1646**

Text and translation of a late 15th-century work. The Irish version is very close to the Old French Queste del Saint Graal; it has some omissions.

QUINZE JOYES DE MARIAGE

Quinze joyes de mariage. The fifteen joys of marriage, tr. by Elisabeth Abbott. London and New York, Orion Press [1959]. vii, 221 p. **1647**

A prose translation of a work ascribed by some to Antoine de la Sale, b. 1388.

Qusṭā ibn Lūqā, al-Ba'albakkī, *c. 820–912.* "Qusta ibn Luqa on the use of the celestial globe," by W. H. Worrell, *Isis,* 35 (1944), 285–93. **1648**

Translation from a manuscript in the McGregor collection, University of Michigan.

R

Raimbaud III, *comte d'Orange, fl. 1155–1173.* The life and works of the troubadour Raimbaut d'Orange [by] Walter T. Pattison. Minneapolis, University of Minnesota Press [1952]. xiv, 225 p. **1649**

Contains text and facing prose translation of Raimbaud's poems, pp. 63–203.

Raimbaut de Vaqueiras, *12th cent.* The poems of the troubadour Raimbaut de Vaqueiras, ed. [and tr.] by Joseph Linskill. The Hague, Mouton, 1964. viii, 349 p. **1650**

Provençal text followed by prose translation of each poem.

Rauðolf's þattr. The story of Rauð and his sons, tr. by Joan E. Turville-Petre. [Kendal, Eng., Viking Society for Northern Research], 1947. 32 p. **1651**

The story dates from around 1200.

Raymundus de Vineis, *1330–1399.* The life of St. Catherine of Siena, tr. by George Lamb. New York, P. J. Kenedy [1960]. 384 p. **1652**

The author is also known as Raymundus de capua.

Regimen sanitatis Salernitanum. The regimen of health of the medical school of Salerno, tr. with a commentary by Pascal P. Parente. New York, Vantage Press [1967]. 93 p. **1653**

Text and prose translation of "the most popular medical book in the Middle Ages," a compilation of aphorisms, *c.* 1100, from various authors.

Reynard the Fox. The history of Reynard the Fox, tr. and printed by William Caxton in 1481, ed. with an intro. and notes by Donald B. Sands. Cambridge, Harvard University Press, 1960. viii, 224 p. **1654**

The edition has modernized spelling and punctuation. The bibliography, pp. 191–200, contains a list of editions and translations. For other translations, see items 1459 and 1461 above.

—— The scandalous adventures of Reynard the fox, a modern American version by Harry J. Owen. New York, Knopf, 1945. xvii, 115 p. **1655**

A retelling in modern idiom, based on Caxton and Goethe texts.

Rhygfarch, *1056–99.* Rhigfarch's life of St. David, the basic mid-twelfth-century Latin text with a translation by John W. James. Cardiff, University of Wales Press, published on behalf of the Board of Celtic Studies, 1967. xlix, 49 p. **1656**

Text based on twenty-nine manuscripts, newly edited, followed by translation.

Richard of Devizes, *fl. 1191.* The chronicle of Richard of Devizes of the time of King Richard the First, ed. by John T. Appleby. London and New York, Nelson [c. 1963]. xxvi, 1–84, 1–84, [85]–106 p. *Medieval texts.* **1657**

Text and facing translation of a chronicle covering the years 1189–92 and King Richard's crusade. The translation seems to be the author's revision of that of J. A. Giles; *cf.* Farrar and Evans, item 3292.

Richard of St. Victor, *d. 1173.* Benjamin Minor, tr. from Latin by S. V. Yankowski. Ausbach [privately printed by Elisabeth Kottmeier and E. G. Kostetzky], 1960. 97 p. **1658**

This translation has not been seen; it is listed in the Library of Congress but has been temporarily lost.

—— Selected writings on contemplation, tr. by Clare Kirchberger. London, Faber & Faber [1957]. 269 p. **1659**

Contains translation of excerpts from Benjamin Major, Benjamin Minor, Mystical notes on the Psalms, On the extermination of evil.

Rigaldus, Odo, *abp. of Rouen, d. 1275.* The Register of Eudes of Rouen, ed. with intro., notes, and appendix by Jeremiah F. O'Sullivan; tr. by Sydney M. Brown. New York, Columbia University Press, 1964. xxxvi, 779 p. *Records of civilization*, 72 **1660**

Eudes Rigaud's calendar of his visitations covers the period 1248–69. An appendix includes a translation of the Statutes of Pope Gregory IX on the reformation of monks of the order of St. Benedict.

Robert of Bridlington, *d. 1167, supposed author.* The Bridlington dialogue, an exposition of the Rule of St. Augustine, . . . tr. by a Religious of C.S.M.V. London, Mowbray, 1960. 202 p. (duplicate numbering). **1661**

Text and facing translation of a work known only since 1932, from Bodleian ms. Lat. th. d. 17; contains an abridged translation of the Rule of St. Augustine, as well as Robert's exposition. Robert is also known as Robert the Scribe.

Robert de Handlo, *fl. 1326.* Robert de Handlo, tr. and ed. by Luther Dittmer. New York, Institute of Medieval Music [1959]. 44 p. *Musical theorists in translation*, 2. **1662**

Translation of the Rules of Robert de Handlo, a compilation of 1326 concerning the principles of mensuration of polyphonic music, a manual for the practising musician.

Rojas, Fernando de, *d. 1541.* The Celestina, in The classic theatre, ed. by Eric Bentley. Garden City, N.Y., Doubleday (Anchor), 1959. 4 v. Vol. 3, Spanish. **1663**

The editor has adapted Mabbe's 17th-century translation and divided the work into five acts.

—— The Celestina, a novel in dialogue, tr. from the Spanish by Lesley Byrd Simpson. Berkeley, University of California Press, 1955. x, 162 p. **1664**

A translation of the sixteen-act version of the Celestina (written 1499), also known as the Tragicomedy of Calisto and Melibea.

—— Celestina, a play in twenty-one acts, tr. by Mack H. Singleton. Madison University of Wisconsin Press, 1958. xv, 299 p. **1665**

A prose translation of the entire work; the last five acts were added after the first edition of 1499, apparently by Rojas.

—— Celestina, or the Tragi-comedy of Calisto and Melibea, tr. by Phyllis Hartnoll. London, Dent; New York, Dutton [1959]. xii, 211 p. *Everyman's library.* **1666**

A translation of the twenty-one-act version.

—— The Spanish Bawd, La Celestina, being the tragi-comedy of Calisto and Melibea, intro. and tr. by J. M. Cohen. Baltimore, Penguin Books [1964]; New York, New York University Press, 1966. 247 p. **1667**

A translation of the twenty-one act version.

Rolle, Richard, *of Hampole, 1290?–1349.* Selected writings, tr. and arranged by John G. Harrell. London, S.P.C.K., 1963. xxiii, 72 p. **1668**

Contains translations of several Latin works and modernizations of the Middle English ones, arranged topically. Although the title page lists the editor as the translator, much of the translation is acknowledged to be from previously published sources.

Roman de la Rose. The Romance of the Rose, by Guillaume de Lorris and Jean Meun, tr. into English verse by Harry W. Robbins, ed. and with an intro. by Charles W. Dunn. New York, Dutton, 1962. xxxiii, 472 p. **1669**

This is apparently the first complete translation into English.

Roman de Laurin. Le roman de Laurin, fils de Marques le Sénéchal . . ., an unpublished thirteenth-century prose romance, by Lewis Thorpe. Cambridge [Eng.], Bowes & Bowes [1950]. 2 v. *University of Nottingham research publication,* 1. **1670**

The text is in Vol. 2; a detailed summary of the romance appears in Vol. 1, Appendix IV, pp. 261–301. The work is part of the French cycle about the Seven Sages.

Royal chronicle of Abyssinia. The glorious victories of ʻAmda Ṣeyon, king of Ethiopia, tr. and ed. by G. W. B. Huntingford. Oxford, Clarendon Press, 1965. xii, 142 p. **1671**

The chronicle is translated from Geʻez, a dialect of Ethiopic; also translated are four Soldiers songs, from Amharic, the descendant of Geʻez. King Ṣeyon died in 1344.

Rufinus Tyrannius, *Aquileiensis, c. 345–410.* A commentary on the Apostles' Creed, tr. and annotated by J. N. D. Kelly. London, Longmans, Green; Westminster, Md., Newman Press, 1955. 166 p. *Ancient Christian writers,* 20. **1672**

This is one of the few original works of Rufinus, who was known as a translator primarily. During the Middle Ages his commentary was attributed to St. Cyprian or St. Jerome, according to the editor.

—— Rufinus of Aquileia, his life and works, ed. by Francis X. Murphy. Washington, Catholic University of America Press, 1945. xviii, 248 p. *Catholic University studies in medieval history,* 6. **1673**

Contains *passim* a good deal of translation as well as summary of biographical parts of his Apologia in S. Hieronymum and Apologia ad Anastasium papam, and of his prefaces.

—— *supposed author.* Rufini presbyteri Liber de fide, tr. by Mary W. Miller;

a critical text and translation with intro. and commentary. Washington, Catholic University of America Press, 1964. xxii, 203 p. *Patristic studies*, 96. **1674**

Text from a unique manuscript; translation is the first into any modern language, the editor says. Though the work is attributed to Rufinus of Aquileia, the editor thinks it is not by him but by a Rufinus of "Syria," *i.e.*, Palestine, a Pelagian-disposed priest of the late 4th or early 5th century, identified by the Library of Congress as Rufinus Syrus, *fl.* 390–401.

al-Ruhāwī, Isḥaq ibn 'Alī, *9th cent.* Medical ethics of medieval Islam with special reference to al-Ruhāwī's "Practical ethics of the physician," by Martin Levey. Philadelphia, American Philosophical Society, 1967. *Transactions of the American Philosophical Society*, n.s., v. 57, pt. 3 (1967), 100 p. **1675**

Contains a translation of al-Ruhāwī's work, the "only medieval Arabic work known to have considered the aspects of medical ethics on a broad scale."

Ruiz, Juan, *arcipreste de Hita, fl. 1343.* "Two Spanish masterpieces, the Book of good love and the Celestina," by María Rosa Lide de Malkiel, *University of Illinois Studies in Language and Literature*, 43 (1961), 35–50. **1676**

Contains new translation of a long passage from the Book of good love.

Runes. "The Kensington stone," by E. Moltke; English translation by J. R. B. Gosney, *Antiquity*, 25 (1951), 87–93. **1677**

Text and translation of the inscription and Moltke's argument that it is not medieval but a 19th-century forgery.

—— Norse medieval cryptography in runic carvings, by Alf Mongé and O. G. Landsverk. Glendale, Cal., Norseman Press [1967]. 224 p. **1678**

This work has as its purpose to demonstrate the authenticity of American runic inscriptions, including the Kensington stone. It contains transliteration and translation *passim* of many runes both in America and elsewhere.

—— Runes, an introduction, by Ralph W. V. Elliott. Manchester, Manchester University Press, 1959. xvi, 124 p. **1679**

Contains translation of runes, *passim*. A corrected edition was issued in 1963.

—— The Runes of Sweden, by Sven Jansson, tr. by Peter G. Foote. London, Phoenix House; New York, Bedminster Press, 1962. 165 p. **1680**

Translation *passim* of runes dating from 3d century; most are from 9th-11th centuries.

Ruodlieb. Ruodlieb, the earliest courtly novel, after 1050, intro., text, translation, commentary, and textual notes by Edwin H. Zeydel. Chapel Hill, University of North Carolina Press [1959]. 165 p. *University of North Carolina studies in the Germanic languages and literatures*, 23. **1681**

Text and facing translation.

—— The Ruodlieb, the first medieval epic of chivalry from eleventh-century Germany, tr. from the Latin with an intro. by Gordon B. Ford, Jr. Leiden, Brill, 1965. 104 p. **1682**

The text, edited by Ford, was separately published by Brill in 1966.

Russia. *Historical sources.* Medieval Russia, a source book, 900–1700, ed. by

Basil Dmytryshyn. New York, Holt, Rinehart, and Winston [1967]. viii, 312 p. 1683

Contains translation of excerpts from chronicles, letters, and documents by both Russians and other European observers; the longest excerpt is from the Russian Primary Chronicle; and the Song of Prince Igor's campaign is translated by the editor, pp. 71–86. Foreign observers include Giovanni de Plano Carpini, Willem van Ruysbroek, and Ambrogio Cantarini.

—— Medieval Russian laws, tr. by George Vernadsky. New York, Columbia University Press, 1947. 106 p. *Records of civilization,* 41. 1684

Contains translation of Pravda Russkaia, Russian law, and of the charters of Pskov, Novgorod, and Dvina Land.

—— Muscovite judicial texts, 1488–1556, compiled, tr., and ed., with annotations and selected glossary by Horace W. Dewey. Ann Arbor [University of Michigan, Department of Slavic Languages and Literatures], 1966. v, 94 p. *Michigan Slavic materials,* 7. 1685

The White Lake charter of 1488, the 1497 Sudebnik (the first national code of law), and four 15th-century "immunity" charters are translated.

—— Readings in Russian civilization, ed. by Thomas Riha. Chicago and London, Chicago University Press [c. 1964]. xxxi, 873 p.; 3 v. in 1. Vol. 1, Russia before Peter the Great, 900–1700. 1686

Contains excerpts from the Russian Primary chronicle, Russian laws, the chronicle of Novgorod, the byliny, and the life of St. Sergius by St. Epiphanius. For a complete translation of the Primary chronicle, see item 1621 above.

—— Readings in Russian history, compiled and ed. by Warren B. Walsh. Syracuse, N.Y., Syracuse University Press [c. 1948]. Revised editions 1950, 1959, 1963. 1687

Contains about twenty pages of excerpts from the Russian Primary Chronicle (in 4th edition only), the Novgorod Chronicle, the Russkaia Pravda, and a 13th-century description of the Tartars.

Russian literature. *Collections.* History of early Russian literature, by Nikolaĭ K. Gudziĭ, tr. by Susan W. Jones. New York, Macmillan, 1949. xix, 545 p. 1688

Contains throughout extensive paraphrase and summary, with illustrative quotations, from many works not elsewhere translated; particularly important for indication of works translated into Russian during the medieval period.

—— Medieval Russia's epics, chronicles, and tales, ed., tr., and with an intro. by Serge A. Zenkovsky. New York, Dutton, 1963. 436 p. 1689

Includes translations previously published by others but revised by the editors, who have furnished much new translation of works from 1030–1700, some written in Church Slavonic, others in Russian.

—— The Penguin book of Russian verse, introduced and ed. by Dimitri Obolensky, with plain prose translation of each poem. Baltimore, Penguin Books [1962]. 444 p. 1690

The first fifty-one pages contain translation from Slovo o polku Igoreve (Song of Prince Igor), and of selected byliny and stikhi (oral heroic and religious poems, respectively).

—— A treasury of Russian literature, ed. by Bernard G. Guerney. New York, Vanguard, 1943. xx, 1048 p. **1691**

Contains forty-four pages of medieval works in translation: excerpts from Friar Nestor and A. Nikitin, a selection about Solomon from the Apocrypha, two folk epics, and an abridged translation of The Tale of Prince Igor's Campaign by an unnamed translator, apparently the editor.

—— A treasury of Russian spirituality, ed. by Georgiĭ P. Fedotov. New York, Sheed & Ward, 1948. xvi, 501 p. **1692**

Contains Nestor's life of St. Theodosius, an excerpt from a sermon of St. Theodosius, "On patience and love," Epiphanius' life of St. Sergius, and selections from St. Nilus Sorsky (*c.* 1433–1508). Another work by Fedotov, The Russian religious mind, Harvard University Press, 1946–66, 2 v., contains many excerpts in translation *passim.*

—— The Ukrainian poets, 1189–1962, tr. by C. H. Andrusyshen and Watson Kirkconnell. [Toronto], University of Toronto Press for the Ukrainian Canadian Committee, 1963. xxx, 500 p. **1693**

Contains a translation of the Tale of Prince Igor's campaign, pp. 4–21.

S

Saadiah ben Joseph, *gaon, 892?–942.* The book of beliefs and opinions, tr. from the Arabic and the Hebrew by Samuel Rosenblatt. New Haven, Yale University Press, 1948. xxxii, 496 p. *Yale Judaica series,* 1. **1694**

The translation of Kitāb al-'Amānāt is from an Arabic manuscript containing many Hebrew words; this manuscript has been correlated with Hebrew versions of it.

—— The book of doctrines and beliefs, tr. by Alexander Altman. Oxford, East and West Library, 1946; New York, Crown, 1948. 191 p. *Philosophica Judaica.* **1695**

An abridged version of Kitāb al-'Amānāt.

—— "Saadia on the scroll of the Hasmonaeans," by S. Atlas and Moshe Perlmann, *Proceedings of the American Academy for Jewish Research,* 14 (1944), 1–23. **1696**

Contains text and facing translation of Saadiah's preface to his commentary on the Maccabean wars, from a 12th-century manuscript.

—— Sa'dyah Gaon on the influence of music, by Henry George Farmer. London, Probsthain, 1943. xi, 109 p. **1697**

Text and translation of musical passages from Saadiah's Kitāb al-'Amānāt, with three Hebrew versions of the 12th century; also contains translation from al-Kindī and excerpts from other Arabic and Hebrew writers on musical theory.

Sacro Bosco, Joannes de, *fl. 1230.* The sphere of Sacrobosco and its commentators, by Lynn Thorndike. Chicago, University of Chicago Press, 1949. x, 496 p. *Corpus of medieval scientific texts,* 2. **1698**

Contains text and translation of Tractatus de sphera by Sacro Bosco and the Commentary by Robertus Anglicus, written in 1272, as well as the text only of futher commentaries.

Sa'dī, *1184–1292.* The Gulistan or Rose garden of Sa'di, tr. by Edward

Rehatsek, ed. with preface by W. G. Archer, intro. by G. M. Wickens. London, Allen & Unwin, 1964; New York, Putnam [1965]. 265 p. **1699**

Rehatsek's translation, privately printed in India in 1888 without his name and used by Burton also without the name (*cf.* Farrar and Evans, item 3375) is here corrected and improved.

—— Kings and beggars, the first two chapters of Sa'di's Gulistan, tr. with intro. and notes by A. J. Arberry. London, Luzac, 1945. 110 p. **1700**

Ch. 1, On the character of kings, and Ch. 2, On the manners of dervishes are translated.

Saints' lives. *Collections.* Anglo-Saxon missionaries in Germany, ed., tr. by C. H. Talbot. New York, Sheed & Ward [1954]. xx, 234 p. **1701**

Contains translation of The life of St. Willibrod, by Alcuin; of St. Boniface by Willibald; of St. Sturm by Eigil, Abbot of Fulda; of Leoba by Rudolf, Monk of Fulda; of St. Lebuin, anon. and Huebald of St. Amand; the Hodoeporicon of St. Willibald (record of a pilgrimage to the Holy Land) by Huneberc of Heidenheim; and letters of St. Boniface.

—— Anglo-Saxon saints and heroes, tr. by Clinton Albertson. New York, Fordham University Press [c. 1967]. xv, 347 p. **1702**

Contains life of St. Cuthbert; life of Wilfred by Eddius; life of St. Guthlac by Felix; lives of the abbots, by Bede; life of Ceolfrith; life of St. Willibrod by Alcuin; life of St. Boniface by Willibald, all from Northumbria, 670–730. The translations are somewhat abridged but omitted parts are summarized.

—— Charlemagne's cousins; contemporary lives of Adalard and Wala, by Saint Paschasius Radbertus, tr., with intro. and notes, by Allen Cabaniss. [Syracuse, N.Y.], Syracuse University Press [1967]. vii, 266 p. **1703**

Translation of Vita sancti Adalhardi and Vita Walae seu Epitaphium Arsenii. Adalard, Wala, and Paschasius were all monks of Corbie.

—— Early Christian biographies, tr. by Roy J. Deferrari *et al.* [New York], Fathers of the Church [c. 1952]. xiv, 407 p. *Fathers of the Church,* 15. **1704**

Contains Pontius, life of St. Cyprian; Paulinus, life of St. Ambrose; Bishop Possidius, life of St. Augustine; St. Athanasius, life of St. Anthony; St. Jerome, life of St. Paul, the first hermit; St. Jerome, life of St. Hilarion; St. Jerome, life of St. Malchus; St. Ennodius, life of St. Epiphanius; St. Hilary, A sermon on the life of St. Honoratus.

—— Lives and legends of the Georgian saints, selected and tr. . . . by David Marshall Lang. London, Allen & Unwin; New York, Macmillan [1956]. 179 p. *Ethical and religious classics of East and West,* 15. **1705**

Contains life of St. Nino, 10th–11th cent.; story of the Nine martyred children of Kola from a 10th-century manuscript; the passion of St. Shushanik, from a 4th–5th cent. work, the earliest surviving work of Georgian literature; life of Peter the Iberian (*i.e.,* from Eastern Georgia), 409–488; of David of Garesja by Arsenus II, Catholicos of Georgia, 955–80; St. Eustace the Cobbler; Abo of Tiflis; Gregory of Khandzta; Athonites; Queen Ketevan. Most of the works were written in Georgian, some in Syrian.

—— Lives of the saints, tr. by J. F. Webb. Baltimore, Penguin Books [1965]. 206 p. **1706**

Contains translation of the Voyage of St. Brendan; Bede's Life of Cuthbert; Eddi's Life of Wilfrid.

—— Saints' lives and chronicles in early England; together with first English translation of the oldest life of Pope St. Gregory the Great by a monk of

Whitby, and The life of St. Guthlac of Crowland by Felix, tr. by Charles Williams Jones. Ithaca, N.Y., Cornell University Press, 1947. xiii, 232 p. *Romanesque literature,* 1. **1707**

The translation appears on pp. 95–160.

—— Three Byzantine saints, tr. by Elizabeth Dawes and Norman H. Baynes. Oxford, Blackwell, 1948. xiv, 275 p. **1708**

Lives of St. Theodore of Sykeon; St. Daniel the Stylite; and of St. John the Almsgiver, patriarch of Alexander, by Leontius, bp. of Neapolis in Cyprus.

—— Two Armenian passions of saints in the Sassanian period, tr. from Armenian with notes by Louis H. Gray, *Analecta Bollandia,* 67 (1949), 361–76. **1709**

Translation of Armenian texts, probably translated from Syriac, of lives of St. Bardišoy, martyred in the reign of Sāpōr II (309–379); and St. Atom, martyred in the reign of Yazkert II (438–57), according to the translator. The lives were homilies meant to be read on the saints' feasts, 26 October and 19 August, respectively, and date from *c.* 6th century.

—— The Western Fathers; being the lives of SS. Martin of Tours, Ambrose, Augustine of Hippo, Honoratus of Arles, and Germanus Auxerre, tr. and ed. by Frederick Russell Hoare. New York, Sheed & Ward, 1954. xxxii, 320 p. **1710**

Contains the life of St. Martin, by Sulpicius Severus; three letters and two dialogues by Sulpicius Servus; life of St. Ambrose by Paulinus Mediolanensis; life of St. Augustine by St. Possidius, bp. of Calama; life of St. Honoratus of Arles by St. Hilary, bp. of Arles; life of St. Germanus Auxerre, by Constantius of Lyons.

Saltair na Rann. The fifteen signs before doomsday, by William W. Heist. [E. Lansing], Michigan State College Press, 1952. 231 p. *Studies in languages and literature.* **1711**

Contains text and facing translation of strophes 153–162 of Saltair na Rann, the "Psalter of Quatrains" from the late 10th century. For Welsh versions of the poem, see item 1963 below.

—— "Scél Saltrach na Rann," by Myles Dillon, *Celtica,* 4 (1958), 1–43. **1712**

Text and facing translation of a prose version of the Saltair na Rann, distinct from the text found in the Book of Hy Many and the Leabhar Breac; this version has the story of Abraham, Joseph, and Moses from Genesis, with the *incipit* Epistil matusalem.

Salvianus, *5th cent.* The writings of Salvian, the presbyter, tr. by Jeremiah F. O'Sullivan. New York, Cima Publishing Co. [c. 1947]. 396 p. *Fathers of the Church,* 3. **1713**

Contains The governance of God, Letters, The four books of Timothy to the church.

al-Samarqandī, Najib al-Dīn, Muḥammed ibn 'Alī, *d. 1222.* The medical formulary of al-Samarqandī and the relation of early Arabic simples to those found in the indigenous medicine of the Near East and India, tr. by Martin Levey and Noury al-Khaledy. Philadelphia, University of Pennsylvania Press [1967]. 382 p. **1714**

Text and translation of al-Aqrābādhīn, work written in Arabic but including technical terms in many other languages.

Samuel ibn Abbas al-Maghribī, *12th cent.* Samu'al al-Maghribī Ifḥam al-Yahūd, Silencing the Jews, ed. and tr. by Moshe Perlmann. New York, American Academy for Jewish Research, 1964. 104 p. + Arabic text. *Proceedings of the American Academy for Jewish Research,* 32 (1964). **1715**

An anti-Jewish tract by a Jewish convert to Islam; this includes his autobiography and letters to and from critics of an earlier version of his polemic.

Sanā'ī, of Ghazni, *d. c. 1150.* A Persian forerunner of Dante, by Reynold A. Nicholson. Towyn-on-Sea, N. Wales, Printed by J. W. Williams, 1944. 8 p. **1716**

Verse translation of extracts from Sair al-'ibād ilā al-ma'ad, "The journey of God's creatures (mankind) to the afterworld," a Persian mystic's description of his journey to Paradise. This translation was first published in 1943 in *Transactions of the Bombay Branch of the Royal Asiatic Society*. The Widener library copy has the note, "corrected by the author."

Sannazaro, Jacopo, *1458–1530.* Arcadia and Piscatorial eclogues, tr. with an intro. by Ralph Nash. Detroit, Wayne State University Press, 1966. 220 p. **1717**

Contains translation from Italian of the Arcadia, written probably by 1489; and text and facing translation from Latin of the Piscatorials, the first drafts of which, according to the translator, were probably written before 1501.

Sāwīrus ibn al-Muqaffa', *bp. of el Ashmunein, fl. 955–87.* History of the patriarchs of the Egyptian church, known as the history of the Holy Church, by Sāwīrus ibn al Mukaffa', bishop of al-Asmūnīn, tr. and annotated by Aziz Suryal Atiya, Yassa Abd al-Masih, and O. H. E. Khs.-Burmester. Cairo, Société d'archéologie copte, 1943. 2 v. *Textes et documents.* **1718**

Arabic text and translation of the entire work, through 1066 A.D. The author's name in Farrar and Evans is given as Severus ibn al-Mukaffa', Anba, *bp. of Ushmunain, fl.* 950.

School of self-knowledge. The school of self-knowledge, a symposium from medieval sources, tr. . . . by Geoffrey Webb and Adrian Walker. London, Mowbray [1956]. 48 p. **1719**

Contains devotional works by Cistercians of the late 12th and early 13th centuries: Liber de cognitione sui, by Hélinand of Froidmont; and two anonymous works: Meditatio piissima and Domus interior.

Scientific Works. The alchemists, founders of modern chemistry, by Taylor F. Sherwood. New York, Henry Schuman, 1949. x, 246. **1720**

Has alchemical formulae from Europe, Islam, England, as well as a translation of the "Emerald table" of Hermes Trismegistus.

—— Archimedes in the Middle Ages [by] Marshall Clagett. Madison, University of Wisconsin Press, 1964–. v. 1 *University of Wisconsin publications in medieval science,* 6. **1721**

Vol. I, The Arabo-Latin tradition, contains translations of texts from Arabic and Latin, both translations of Archimedes into those languages and also related works which show use of Archimedes' principles and the degree to which they were understood. Latin texts are from 12th–15th century manuscripts; the Latin is given facing the translation. Some of the authors translated are Plato of Tivoli, Gerard of Cremona, Albert of Saxony, and an Arabic scientific work, the so-called Verba filorum of Banū Mūsā ibn Shākir (three 9th-century brothers). The translations were made by the author for this volume. Vol. 2 is to contain William of

Moerbeke's translation of Archimedes, which was independent of the Arabic tradition and straight from Greek manuscripts.

—— The autobiography of science, excerpts ranging from Hippocrates to Einstein, ed. by Forest R. Moulton and Justus J. Schifferes. Garden City, N.Y., Doubleday, 1950. 748 p. **1722**

Only pp. 34–46 contain translation from medieval works, including excerpts from Roger Bacon, Guy de Chauliac, the Regimen of Salerno, and Leonardo da Vinci's On flight.

—— "An early medieval water-clock, by Francis Maddison, *et al.*, *Antiquarian Horology,* 3 (1962), 348–53. **1723**

Contains a translation of what the translators think may be the earliest medieval description of a water-clock, from a Latin manuscript of the 10th–11th century, Ms. Ripoli 225 (Barcelona).

—— "A fourteenth-century cosmology," by George Boas, *Proceedings of the American Philosophical Society,* 98 (1954), 50–59. **1724**

Contains a summary and extensive quotations in translation from a work written 1375–78 perhaps by a "Venetian named Trivisano," which is a "fair sample of learned opinion" in the 14th century.

—— "A Greek gunner's manual," by G. Morgan, *Annual of the British School at Athens,* 49 (1954), 57–71. **1725**

Contains text and English translation from Bodleian Ms. Laud 23 of a craftsman's manual; although the manuscript is 16th-century, the material is medieval, according to the translator.

—— "Hafod 16, a medieval Welsh medical treatise," ed. and tr. by Ida B. Jones, *Études Celtiques,* 7 (1955), 46–75, 270–339; 8 (1958), 66–97, 346–93. **1726**

Text and facing English translation.

—— A history of Greek fire and gunpowder, by James R. Partington. Cambridge [Eng.], Heffer, 1960. xvi, 381 p. **1727**

Contains a translation, pp. 42–61, of Liber ignium ad comburendos hostes, as well as translation of excerpts from later works indebted to it by Roger Bacon, Albertus Magnus, and Michael Scot.

—— A history of Western technology, by Friedrich Klemm, tr. by Dorothea W. Singer. London, Allen & Unwin, 1959. 401 p. **1728**

Part 2, The Middle Ages, has extensive quotations in translation illustrating attitudes toward technical achievement, pp. 55–107.

—— Latin treatises on comets between 1238 and 1368 A.D., by Lynn Thorndike. Chicago, University of Chicago Press, 1950. ix, 274 p. *Corpus of medieval scientific texts,* 3. **1729**

Contains texts of several treatises and translation of those by Albertus Magnus and Thomas Aquinas.

—— Leechdoms, wortcunning, and starcraft of early England . . . , documents illustrating the history of science in this country before the Norman Conquest, ed. by Thomas Oswald Cockayne, intro. by Charles Singer. London, Holland Press, 1961. 3 v. **1730**

The 1961 revised edition of the work originally published in 1864–66 contains the facsimile text and translation of such works as the Herbarium of Apuleius Platonicus (vol. 1) and Lacnunga (vol. 3). *Cf.* Farrar and Evans, items 343, 1425, 2309, 2391, and 2395. For other translations of Lacnunga, see above, items 1205, 1206.

—— "The Manichaean fasts," by W. B. Henning and S. H. Taqizadeh, *Journal of the Royal Asiatic Society,* 1945, 146–64. **1731**

Contains transcription and translation of Sogdian Manichaean calendar tables dating from 9th and 10th centuries.

—— "Medical ethics and etiquette in the early Middle Ages, the persistance of Hippocratic ideals," by Loren C. MacKinney, *Bulletin of the History of Medicine,* 24 (1952), 1–31. **1732**

Contains many excerpts in translation.

—— A medical history of Persia and the Eastern Caliphate, from the earliest times until the year A.D. 1932, by Cyril Elgood. Cambridge [Eng.], Cambridge University Press, 1951. xii, 616 p. **1733**

The author has translated many excerpts from Arabic and Persian works.

—— "A medieval German wound man: Wellcome Ms 49," ed. and tr. by Boyd H. Hill, Jr., *Journal of the History of Medicine,* 20 (1965), 334–57. **1734**

Text and facing translation of a Middle High German work of *c.* 1420; it lists treatments for problems illustrated by the "wound man," a drawing of a body illustrating blows and lacerations by weapons such as clubs and knives.

—— "A medieval physician's Vade mecum," by C. H. Talbot, *Journal of the History of Medicine,* 16 (1961), 213–33. **1735**

Latin text and translation of a work dated late 14th- or early 15th-century, containing medical diagnosis.

—— The medieval science of weights (scientia de ponderibus); treatises ascribed to Euclid, Archimedes, Thabit ibn Qurra, Jordanus de Nemore, and Blasius of Parma, ed. with intro. and notes, by Ernest Addison Moody [and] Marshall Clagett. Madison, University of Wisconsin Press, 1952. x, 438 p. **1736**

Text and facing translation of works which are not merely Latin translations from the Greek or Arabic but which, according to the editors, involve proof of or commentary on the originals. Jordanus de Nemore, 13th century, is sometimes identified as Jordan of Saxony, according to the editors, and Blasius of Parma is Blaise Pelacani, d. 1416.

—— "Procreation, pregnancy, and parturition, extracts from a Middle English metrical encyclopedia," by R. E. Nichols, Jr., *Medical History,* 11 (1967), 175–81. **1737**

Contains a translation of eight questions and answers from Hugh of Campadene's version of a French work, Sidrak and Bokkus, a medieval romance and book of knowledge.

—— Readings in early anthropology, ed. by James S. Slotkin. Chicago, Aldine Publishing Co., 1965. xvii, 530 p. **1738**

Translation of brief excerpts emphasizing "social anthropology or comparative study of cultures," from twenty-two medieval authors, in about forty-five pages.

—— Readings in pharmacology, ed. by B. Holmstedt and G. Liljestrand. Oxford, Pergamon; New York, Macmillan, 1963. x, 395 p. **1739**

Includes new translation of brief excerpts from Alexander of Tralles (6th century) Avicenna, Matthaeus Platearius (*fl.* mid-12th century), and Rhazes (Muḥammed ibn Zakarīyā, Abū Bakr, al-Rāzī).

—— "A Salernitan student's surgical notebook," by Henry E. Sigerist, *Bulletin of the History of Medicine,* 14 (1943), 505–16. 1740

Text and translation from a 12th-century manuscript of Italian origin.

—— Science, medicine, and history, essays on scientific thought and medical practice in honour of Charles Singer, ed. by Edgar A. Underwood. London, Oxford University Press, 1953. 2 v. 1741

Vol. 1, pp. 143–265, has translation *passim* in articles on medieval medical writings from Iceland, Persia, Germany, Italy, England.

—— The science of mechanics in the Middle Ages, by Marshall Clagett. Madison, University of Wisconsin Press, 1959. xxix, 711 p. *University of Wisconsin publications in medieval science,* 4. 1742

Contains translations from some twenty medieval authors, writing in Latin or translating Greek and Arabic into Latin. The works are occasionally abridged; translation is largely by the author. Among the medieval authors are Jordanus de Nemore, Gerard of Brussels, Thomas Bradwardine, and John Buridan.

—— "Some eleventh-century medical questions posed by Ibn Buṭlān and later answered by Ibn Ithirdī *fl.* 1113–4," by Martin Levey, *Bulletin of the History of Medicine,* 39 (1965), 495–507. 1743

Translation from Ibn Buṭlān's Treatise on medical table talk, written *c.* 1050, and from Ibn Ithirdī's commentary written about fifty years later.

—— Source book of medical history, compiled with notes by Logan Clendening. New York and London, P. B. Hoeber [c. 1942]. xiv, 685 p. 1744

Excerpts on pp. 76–83 from old translations of the Regimen of Salerno and works of John of Gaddesden (1280–1361), John of Arderne (1307–80), Bartholomew Anglicus (12th century), and Guy de Chauliac, 1300–68.

—— Studies in Arabic and Persian medical literature, by Muhammad Z. Siddíqí. [Calcutta], Calcutta University Press, 1953. xlviii, 173 p. 1745

Contains description, outline, and much paraphrase of the "Firdausu'l-Hikmat or Paradise of Wisdom" by 'Ali b. Rabban written *c.* 830; and a translation of "Clinical cases mentioned by al-Razí and others." The al-Rāzī referred to is Muḥammad ibn Zakarīyā, Abū Barr, al-Rāzī, d. *c.* 923.

—— The treasury of mathematics, ed. by Henrietta O. Midonick. New York, Philosophical Library [c. 1965]. xxi, 820 p. 1746

An anthology of readings, largely from previously published translations, but over half the entries are from medieval authors, including Bonfils, al-Khwārizmī, Metrodorus, Omar Khayyam, Pappus, and Proclus.

—— "A weather record for 1399–1406 A.D.," by Lynn Thorndike, *Isis,* 32 1949), 304–23 and 57 (1966), 90–99. 1747

Both articles contain paraphrase of a daily weather record from Basel Latin Ms. F.III.8. Modern computation of the data indicates the location of the observations probably to have been the Doubs Valley near Besançon in France.

—— "A Welsh treatise on horses," by Cecile O'Rahilly, *Celtica*, 5 (1960), 145–60. **1748**

Text and translation of a work of unknown date found in a 16th-century manuscript; it is a product of the 15th or 16th century.

Scillacio, Nicocolò, *fl. 1450.* N. Syllacius de insulis Meridiani atque Indici maris Nuper inventis . . . , with a translation into English by John Mulligan. New York [n.p.], 1859. xviii, 105, lxiii p. **1749**

Text and facing translation of the entire work. Appendix A contains a translation of "A Letter addressed to the Chapter of Seville by Doctor Chanca, native of that city and physician to the fleet of Columbus, in his second voyage to the West Indies, describing the principal events . . . ," written apparently in January, 1494. The introduction is signed J. L., *i.e.,* James Lenox, editor. This work, published in an edition of 102 copies, was not noted in Farrar and Evans; two copies are in the Harvard libraries.

Scotland. *Historical sources.* A source book of Scottish history, ed. and tr. by William C. Dickinson, Gordon Donaldson, and Isabel Milne. London, New York, Nelson, 1952–54. 3 v. **1750**

Vol. 1 covers to 1424; vol. 2, 1424–1567. Contains translation from documents (charters are abstracted rather than translated), annals, chronicles, church records, travel books, many directly from manuscript sources. The translators are not always indicated and apparently the editors have supplied many of the translations.

Scott, Michael, *1175?–1234?* Michael Scot, by Lynn Thorndike. [London], Nelson [1965]. 143 p. **1751**

Translation *passim* from Scott's works, apparently not elsewhere translated.

Sermons. *Collections.* Master sermons through the ages . . . , ed. by William Alan Sadler. London, S.C.M. Press; New York, Harper, 1963. xix, 222 p. **1752**

Has one sermon each from Augustine, Chrysostomus, Thomas Aquinas, pp. 157–74; all are about the church seasons.

—— No uncertain sound, sermons that shaped the pulpit tradition, ed. by Ray C. Petry. Philadelphia, Westminster Press, 1948. xiii, 331 p. **1753**

New translations for this volume from twenty-six medieval writers, mostly Christian.

—— The Sunday sermons of the great Fathers . . . , ed. and tr. by Martin F. Toal. Chicago, Regnery [1958–63]. 4 v. **1754**

First published 1955 under the title Patristic homilies on the Gospels; arranged according to the Christian year. Most selections include a commentary from Thomas Aquinas' Catena aurea.

—— The world's great sermons, ed. by S. E. Frost, Jr. Garden City, N.Y., Halcyon house [1943]. xiii, 395 p. **1755**

Contains translations of sermons by thirteen medieval authors; no indication of translators.

Seven sages. The book of the wiles of women, tr. by John E. Keller. Chapel Hill, University of North Carolina Press, 1956. 60 p. *University of North Carolina studies in the Romance languages and literatures,* 27. **1756**

A translation of the Libro de los engamos e los asayamientos de las mugeres, a translation into Spanish made in 1253 from the Arabic. The specific Arabic version is unidentified, but this work contains sixteen of the twenty-nine tales found in the Arabian Nights; it is also known as the Book of Sindibad or Sindbad, the philosopher.

Severian of Gabala, *d. after 408.* "Homily on the nativity of our Lord by Severian, Bishop of Gabala," by Cyril Moss, *Bulletin of the School of Oriental and African Studies,* 12 (1948), 555–66. **1757**

Syriac text and translation of newly discovered homily.

Shabestarī, Maḥmūd ebn 'Abd al-Karīm, *d. c. 1320.* Gulshan i raz: the mystic rose Garden of Sa'd ud Din Mahmud Shabistari, the Persian text, with an English translation and notes, chiefly from the commentary of Muhammad bin Yahya Lahiji, by E. H. Whinfield. London, Trübner, 1880. **1758**

Although this work is entered in Farrar and Evans (item 2611), there is no cross-reference to the name Shabestari under which the Library of Congress now enters the author nor to Lahiji, *fl.* 1474.

al-Shāfi'ī, Muḥammad ibn Idrīs, *767 or 768–820.* Islamic jurisprudence; Shafi'ī's Risāla, tr. with an intro., notes, and appendices, by Majid Khadduri. Baltimore, Johns Hopkins Press, 1961. xiv, 376 p. **1759**

A translation of the complete Kitāb al-Risāla or Fī uṣul al-Fiqh, "Roots or sources of the law."

—— Ash-Shāfi, Risālah, basic ideas (with translations of the chapters on "An-Nāsikh wa'al-Mansūkh"), tr. by Khalil I. Semaan. Lahore, Ashraf, 1961; x, 69 p. **1760**

A summary of the complete work, with a translation of Part III, The principle of abrogation. See also an article by Semaan, "Al Nāsikh Wa-al-mansūkh," *Islamic Quarterly,* 6 (1961), 11–29.

Shanūdah, Anba, *Saint, d. 451?, supposed author.* Pseudo-Shenoute on Christian behavior, ed. and tr. by K. H. Kuhn. Louvain, Secretariat du Corpus SCO, 1960. 2 v. *Corpus scriptorum Christianorum orientalium,* 206–7; *Scriptores Coptici,* 29, 30. **1761**

Coptic text in vol. 29, translation in vol. 30, of a sermon attributed to Shanūdah or Shenoute, abbot of the White Monastery, in the heading of the manuscript as well as in the Arabic manuscript; but the editor doubts the ascription. This may be an original Coptic work rather than a translation from the Greek, in the editor's opinion.

al-Shaybūni, Muḥammad ibn al-Ḥasan, *c. 750–804 or 805.* The Islamic law of nations: Shaybānī's Siyar, tr. with an intro., notes, and appendices by Majid Khadduri. Baltimore, Johns Hopkins Press [1966]. xviii, 311 p. **1762**

Contains also translation from two works on taxation, al-Shaybāni's Kitāb al-Kyarāj and Dāwūd b. Rushayd's Book on Ushr (tithe).

Shirakatsi, Ananiya, *7th cent.* The trade and cities of Armenia in relation to ancient world trade, H. A. Manandian, tr. by Nina G. Garsonian, Lisbon, Livraria Bertrand, 1946; 2d ed., 1965. **1763**

Contains translation of excerpts from historical and geographical sources from antiquity to 15th cent., including the Itinerary of Ananiya.

Shirwood, William, *fl. 1260.* William of Sherwood's Introduction to logic, tr. by Norman Kretzman. Minneapolis, University of Minnesota Press; London, Oxford University Press [c. 1966]. xiii, 187 p. **1764**

A translation of "Introductiones Magistri Guilli de Shyreswode in logicam."

Sidonius, C. Sollius Modestus Apollinaris, *d. c. 489.* . . . Poems and letters; with an English translation, intro. and notes by William B. Anderson. Cambridge, Harvard University Press; London, Heinemann, 1936–65. 2 v. *Loeb classics.* **1765**

Text and facing translation. Vol. 2 appeared in 1965, six years after the death of William B. Anderson. The manuscript was prepared for press by E. H. Warmington. *Cf.* Farrar and Evans, item 3502.

Skeireins. The Gothic commentary on the gospel of John, skeireins aiwaggeljons þairh iohannen, a decipherment, edition, and translation by William H. Bennett. New York, Modern Language Association of America, 1960. xii, 144 p. *Monograph series,* 31. **1767**

Text and translation in double columns. *Skereins* is the *incipit* of the commentary.

Slovo o polku Igoreve.

For translations of parts of the epic and for critiques, see Avrahm Yarmolinsky, "The Slovo in English," in Russian epic studies, ed. by Roman Jakobson and Ernest J. Simmons, Philadelphia, American Folklore Society, 1949, pp. 203–23. (Memoirs of the American Folklore Society, 42, 1947). See also *Russian literature. Collections.*

1768

—— La geste du Prince Igor, épopée russe du douzième siècle, ed. and tr. by Henri Grégoire and others. New York, School of Advanced Studies, 1948. 343 p. *Annuaire de l'institut de philologie et d'histoire orientales et slaves,* 8. **1769**

Contains Russian text reconstructed by Ramon Jakobson and facing English translation by Samuel H. Cross.

—— Prince Ihor's raid against the Polovtsi, tr. by Paul C. Crath, versified by Watson Kirkconnell. Saskatoon, Saskatchewan, published by the Mohyla Ukrainian Institute, 1947. iii, 14 p. **1770**

An abridged and purposefully non-literal translation.

—— The song of Igor's campaign, an epic of the twelfth century, tr. by Vladimir Nabokov. London, Weidenfeld and Nicolson, 1961; New York, Vintage Books [c. 1960]. 135 p. **1771**

A complete translation.

Smpad, Contable, *1208–76.* "The Armenian chronicle of the Constable Smpad or of the 'Royal Historian,'" by Serapie Der Nersessian, *Dumbarton Oaks Papers,* 13 (1959), 143–68. **1772**

Contains translation from a new edition of the chronicle based on an early manuscript. The chronicle treats of the fall of Jerusalem and has more material on the years 1163–75 than other versions.

Snorri Sturluson, *1178–1241.* Heimskringla; history of the kings of Norway, tr. with intro. and notes by Lee M. Hollander. Austin, published for the American-Scandinavian Foundation by the University of Texas Press [1964]. xxvi, 854 p. **1773**

—— Heimskringla: sagas of the Norse kings, tr. by Samuel Laing; rev. with intro. and notes by Peter Foote. London, Dent; New York, Dutton [1961]. xxxii, 461 p. *Everyman's library.* 1774

Laing's translation (see Farrar and Evans, item 3514) has been revised to show the interpolations he made in the 19th-century text. The original plates have been reprinted, but corrections are noted in an appendix and about half the footnotes have been rewritten, according to the editor.

—— King Harald's Saga: Harald Hardradi of Norway, from Snorri Sturluson's 'Heimskringla', tr. with an intro. by Magnus Magnusson and Hermann Pálsson. Harmondsworth [Eng.], Penguin Books, 1966. 187 p. 1775

—— The prose Edda of Snorri Sturluson, tales from Norse mythology, intro by Sigurður Nordal; sel. and tr. by Jean I. Young. Cambridge [Eng.], Bowes and Bowes, 1955; Berkeley, University of California Press, 1964. 131 p. 1776

An abridged translation. Includes all of Part 1; omits catalogs of kennings in Part 2 on Poetic diction and all of Part 3. For a translation of the parts on poetic theory, *see Edda Snorra Sturlusonar, Norren staffraeði,* item 591 above.

Sottovagina, Hugh, *d. 1139?* Hugh the Chantor, the history of the church of York, 1066–1127, tr. with intro. by Charles Johnson. London, Nelson, 1961. xvii, 132, 132, 134–38 p. *Medieval texts.* 1777

Text and facing translation of a work reporting the "contest for the primacy of Britain between the sees of Canterbury and York."

Spain. *Historical sources.* Spanish life in the late Middle Ages, sel. and tr. by Kenneth R. Scholberg. Chapel Hill, University of North Carolina Press [1966]. 180 p. *University of North Carolina, Studies in the Romance languages and literatures,* 57. 1778

Contains translation of selections in Latin and Spanish from Castilian prose writers about life in and around the court of King Juan II of Castile, 1405–54. Thirteen authors are represented, only two of whose work seems to have been translated before.

—— "Two twelfth-century Latin charters from rural Catalonia in the Lea Library," tr. by John F. Bent, *University of Pennsylvania Library Chronicle,* 28 (1962), 14–25. 1779

Translation of two manuscripts on feudal land tenure and inheritance; text and facsimile included.

Spanish literature. *Collections.* An anthology of Spanish literature in English translation, ed. by Seymour Resnick and Jeanne Pasmantier. London, J. Calder; New York, Ungar, 1958. Vol. 1, Cid to Gracian, xxv, 608 p. 1780

Contains selections from some twenty-three medieval authors, by various translators.

—— Arabic-Andalusian Casidas, tr. with an intro. by Harold Morland. London, Phoenix, 1949. 57 p. 1781

Poems of the 9th to 13th century translated into verse.

—— Early Spanish plays, ed. by Robert A. O'Brien. New York, Las Americas, 1964. 2 v. 1782

Contains translation by various translators (apparently new for this volume) of Auto de los reyes magos, *c.* mid-12th century; Gomez Manrique's The birth of our Lord; Rodrigo Cota's Dialog between love and an old man (the latter two, 15th century).

—— Eight Spanish plays of the Golden Age, tr., ed., and intro. by Walter F. Starkie. New York, Modern Library [c. 1964]. xvliii, 328 p. **1783**

Contains translation of the Mystery of Elche, a 15th-century play of the Assumption, and of The Gallant, the bawd, and the fair lady from El Libro do Buen Amor of Juan Ruiz, Archpriest of Hita.

—— Hispano-Arabic poetry and its relations with the old Provençal troubadours, by A. R. Nykl. Baltimore, J. H. Furst Co., 1946. xxvii, 416 p. **1784**

Translation of selected poems written 711–1492 by some three hundred poets.

—— Literature of the Spanish people from Roman times to the present day, by Gerald Brenan. Cambridge [Eng.], Cambridge University Press, 1951. xviii, 496 p. **1785**

Contains *passim* translation and text of some thirty-five medieval poems or extracts.

—— Medieval lyrics in Spain and Portugal, by John B. Trend. Cambridge [Eng., Printed by R. I. Severs], 1952. 25 p. **1786**

Contains translation and paraphrase of some 14th- and 15th-century Spanish lyrics as well as of 16th-century Spanish and Portuguese versions of ballads which may belong to an earlier tradition. A copy of this apparently rare work is in the Yale University Library.

—— "The oldest Spanish poetry," by John B. Trend, pp. 415–28 in Hispanic Studies in honour of I. Gonzáles Llubera, ed. by Frank Pierce. Oxford, Dolphin Book Co., 1959. 444 p. **1787**

Contains translation of mozarabic poems of the late 11th and early 12th centuries; written in Hebrew or Arabic characters, these are strophic poems with a refrain, known as muwaṣṣahs. See also items 115, 121, 122, and 845 above.

—— The Penguin book of Spanish verse, with plain prose translations of each poem, ed., tr. by John M. Cohen. Harmondsworth [Eng.], Penguin Books [1956]. xxxvi, 441 p. **1788**

Contains text and translation from many medieval poems and romances, pp. 1–97.

—— Spanish ballads, ed. and tr. by William S. Merwin. Garden City, N.Y., Doubleday; London, Abelard-Schuman [1961]. 158 p.; 127 p. **1789**

The London edition appeared under the title Some Spanish ballads. Included are translations of Spanish and Moorish romances and cantares from the 14th century on.

—— Ten centuries of Spanish poetry, an anthology in English verse with original texts from the XIth century to the generation of 1898, ed. by Eleanor L. Turnbull. Baltimore, Johns Hopkins University Press [1955]. xv, 452 p. **1790**

Texts and facing translation by many translators, including the editor.

Stephen, King of England, *1105–54.* Gesta Stephani, the deeds of Stephen, King of England, tr. by Kenneth R. Potter. London and New York, Nelson [1955]. xxxii, 159–159, 161–63 p. *Medieval texts.* **1791**

Text and facing translation; text based on a manuscript discovered while the work was in progress, Valenciennes Ms. 793, which includes the last part of the work, previously lost.

Strassburg manuscript. The Strasburg manuscript, a medieval painters' handbook, tr. from the Old German by Viola and Rosamund Borradaile; editors' text tr. into German by Johanna M. Franck, foreword by John Harthan. London, Alec Tiranti, 1966; New York, Transatlantic Arts, 1966. 116 p. **1792**

The Old High German text was made from a transcript in the National Gallery, London, which was made before the manuscript was destroyed in 1870. Portions of the work are instructions of Heinrich von Lübegge and Andres von Colmar.

Suger, *abbot of Saint Denis, 1081–1151.* Abbot Suger, On the Abbey-church of St.-Denis and its art treasures, ed., tr., and annotated by Erwin Panofsky. Princeton, Princeton University Press, 1946. xiv, 250 p. **1793**

Text and facing translation of the complete work.

Suso, Heinrich, *1300?–1366.* The exemplar; life and writings of Blessed Henry Suso, Complete edition based on mss. with a critical intro. and explanatory notes by Nicholas Heller, tr. from the German by Ann Edward. Dubuque, Iowa, Priory Press [1962]. 2 v. **1794**

The text appeared in Des Mystikers Heinrich Seuse, 1925, and is not included here. The vita seems to be partly autobiographical, partly the work of anonymous biographers, apparently compiled by Suso's friend Elsbeth Stagel.

—— The letters of Henry Suso to his spiritual daughters, tr. by Kathleen Goldmann. London, Blackfriars, 1955. 76 p. **1795**

Translation from Latin of twenty-three letters in Das grosse Briefbuch collected by Suso's correspondent Elsbeth Stagel.

—— The life of the servant, tr. by James M. Clark. London, J. Clarke and Co., 1952. 150 pp. **1796**

The translation is based on a critical text of 1913, whereas the previous translation by Knox (see Farrar and Evans, item 3539) was based on an edition of 1829. This is essentially Suso's autobiography.

—— The little book of eternal wisdom and the little book of truth, tr. by James M. Clark. London, Faber & Faber; New York, Harper [1953]. 212 p. **1797**

The translation is from the German version by Suso; both works are from the Exemplar.

Sylvester II, *pope, d. 1003.* The letters of Gerbert, with his papal privileges as Sylvester II, tr. with an intro. by Harriet Pratt Lattin. New York, Columbia University Press, 1961. x, 412 p. *Records of civilization*, 60. **1798**

Includes letters to and from Gerbert, as well as translation of thirty-one papal documents.

Symon Simeonis, *fl. 1322.* Itinerarium Symonis Semeonis ab Hibernia ad Terram Sanctam, ed. and tr. by Mario Esposito. Dublin, Institute for Advanced Studies, 1960. ix, 127 p. *Scriptores Latini Hiberniae,* 4. **1799**

Text and facing translation of a journey to Jerusalem in 1323, from a manuscript of *c.* 1335–52. An unusual aspect of the record is that prices and values of money are given.

T

al-Ṭabarī, *838–923.* . . . The reign of al-Mu'tasim, tr. and annotated by Elma Marin. New Haven, American Oriental Society, 1951. xvii, 142 p. *American Oriental series,* 35. **1800**

Translation of annals covering the reign of Abbasid ruler who died in 842. The translator intended to continue the record of the reign of al-Mu'tasim's two sons until 861, but no further volumes have appeared. The annals include some letters but little comment. The author's full name, formerly used by the Library of Congress, is Abū Ja'far Muḥammad ibn Jarīr al-Ṭabarī.

al-Taftāzānī, Mas'ūd ibn 'Umar, *1322–1389?* A commentary on the creed of Islam; Sa'd al-Dīn al-Taftāzānī on the creed of Najm al-Dīn al-Nasafī, tr. with intro. and notes by Earl Edgar Elder. New York, Columbia University Press, 1950. xxxii, 187 p. *Records of civilization,* 43. **1801**

The translation of al-Nasafī's creed appears in bold type, with al-Taftāzānī's comment below each item. According to a review in *Speculum* (1950), p. 565, this work "has for centuries been a standard text-book of Sunnite theology."

Ṭāhir, *of Hamadān, 11th cent.* The Rubáiyyát of Bábá Táhir Oryán of Hamadán, rendered from Persian verse into English verse by Mehdi Nakosteen. Boulder, University of Colorado Press [1968? c. 1967]. 54 p. **1802**

Persian text reproduced in Dr. Nakosteen's handwriting, with facing translation.

Talkyng of the love of God. A talking of the love of God, ed. from Ms Vernon (Bodleian 3938) and collated with Ms Simeon (Brit. Mus. Add. 22283) by [Cecilia Maria Westra.] The Hague, Nijhoff, 1950. xxi, 171 p. **1803**

Middle English text and facing translation of a mystical work.

Talmud. The Talmud, tr. by Maurice Simon, ed. by I. Epstein. London, Soncino Press, 1960– . **1804**

This Hebrew-English edition is based on the Wilna edition of the Talmud. Another translation alone was published by Soncino 1935–52. Although it was not included by Farrar and Evans, the Talmud is included here because it was compiled and written down, at least in part, during the medieval period, and because most modern editions include the medieval commentaries of Rashi, Maimonides, and Samson of Sens. No attempt is made here to include all translations of parts of the Talmud; medieval commentaries published alone are noted under their authors. See also *Mishnah*, *Midrash*, and *Judaism*.

—— The Talmud, with English translation and commentary, ed. by A. Ehrman, tr. by Esther J. Ehrman *et al.* Jerusalem-Tel Aviv, El-Am [*i.e.,* Talmud Publishing Society], 1965– . **1805**

Known as the El-AM edition, this translation with Hebrew text is being published in separate fasicles.

—— Hammer on the rock, a short midrash reader, ed. by Nahum N. Glatzer [tr. by Jacob Sloan]. New York, Schocken Books [1948]. 128 p. **1806**

This often reprinted selection includes material from the non-legal parts of the Talmud, the Haggadah, and the Midrash.

—— Our sages say, stories and sayings from the Babylonian Talmud, compiled and arranged by Joseph Apfel. Leeds, J.J.A., 1952. vii, 271 p. **1807**

Selected Rabbinic sayings and parables arranged topically.

Tamīm ibn Baḥr, *9th cent.* "Tamīm ibn Baḥr's journey to the Uyghurs," by V. Minorsky, *Bulletin of the School of Oriental and African Studies,* 12 (1947–48), 275–305. **1808**

Arabic text and translation of record of a journey *c.* 821 to Mongolia; a record of an actual journey, according to the editor, this work became a source for later Arabic works. The Uyghurs inhabited an ancient Turkish kingdom of central Asia.

Tauler, Johannes, *c. 1300–61.* Signposts to perfection, sel., ed., and tr. by Elizabeth Strakosch. London, Blackfriars; St. Louis, Herder, 1958. xxxix, 140 p. **1809**

Has translation of twenty-one sermons selected from the eighty-four known by Tauler, arranged according to the liturgical calendar.

—— Spiritual conferences, tr. and ed. by Eric Colledge and M. Jane. St. Louis, Herder [1961]. 283 p. **1810**

Translation of selections from Die Predigten Taulers, edited in 1910; only half of the sermons attributed to Tauler are genuinely his, according to the editors.

——, *supposed author.* The book of the poor in spirit, by a Friend of God (A guide to Rhineland mysticism), tr. by Carl F. Kelley. London, Longmans, Green; New York, Harper, 1954. 288 p. **1811**

A translation of a work formerly translated by J. R. Morrell as "The following of Christ" (see Farrar and Evans, notes to item 3575); the original is cited as Nachfolgung des Armen Lebens Christi, 1621, by the Index Translationum, and as Von den geistligen Armut by the British National Bibliography. The translator says that he has worked not from manuscripts but from 19th-century German editions; he does not specify which ones.

Taxster, John de, *d. 1265?, supposed author.* The chronicle of Bury St. Edmunds, 1212–1301, ed. with intro., notes, and translation by Antonia Grandsen. London, Nelson [1964]. xlv, 164, 164, [165]–187 p. *Medieval texts.* **1812**

Text and facing translation of the Chronica Buriensis, attributed to John de Taxster, and two other unknown monks.

Tertullianus, Quintus Septimius Florens, *c. 150–240.*

COLLECTIONS

—— Apologetical works, and Minucius Felix: Octavius, tr. by Rudolph Arbesmann *et al.* New York, Fathers of the Church, 1950. xix, 430 p. *Fathers of the Church,* 10. **1813**

Contains Tertullian's Apology, Testimony of the soul, To Scapula, On the soul.

—— Disciplinary, moral, and ascetical works, tr. by Rudolph Arbesmann *et al.* New York, Fathers of the Church, 1959. 323 p. *Fathers of the Church,* 40. **1814**

Contains To the martyrs, Spectacles, the Apparel of women, Prayer, Patience, the Chaplet, Flight in time of persecution.

—— Treatises on marriage and remarriage: To his wife, An exhortation to chastity, Monogamy, tr. and annoted by William P. Le Saint. Westminster, Md., Newman Press, 1951. vii, 196 p. *Ancient Christian writers,* 13. **1815**

—— Treatises on penance: On penitence and On purity, tr. and annotated by William P. Le Saint. Westminster, Md., Newman Press, 1959. vi, 330 p. *Ancient Christian writers,* 28. **1816**

The text (not included) has been newly edited from manuscripts discovered in 1916 and 1946.

TERTULLIANUS

SINGLE WORKS

—— The treatise against Hermogenes, tr. and annotated by J. H. Waszink. Westminster, Md., Newman Press, 1956 [i.e. 1957]. vi, 178 p. *Ancient Christian writers,* 24. **1817**

Hermogenes was a heretic, *fl. c.* 200.

—— . . . Adversus Praxeam liber: Tertullian's treatise against Praxeas, ed. and tr. by Ernest Evans. London, S.P.C.K., 1948. viii, 342 p. **1818**

Text and translation.

—— De baptismo liber, Homily on baptism, ed. with an intro., translation, and commentary by Ernest Evans. London, S.P.C.K., 1964. xl, 122 p. **1819**

Text and facing translation.

—— De carne Christi liber, treatise on the incarnation, ed. and tr. with intro. and commentary by Ernest Evans. London, S.P.C.K., 1956. xliii, 197 p. **1820**

—— De idololatria, ed. by Pieter Gijsbertus van der Nat [tr. by P. H. van Huizen]. Leiden, Saint Lucas Society, 1960. 23, 148 p. **1821**

Text and translation.

—— Tract on the prayer, the Latin text with critical notes, ed. and tr. by Ernest Evans. London, S.P.C.K., 1953. xviii, 69. **1822**

Text and facing translation of De oratione liber.

Thābit ibn Qurrah al Harrānī, *d. 901.* "Thâbit ben Qurra, On the solar year and On the motion of the spheres," tr. and commentary by O. Neugebauer, *Proceedings of the American Philosophical Society,* 106 (1962), 264–99. **1823**

The translation is based on the Latin versions edited by F. J. Carmody in 1960.

Themistius, *4th cent.* "Themistius' first Oration," by Glanville Downey, *Greek, Roman, and Byzantine Studies,* 1 (1958), 49–69. **1824**

Themistius was a teacher of Aristotle's and Plato's works. For the translation into Arabic by Isḥāk ibn Ḥunain, see "An Arabic translation of the Commentary of Themistius," by M. C. Lyons, *Bulletin of the School of Oriental and African Studies,* 17 (1955), 426–35.

Theodorus, *bp. of Mopsuestia, c. 350–c. 428.* Manhood and Christ, a study of the Christology of Theodor Mopsuestia, by R. A. Norris. Oxford, Clarendon Press, 1963. xv, 274 p. **1825**

Contains translation from Theodorus' works and others' on the relationship of body and soul as well as on Christology; based on a newly edited text of Theodorus' work thought to have been lost until discovered in the 1930s and 40s.

—— Theodorus of Mopsuestia, exegete and theologian, by Rowan A. Greer. Westminster [London], Faith Press [1961]. 173 p. **1826**

Contains translation *passim* by the author of excerpts from Theodore's works, especially his Commentary on St. John, not elsewhere translated. The translation is from a Syriac version of the original.

Theodosius, *abp. of Alexandria, d. 566.* A panegyric on John the Baptist attributed to Theodosius, Archbishop of Alexandria, ed. and tr. by K. H. Kuhn.

Louvain, Secretariat du Corpus SCO, 1966. 2 v. *Corpus scriptorum Christianorum orientalium,* 268–69; *Scriptores Coptici,* 33, 34. **1827**

Coptic text in vol. 33, translation in vol. 34, of a sermon.

Theologia deutsch. Theologica Germanica, by Joseph Bernhart; intro. and notes tr. from German by Willard R. Trask. [New York], Pantheon Books [1949]. 240 p. **1828**

The translation of Susanna Winkworth "completely revised to conform with the modern German version of Joseph Bernhart." See Farrar and Evans, item 3616.

Theophilus, *called also* **Rugerus,** *fl. 12th cent.* The various arts, ed. and tr. by C. R. Dodwell. London, Nelson, 1961. lxxvii, 178 p. *Medieval texts.* **1829**

Text edited from manuscripts and facing translation of De diuersis artibus.

—— On divers arts, the treatise of Theophilus, tr. by John G. Hawthorne and Cyril S. Smith. [Chicago], University of Chicago Press [1963]. xxxv, 216 p. **1830**

This translation had been completed when Dodwell's appeared; the editors, a classicist and a metallurgist, collated their printed text with Dodwell's newly established one and issued the translation since it differs in many respects from Dodwell's.

Thomas à Kempis, *1380–1471.* The imitation of Mary, extracts from the original works of Thomas à Kempis, sel. and ed. by Albin de Cigala; tr. from the French ed. by a Dominican sister. Westminster, Md., Newman Press [c. 1948]. iv, 114 p. **1831**

Selections from various works of Thomas arranged to tell the life of Mary.

—— In praise of the Blessed Virgin Mary, tr. by Robert E. Patterson. Milwaukee, Bruce Publishing Co. [1956]. 52 p. **1832**

Translation of discourses 21–24 of the Sermones ad novicios. For translations of the Imitatio Christi, see items 987–97 above.

Thomas Aquinas, *Saint, 1225?–1274.*

COLLECTIONS

—— The life of Saint Thomas Aquinas: biographical documents, ed. and tr. by Kenelm Foster. London, Longmans, Green; Baltimore, Helicon Press [1959]. xii, 172 p. **1833**

Contains Bernard Gui, Vita; excerpt from Tolomeo of Lucca; excerpts from the Vitae fratrum and the Cronica brevis of Gerard de Frachet; a letter of the Faculty of Arts, University of Paris; an excerpt from the canonisation enquiry; and a sonnet ascribed to Thomas.

—— Selected writings of St. Thomas Aquinas: The principles of nature, On being and essence, On the virtues in general, On free choice, tr. by Robert P. Goodwin. Indianapolis, Bobbs-Merrill [1965]. xxi, 162 p. **1834**

—— The Trinity and The unicity of the intellect, by St. Thomas Aquinas, tr. by Rose Emmanuella Brennan. St. Louis and London, Herder, 1946. v, 289 p. **1835**

Translation of Expositio super Boetium De trinitate and of De unitate intellectus.

THOMAS AQUINAS

SINGLE WORKS

—— [Catena aurea] The golden chain; selections from the "Catena aurea" of St. Thomas Aquinas for Lent and Eastertide, tr. by a Religious of C.S.M.V. London, Mowbray; New York, Morehouse-Gorham [1956]. 90 p. **1836**

A compilation by Thomas of commentaries on the Gospels from 3d- to 9th-century Fathers.

—— [De ente et essentia] On being and essence, tr., with an intro. and notes, by Armand Augustine Maurer. Toronto, Pontifical Institute of Mediaeval Studies, 1949. 63 p. **1837**

—— [De ente et essentia] . . . On being and essence, a translation and interpretation by Joseph Bobik. [Notre Dame, Ind.], University of Notre Dame Press [1965]. xv, 286 p. **1838**

Text and translation with extensive commentary interspersed. For another translation and the commentary of Thomas de Vio (Cajetan), see item 1941 below.

—— [De fide et spe (Compendium theologiae)] Compendium of theology by St. Thomas Aquinas, tr. by C. Vollert. St. Louis, Herder [1947]. xx, 366 p. **1839**

The Compendium is Thomas' own summary of Christian theology, written after the two great Summas; he did not live to complete it. It was later known by the title De fide et spe.

—— [De modo studendi] How to study, being the letter of St. Thomas Aquinas to Brother John, ed. and tr. by Victor White. London, Blackfriars, 1947. 43 p. **1840**

Text and translation in double columns, only seven pages long; most of this volume is exposition by the editor.

—— [De motu cordis] "St. Thomas Aquinas on the movement of the heart," by Vincent R. Larkin, *Journal of the History of Medicine,* 15 (1960), 22–30. **1841**

Contains translation of what the editor identifies as a letter of St. Thomas.

—— [De principiis naturae] . . . De principiis naturae, ed. by R. J. Henle and V. J. Bourke [tr. by Leo Kane]. St. Louis, St. Louis University Press, 1947. 91 p. **1842**

Text and facing translation.

—— An introduction to the philosophy of nature, compiled by R. A. Kocourek. St. Paul, North Central Publishing Co. [c. 1948]; rev. ed., 1956. 193 p. **1843**

Contains a translation of De principiis naturae and of Thomas' Commentary on the first two books of Aristotle's Physics.

—— . . . The principles of nature, tr. by Pierre H. Conway. Columbus, Ohio, College of Saint Mary of the Springs, 1963. 11 p. **1844**

This work has not been seen; it seems to be an abridged version. For another translation, complete, of De principiis, see item 1883 below.

—— [De regno; ad regem Cypri] On kingship, To the King of Cyprus, tr. by

Gerald B. Phelan, rev. by I. T. Eschmann. Toronto, Pontifical Institute of Mediaeval Studies, 1949. xxxix, 119 p. **1845**

The translation, published under the title On the governance of rulers in 1935 (*cf.* Farrar and Evans, item 3655), has been revised in the light of the manuscripts; a new text has been established by the editor, though not published here. Appendix II contains translation of parts of Thomas' other works on this subject. De regno and Ad regem Cypri were bound with a work of Thomas' disciple Tolomeo of Lucca in the 14th century, according to the editor, and the compilation given the title of Tolomeo's work, De regimine principium.

—— [Expositio . . . Aristotelis] . . . Proems and first lectures of the expositions of Aristotle, tr. by Pierre H. Conway and R. F. Larcher. Columbus, Ohio, Alum Creek Press [1965]. iv, 36 p. **1846**

Thomas' introductions to twelve commentaries on Aristotle.

—— [Expositio . . . Aristotelis] De anima, in the version of William of Moerbeke; and The commentary of St. Thomas Aquinas, tr. by Kenelm Foster and Silvester Humphries, with an intro. by Ivo Thomas. New Haven, Yale University Press, 1951. 504 p. *Rare masterpieces of philosophy and science.* **1847**

Both Moerbeke's Latin version of De anima, used by Thomas, and Thomas' commentary are translated. This commentary or *lectio* is to be distinguished from Thomas' De anima which is one of the Quaestiones disputatae.

—— [Expositio . . . Aristotelis] The commentary of St. Thomas Aquinas on Aristotle's treatise on the soul, tr. by R. A. Kocourek. [St. Paul, Minnesota, College of St. Thomas, 1947. 61 p.] **1848**

According to the Library of Congress, there was another issue of this work in Minneapolis, 1947, 76 p.; the copy seen at Widener Library had sixty-one pages and no title page or introductory material.

—— [Expositio . . . Aristotelis] Exposition of Aristotle's treatise On the heavens, tr. by R. F. Larcher and Pierre H. Conway. Columbus, Ohio, College of St. Mary of the Springs, 1963–64. 2 v. **1849**

A translation of Thomas' commentary on De caelo.

—— [Expositio . . . Aristotelis] Exposition of Aristotle's treatise On generation and corruption, Book I (cc. 1–5), tr. by R. F. Larcher and Pierre H. Conway. Columbus, Ohio, College of St. Mary of the Springs, 1964. 64 p. **1850**

—— [Expositio . . . Aristotelis] "On the combining of the elements," tr. by Vincent R. Larkin, *Isis,* 51 (1960), 67–72. **1851**

Thomas' commentary on Aristotle's De generatione, Book I, ch. 10, De mixtione elementorum.

—— [Expositio . . . Aristotelis] Aristotle, On interpretation, commentary by St. Thomas and Cajetan, tr. with an intro. by Jean T. Oesterle. Milwaukee, Marquette University Press, 1962. xiii, 271 p. *Medieval philosophical texts in translation,* 11. **1852**

Aristotle's Peri Hermeneias is translated from the Greek, the commentaries from Latin.

—— [Expositio . . . Aristotelis] Commentary on the Metaphysics of Aristotle, tr. by John P. Rowan. Chicago, Regnery, 1961. 2 v. (xxiii, 955 p.) **1853**

The translation is based on a 1950 edition of the text (not included) and includes translation of the Latin text presumably used by Thomas, that of William of Moerbeke. Another version of Thomas' commentary alone, a summary with "key points and main developments in St. Thomas' own words," is that of Pierre H. Conway, Columbus, Ohio, College of St. Mary of the Springs, 1963, xiv, 228 p.

—— [Expositio . . . Aristotelis] Latin treatises on comets, between 1238–1368, ed. and tr. by Lynn Thorndike. Chicago, University of Chicago Press [1950]. ix, 274 p. **1854**

Texts of several treatises and translations of those of Albertus Magnus and Thomas Aquinas, pp. 77–86; Lectiones 8–10 are translated. The treatise on comets is part of Thomas' commentary on Aristotle's De meteorologica, book 1.

—— [Expositio . . . Aristotelis] Exposition of Aristotle's treatise On meteorology, book I–II (cc. 1–5), Index I–II, tr. by R. F. Larcher and Pierre H. Conway. Columbus, Ohio, College of St. Mary of the Springs, 1964. iv, [45] p. **1855**

—— [Expositio Aristotelis] Commentary on the Nicomachean ethics, tr. by C. I. Litzinger. Chicago, Regnery [1964]. 2 v. **1856**

Includes a translation of the Latin text of Aristotle by William of Moerbeke used by Thomas. Each volume contains five books.

—— [Expositio . . . Aristotelis] St. Thomas Aquinas, on Aristotle's Love and friendship, Ethics, books viii–ix, tr. by Pierre Conway. Providence, R.I., Providence College Press, 1951. xvi, 132 p. **1857**

A selection from the commentary on the Nichomachean Ethics. Includes a translation of the Latin text of Aristotle used by Thomas.

—— [Expositio . . . Aristotelis] Exposition of the Physics of Aristotle, tr. by Pierre H. Conway and R. F. Larcher. Columbus, Ohio, College of St. Mary of the Springs, 1958–63. 2 v. **1858**

Vol. 1 contains a detailed summary of books 1 and 2; vol. 2 has a translation of books 3–8 and Thomas' index. For another translation of books 1 and 2, see above, item 1843.

—— [Expositio . . . Aristotelis] Commentary on Aristotle's Physics, tr. by Richard J. Blackwell, Richard J. Spath, and W. Edmund Thirlkel; intro. by Vernon J. Bourke. New Haven, Yale University Press; London, Routledge & Kegan Paul [1963]. xxxii, 599 p. *Rare masterpieces of philosophy and science.* **1859**

A translation of the entire commentary.

—— [Expositio . . . Aristotelis] Exposition of the posterior analytics of Aristotle, tr. by Pierre Conway. Quebec, La libraire philosophique, M. Doyon, 1956. xvi, 449 p. **1860**

A complete and literal translation, according to the editors, except that technical terms are kept in Latin.

—— [Expositio in Dionysium] "Medieval Aesthetic II, St. Thomas on Dionysius," tr. by Ananda K. Coomaraswamy, *Art Bulletin,* 20 (1938), 66–77. **1861**

A translation of Ch. 4, lecture 5, not listed by Farrar and Evans.

—— [Expositio super Boethium . . .] The division and methods of the sciences [by] St. Thomas Aquinas. Questions v and vi of his Commentary on the De Trinitate of Boethius, tr. with intro. and notes by Armand Maurer. Toronto,

Pontifical Institute of Mediaeval Studies, 1953. xxxvi, 96 p. 2d ed. rev., 1958; 3d ed. rev., 1963. **1862**

The revised editions have not been seen.

—— [Quaestiones disputatae, De anima] The Soul, a translation of St. Thomas Aquinas's De anima by John Patrick Rowan. St. Louis, Herder, 1949. viii, 291 p. **1863**

This is not the same work as Thomas' commentary on Aristotle's De anima, *q.v.* above, items 1847, 1848.

—— [Quaestiones disputatae, De caritate] On charity (De caritate), tr. with an intro., by Lottie H. Kendzierski. Milwaukee, Marquette University Press, 1960. 115 p. *Medieval philosophical texts in translation,* 10. **1864**

—— [Quaestiones disputae, De spiritualibus creaturis] On spiritual creatures, tr. with an intro. by Mary C. Fitzpatrick and John J. Wellmuth. Milwaukee, Marquette University Press, 1949. 135 p. *Medieval philosophical texts in translation,* 5. **1865**

—— [Quaestiones disputatae, De veritate] Truth, tr. from the definitive Leonine text, by Robert J. Mulligan, James V. McGlynn, and Robert W. Schmidt. Chicago, Regnery, 1952–54. 3 v. **1866**

Vol. 1 contains translation of Questions 1–9; Vol. 2, Questions 10–20; Vol. 3, Questions 21–29. This translation is referred to as the "West Baden translation" and is the first complete translation into any language, according to the editors.

—— [Quaestiones disputatae, De veritate] The teacher (Truth, question eleven). The West Baden translation, with an intro. by James Collins. Chicago, Regnery [1954]. xi, 45 p. **1867**

Another excerpt from the West Baden translation (both translations by James V. McGlynn) was edited by James Collins for Regnery in 1954: it included Questions 10 and 11 (The teacher, The mind, and Truth; xxiii, 227 p.). This seems to be the same work that Farrar and Evans labeled De magistro; *cf.* item 3652.

—— [Quaestiones disputatae, De virtutibus] On the virtues (in general), tr. with intro. and notes by John P. Reid. Providence, R.I., Providence College Press, 1951. xxix, 188 p. **1868**

Based on 1949 "Marietti" edition; text not included. The translation is of only a part of Thomas' treatise; the translator notes that this is the first English version of this work, which is to be distinguished from a selection from the Summa theologica with the same title; see item 1876 below.

—— [Summa contra Gentiles] On the truth of the Catholic faith. Summa contra Gentiles, tr., with an intro. and notes, by Anton C. Pegis. Garden City, N.Y., Image Books [1955–57]. 4 v. in 5. **1869**

Vol. 1, God, tr. by Pegis; vol. 2, Creation, tr. by James F. Anderson; vol. 3, Providence (published in two parts), tr. by Vernon J. Bourke; vol. 4, Salvation, tr. by Charles J. O'Neil.

—— [Summa theologica] Summa theologiae, Latin text and English [tr. by Dominicans of the English Province, ed. by Thomas Gilby]. [Cambridge Eng.], Blackfriars; New York, McGraw-Hill, 1964– . **1870**

This new translation has facing text and when completed will include the entire Summa, in an estimated sixty volumes. The older translation without text for the English Dominican Fathers by Lawrence Shapcote (*cf.* Farrar and Evans, item 3660) was reissued as the "first American edition" by Benziger Bros., New York, 1947–48, in three volumes; a revised version by Daniel J. Sullivan was published as Vols. 19 and 20 of Great Books of the Western World, 1952 (Chicago, Encyclopedia Britannica).

—— Nature and grace; selections from the Summa theologica of Thomas Aquinas, tr. and ed. by A. M. Fairweather. Philadelphia, Westminster Press [1954]. 386 p. *Library of Christian classics,* 11. **1871**

Contains Part 1, Questions 1–4, 20–23; Of Sin, Prima secundae, Questions 82, 85; Treatise on grace, Prima secundae, Questions 109–14; Treatise on the theological virtues, On faith, Secunda secundae, Questions 1–7; On hope, Secunda secundae, Questions 17–21; On charity, Secunda secundae, Questions 23, 27.

—— Treatise on God, sel. and tr. by James F. Anderson. Englewood Cliffs, N.J., Prentice-Hall, 1963. 180 p. **1872**

Selections largely from First Part, Part I, exemplify Thomas' natural theology; based on the Leonine text edited in 1948.

—— Treatise on happiness, tr. by John A. Oesterle. Englewood Cliffs, N.J., Prentice-Hall, 1964. xvi, 208 p. **1873**

Includes the treatise on happiness and the treatise on human acts from the Summa theologica, Questions 1 and 21 of the Prima secunda. Text from 1955 Leonine edition, not included.

—— Treatise on law, Summa theologica, questions 90–97; On truth and falsity, Summa theologica, pt. 1, questions 16–17; On human knowledge, Summa theologica, questions 84–88; intro. to Treatise on law by Stanley Parry. Chicago, Gateway Editions; distributed by Regnery [c. 1949]. x, 244 p. **1874**

The translation is that of Lawrence Shapcote. A new abridged edition (not seen) of this selection appeared in 1965 (116 p.).

—— Treatise on man, tr. by James F. Anderson. Englewood Cliffs, N.J., Prentice-Hall, 1962. xiv, 178 p. **1875**

Translation of Questions 75–88 of part 3 of the First Part.

—— Treatise on the virtues, tr. by John A. Oesterle. Englewood Cliffs, N.J., Prentice-Hall, 1966. xvii, 171 p. **1876**

A translation of Questions 49–67 of part 2, I–II, De virtutibus in communi. In spite of the identical title, this selection is not the same as the Treatise on the virtues which is a part of the Quaestiones disputatae; see item 1868 above.

—— [Super epistolas S. Pauli lectura] Aquinas Scripture series. Albany, Magi books [1966–]. **1877**

Vol. 1 contains the Commentary on St. Paul's Epistle to the Galatians, tr. by F. R. Larcher; vol. 2, Commentary on St. Paul's Epistle to the Ephesians, tr. by M. L. Lamb; both appeared in 1966. Further volumes will appear in this series, according to the introduction.

—— [Tractatus de substantiis separatis] Treatise on separate substances [tr. from] a newly-established Latin text based on twelve medieval mss. [by] Francis J. Lescoe. W. Hartford, Conn., St. Joseph's College [c. 1959]. x, 138 p. **1878**

The edition of the Latin text appeared in 1961, and an edition with facing translation and text in 1963. The treatise is about angels.

SELECTIONS

—— Basic writings of Saint Thomas Aquinas, ed. and annotated with an intro., by Anton C. Pegis. New York, Random House [1945]. 2 v. **1879**

Selections largely from the Summa theologica and Summa contra gentiles, in a revised and corrected version of Lawrence Shapcote's translation for the English Dominican Fathers; see Farrar and Evans, item 3660. This selection was reprinted as Introduction to St. Thomas Aquinas by the Modern Library, 1948.

—— The human wisdom of St. Thomas Aquinas, a breviary of philosophy from his works, arranged by Josef Pieper, tr. by Drostan MacLaren. New York, Sheed & Ward, 1948. xii, 111 p. **1880**

I have not seen this work, which seems to be a translation by Pieper from a German version rather than directly from the sources.

—— An introduction to the metaphysics of St. Thomas Aquinas. Texts sel. and tr. by James F. Anderson. Chicago, Regnery, 1953. 137 p. **1881**

A selection from several works, newly translated.

—— Philosophical texts, sel. and tr. with notes and an intro., by Thomas Gilby. London and New York, Oxford University Press, 1951. xxii, 405 p. Repr. 1956, 1960 by Galaxy Books. **1882**

A selection from various works, grouped topically and arranged in the order of the Summa theologica; many translated into English for the first time, according to the translator.

—— The pocket Aquinas; selections from the writings of St. Thomas, ed., with some passages newly tr., and a general intro., by Vernon J. Bourke. New York, Washington Square Press [1960]. 372 p. **1883**

Topically arranged selections. Includes new translation of De principiis naturae, complete.

—— The political ideas of St. Thomas Aquinas, representative selections, ed. with an intro. by Dino Bigongiari. New York, Hafner, 1953. 217 p. **1884**

Selections from the Summa theologica and De regimine principium (De regno); previously published translation with some revisions by editor.

—— St. Thomas Aquinas on analogy, a textual analysis and systematic synthesis, by George P. Klubertanz. Chicago, Loyola University Press, 1960. vii, 319 p. **1885**

Selected texts appear on pp. 157–293, and Ch. 6 is a systematic summary of them; not a translation but a fairly close paraphrase.

—— Selected political writings, ed. with an intro. by A. P. D'Entrèves, tr. by J. G. Dawson. Oxford, Basil Blackwell, 1948. xxxvi, 199 p. **1886**

Text and facing translation of selections from the Summa contra Gentiles, Summa theologica, Commentary on the Sentences of Peter Lombard, Commentary on Aristotle's Ethics and on the Politics; and treatises On princely government and On the government of Jews. Part of Thomas' commentary on Aristotle's Politics (Book III, Lectures 1–6) is translated in Lerner and Mahdi, Medieval Political Philosophy, pp. 297–334, by E. L. Fortin and Peter D. O'Neill. See above, item 1585.

—— Sermon matter from St. Thomas Aquinas on the epistles and gospels of the

THOMAS AQUINAS

Sundays and feast days (Advent to Easter), by C. J. Callan. St. Louis, Herder, 1950. vii, 311 p. **1887**

Translations of twenty-eight sermons taken from various sources, some from commentaries which cannot clearly be called sermons; no translator is named and there is some indication that the author is paraphrasing rather than translating.

—— Theological texts, sel. and tr. with notes and an intro., by Thomas Gilby. London and New York, Oxford University Press, 1955. xvii, 423 p. **1888**

Selected excerpts from various works, arranged according to the plan of the Summa theologica.

SPURIOUS AND DOUBTFUL WORKS

—— Aurora consurgens: a document attributed to Thomas Aquinas on the problem of opposites in alchemy, ed., with a commentary, by Marie-Louise von Franz. A companion work to C. G. Jung's Myserium coniunctionis. Tr. by R. F. C. Hull and A. S. B. Glover. [New York], Pantheon Books [1966]. xv, 555 p. *Bollingen series*, 77. **1889**

The entire work published in German (1957) has been translated by Hull and Glover; Latin text and translation of the Aurora consurgens, pp. 32–149. The work is reputed to be the last work of St. Thomas, perhaps dictated on his deathbed, and, according to Jung and the editor, is not a practical treatise on alchemy but a mystical work using alchemical symbols.

—— The divine ways, a little work of St. Thomas Aquinas, tr. . . . by Raissa Maritain and Margaret Sumner. [Windsor, Ont., Basilian Press, 1944.] 3, 41 p. **1890**

Thomas of Celano, *fl. 1257, supposed author.* The legend and writings of Saint Clare of Assisi; intro., translation and studies by Ignatius Brady. St. Bonaventure, N.Y., Franciscan Institute, 1953. xiv, 177 p. **1891**

The medieval texts are in the translation of Paschal Robinson, revised by Brady; the studies are translated from the German of Lothar Hardich. Documents translated are the Legend of St. Clare, written, supposedly by Thomas, soon after her canonization in 1255; two ecclesiastical documents including the bull of canonization; letters of Clare to Cardinal Hugolino (Pope Gregory IX) and St. Agnes; Clare's Rule, Testament, and Blessing.

Thomas of Metsopʻ, *vardapet, d. c. 1448.* "Thomas of Metsopʻ on the Timurid-Turkman wars," by V. Minorsky, pp. 145–70 in Professor Muhammad Shafiʼ presentation volume, ed. by S. M. Abdullah. Lahore, Majlis-e Armughan-e-ʻIlmi, 1955. **1892**

A "condensed paraphrase" translated from an Armenian work covering 1405–38.

Timoetheus of Gaza, *fl. 491–518.* . . . On animals . . ., fragments of a Byzantine paraphrase of an animal-book of the 5th cent. A.D., tr. with commentary and intro. by Friedrich S. Bodenheimer and Alexander Rabinowitz. Paris, Académie Internationale d'Historie des Sciences, 1949; Leiden, Brill. *Collection de traveaux de l'Académie internationale*, 3. **1893**

A prose paraphrase of the original poem, in a 14th-century manuscript, is translated. The work is largely "lore" rather than scientific description; about one third of it parallels closely Aristotle's Historia animalium, Books 6, 8, 9; very few parallels to the Physiologi.

Tinctoris, Jean, *d. 1511.* The Art of counterpoint (Liber de arte contrapunti), tr. and ed. with an intro. by Albert Seay. Rome, American Institute of Musicology, 1961. 141 p. **1894**

Professor Seay has translated another work by Tinctoris, the De natura et propretate tonorum: Concerning the nature and propriety of tones, Colorado Springs, Colorado College Music Press, 1967, 42 p. plus twenty-two musical examples.

—— Dictionary of musical terms by Johannes Tinctoris, tr. by Carl Parrish. [New York], Free Press of Glencoe [c. 1963.] xi, 108 p. **1895**

Text and facing translation of Terminorium musicae diffinitorium, written probably 1474–76, according to the translator.

—— "The *Proportionale musices* of Johannes Tinctoris," tr. into English with an intro. by Albert Seay, *Journal of Music Theory,* 1 (1957), 22–75. **1896**

Tortelli, Giovanni, *1400–66.* . . . On medicine and physicians; Gian. Giacomo Bartolotti, On the antiquity of medicine, two histories of medicine from the fifteenth century, ed. and tr. by Dorothy Schullian and Luigi Belloni. [Milan, Industrie Grafiche Italiane Stucchi, 1954]. xliv, 226 p. **1897**

The Latin texts are followed by translations into English and into Italian.

Towneley plays. The Wakefield mystery plays, ed. [and tr.] by Martial Rose. London, Evans Bros. [1961] 464 p. Garden City, N.Y., Doubleday, 1962. 552 p. **1898**

A modernized acting version of twenty plays.

—— The Wakefield shepherds' play, adapted and abridged by H. Coward. London, S. French [1960]. 34 p. **1899**

An acting version of the Second Shepherds' play.

Transmundus, *monk of Clairvaux, fl. 1185, supposed author.* "The letter collections attributed to master Transmundus, papal notary and monk of Clairvaux in the late twelfth century," by Sheila J. Heathcote, *Analecta Cisterciana,* 21 (1965), 35–109, 167–238. **1900**

No translation but many letters are summarized in detail.

Travel literature. *Collections.* The African past, chronicles from antiquity to modern times, ed. by Basil Davidson. Boston, Little, Brown [1964]. xix, 392 p. **1901**

Contains excerpts of documents from Arabic travelers, 9th–15th centuries, and from Vasco da Gama and Ruy de Pina, both of whom traveled to Africa in 1497.

—— Arab seafaring in the Indian Ocean in ancient and early medieval times, by George F. Fadlo. Princeton, Princeton University Press, 1951. viii, 131 p. *Princeton Oriental studies,* 13. **1902**

Has translation *passim* and in appendices from many sources, including Buzurg ibn Shariyar of Ramhurmaz, 10th century, and Ibn Jubayr, 12th century.

—— East African coast, selected documents from the first to the early nineteenth century, ed. and tr. by Grenville S. P. Freeman-Grenville. Oxford, Clarendon Press, 1962. x, 314 p. **1903**

Has translation of brief excerpts from Arabic travel documents of 10th–15th centuries, pp. 9–

33; and from Vasco da Gama, pp. 50–58. The translation is largely by the editor, partly from intermediary French translations.

—— Ethiopian itineraries, circa 1400–1524 . . ., ed. by O. G. S. Crawford [tr. by C. A. Ralegh Radford]. Cambridge [Eng.], Cambridge University Press, for the Hakluyt Society, 1958. xxxix, 230 p. *Hakluyt Society,* 2d series, 109. **1904**

The itineraries include those collected by Alessandro Zorzi from oral sources 1519–24 and a few recorded earlier; they represent actual rather than imaginary journeys, the editor thinks.

—— Great adventures and explorations from the earliest times to the present as told by the explorers themselves, ed. by Vilhjalmur Stefansson and Olive Rathburn Wilcox. New York, Dial Press, 1947. xii, 788 p. **1905**

Has translations from Icelandic sources by the editor and from other sources by various translators.

—— "A Jewish merchant in China at the beginning of the tenth century," by Elkan N. Adler in *Abhandlungen zur Erinnerungen H. P. Chajes,* Vienna, 1933, pp. 1–5. **1906**

This translation from a work of an Arabian Jew of Oman who died before 932 supplements Adler's earlier volume, Jewish travellers, 1930, and was omitted by Farrar and Evans.

—— The Mongol mission: narratives and letters of the Franciscan missionaries in Mongolia and China in the thirteenth and fourteenth centuries, ed. by Christopher H. Dawes, tr. by a nun of Stanbrook Abbey. New York, Sheed & Ward, 1955. xxxix, 246 p. **1907**

Includes translation of John of Plano Carpini, History of the Mongols, pp. 3–73; two bulls of Innocent IV addressed to the Emperor of the Tartars (Dei patris immensa, Cum non solum), pp. 73–76; the narrative of Brother Benedict the Pole, pp. 79–86; the journey of William of Rubruck [Ruysbroek], pp. 89–220; and letters of John of Monte Corvino, Brother Peregrine, and Andrew of Perugia.

—— Portuguese voyages, 1498–1663, ed. by Charles D. Ley. London, Dent; New York, Dutton [1947]. xxii, 360 p. *Everyman's library.* **1908**

Includes excerpts from Vasco da Gama and Pedro Vaz de Camintia.

—— The spring voyage: the Jerusalem pilgrimage in 1458, by Rosamund Joscelyne Mitchell. London, J. Murray, 1964. 212 p. **1909**

Contains translation of excerpts from six participants in the pilgrimage, including Roberto da Sanseverino and Gabriele Capodilista. A report of a later journey (1495) from Venice to Jerusalem by a disciple of Rabbi Obadiah of Bertinoro, appeared in Roads to Zion; four centuries of travellers' reports, tr. by Israel Meir Lask, New York, Schocken Books 1948, 117 p.

—— Visit to the holy places of Egypt, Sinai, Palestine, and Syria in 1384 by Frescobaldi, Gucci, and Sigoli, English version by Theophilus Bellorini and Eugene Hoade, with an intro. by Bellarmino Bagatti. Jerusalem, Franciscan Press, 1948. 207 p. *Publicaczioni dello Studium Biblicum Franciscanum,* 6. **1910**

Trevor, John, *bishop, fl. 1380.* Medieval heraldry, some fourteenth-century heraldic works, ed. and tr. by Evans J. Jones, foreword by Anthony R. Wagner. Cardiff, Wales, William Lewis, 1943. lxvi, 260 p. **1911**

Text and translation of Llyfr Arfan, Book of arms, which the editor thinks is not a translation from the Tractatus de armis of Johannes de Bado Aureo but an original work based on several sources; in fact, Jones suggests that Trevor was Johannes de Bado Aureo, also known as John of Guildford, and was the author of "Tretis on armes" by John [Vade]. The Latin text of the Tractatus de armis is also included.

al-Ṭūsī, Naṣir al-Dīn Muḥammad ibn Muḥammad, *1201–74*. "The death of the last 'Abbasid caliph, a contemporary Muslim account," by John Andrew Boyle, *Journal of Semitic Studies,* 6 (1961), 145–61. **1912**

Translation of al-Ṭūsī's work found in the appendix of one manuscript of Joveyni's 'Ata-Malik Juvaini, a much earlier version than any previously known of the famous story about the order to the Caliph to eat his gold plates by Prince Hülegü, an event which, according to Professor Boyle, "marked the extinction of the Islamic world empire."

—— "The longer introduction to the 'Zȳ-l-Īlkhānī' of Naṣir-ad-Dīn Ṭūsī," by John Andrew Boyle, *Journal of Semitic Studies,* 8 (1963), 244–54. **1913**

The shorter introduction translated by A. J. Arberry is given, as well as the text and translation of the longer introduction by Professor Boyle.

—— The Nasirean ethics by Nasīr ad Dīn Tūsī, tr. by G. M. Wickens. London, Allen & Unwin, 1964. 352 p. UNESCO *collections of representative works, Persian series.* **1914**

No text, but Persian phrases are cited in the notes; according to the editor, this is the first translation into any Western language of the best known Persian if not Islamic ethical digest, written *c.* 1235.

—— The rawdatu't-taslim, commonly called Tasawwurat, Persian text ed. and tr. into English by W. Ivanow. Leiden, Brill, 1950. lxxxviii, 249, 160 p. *Ismaili Society,* series A, 4. **1915**

Persian text and translation of an encyclopedic treatise on Ismailism and ethics; material also on astronomy, medicine, physics. According to the editor, Ismaili philosophy "is generally treated as the Islamic paraphrase of the speculations of Plotinus."

—— "A statement on optical reflection and 'refraction' attributed to Naṣīr ud-Dīn-aṭ-Tūsī," tr. by H. J. J. Winter and W. 'Arafat, *Isis,* 42 (1951), 138–42. **1916**

Translation from two manuscripts in the John Rylands library.

U

'Ubaid, Nizam al-Dīn, Zākānī, *1300–71, supposed author.* Rats against cats, by Nezzà àmeddin Obeyd, tr. by Mas'uud Farzààd. London, Priory Press [preface, 1945]. 23 p. **1917**

Attributed to 'Ubaid, the fable is known as Kiṣṣah i mūsh u Gurban. I have not seen this work, a copy of which is in the University of Chicago library.

Ulrich von Zatzikhoven, *fl. c. 1200.* Lanzelet, a romance of Lancelot, tr. by Kenneth G. T. Webster, revised by Roger S. Loomis. New York, Columbia University Press, 1951. viii, 238 p. *Records of civilization,* 47. **1918**

Since the translator died before the book was published, Professor Loomis revised the translation, provided additional notes, and wrote the introduction.

V

Valerianus, *Saint, bp. of Cimiez, fl. 1439–55.* Saint Peter Chrysologus, selected sermons, and Saint Valerian, homilies, tr. by George E. Ganss. New York, Fathers of the Church, 1953. viii, 454 p. *Fathers of the Church,* 17. **1919**

Valerius, *Saint, abbot of San Pedro de Montes, fl. 655.* Valerio of Bierzo, an ascetic of the late Visigothic period, by Consuelo M. Aherne. Washington, Catholic University of America Press, 1949. x, 211 p. *Catholic University studies in medieval history,* n.s., 11. **1920**

Text and translation of Valerio's autobiography, pp. 65–161.

——, *supposed author.* . . . The vita Sancti Fructuosi, text with a translation, intro., and commentary by Frances C. Nock. Washington, Catholic University of America Press, 1946. vii, 163 p. *Catholic University studies in medieval history,* n.s., 7. **1921**

The editor does not think that this life of St. Fructuosus, archbishop of Braga, *d. c.* 665, is by Valerius.

Vatnsdœla saga. The Vatnsdalers' saga, tr. by Gwyn Jones. Princeton, Princeton University Press [1944]. 158 p. **1922**

A family saga of the "men of Waterdale."

Venette, Jean de, *b. 1307.* The chronicle of Jean de Venette, tr. by Jean Birdsall, ed. with intro. and notes by Richard A. Newhall. New York, Columbia University Press, 1953. 354 p. *Records of civilization,* 50. **1923**

The chronicle covers the years 1340–68; in the 15th century it was copied as part of the Latin chronicle of Guillaume de Nanges and was regarded as his until 1735. Although the present volume contains no text, the translation is based upon a comparison of the manuscript (British Museum Arundel 28) with the printed text of 1843, and the differences are cited.

Vengeance de la mort de Nostre Seigneur. The oldest version of the twelfth-century poem, La venjánce Nostre Seigneur, ed. by Loyal A. T. Gryting. [Ann Arbor], University of Michigan Press; London, Cumberlege, 1952. x, 143 p. *University of Michigan contributions in modern philology,* 19. **1924**

This edition does not contain a translation but does have a sixteen-page summary of the poem in English.

Verba seniorum. "Further leaves from the Arabic ms. in Coptic script of the Apopthegmata Patrum," by O. H. E. Khs.-Burmester, *Bulletin de la Soiciété archaéologique copte,* 18 (1965–66), 51–64. **1925**

Text, transliteration, and translation of fragments of a 13th- or 14th-century manuscript.

—— The Hermits, a translation of the Verba seniorum, "Sayings of the Fathers," by Charles Kingsley in Cyclopedia of religious literature. New York, John B. Alden, 1883. 2 v. **1926**

The first part of this work, omitted by Farrar and Evans, is a translation of an abridged version of Rosweyde's edition of the Vitae patrum; the second part (Vol. 1, pp. 223–339) on "The Hermits of Europe" contains paraphrased or summarized lives of western European saints.

—— The wisdom of the desert: sayings from the Desert Fathers of the fourth century, tr. by Thomas Merton. London, Hollis and Carter; New York, New Directions [c. 1960], 1961. ix, 83 p. 1927

A "free and informal redaction" of selections.

—— The wisdom of the desert, by James O. Hannay. [New York?], Thomas Whittaker, 1904. 1928

This volume, not in Farrar and Evans, contains selections from the Egyptian monks organized by topic, translated from Migne and Rosweyde's edition.

Vespucci, Amerigo, *1451–1512.* The letters of Amerigo Vespucci and other documents illustrative of his career, tr. with notes and an intro. by Clements R. Markham. London, Hakluyt Society, 1894. xliv, 121 p. 1929

Contains letters about two voyages to America, one in 1497–98 which may be fictitious, and one in 1499–1500. For a discussion of the authenticity, see G. R. Crone, The discovery of America, New York, Weybright and Talley, 1969.

Villard de Honnecourt, *13th cent.* The sketchbook of Villard de Honnecourt, ed. by Theodore Bowie. Bloomington, Indiana University Press [1962, c. 1959]. 144 p.; earlier ed., 1959, 80 p. 1930

The Old French captions to the drawing are translated by the editor. In the first edition (not seen), the captions appear in a list; in the second, they appear opposite a facsimile of the original. Villard's drawings are largely architectural ones of cathedrals at Cambrai, Rheims, and Laon, but some are of sculpture and furniture.

Villon, François, *b. 1431.* . . . Ballades, selected by André Deutsch and Mervyn Savill. [London], Allan Wingate [1946]. 95 p. 1931

Various translators are represented, including the editors; text and facing translation.

—— Complete works, tr. with a biography and notes by Anthony Bonner, with an intro. by William Carlos Williams. New York, D. McKay Co. [1960]. xxvi, 228 p. 1932

Text and facing verse translation. Includes the rondeau for voice and two instruments (Mort, j'appelle) by an anonymous composer.

—— I laugh through tears, the ballades of François Villon, tr. by G. P. Cuttino. New York, Philosophical Library [1955]. xiv, 65 p. 1933

Includes "all of the ballades except those in the Jargon," in verse translation.

—— Poems, a new translation with an intro. by Galway Kinnell. [New York], New American Library [1965]. 224 p. 1934

Text and facing verse translation.

—— Poems, including "The testament," tr. in the original verse forms by Norman Cameron. London, Jonathan Cape [1953]; New York, Harcourt, Brace & World [1966]. 134 p. 1935

—— Poems of François Villon, tr. by H. B. McCaskie. London, Cresset Press [1946]. 243 p. 1936

Text and facing translation in verse of poems in The legacy, The testament, and Diverse poems.

Vincentius Ferrerius, *Saint, c. 1350–1419.* A Christology from the sermons of

VINCENTIUS FERRERIUS

St. Vincent Ferrer of the Order of Preachers, sel. and tr. by S. M. C. London, Blackfriars, 1954. viii, 211 p. **1937**

Includes translation of selected sermons on the life of Jesus.

—— A treatise on the spiritual life, with a commentary by J. Morrell, tr. by the Dominican Nuns, Corpus Christi Monastery, Menlo Park, California. Westminster, Md., Newman Press, 1957. 175 p. **1938**

The 17th-century commentary by Julienne Morrell, as well as Vincent Ferrer's treatise, is translated.

Vinsauf, Geoffrey de, *fl. 1200.* Poetria nova, tr. by Margaret F. Nims. Toronto, Pontifical Institute of Mediaeval Studies, 1967. 110 p. **1939**

Vio, Tommaso de, *called* Gaetano, cardinal, *1469–1534.* The analogy of names, and The concept of being, tr. and annotated by Edward A. Bushinski, in collaboration with Henry J. Koren. Pittsburgh, Duquesne University Press, 1953. x, 93 p. *Duquesne studies, philosophical series,* 4. **1940**

A translation of De nominum analogia, written 1498; a systematic explanation of Thomas Aquinas' theory of analogy. Most of de Vio's writings on philosophy fall before 1500, his theological and exegetical works later; the De conceptu entis translated here is dated 1509. He is usually known to English speakers as Cajetan.

—— Commentary on being and essence: In De ente et essentia d. Thomas [sic] Aquinatis [by] Cajetan, tr. from the Latin with an intro. by Lottie H. Kendzierski and Francis C. Wade. Milwaukee, Marquette University Press, 1964. 355 p. *Medieval philosophical texts in translation,* 14. **1941**

Includes a translation of Thomas Aquinas' De ente et essentia along with Cajetan's commentary, which was written between 1494 and 1499.

Völsunga saga. The saga of the Volsungs, ed. and tr. by R. G. Finch. [London], Nelson [1965]. xlii, 84, 84, [85]–97 p. *Icelandic texts.* **1942**

Text and facing translation of one of the fornaldarsögur, "sagas of ancient times." This saga is essentially a retelling of the Edda material about Sigurd and Brynhild.

W

Walahfrid Strabo, *807?–849.* Hortulus, tr. by Raef Payne, commentary by Wilfrid Blunt. Pittsburgh, Hunt Botanical Library, 1966. xi, 91 p. **1943**

Facsimile, transliteration and facing translation of a work on botany.

Walter, Daniel, *fl. 1170.* The life of Ailred of Rievaulx, tr. by F. M. Powicke. London, Nelson, 1950; New York, Oxford University Press, 1951. cii, 81, 81, [82]–88 p. *Medieval classics.* **1944**

Text and facing translation of the vita and of Daniel's Epistola ad Mauricium, his apologia for his life of Ailred [Ethelred].

Walthari of Aquitaine, *legend.* Walter of Aquitaine, materials for the study of his legend, tr. by F. P. Magoun, Jr., and H. M. Smyster. New London, Connecticut College Bookshop, 1950. 62 p. *Connecticut College monograph,* 4. **1945**

A revision with additional material of a 1941 work; *cf.* Farrar and Evans, items 868, 1279, and 1351. New material includes Old English Waldere fragments I and II, the Graz and Vienna fragments of the Middle High German romance Walter and Hildegund, and Walcerz in Polant, four Polish works, only one of which is medieval. The material in the 1941 work has been revised.

Walther von der Vogelweide, *12th cent.* Poems of Walther von der Vogelweide, thirty new English renderings by Edwin H. Zeydel and Bayard Q. Morgan. Ithaca, N.Y., Thrift Press [c. 1952]. 78 p. **1946**

This edition contains text and a translation into modern German as well as translation into English.

Welsh literature. *Collections.* An anthology of Welsh verse in translation, ed. by Gwyn Williams. London, Faber & Faber [1959]. 128 p. **1947**

Includes eleven medieval poems, by various translators.

—— "The Black Book of Carmarthen 'Stanzas of the Graves,'" by Thomas Jones, *Proceedings of the British Academy,* 53 (1967), 97–137. **1948**

Contains translation of the "Englynion y Beddau, neu Beddau Milwyr Ynys Prydain," "The Graves of the Warriors of the Island of Britain," 9th or 10-century poems found in the Black Book of Carmarthen, the Red Book of Hergest, Peniarth Ms. 98B, and Wrexham Ms. I, all the known "Stanzas of the Graves."

—— A book of Wales, ed. by D. M. and E. M. Lloyd. London, Collins [1953]. 384 p. **1949**

Includes many brief excerpts from poetry, chronicles, and other literature, all previously translated.

—— "The Brogyntyn Welsh manuscripts," by E. D. Jones, *National Library of Wales Journal,* 6 (1949–50), 149–61; 309–28. **1950**

Translation, with text and notes, of poems from a 17th-century manuscript; poems date back to 1282 and earlier.

—— The burning tree, poems from the first thousand years of Welsh verse, sel. and tr. by Gwyn Williams. London, Faber & Faber [1956]. 234 p. **1951**

Welsh poetry from 600 to 1600, text and facing translation.

—— A collection of Welsh riddles, by Vernam Hull and Archer Taylor. Berkeley, University of California Press, 1942. *University of California publications in modern philology,* 26. **1952**

Contains on pp. 225–325 translation of riddles which have come down through oral tradition.

—— "The court poets of the Welsh princes," by J. Lloyd-Jones, *Proceedings of the British Academy,* 34 (1948), 167–97. **1953**

Contains translation of poems of the Gogynfirdd, bards of the 12th and 13th centuries.

—— The development of Welsh poetry, by H. Idris Bell. Oxford, Clarendon Press, 1936. xi, 192 p. **1954**

Although this work was omitted by Farrar and Evans, it includes much translation *passim,* usually with Welsh text cited.

WELSH LITERATURE

—— A history of Welsh literature, by Thomas Parry, tr. by H. Idris Bell. Oxford, Clarendon Press, 1955. viii, 534 p. 1955

Contains translation of many works, some in "rhythmical prose," others in poetry, including Bell's revision of his earlier translation of the poems of Dafydd ap Gwilym; *cf.* Farrar and Evans, item 1172. Parry's book was published in 1944 under the title Hanes Llenyddiaeth Gymraeg hyd 1900.

—— An introduction to Welsh poetry, from the beginnings to the sixteenth century, by Gwyn Williams. London, Faber & Faber [1953]. 271 p. 1956

Contains translation *passim* with Welsh text of many poems, some "not very widely known."

—— Lectures on early Welsh poetry, by Ifor Williams. Dublin, Dublin Institute for Advanced Studies, 1944. 76 p. 1957

Includes *passim* translations by the author of some twenty poems or excerpts.

—— Medieval Welsh lyrics, tr. by Joseph P. Clancy. New York, St. Martin's Press; London, Macmillan, 1965. ix, 289 p. 1958

Most of the selections are from the 14th and 15th centuries.

—— The Penguin book of Welsh verse, tr. by Anthony Couran. [Harmondsworth, Eng.] Penguin Books [1967]. 286 p. 1959

Text and translations of poems from thirty-four medieval Welsh poets, pp. 73–188.

—— Presenting Welsh poetry, an anthology of Welsh verse in translation and of English verse by Welsh poets, ed. by Gwyn Williams. London, Faber & Faber, 1959. 128 p. 1960

Poems from 600–15th century by various translators appear on pp. 17–37. This work overlaps somewhat with the editor's The rent that's due to love.

—— The rent that's due to love, a selection of Welsh poems, tr. and compiled by Gwyn Williams. London, Editions Poetry, [1950]. 126 p. 1961

Text and facing translation of medieval poems on pp. 10–39.

—— Triodd ynys prydein, the Welsh triads, ed. and tr. by Rachel Bromwich. Cardiff, University of Wales Press, 1961. cxliv, 555 p. 1962

Text and translation usually on same page for ninety-six triads, with notes interspersed.

—— "Welsh prose versions of the Fifteen signs before Doomsday," by William W. Heist, *Speculum,* 19 (1944), 421–32. 1963

Welsh text and English translation at bottom of page from several manuscripts, all belonging to the European types of the legend. For the Irish version of the poem, see item 1711 above.

Whiterig, John, *supposed author, d. 1371.* The monk of Farne, the meditations of a fourteenth-century monk, tr. by a Benedictine of Stanbrook [ed. by Hugh Farmer]. London, Longmans; Baltimore, Helicon Press [1961]. vii, 155 p. 1964

Translation of six meditations by a solitary monk on Farne island.

William of Malmesbury, *d. 1143.* The Historia novella, tr. by K. R. Potter. London, Nelson [1955]. xliii, 77, 77, [78]–84 p. 1965

Text and facing translation of a history covering largely the reign of Stephen, king of England, up to 1142.

Wirekerus, Nigellus, *c. 1130–c. 1200.* The book of Daun Burnel the ass: Nigellus Wireker's Speculum stultorum, tr. with an intro. and notes by Graydon W. Regenos. Austin, University of Texas Press [c. 1959]. 165 p. **1966**

The author is also known as Nigel Longchamp.

—— A mirror for fools; the book of Burnel the Ass, by Nigel Longchamp, tr. by J. H. Mozley, preface by Paul E. Beichner. [Notre Dame, Ind.], University of Notre Dame Press; Oxford, Blackwell [1963]. xxvi, 143 p. **1967**

A translation based on separately published text (ed. J. H. Mozley and Robert R. Raymo, Berkeley, University of California Press, 1960); slightly abridged.

Wittenweiler, Heinrich, *15th cent.* Wittenwiler's Ring, and the anonymous Scots poem Colkelbie sow; two comic-didactic works from the fifteenth century, tr. by George Fenwick Jones. Chapel Hill, University of North Carolina Press [1956]. xii, 246 p. *University of North Carolina studies in Germanic languages and literatures,* 18. **1968**

Colkelbie sow is from the Bannatyne manuscript.

Wolfram von Eschenbach, *12th cent.* Parzival, tr. by Helen M. Mustard and Charles E. Passage. New York, Vintage Books [1961]. lvi, 443 p. **1969**

A complete prose translation.

—— Parzival, tr. into English verse with intro., notes and connecting summaries, by Edwin H. Zeydel in collaboration with Bayard Quincy Morgan. Chapel Hill, University of North Carolina Press, 1951. xi, 370 p. *University of North Carolina studies in the Germanic languages and literatures,* 5. **1970**

This is an abridged translation; about half the poem is given in summary.

—— Studies of Wolfram von Eschenbach with translations in English verse of passages from his poetry, by Margaret F. Richey. Edinburgh, Oliver & Boyd [1957]. x, 226 p. **1971**

Translation of excerpts from Parzival, Willehalm, and Titurel, pp. 175–221.

Wycliffe, John, *d. 1384.* The prosecution of John Wyclyf, by Joseph Dahmas. New Haven, Yale University Press, 1952. xi, 167 p. **1972**

Some works of Wycliffe and documents about his trial are translated *passim.*

Y

Yaḥyā ibn Ādam, *d. 818.* Yaḥyā ben Ādam's Kitāb al-Kharāj, ed., tr. and provided with an intro. and notes by A. Ben-Shemesh. Leiden, Brill, 1958. x, 172 p. **1973**

This is Vol. 1 of the editor's Taxation in Islam; for Vol. 2, see Qudāmah ibn Ja'far, al Kātib, al-Baghdādī, item 1645 above. Yaḥyā's work is a book of hadith (traditions) one of the most ancient Islamic books to come down to us, according to the editor; it represents pre-Greek influence and deals with the legal position of non-Muslims as well as Muslims about land tenure and taxation.

Yaḥyā ibn Muḥammad, *called* **Ibn al-'Auwam,** *12th* cent. "Ibn al-Awwām's Kitāb al-Filaḥah," by M. Abdur Rahman Khan, *Islamic Culture,* 24 (1950), 200–17. **1974**

This work, said by Khan to be the "most outstanding and monumental medieval contribution to scientific agriculture," is summarized in this article; existing translations into Spanish (1802) and French (1864–67) preceded the edition of 1927 and according to Professor Hitti, Khan says, are totally inadequate.

al-Ya'qūbī, Aḥmad ibn Abī Ya'qūb, *d. 897?* "The adaptation of men to their time, an historical essay by al-Ya'qūbī," tr. by W. Millward, *Journal of the American Oriental Society,* 84 (1964), 329–44. **1975**

Al-Ya'qūbī is also known as Ibn Wādih al-Ya 'qūbī. The translation is based on a text edited by the translator, previously published in Beirut.

Yāqūt ibn 'Abd Allāh al-Hamawī, *1179?–1229.* The introductory chapters of Yāqūt's Mu'jam al-Buldān, tr. by Wadie Jwaideh. Leiden, Brill, 1959. xvi, 79 p. **1976**

Translation of Yāqūt's compilation of astronomical, geographical, and philosophical information up to the 13th century, an important source for later works, according to the translator. The introductory chapters translated here draw extensively on al-Bīrūnī; they outline the entire work, explain cosmological and geographical terms, and include stories of peoples and countries.

York plays. The York cycle of mystery plays, a complete version, by J. S. Purvis. London, S.P.C.K.; New York, Macmillan, 1957. 384 p. **1977**

A shorter version of the cycle was published by S.P.C.K. in 1951 (200 p.) and a selection, The flood: the Fishers' and Mariners' play, in 1954 (15 p.) by the York Festival Society.

—— The York nativity play, adapted by E. Martin Browne. London, S.P.C.K., 1952. vii, 28 p. **1978**

Z

Žižka, Jan, *c. 1360–1424.* The very pretty chronicle of John Žižka, the servant of King Wenceslas, tr. by Frederick G. Heymann in John Ziska and the Hussite Revolution. Princeton, Princeton University Press, 1955. x, 521 p. **1979**

The chronicle, covering the years 1434–36, is translated on pp. 3–10, with some omissions.

Zohar. Zohar, the book of splendour, basic readings from the Kabbalah, ed. and tr. by Gershom G. Scholem [aided by Sherry Abel]. London, Bailey Bros., 1963. 125 p. **1980**

New translation of selections.

Index

The numbers given are those of individual entries, not pages. Boldface numbers immediately following a heading in the Index indicate a main entry in the Bibliography. Cross references are made to other index headings as well as to main entries.

INDEX

INDEX

Andrew of Perugia, bp. of Zaiton, 1907
Andrews, Avery D., 1611
Andrews, Elizabeth Buermann, 1614
Andrusyshen, C. H., 1693
Angela, Saint, of Foligno, 1442
Anglo-Latin literature, 630
Anglo-Norman literature, 714, 715
Anglo-Saxon chronicle, **76–78**, 608; *see also* Hugh Candidus
Anglure, Ogier VIII, seigneur d', **79**
Animals, of Egypt, 5; Aristotle on, 138; satire using, 586, 632; Arabic poem on, 1642; Welsh treatise on, 1748; Timotheus of Gaza on, 1893; *see also* Bestiary; Physiologus; Reynard the Fox.
Ankori, Zvi, 1150
Annales Gandenses, **80**
Annals of Innisfallen, **81**
Anonymous IV, **82**
Anonymous VII, **83**
al-Anṣāri, 'Umar ibn Ibrahim al-Awsī, *see* al-Awsī
Anṣāri (Arabic) poems, 843
Ansari, A. S. B., 1190
Anselm, Saint, **84–88**, selections from, 440, 445, 1576, 1579, 1590; Proslogion, 449; life of, by Eadmer, 583, 585
Anthemius, **89**
Anthologia graeca, **90**, 1285
Anthropology, 1738
Antoine de la Sale, 1647
Antonio, abp. of Florence, 896
Antichrist, *see* Ludus de Antichristo
Antioch, comments on by Libanius, 132–33
Antiochenes, epistles to, 158
Antonio Averlino, *see* Filarete
Antonio Mario, 1270
Antonius, Saint, life of, by Athanasius, 156, 1704; in the Philokalia, 417
al-Anvār, Qāsim, **91**
Apel, Willi, 1422
Apfel, Joseph, 1807
Aphorisms, of Hippocrates, 1400; of Muḥammad the Prophet, *see* Muḥammad; *see also* Gnomic sayings; Verba seniorum
Apicius, **92**
Apocalypse, version of by St. Beatus, 265; of Falashas, 675
Apocrypha of the New Testament, **93–102**; selections, 437; Coptic Acts of the Apostles, 493; Russian excerpt from, 1691; *see also* Apostolic Fathers; Christian literature, collections; Dead Sea Scrolls; and individual apocrypha: Andrew, Bartholomew, Daniel, Nicodemus, Peter, Philip, Thomas
Apocrypha of the Old Testament, Aramaic Genesis, 561
Apollinarian controversy, 404
Apollonius of Tyre, **103**
Apopthegmata patrum, *see* Verba seniorum
Apostolias, Michael, **104**
Apostolic Fathers, **105–108**; selections, 412, 414, 415, 416, 423, 434, 437, 446; *see also* Christian literature, collections
Appleby, John T., 1657
Apuleius Platonicus (or Barbarus), 1730
Arabia, 130
Arabian Nights, **109–114**; Spanish version of, 1756
Arabic literature, collections, **115–28**, 731, 1241, 1249, 1257, 1259, 1271, 1280, 1281; theory of by al-Bāqillānī, 252; about the British Isles, 600; pre-Islamic, 1409; bibliography of, 1643; *see also* Islamic literature; Mu'allaqāt; Persian literature
Arabs, historical sources, **129–30**; *see also* Islamic literature
'Arafat, W., 843, 1916
Arama, Isaac, 1110
Aramaic texts, **131–34**
Arand, Louis A., 203
Arasteh, A. Reza, 1091
Arberry, Arthur J., 28, 112, 117, 125, 139, 238, 678, 687, 830, 833, 930, 931, 936, 960, 1048, 1069, 1072, 1087, 1090, 1094, 1095, 1096, 1195, 1198, 1403, 1415, 1416, 1430, 1489, 1490, 1491, 1493, 1538, 1540, 1542, 1544, 1548, 1643, 1700, 1913,
Arbesmann, Rudolph, 176, 738, 1813, 1814
Archelaos, alchemist, **135**
Archer, Gleason L., Jr., 860
Archer, W. G., 1699
Archery, Arabic book on, 1191
Archilletes and Synkltikē, Coptic poem, 497; legend, 498
Archimedes, 1721, 1736
Archipoeta, 1283
Architecture, Gothic theory of, 146; treatise on by Filarete, 695; Icelandic work on, 985; description of church at Constantinople, 1474; Persian inscriptions and, 1541; Abbot Suger on, 1793; Villard de Honnecourt on, 1930; *see also* Art
Arculf, 38
Arent, A. Margaret, 1214
Arethas, abp. of Caesarea, **136–37**
Arianism, in St. Hilarius of Poitiers, 865
Arienti, Sabadino Degli, Giovanni, 1273
Aristotle, **138–39**; commentary on by Abraham bar Hiyya, 16; on De anima, by Avempace, 226; by Averroës, 231–33; by

INDEX

INDEX

Benedictines, 1660
Benedictines of Stanbrook Abbey, 58, 69, 445
Benedictus, Saint, abbot of Monte Cassino, **270–74**; rule of, 448, 605, 1253; life of by Gregory the Great, 795–96
Benedictus Crispus of Milan, **275**
Benedictus le puncteur, 287
Benjamin, abp. of Pittsburgh, 1307
Benjamin, Anna S., 193
Benko, S., 645
Bennett, William H., 1767
Ben-Shemesh, Aharon, 1645, 1973
Bent, John F., 1779
Bentley, Eric, 1663
Bentley, Gerald E., 662
Belt, Elmer, 1221
Bennett, Josephine W., 1352
Benzi, Ugo, **276**
Beowulf, **277–86**, 617, 620–21, 623, 635, 638, 1250, 1265, 1267
Berechiah ben Natronai, ha-Nakdan, **287**
Bergh, Simon van den, 235, 779
Bergin, Thomas G., 540, 826, 1076, 1082, 1564, 1566–67
Berko, Matthew A., 1315
Bernadet, 702
Bernard, Brother, **288**
Bernard Gui, *see* Gui, Bernard
Bernard of Clairvaux, Saint, **289–98**, 428, 445, 1576
Bernardino da Siena, Saint, **299–300**
Bernart de Ventadorn, **301**, 722, 1279
Berners, John Bourchier, Lord, 733
Bernhart, Joseph, 1828
Bernt, Alois, 1120
Béroul, 732
Berry, Virginia Gingerick, 1486
Berta of Hungary (poem), 1267
Berthold, Fred, 1135
Bertinoro, Obediah, 1382
Bertrand de Bar-sur-Aube, 732
Bertrand de Born, 1279
Bertrand de Mignanelli, **302–303**
Besa, abbot of Athribis, **304**
Besharov, Justina, 395
Best, R. I., 1029
Bestiary, **305**; *see also* Animals; Physiologus; Zoology
Bettenson, Henry, 412, 414
Bévenot, Maurice, 514
Bewnans Meryasek, *see* Cornish plays
Beyenka, Mary Melchior, 67
Beyer, Harald, 975
Biancolli, Louis, 545
Bible, commentary on, by St. Basilius, 258; by Cassiodorus Senator, 358; Jewish, 1139; by Karaite Jews, 1149; by Nicolas de Lyre, 1467; by Rashi, 1467; by Thomas Aquinas, 1887; *see also* individual books: Genesis, John, etc.; Apocrypha; Creeds; Judaism; New Testament; Talmud
Bickersteth, E., 462
Bickersteth, Geoffrey L., 544
Bidpai, Hebrew version of tales of, 1379
Biel, Gabriel, 1577
Bieler, Ludwig, 573, 658, 1015, 1524, 1535
Biggs, Anselm G., 749
Bigongiari, Dino, 218, 1884
Billy, Method C., 325
Binchy, D. A., 1535
Binyon, Laurence, 528, 1258
Biography, of Abān ibn 'Abd al-Hamīd al-Lāḥiqī, 4; of Avicenna, 241; of Buddha, 254–55; of Ugo Benzi, 276; of Barqūq, sultan of Egypt, 302; of Tamerlane, 303; of Boccaccio, 313–15; of Cristoforo Colombo, documents for, 483; of Di'bil b. 'Alī, 571; of Edward II, king of England, 594; of Emma, queen of England, 597; English, selected, 631; of Henry IV, Holy Roman emperor, 761; of Ḥasan Dihlavi, 842; of Secundus the philosopher, 871; of an Icelandic physician, 898; of Baybars I, of Egypt, 913; of Assassins, 916; of Rāṣid al-Dīn, 916; of 'Abd al-Raḥman, Caliph of Cordova, 918; of Ibn al-Nāfis, 955; of Jalāl al-Dīn Rūmī, 1088; of Johannes Mercurius Corrigiensis, 1122; of Josephus, 1132; of al-Junayd, 1164; of Muḥammad, the prophet, 1408; of Friedrich Barbarossa, 1513; of Proclus, 1625; *see also* Kormáks saga, 1201; Autobiography; Jesus, biography
Biology, of Abraham, ben David, ha-Levi, 17; of Aristotle, 138; *see also* Animals; Botany; Zoology
Birdsall, Jean, 1923
Birnbaum, Philip, 10, 1323, 1394
al-Bīrūnī, **306–10**, 1054; *see also* Yāqūt ibn 'Abd al-Hamawī
Bishop, Eric F. F., 261
Bishop, Morris, 1557, 1561
Bittar, E. Edward, 955
Black, Matthew, 1306
Blackburn, Paul, 466
Blackman, Philip, 1381
Blackwell, Richard J., 1859
Blaisdell, Foster W., 647
Blaithmaic, Saint, **311**, 1012
Blake, Norman F., 1129
Blake, Robert P., 810
Blakeney, E. H., 1208

Blakney, Raymond B., 590
Blanchard, Harold H., 1079
Blasius Pelacani of Parma, 1736
Blindheim, Joan Tindale, 71
Blum, Fred, 1420
Blum, Owen J., 1606
Blumberg, Harry, 231
Blunt, Wilfrid, 1943
Boak, Arthur E. R., 1629
Boas, George, 321, 1724
Bobik, Joseph, 1838
Boccaccio, Giovanni, **312–16**, 1077, 1079–82, 1245, 1273
Bodel, Jean, 721
Bodenheimer, Friedrich S., 17, 764, 957, 1893
Bodenstedt, Mary I., 1330
Boehner, Philotheus, 322, 1484
Boethius, **317**, 1274; commentary on by Thomas Aquinas, 1835, 1862
Bohemia, 469
Bohemian Plowman, the, *see* Johannes de Tepla
Boiardo, Matteo Maria, 1270
Bolland, Joseph, 1098
Bologna, university of, 892; Spanish college at, 1084
Bolton, Harry F., 996
Bolton, W. F., 630
Bombaci, Alessio, 1540
Bonaventura, Saint, Cardinal, **318–27**, 428, 449, 1590
Bone, Gavin, 277, 616
Bonet, Honoré, **328**
Bonfils, Immanuel ben Jacob, **329**, 1746
Bonifacio Calvo, *see* Calvo, Bonifacio
Bonifacius, Saint, abp. of Mainz, 1701–1702
Bonner, Anthony, 1932
Book of Hy Maine, Book of Leinster, *see* Cuchulain cycle
Book of O'Hara, **330**
Book of rights, Book of Magauran, etc., *see* Leabhar gabhála, Leabhar méig, etc.
Books, Arabic making of, 1417
Borah, M. I., 842
Borgia, Rodrigo, *see* Alexander VI, Pope
Borgognoni, Teodorico, bp., **331**
Borradaile, Viola and Rosamund, 1792
Borroff, Marie, 747
Bosanquet, Geoffrey, 583
Botany, of Egypt, 5; of Ibn Miskawaih, 950; of Walahfrid Strabo, 1943; *see also* Pharmacology
Bougerol, Jacques G., 323
Bourke, Vernon J., 171, 184, 221, 1842, 1859, 1869, 1883
Boustronious, George, **332**
Bouyer, Louis, 406
Bowen, John C. E., 1495, 1547
Bowie, Theodore, 1930
Boyajian, Zabelle C., 141
Boyde, P., 529
Boyle, John A., 1133, 1912–13
Bozon, Nicole, **333–35**
Braakhuis, H. A. G., 1595
Bradwardine, Thomas, abp. of Canterbury, **336–37**, 1577, 1742
Brady, Ignatius, 468, 1891
Brands þattr örva, 980
Brandt, Walther I., 579
Brant, Sebastian, **338–39**
Brantingham, Thomas, 502
Brantl, George, 401
Braude, Morris, 1136, 1403
Braude, William G., 1376
Braulio, bp. of Saragossa, 1038
Brecher, Chaim M., 1393
Brenan, Gerald, 1785
Brendan, Saint, voyage of, 1706
Brengle, Richard L., 149
Brennan, Rose, E., 1835
Brentano, Robert, 875
Breton literature, *see* Celtic literature
Brevicoxa, John, 1577
Brian family, 1216
Bricriu's feast, 1027
Briffault, Robert, 731, 1281
Bright, James W., 636
Brinner, William M., 963
Brinton, Howard H., 475
Bristol, Little red book of, 607
Brittain, Fred, 1274
Broadhurst, R. J. C., 942
Brock, Sebastian, 1482
Brome Abraham and Isaac, 622, 1433–36, 1438, 1440–41
Bromwich, Rachael, 1962
Brooke, C. N. L., 1124
Brooklyn Confraternity of the Precious Blood, 987
Brother Bernard, *see* Bernard
Broughton, Bradford B., 639
Brown, Calvin S., 1261
Brown, Louise Fargo, 888
Brown, R. Gene, 1515
Brown, Raphael, 706–707
Brown, Ruth Allison, 180
Brown, Sydney M., 1660
Browne, C. A., 135
Browne, E. Martin, 1441, 1978
Browne, Lewis, 1157
Bruce, the, 253
Brucker, Gene, 1609

Brunanburgh (Old English poem), *see* English literature, collections
Brundage, James A., 503, 852
Brunetto Latini, 894
Bruno, Saint, 442
Brut y tywvsogion, **340–41**
Buchanan, E. S., 265
Buchanan, James J., 317
Buck, Philo M., Jr., 1239
Buddha, life of (legend), *see* Barlaam and Joasaph
Bühler, Curt F., 368
Buehne, Sheema Z., 840
Bukhara, history of, 1447
al-Bukhārī, Muḥammad ibn Ismā'īl, 342, 1055
Bunim, Irving M., 12
Burch, monastery of (Peterborough), *see* Hugh Candidus
Burch, George B., 1576
Burchard, Johann, bp. of Orta and Cività Castellana, **343**
Burgundy, history, *see* Lex Burgundionum, 1231
Burhān ad-Dīn ibn al-Firkāh al-Fazāri, *see* Ibn al-Firkāh
Burhān al-Dīn, **344**
Buridan, Jean, **345**, 1742
Burke, Nora, 797
Burke, Richard J., 1237
Burleigh, John H. S., 165, 202
Burley, Walter, 1590
Burmester, O. H. E. Khs.-, 102, 1294, 1296–97, 1301–1302, 1718, 1925
Burnaby, John, 167
Burton, Richard F., 111
Bury, John B., 1624
Bury St. Edmunds Abbey, chronicle of, 1812
Bushinski, Edward A., 1940
Bussard, Hubertus L. L., 1505
Butler, H. E., 1124
Butler, Mary M., 1263, 1440
Buzurg ibn Shahriyār, 129, 1902
Byrne, Francis J., 1012
Byrnes, Aquinas, 909
Byzantine empire, historical sources, **346–51**, 7, 104, 136–37, 490, 1361, 1466, 1473, 1575, 1596, 1628–30, 1637; Jews in, 1107; Karaite Jews in, 1150; legendary fate of, 1219; *see also* Digenes Acritas; Lesbos, chronicle of; Russia, historical sources

C

Cabaniss, Allen, 419, 1328, 1519
Cabasilas, Nicolas, abp. of Thessalonica, **352–53**
Cachia, Pierre, 665
Caedmon, hymn of, and Caedmonian poems, *see* English literature, collections
Caenegem, R. C. van, 611
Caesarius, Saint, bp. of Arles, **354–55**, 442, 807
Cain and Abel, by St. Ambrosius, 66
Cáin Domnaig, **356**
Cairns, Huntington, 1256
Cajetan, *see* Vio, Tommaso de
Calder, William M., 1234
Calendar, 309, 567, 1731
Callahan, Virginia Woods, 800
Callan, C. J., 1887
Callus, Daniel A. P., 813
Calvo, Bonifacio, **357**
Cambrai, cathedral of, 1930
Cambridge songs, 1283
Cambyses (Coptic romance), 497
Cameron, Averil, 1628
Cameron, James K., 398
Cameron, Norman, 1935
Campbell, Alistair, 597, 656
Campbell, Eldridge, 331
Campbell, Jackson J., 667
Campbell, Roy, 546
Campbell, Thomas S., 576
Cantarini, Ambrogio, 1683
Cantor, Norman F., 887
Caplan, Samuel, 1142
Caponigri, Robert, 1604
Caradoq of Llancarvan, 341
Carbone, Ludovico, 1083
Carleton, A. P., 211
Carmarthen, Black book of, 1948
Carmichael, Douglas, 1605
Carmina Burana, 1253, 1274–75, 1282–83
Carmody, Francis J., 1601
Carney, James, 311, 511, 1010, 1012, 1021, 1031
Caro, Isaac, 1110
Caroline war, the, 269
Carolingian empire, 893; *see also* Charlemagne
Carols, Latin and Middle English, 1424
Carpenter, Robert, 1613
Carpianus, epistle to, 661
Carroll, Paul, 863
Carson, George B., Jr., 888
Carson, Molloy, 1005
Carthaigh's book, 1001
Casey, Robert P., 158, 420
Cassianus, Joannes, excerpts from the conferences of, 448
Cassiodorus Senator, Flavius Magnus Aurelius, **358**; on music, 1428
Cassirer, Ernst, 1559, 1594

Cistercians, 1718; anonymous works by, 298; works of, 406; rule of, 650
Cities, 118, 123, 884, 917; *see also names of individual cities, e.g.*, Baghdad; Constantinople; Damascus, *etc.*
Clagett, Marshall, 1721, 1736, 1742
Clairvaux, monk of, *see* Transmundus, 1900
Clancy, Joseph, P., 1958
Clara of Assissi, Saint, **468**, 1891
Claretus de Solencia, **469**
Clark, Ernest G., 1035
Clark, James M., 589, 1796–97
Clark, Kenneth, 1225
Clarkson, John F., 405
Claudius, Saint, martyr, **470**
Claudius of Turin, 419
Cleanness (Middle English poem), 1531
Clemens, Romanus, Saint, **471**, 105, 107–108, 414–15
Clemens, Titus Flavius, Alexandrinus, **472–74**, 399, 1578
Clement V, pope, 876
Clement VI, pope, letter to, 1560
Clement of Alexandria, *see* Clemens, Titus Flavius, Alexandrinus
Clement of Rome, *see* Clemens, Romanus
Clendening, Logan, 1744
Clopinel, *see* Jean de Meun
Cloud of unknowing, **475–78**, 1442; author of, 578
Cnut, king of England, 597
Cockaigne, land of (Middle English poem), 635
Cockayne, Thomas O., 1730
Codex Theodosianus, **479**
Codrington, Humphrey W., 1292
Coghill, Nevill, 379, 1213
Cohen, Boaz, 1390
Cohen, Gerson D., 17, 19
Cohen, John M., 1667, 1788
Cole, William, 1251
Coleman-Norton, P. R., 438
Colet, John, **480**
Colgrave, Bertram, 689
Colkelbie sow (Scots poem), 1968
Colledge, Eric, 429, 868, 1097, 1099, 1460–61, 1810
Colleran, Joseph M., 163
Collins, James, 1867
Collins, Rowland L., 284
Colombo, Christoforo, **481–83**; *see also* Scillacio, Nicocolò
Colonna, Egidio, abp., **484–85**, 1583
Colson, F. H., 1573
Colton, James, 331
Colum, Padraic, 1007
Columba, Saint, of Iona, **486**; life of by St. Adamnan, 37
Columban, Saint, **487–89**, 894
Combat at the ford (Irish), 1013
Comets, treatises on by Albertus Magnus and Thomas Aquinas, 54
Commerce, *see* Economics
Comnenus, Andronicus, 1177
Compostella, council of, 749
Conant, Virginia, 694
Conder, Alan, 729
Conlon, Walter M., 906
Connolly, R. H., 63
Conrad II, Holy Roman emperor, 761
Constance, council of, 408, 1106, 1556
Constantine, bp. of Assiut, 470
Constantinople, 48, 452, 1126, 1202, 1219, 1474, 1912
Constantinus I, emperor, life of, by Eusebius, 662; Donation of, 873
Constantinus VII Porphyrogenitus, emperor of the East, **490**
Constantius II, Flavius Julius, **491**, 7; letter to from St. Cyrillus, 521
Constantius of Lyons, 1710
Conti, Nicolò de, 1617
Conway, M. George Edward, 512, 518
Conway, Pierre H., 1844, 1846, 1849–50, 1853, 1855, 1857–58, 1860
Cook, Genevieve M., 642
Cooke, Franklin O., 703
Cookery, 92, 1614
Coomaraswamy, Ananda K., 1861
Cooper, Eve Marie, 706
Coopland, G. W., 328, 1503
Coover, James, 1419
Coptic church, canon law of, 523; liturgy and ritual of, 1294–1302, *see also* Mennas, St.
Coptic texts, **492–99**, 94–99, 102, 461, 788, 1761, 1827, 1925
Corbett, James A., 411, 433, 1622
Corbie, monastery of, 1519
Corbin, Henry, 237
Cordeliers, chronicle of, 1102
Cordova, caliph of, 918
Cornish literature, 370
Cornish plays, **499–500**, 640, 1441; Death of Pilate, 1263, 1433, 1440
Corpus juris civilis, **501**; *see also* Codex Theodosianus
Corrigan, Felicitas, 207
Corrigan, Francis X., 634
Cota, Rodrigo, 1782
Councils, church, 404, 409; Council of Constance, *see* Constance, council of, etc.
Couran, Anthony, 1959

D

INDEX

E

F

G

Greenwood, Omerod, 744
Greer, Rowan A., 1826
Grégoire, Henri, 1361, 1769
Gregorius I, Saint, the Great, pope, **795–99**, 419, 445, 1527; life of, 1707
Gregorius VII, Saint, pope, 445
Gregorius, Saint, bp. of Nyssa, **800–804**, 404
Gregorius, Saint, bp. of Tours, **805**, 705
Gregorius IX, pope, 1660, 1891
Gregorius (Oedipus legend, German), 839–40
Gregorius de Arimino, **806**
Gregorius Nazianzenus, Saint, **807–808**, 404; scholia on, 1482; commentary on by Maximus Confessor, 1366
Gregorius Palamas, Saint, abp. of Thessalonica, **809**, 417
Gregory of Khandzta, Saint, 1705
Gregory of Langres, Saint, life of, 805
Gregory of Narck, Saint, 141
Gregory of Rimini, *see* Gregorius de Arimino
Grigor of Akanc', **810**
Grigoris of Aghtamar, 141
Grocheo, Johannes de, **811**
Grœnlander saga, 70–71
Grosseteste, Robert, bp. of Lincoln, **812–14**
Grossman, Philip, 1391
Grunebaum, G. E. von, 118, 252, 344
Gryting, Loyal A. T., 1924
Guarini, Battista, 1075
Guarino, Guido A., 313
Gucci, Giorgio, 1910
Gudmund the Good, *see* Guðmundar saga
Gudrun, **815**
Gudzii, Nikolai K., 1688
Guerney, Bernard G., 1691
Guest, Rhuvon, 958
Gui, Bernard, 886, 1276, 1833
Gui de Chauliac, 1276, 1722, 1744
Guibert of Nogent, 419
Guido Aretinus, on music, 1428
Guigo II, general of the Carthusians, *see* Guiges du Chastel
Guigo de Castro Novo, *see* Guiges du Chastel
Guigues du Chastel, **816–17**
Guilelmus, abp. of Tyre, **818**
Guillaume IX, duke of Aquitaine, **826**
Guillaume, Alfred, 937, 1408
Guillaume (chanson de geste), **819**
Guillaume de Guilleville, **820**
Guillaume de Lorris, **821**
Guillaume de Machault, 717, 719, 723–24, 728
Guillaume de Nanges, 1923
Guillaume de Poitiers, 1251
Guillaume de Saint Thierry, **822–25**; life of St. Bernard, 297
Guillaumont, A., 97
Gumbinger, Cuthbert, 299
Gundersheimer, Werner L., 1074
Gundissalinus, Dominicus, 933
Gundobad, king, laws of, 1231
Gunnlaugs saga Ormstungu, **827**, 973, 983
Guterman, Norbert, 1242
Guthlac, Saint, life of by Felix, 689–90, 1702, 1707
Guttman, Julius, 1395
Guðmundar saga Arasonar, **828**
Gwynn, Aubrey, 1525
Gynecology, of Aetius of Amida, 46

H

Ḥabash al-Ḥāsib, **829**
Hackstaff, L. H., 193
Hadas, Moses, 287, 878
Hadewijch of Antwerp, 1459–60
Haensna-þoris saga, 973
Haf Paikar, 1478
Ḥāfiẓ, **830–33**, 1540, 1548
Ḥāfiẓ Ābrū, **834**
Ḥafs ben Albar al-Qūṭī, **835**
Haft bab (Persian), 1051, 1066
Hague, René, 1127
Haight, Anne L., 899
Hailperin, Herman, 1467
al-Ḥākim al-Nīsabūrī, Muḥammad ibn 'Abd Allāh, **836**
Hales, E. E. Y., 614
Halkin, Abraham S., 919, 1390
Hall, G. D. G., 787
Hall, Louis B., 314
Halliday, Frank E., 500
Hallmundson, Hallberg, 985
Halton, Thomas, 457
Ham, Edward B., 719
Hamarneh, Sami Khalaf, 33
Hamburg, archbishops of, 39
Hamidullah, Muhammad, 950
Hamm, Victor M., 1603
Hamman, Adalbert, 416
Hammond, Lincoln D., 1617
Hand, Thomas A., 210
Handford, S. A., 42
Hannay, James O., 1928
Hannesson, Jóhann S., 592
Hanson, Richard P. C., 1161
Haq, S. Moinul, 959
al-Ḥaqīqī, *see* Jihān Shāh
Harald III Hardradi, king of Norway, 1775
Hardich, Lothar, 1891
Hardie, Colin, 532
Hardy, Edward R., 422

I

Ingstad, Helge, **71**
Innisfallen, Annals of, *see* Annals of Innisfallen
Innocentius II, pope, letter to by St. Bernard, 289
Innocentius III, pope, **998–99**
Innocentius IV, pope, 1907
Innocentius VIII, pope, 1329
Intellect, al-Kindī on, 1188, 1190; *see also* Memory
Iqbal, Afzal, 1088
Iran Society, Calcutta, 309
Ireland, historical sources, **1000–1002**, 81, 784, 1215–17, 1525; wonders of, 1525
Irenaeus, Saint, bp. of Lyons, **1003**, 415, 418, 425
Irish literature, collections, **1004–31**, 101, 799, 1248; *see also* Celtic literature; Cuchulain cycle; Finn macCumaill; Mythological cycle, Irish.
Irvine, Helen Douglas, 360
ʻĪsā ibn Yahyā, 869
Isaac, Brome play of Abraham and, *see* Brome
Isaac Abravanel, 847
Isaac [ben Solomon] Israeli, **1033**
Isaac Judaeus, **1034**
Isaac of Antioch, Saint, 1032
Isaac of Syria, Saint, 417
Isaac of Stella, 1576
Isaacs, H. D., 776
Isbell, Harold, 224
Isḥāk ibn Ḥunain, 1824
Ishmael, 943
Ishōʻbar Nūn, **1035**
Ishō ʻDadh of Merv, 1035
Isidore, son of Basilides, 425
Isidorus, Saint, bp. of Seville, **1036–38**
Isidorus, cardinal of Thessalonica, **1039**
Islam, historical sources, **1040–45**, 657, 967, 1912; *see also* Genizah documents
Islamic literature, collections, **1046–72**, 1445, 1580; *see also* Arabic literature; Koran; Persian literature
Islendings sögufroða, 980
Ismāʻilīyas, 1367, 1449, 1483, 1915; *see also* Islamic literature; Mysticism
Issawi, Charles, 946
Italian literature, collections, **1073–83**, 147, 148, 1270, 1271, 1273, 1593
Italy, historical sources, **1084**, 261, 532, 879, 893, 1043, 1045, 1612; *see also* Rome; Travel literature
Ivanov, Vladimir [vanow, W.], 1051, 1059, 1070, 1367, 1429, 1449, 1915
Ivo of Chartres, 419

J

Jackson, Kenneth, 370
Jacme d'Agramont, **1085**
Jacob, Alfred B., 933
Jacobite church, *see* Liturgy and ritual, West Syrian or Jacobite church, 1320
Jacobs, Joseph, 43
Jacopo Ragona, **1086**
Jacques de Liege, 1428
Jaegher, Paul de, 1442
Jakobson, Ramon, 1769
Jalāl al-Dīn Rūmī, Mawlānā, **1087–95**, 1540
James, Bruno S., 291–92
James, John W., 1656
Jāmī, **1096**, 1540
Jamshīd Ghiyāth al-Dīn al-Kāshī, *see* al-Kāshī
Jamshīdīpūr, Yusūf, 833
Jan van Ruysbroek, **1097–99**, 428, 1442, 1460
Jan Zatecky, *see* Johannes de Tepla
Jane, Cecil, 481–82
Jane, M., 1810
Jansson, Sven, 1680
Janus Cornarius, 46
Jarcho, Saul, 1034
Jarlmanns saga ok Hermanns, 978
al-Jarsīfī, ʻUmar ibn ʻUthman, **1100**
Jay, Eric G., 1510
Jayne, Sears R., 480, 693
Jean de Condé, 721
Jean de la Taille, 1247
Jean de Meun, **1101**
Jean de Venette, *see* Venette, Jean
Jean le Bel, 705
Jeanne d'Arc, Saint, **1102–1104**
Jeffery, Arthur, 921, 1056, 1067, 1199
Jehuda Halevi, *see* Judah, ha-Levi
Jehuda ibn Tibbon, 250
Jenkins, Romilly J. H., 136, 490, 1473
Jennings, Alvin R., 1515
Jensen, Gillian F., 978
Jepson, John J., 198
Jerome, Saint, *see* Hieronymus, Saint
Jerome, M. Francis, 653
Jerome of Moravia, **1105**
Jerome of Prague, **1106**
Jerusalem, journies to, 38, 79, 671–72, 942, 1465, 1799, 1909, 1910; as Moslem shrine, 932; fall of, 1772; *see also* Crusades
Jesus, biography, 101, 326, 462, 654, 1330, 1757; sayings of in Coptic gospel, 97–99; *see also* Apocrypha; Christian literature, collections
Jews, historical sources, **1107–11**, 150, 1132; story of the four captives, 18; inscriptions,

K

Kābbala, by Abraham ben Simeon, 22; selections, 1143; of Moses ben Nahman, 1402
Kaddal, Mohamed, 261
Kadloubovsky, E., 417
Kahane, Henry, 855
Kahane, Renée, 855
Kahle, Paul E., 492
Kai Kā'us ibn Iskander, *see* Kaykāvūs ibn Iskander ibn Qābūs
Kákosy, L., 496
Kalevala, **1167–68**
Kamal al-Dīn, *see* Ibn al-'Adīm
Kamali, Sabih Ahmad, 779
Kaminsky, Howard, 392, 1475
Kaplan, Mordecai M., 15
Karaites, polemic against, by Abraham ben David, ha-Levi, 19; Islamic documents about, 1041; dietary laws of, 1138; literature of, 1149; in Byzantium, 1150; criticism of Christianity by, 1644; *see also* Aaron ben Elijah
Karlin-Hayter, P., 137, 664
Karrer, Otto, 588, 709
Kasher, Menachem Mendel, 1139
al-Kāshī, Jamshīd ibn Mas'ūd, **1170–75**
Katz, Joseph, 1590
Kaufman, Walter A., 1586
Kavanagh, Denis J., 161, 176, 199
Kay, George R., 1078
Kaykāvūs ibn Iskandar ibn Qābūs, 'Unṣur al-Ma'ālī, **1176**
Kays, J. M., 1613
Kazan, S., 1032
Kazis, Israel J., 329
Keele, Kenneth D., 1223
Keenan, Angela E., 518
Keenan, Mary E., 801
Kelley, Carl F., 1811
Kelly, John N. D., 413, 1672
Kelsey, Alice G., 1453
Kempe, Margery, 429
Kendig, 488
Kendzierski, Lottie H., 1864, 1941
Kennedy, Charles W., 617, 624–25
Kennedy, E. S., 306, 308, 1170, 1172–75
Kenner, Hugh, 1279
Kensington stone, the, 1677–78
Kepler, Thomas S., 424, 991, 1372
Ketevan, Queen, 1705
Khadduri, Majid, 1759, 1762
al-Khaledy, Noury, 1714
Khan, M. A. Halder, 1053
Khan, M. Abdur Rahman, 1974
Khan, Yusuf, 1489
Khāqānī, Afẓal al-Dīn Shirrānī, **1177**
Khatchadourian, Haig, 1185–87
al-Khaṭīb al-Tibrīzī, Muḥammad ibn 'Abd, **1178**
al-Khayyāt, Abū al-Ḥusayn ibn Uthmān, **1179**
Kholeif, Fathalla, 1414
Khoneli, Mose, 72
Khs.-Burmester, *see* Burmester, O. H. S.
al-Khwārizmī, Muḥammad ibn Aḥmad, **1180–81**
al-Khwārizmi, Muḥammad ibn Musa, **1182;** commentary on by Ibn al-Muthannā, 952; selections, 1746
Kibre, Pearl, 56, 892
Kidd, B. J., 409, 430
Kimchi, David, **1183**
al-Kindī, **1184–90**, 1597; theory of music, 1697
King, Archdale A., 1291
Kings, Irish, rights of, 1217; on the character of kings, by Sa'dī, 1699–1700; the three kings [Magi], 69, 1117
Kingsley, Charles,, 1926
Kinnell, Galway, 1934
Kinsella, Thomas 508, 1025, 1522
Kiralfy, A. K. R., 613
Kirby, John P., 1258
Kirchberger, Clare, 407, 1659
Kirkconnell, Watson, 1693, 1770
Kirrmann, Ernest N., 1120
Kisch, Guido, 1109, 1111
Kitāb fī bayān faḍl, **1191**
Klein, Hyman, 1391
Klein, Isaac, 1391
Kleist, James A., 106, 471
Klemm, Friedrich, 1728
Klenke, M. Amelia, 334–35
Klibansky, Raymond, 1627
Klien, B. D., 1391
Klubertanz, George P., 1885
Knapp, Janet, 83, 1105
Knight, William F. J., 195
Knights Templar, history, 876
Knott, Betty I., 987
Knott, Eleanor, 1010, 1016, 1024
Knowles, David, 1210
Knox, Ronald, 995
Kobler, Franz, 846
Kocourek, R. A., 1843, 1848
Köprülü, Fuad, 916, 950
Konstantinos Euteles Anagnostes, 520
Koons, Lawrence F., 731, 1281
Kopf, L., 957
Koran, **1192–1200**, 1056, 1067; commentary on by Averroës, 234; by al-Bāqillānī, 252;

INDEX

M

INDEX

McNiff, William T., 619
McNulty, P. A., 353
Macrina, Saint, life of, 800
Macrobius, Ambrosius Aurelius Theodosius, **1335**
Maddison, Francis, 1723
Maenan abbey, 6
Maerlant, Jacob von, 1459
Magauran, Book of, 1216
al-Maghribī, *see* Ibn Sa'īd and Samuel ibn Abbas
Magi, 69, 1117
Magic, in Aramaic incantations, 131–34; Avicenna (?) on, 246; in a Coptic text, 496; in Leabhar na g-cert, 1217; in Mandaean texts, 1347, 1349–50; Anglo-Saxon, *see* Lacnunga; *see also* Alchemy; Kabbala
Magill, Frank N., 405
Magna carta, **1336–37**, 605, 886
Magna carta Hiberniae, 1000
Magnus, king, 145
Magnusson, Magnus, 70, 1481, 1775
Magoun, Francis P., Jr., 636, 1168, 1945
Mahdi, Muhsin, 676, 685, 1585
Maḥmud ebn 'Abd ul-Karīm, Shabistarī, *see* Shabestarī
Mahoney, Mary Hannan, 518
Mahr, August C., 520
Maimonides, *see* Moses ben Maimon
Mainardi, Arlotto, 1083
Maine, George F., 994
Mairet, Philip, 98
Maitra, K. M., 834, 1478
Major, Ralph H., 239, 481
al-Majrīṭī, 1182
Makarem, Sami Nassib, 1367
Makdisi, George, 24, 248, 956
Makrembolites, Alexois, **1338**
Malak'ia, the monk, *see* Grigor of Akanc'
Malchus, Saint, 1704
Malcolmson, Anne B., 1436
Maldive islands, 926
Maldon (Old English poem), *see* English literature, collections
Malfatti, Cesare V., 712
Malīk, Shah, sultan, 365, 922
Malkiel, María Rosa Lide de, 1676
Malmesbury, monk of, 594
Malone, Kemp, 641
Malory, Sir Thomas, **1339**, 149, 1268
Maltese literature, 125
Mamlūk dynasty, 913, 1040, 1045, 1641
Manandian, H. A., 1763
Mandaean texts, **1340–51**; rites, 61; incantations, 132, 134; parallels to Coptic Manichaean psalmbook, 493
Mandeville, Sir John **1352–53**
Manetti, Giannazzo, **1354**, 1593
Mango, Cyril, 1219, 1601
Mani (Manes, Manichaeus), **1355**
Manichaeans, 1549, 1731; St. Augustine on, 194, 196; Coptic psalmbook of, 493
Manrique, Gomez, 1782
Mansoor, Menahem, 561, 563
Mansūr ibn Ba'ra, **1356**
Mantua, *see* Baptista Mantuanus
Manuel II Palaelogus, letters from, 349
Manx literature, *see* Celtic literature
Manzio, Aldo Pio, **1357**
Marcellinus, epistle to, 157
Marchettus de Padua, 1428
Marcionite doctrine, 670
Marcus, Ralph, 1132, 1573
Margaret, Saint, life of, 335
Marie de France, 719, 721–22, 726, 732, 1273
Marin, Elma, 1800
Marinus, of Flavia Neapolis, **1358**, 1625
Marique, Joseph, 105
Maritain, Raissa, 1890
Markham, Clements R., 1929
Markley, Gerald J., 466
Marks, Margaret, 1608
Mark the Ascetic, Saint, 417
Marot, François, 722
Marriage, treatises on by St. Augustine, 168; joys of, 1647; Tertullianus on, 1815
Marsh, Arnold, 1523
Marsilius of Padua, **1359**
Martha, Saint, life of, 335
Marti, Berthe M., 1084
Martin, Saint, bp. of Tours, 1710
Martin, Charlotte H., 722
Martin, John Rupert, 1114
Martines, Julia, 1609
Martinez de Toledo, Alfonso, **1360**
Martyrdom, Origines on, 1507
Martyrs, early Christian, 422; Christian, 446; St. Phocas, 493; *see also* Saints' lives, collections
al-Marwāzī, **1361**
Marx, Alexander, 1108
Marx, Olga, 1144, 1326, 1444
Mary, Virgin, **1362–63**; Akathistos hymn to, 48; commentary on by St. Anselm, 88; poem to by Blaithmac, 311; by Sebastian Brant, 338; homily on the Immaculate Conception by, 398; Assumption of, 400; Eadmer's treatise on the Immaculate Conception by, 584; prayer to, 820; commentary on by St. Hieronymus, 862; Icelandic hymn to, 976, 984; Irish poem on, 1031;

INDEX

N

Nabokov, Vladimir, 1275, 1771
Nachod, Hans, 1559, 1594
Nādir, Albīr N., 1179
Nahib, Pahor, 96
Nahmanides, *see* Moses ben Nahman
Nakosteen, Mehdi, 1802
Nance, R. Norton, 499
al-Narshakhī, Muḥammad ibn Ja'far, **1447**
al-Nasafī, 'Umar ibn Muḥammad, 1801
Nash, Ralph, 1717
Nāṣir al-Dīn Muḥammad ibn Muḥammad, al-Ṭūṣī, *see* al-Ṭūsī
Nāṣir li-'l-Ḥaqq, al-Ḥasan, **1448**
Nāṣir ibn Khusraw Abū Mu'īn, **1449–50**, 1051
Nasorean, *see* Mandaean texts
Naṣr al-Dīn, kwājah. **1451–54**
Nasr, Seyyed Hossein, 1054
Nat, Pieter G. van der, 1821
Nathan ben Joel Palquera, **1455**
Nathan, Rabbi, *see* Aboth de-Rabbi Nathan
Nawab Ali, Syed, 783
Near East, 837, 880; *see also* Islam, historical sources
Nebuchadnezzar, 497
Neckam, Alexander, **1456**
Neeson, Eoin, 507, 1013, 1026
Neidhart von Reuental, **1457**, 754, 1423
Neill, Stephen, 455
Nelson, John C., 1081
Nemesius, bp. of Emesa, **1458**, 521
Nemmers, Erwin E., 319
Nemoy, Leon, 32, 944, 1149, 1391, 1644
Neoplatonism, 912, 1033, 1625–27; *see also* Plato
Nerses, Shnorhali, Saint, 141, 1293
Nestor, friar, 1691–92
Nestorians, *see* Liturgy and ritual, Nestorian or East Syrian Church; Ibn Zur'a
Netanyahu, Benzion, 1110
Netherlands literature, collections, **1459–61**; *see also* Beatrijs
Neugebauer, O., 1182, 1823
Neumann, C. F., 596
Neville, Graham, 460
Newhall, Richard A., 1923
Newman, Jacob, 1402
Newman, Joel, 627
Newman, Louis I., 1155
New Testament, St. Beatus' version of the Apocalypse, 265; *see also* Apocrypha; specific gospels: Peter, Thomas, etc.
Nibelungenleid, **1462–64**, 1250, 1258, 1264, 1267
Niccolò Angèli dal Bùcine, 1083
Niccolò da Poggibonsi, **1465**
Nicephorus, patriarch of Constantinople, **1466**
Niceta of Remesiana, 431
Nicholl, Donald, 532
Nichols, R. E., Jr., 1737
Nichols, Stephen G., Jr., 301
Nicholson, Reynold A., 1092, 1715
Nicodemus, gospel of, 659
Nicolas Cabasilas, *see* Cabasilas
Nicolas de Lyre, **1467**
Nicolaus Cusanus, cardinal, **1468–69**, 428, 1276
Nicolaus Damascenus, **1470**
Nicolaus de Autricuria, **1471**, 1583
Nider, Johannes, **1472**
Niebuhr, H. Richard, 402
Nigel, bp. of Ely, 699
Nikitin, Afanasii, 1691
Nikolaos I, Mystikos, Saint, patriarch of Constantinople, **1473**
Nikolaos Mesaritēs, **1474**
Nikolaus, von Dresden, **1475**
Nikulus Bergsson of Munkathvera, **1476**
Nilus of Syria, Saint, 417
Nilus Sorsky, Saint, 1692
Nims, Margaret F., 1939
Nino, Saint, 1705
Nippur, 132
Ní Shéaghdha, Nessa, 696
Nitida saga, 978
Niẓām al-Mulk, **1477**
Niẓāmī Ganjavī, **1478–79**
Njála, **1480–81**
Nola, Alfonso M. di, 436
Noli, Fan S., 908, 1309, 1312, 1317
Nonnus Panopolitanus, **1482**
Nordal, Sigurður, 1776
Norhadian, B., 1373
Norman, A. F., 1233
Normans, in Italy, 879
Norris, R. A., 1825
Norse, in Dublin, 1217
Norway, history, *see* Snorri Sturluson
Norwegian literature, *see* Icelandic literature
Norwich plays, Adam and Eve, 1439
Notker, 1246
Nott, S. C., 686
Novgorod, chronicle of, 1686–87
N-towne plays, 1433, 1439; Betrayal, 1432
al-Nu'man, Abū Ḥan'fa, **1483**
Nūr, Muḥammad 'Abd al-Mun'im, 948
Nykl, A. R., 122, 1784

O

Oakley, Michael, 995
Oates, Whitney J., 162
Obadiah of Bertinoro, disciple of, 1909
Obeyd, *see* 'Ubaid, Niẓām al-Dīn, Zākānī, 1917
Obolensky, Dimitri, 1690
Oberman, Haiko A., 1577
Obermann, Julian, 1391
Obrecht, Jacob, 1423
O'Brien, Elmer, 1445
O'Brien, Robert A., 1782
Ockeghem, Johannes, 1423, 1425
Ockham, William, **1484**, 440, 1590
O'Connor, Frank, 524, 1014, 1019–20
O'Connor, Patrick, 436
O Cuiu, Brian, 1028
O Daly, Mairin, 1012
Odeberg, Hugo, 643
Odo, Saint, abbot of Cluny, **1485**, 1113, 1428
Odo of Deuil, abbot of Saint Denis, **1486**, 297
O'Donnell, J. Reginald, 431
O'Donovan, Michael, *see* O'Connor, Frank
Oedipus legend, *see* Hartmann, von Aue
Oesterle, Jean T., 1852, 1873, 1876
O'Faolain, Eileen, 1017
Ogg, George, 519
O'Gorman, Richard, 721
O'Hara, Book of, *see* Book of O'Hara
O Hinnse, Seamus, 1001
Ohl, John F., 1423
Old Man of the Mountain, 916
Old Saxon, *see* Heliand
Olinder, Gunnar, 1600
Oliver, Harold H., 661
Oliver, James H., 491
Oliverus, bp. of Paderborn, **1487**
Olson, Clair C., 603
Olszewska, E. S., 828
Olympiodorus, the Younger of Alexandria, **1488**, 525
O'Malley, Charles D., 1222
'Omar Khayyam, **1489–98**; mathematical treatises by, 1746
O'Meara, John J., 177, 784, 1507
O'Neil, Charles J., 1869
O'Neill, William, 1626
Optics, 1532
O'Rahilly, Cecile, 510, 1748
Orderic Vitalis, 879
Ordinalia, *see* Cornish plays
Ordination, prayers from western rites of, 432
O'Reilly, Marie Vianney, 189
Oresme, Nicolas, bp., **1499–1505**
Orfeo (Middle English poem), 621, 629, 632, 1268
Orientus, bp. of Auch, **1506**
Origenes, **1507–10**, 399, 1578; commentary on the Lord's prayer, 416
Orléans, Charles d', 717, 722–24, 728–29, 1245, 1279
Orosius, Paulus, **1511**
Orozco, Alphonsus, 210
Orpheus, Icelandic version of, 985
Oryān, *see* Ṭāhir of Hamadān, 1802
Osborne, E. F., 474
Ossianic poems, **1512**
O'Sullivan, Anne, 1012
O'Sullivan, Ivo, 40
O'Sullivan, Jeremiah F., 1660, 1713
Othman, Ali Issa, 782
Otis, Brooks, 808
Otto III, Holy Roman emperor, 894
Otto, bp. of Freising, **1513**
Oulton, J. E. Leonard, 399
Outler, Albert C., 166
Owen, Harry J., 1655
Owl and the nightingale (Middle English poem), **1514**
Oxford University, 615, 892
Oxyrhyncus papyri, 347

P

Pablo Christiani, 1136, 1146, 1403
Paccioli, Luca, **1515**
Padua, university of, 892
Padwick, Constance C., 1063
Paganism, survival of, 496
Pagans, treatise against by Arnobius Afer, 144
Painting, theory of, by Alberti, 50; Leonardo da Vinci on, 1224–26; manual of, 1792
Pakenham, Edward A. H., 1022
Pakistan, al-Indrīsī on, 986
Palaelogues, Manuel II, *see* Manuel II Palaelogues; Palaeologues dynasty, 350, 1596
Palestine, 26, 837; *see also* Jerusalem; Travel literature
Palladius, bp. of Helenopolis and of Aspona, **1516**; in a redaction by St. Ambrosius, 62
Palmer, G. E. H., 417
Palmer, Paul F., 439
Palmer, Philip M., 1278
Pálsson, Herman, 70, 1481, 1775
Pamiers, 257
Pamphilus, Maurilianus, **1517**
Panikkar, K. M., 1241
Panofsky, Erwin, 1793
Pantano, Salvator, 325
Paolucci, Henry, 219
Papacy, 411, 433, 1123, 1484; *see also* Pius
Papias, fragments of, 105, 107–108

INDEX

Q

R

al-Rāzī, *see* Muḥammad ibn 'Umar; Muḥammad ibn Zakarīya
Rebenack, Edward V., 513
Redentin Easter play, 1434
Redlinger, Joseph, 1319
Redmond, S., 517
Reed, Clara Stillman, 543
Rees, B. R., 348
Reese, Gustave, 1425
Reeves, Charles H., 1472
Reformation, predecessors of, 1577
Reformers, 398
Regenos, Graydon W., 1332, 1966
Regimen sanitatis salernitanum, **1653**, 1722, 1744
Regina Laudis, nun of, 765
Regiomontanus, *see* Müller, Johannes
Regularis concordia, 45
Rehatsek, Edward, 938, 1699
Reichert, Victor E., 838
Reid, John P., 1868
Reincarnation, 1592
Reinhold, H. A., 1444
Religious of C.S.M.V., 86, 154, 157, 288, 290, 293–95, 655, 902, 905, 1836
Remigius, 419
Renaissance, a Byzantine view of, 104; *see also* Historical sources, collections; Italian literature; Literature
Renart, Jean, 726, 732
Rescher, Nicholas, 685, 962, 971, 1180, 1185–87, 1597
Resnick, Seymour, 1780
Rexroth, Kenneth, 1275
Reynard the Fox, **1654–55**, 1459, 1461
Reynolds, Barbara, 538
Rhazes, see Muḥammad ibn Zakarīya
Rheims, cathedral of, 1930
Rhetoric, of Beda Venerabilis, 266
Rhydderch, White book of, 1334
Rhygfarch, **1656**
Ribalow, Harold U., 1142
Ricci, James V., 46
Richard I, king of England, 506, 1657
Richard II, king of England, 794
Richard Coeur de Lion (Middle English romance), 639
Richard of Devizes, **1657**
Richard of St. Victor, **1658–59**, 428
Richards, Melville, 575
Richardson, Cyril C., 160, 404, 415
Richardson, Herbert, 88
Richental, Ulrich, 408
Richey, Margaret F., 757, 841, 1971
Richter, Irma A., 1226
Rickert, Edith, 603
Riddles, Arabic and Persian, 126; Bohemian, 469; Anglo-Saxon, 626, 637, 668; Irish, 1008; literary, 1257; Welsh, 1952; *see also* Heiðreks saga
Ridley, Maurice R., 742
Riedl, John O., 484
Riesenberg, Peter, 884
Rigaldus, Odo, abp. of Rouen, **1660**
Riggs, Charles T., 1202
Riha, Thomas, 1686
Rinuccio da Castiglione of Arezzo, 41
Robbins, Harry W., 821, 1101, 1669
Robbins, Rossell H., 371
Robert de Boron 732,, 1536
Robert de Handlo, **1662**
Robert of Bridlington, **1661**
Roberto da Sanseverino, 1909
Robertson, A. J., 598
Robertson, D. W., Jr., 187
Robertson, Edward, 1383
Robertus Anglicus, 1698
Robinson, Paschal, 1891
Robson, James, 836, 915, 1178
Roche, Evan, 581
Rochedieu, Charles A., 753
Roger, monk of Pontigny, 701
Roger of Wendover, 604
Rogers, Francis M., 1329
Rojas, Fernando de, **1663–67**
Roland, Chanson de, *see* Chanson de Roland
Rolle, Richard, of Hampole, **1668**, 428–29, 1442
Roman de la Rose, **1669**
Roman de Laurin, **1670**
Roman empire, laws concerning the Christian church, 438; suggestions for reform in, 568; history, 1624; *see also* Laws
Romances, Georgian, 72; Parthian, 151; of Alexander the Great, 329; Cambyses (Coptic), 497; Provençal, 559; Middle English, 620–21, 629, 631–33, 635, 639; French, 703, 726, 732, 821, 1518, 1536, 1669–70, 1682; by Heliodorus of Emesa, 851; Icelandic, 978; Irish, 1006; collections, 1268; by Ulrich van Zatzikhoven, 1918; *see also* Arthur, king; Chrestien de Troyes
Romania, empire of, 1235
Romans, letter to, by St. Ignatius, 220
Romanos, Eastern Orthodox monk, 1303
Romb, Anselm, 325
Rome, sermon on by St. Augustine, 189; history, 878; in writings of Dante and others, 1073; journey to from Iceland, 1476; *see also* Travel literature
Romulus collection, 41

Roovere, Anthois de, 1459
Rosán, Laurence J., 1358, 1625
Roscellinus, two letters concerning, by St. Anselm, 88
Rose, John, 333
Rose, Martial, 1898
Rosenbaum, Elisabeth, 92
Rosenberg, James L., 745
Rosenblatt, Samuel, 1694
Rosenblum, Morris, 1333
Rosenthal, Erwin I. J., 229, 1591
Rosenthal, Franz, 47, 123, 917, 947, 1052
Rosenwald, Lessing J., 698
Rositzke, Harry A., 78
Ross, James B., 734, 1276
Rossetti, Dante G., 528
Roth, Cecil, 1325
Rouen, charter of, 886
Royal chronicle of Abyssinia, **1671**
Rowan, John P., 1853, 1863
Rowley, P. B., 605
Rubā'īyāt, of Jalāl al-Dīn Rūmī, 1090; of 'Omar Khayyam, 1489–97; of Ṭāhir of Hamadān, 1802
Rubruk, William, *see* Ruysbroek, Willem van
Rudaki, 1545
Rudolf, monk of Fulda, 1701
Rufinus Syrus, *see* Rufinus Tyrannius, Aquileiensis
Rufinus Tyrannius, Aquileiensis, **1672–73**; polemic against by St. Hieronymus, 862; commentary on the Song of Songs, 1509
al-Ruhāwī, Isḥaq ibn 'Alī, **1675**
Ruin, the (Old English poem), 616, 623, 641
Ruiz, Juan, **1676**, 1251, 1783
Rūmī, *see* Jalāl al-Dīn Rūmī
Runciman, Stephen, 490
Runes, **1677–80**
Runes, Dagobert, 1599
Runic poem (Old English), 638
Ruodlieb, **1681–82**
Rupert of Deutz, 419
Russell, Diarmuid, 1027
Russell, Robert P., 161, 197, 222
Russia, historical sources, **1683–87**, 1575, 1621; *see also* Byzantine empire; Caucasus
Russian literature, collections, **1688–93**; mystical works, 447; *see also* 1768–71; Armenian literature; Georgian literature
Russian primary chronicle, *see* Povest' vremennykh let
Rutebeuf, 719, 721
Ruthenian rescension, *see* Liturgy and ritual, Eastern Orthodox church
Rutledge, Denys, 577
Ruy de Pina, 1901
Ruysbroek, Jan, *see* Jan van Ruysbroek
Ruysbroek, Willem van, 1907
Ruzbihan, 1548
Ryan, John K., 173
Ryder, Frank G., 1464
Ryder, John H., 1308

S

Saadiah ben Joseph, **1694–97**, 1598
Saato, Frederick, J., 1304
Sachetti, Franco, 1273
Sacro Bosco, Joannes de, **1698**
Sa'd al-Dīn al-Warāwīnī, 1364
Sadeque, Syedah Fatima, 913
Sa'dī, **1699–1700**, 1540, 1548
Sadler, William A., 1752
Säve-Söderbergh, T., 493
Saffouri, Mohammed, 306
Sagas, Auðunar, 225; Egils, 595; Erex, 647; Eyrbyggja, 669; Gísla Súrssonar, 786; Gunnlaugs, 827; Guðmundar, 828; Heiðreks Kronungs, 849; Hrafnkels Freysgoða, 897, 973, 1286; Hrafns Sveinbjarnasonar, 898; Jómsvikinga, 1128–29; Kormáks, 1201; Thorgeir and Thormod, 1201; Rauðolfs, 1651; of Snorri Sturluson, 1773–76; Vatnsdœla, 1922; Volsunga, 1942; *see also* America, Norse discovery of; Icelandic literature, collections
Sage, Carleton M., 49
Sā'id ibn Aḥmad, al-Andalusī, *see* Ibn Sa'īd, Alī ibn Mūsā
Sa'īd ibn al-Biṭrīq, *see* Eutychius
Saidan, A. S., 27
St. Albans, monk of, 451
St. Bertin, monk of, 593
St. Denis, abbey church of, 1793
St. Erkenwald (Middle English poem), 748
St. Nicholas play, 1436
St. Sophia, Council of, 1466
Saints, letters from, 424
Saints' lives, collections, **1701–10**; Russian, 417; selected Christian, 426, 886; Eastern, 427; English, 606, 608, 614; of Sufis, 687–88; in Spain, 1527; Celtic, 1248; funeral orations on St. Basilius, St. Caesarius, and St. Gorgonia, 807; Verba seniorum, 1925–28; individual saints: Hugh of Lincoln, 36; Columba, 37; Eulogius by Paulus Albarus, 49; Andrew, apostle, 75; Polycarp, martyr, 105, 107–108; Bernard of Clairvaux, 297; women saints, by Nicole Bozon, 334–35; Caterina da Genova, 359; Christina of Markyate (St. Theodora), 451; Claudius, martyr, 470;

INDEX

Shuman, Ronald B., 1472
Shushanik, Saint, 1705
Sicily, Norman kingdom of, 942
Siddíqí, Muhammad Z., 1745
Sidonius, C. Sollius Modestus Apollinaris, **1765**
Siger de Brabant, 1583
Sigerist, Henry E., 143, 1740
Sigoli, Simone, 1910
Sigrgarðs sagas, 978
Silverstein, Shrago, 763
Simon, bp. of Vladimir, 420
Simon, Maurice, 1804
Simon Magus, 1278
Simplician, epistle to, 165
Simpson, Jacqueline, 979
Simpson, Lesley B., 464, 1360, 1664
Simpson, William W., 1322
Sinai, 672, 1040–41, 1043, 1465, 1910
Sinclair, Andrew, 90
Sinclair, John D., 535
Sindbad, Book of, 1756
Sindbad the sailor (Arabian nights), 113
Singer, Burns, 1618
Singer, Charles, 1205, 1223, 1730, 1741
Singer, Dorothea W., 1728
Singer, Simeon, 1324
Singleton, Mack H., 1665
Sitwell, Gerard, 73, 866, 1113, 1485
Skeels, Dell, 1536
Skeireins, **1767**
Skelton, John, 1616
Skelton, R. A., 482
Skinner, John V., 589
Slessarev, Vserolod, 1623
Sloan, Jacob, 1326
Slotkin, James S., 1738
Slovo o polku Igoreve, **1768–71**, 395, 1267, 1275, 1683; *see also* Russian literature, collections
Smart, Ninian, 1579
Smith, A. S. D., 499
Smith, Cyril S., 1830
Smith, Joseph P., 1003
Smith, Margaret, 780, 1068, 1071
Smith, Marion Badwell, 388
Smith, Sidney, 130
Smith, W. K., 1610
Smoldon, William L., 857
Smpad, Constable, **1772**
Smyser, Hamilton M., 1945
Smyth, Joseph H., 119
Smyth, Nathan A., 373
Snorri, Sturluson, **1773–76**, 595
Snyder, Louis L., 760
Sobhy, George, 567
Socrates, commentary on by Jean Buridan, 345; oration on by Libanius, 1234
Sogdian language, 1549
Solomon, Odes of, 911
Solomon ben Isaac, *called* Rashi, 1142, 1467
Solomon ibn Gabirol, *see* Ibn Gabirol
Somogyi, Joseph de, 116
Song of Songs, commentary on by St. Ambrose, 65; by Origenes, 1509
Sonnedecker, Glenn, 33
Sophists, 346
Soranos of Ephesos, 223
Sorley, Herbert T., 1269
Sottovagina, Hugh, **1777**
Soul, St. Augustine on, 163; Avempace on, 226; Avicenna on, 240–41, 245; Ibn Kammūnah on, 944; Mandaean view of after death, 1345; Ismā'ilīya work on, 1449; Patrick, bp. of Dublin, on, 1525; Persian work on, 1545; Theodorus of Mopsuestia on, 1825; Thomas Aquinas on, 1847–48, 1863
Southern, R. W., 583, 585
Spain, historical sources, **1778–79**; legend about Muslim Spaniards, 18–19; Council of Compostella, 749; letter of al-Muqtadir, 1049; Jews in, 1110; *see also* Paulus Diaconus
Spanish College at Bologna, 1084
Spanish literature, collections, **1780–90**, 117, 121–22, 960, 1275, 1443; *see also* Mozarabic literature
Spann, Marcella, 1244
Sparrow, Carroll M., 191
Spath, Richard J., 1859
Spencer, John R., 50, 695
Spender, Stephen, 1251
Spiegel, Shalom, 1151
Spinka, Matthew, 398, 907, 1556
Spitz, Samuel, 1155
Sprengling, Martin, 911
Squire, Elsbeth, 1794–95
Stahl, William H., 1335
Stanley-Wrench, Margaret, 391
Stannard, Jerry, 275
Stapleton, H. E., 969
Starkie, Walter F., 1783
Staupitz, Johann von, 1577
Stearns, Marshall W., 853
Stearns, Raymond P., 1077
Steele, Robert, 729
Stefanski, Elizabeth, 494
Stefansson, Vilhjalmur, 1905
Steidle, Basilius, 272
Steiner, George, 1275

W

INDEX